A Childhood in Bohemia

and the flight to the West

Erika Storey, nee Schroll, a Sudeten German, was born in the German medieval town of Saaz in Bohemia. She now lives in the South East of England, having gone through eventful times for much of her life. World famous for its hops, Saaz was a prosperous, beautifully situated town amongst its sister towns in Bohemia and Moravia. The author spent an interesting childhood there, unaware that, through the political upheaval of the Second World War, her family's existence was soon to undergo a dramatic change, with nowhere to go and struggling to survive.

A Childhood in Bohemia

and the flight to the West

Erika Storey
edited by Ellen Storey

Arena Books

First published simultaneously in Great Britain & the USA in 2009 by Arena
Books

Arena Books
6 Southgate Green
Bury St. Edmunds
IP33 2BL

www.arenabooks.co.uk

Distributed in America by Ingram International, One Ingram Blvd., PO Box 3
LaVergne, TN 37086-1986, USA.

Storey, Erika
    A Childhood in Bohemia and the flight to the West
        1. Storey, Erika – Childhood & youth. 2. World War,
        1939-1945 – Social aspects – Czech Republic – Bohemia.
        3. World War, 1939-1945 – Deportations from Czechoslovakia.
        4. World War, 1939-1945 – Refugees – Germany - Biography
        5. World War, 1939-1945 – Personal narratives, Czech
    I. Title II. Storey, Ellen.
    940.5'3161'092-dc22

ISBN 978-1-906791-34-6

BIC classifications: BGH, BTP, BTM.

Printed & bound by Lightningsource UK

Cover design
Jason Anscomb
Orig paintings by Christine Storey
Typeset in Times New Roman

Dedicated

to
my parents, **Josefine & Ferdinand** &
my children, **Christine, Joseph, Marion & Ellen,**
with thanks to them & my husband, **Maurice**
*

Also, in memory of my sister,
Elisabeth
*

CONTENTS

***

Foreword

L ife is a dangerous and risky business. Every generation has tried to safeguard, improve and protect it. When men lived in caves and trees, everything could endanger their lives - from earthquakes, volcanoes and floods to poisonous berries or the wrath of a dangerous beast. It was every man for himself then and we have come a long way since then.

Now we are underwritten and insured against every possible risk; our health is checked, our food and water tested; we have many rights, and our lives, which last a good deal longer, are made ever more convenient. In fact, we have never had it so good.

But all the time we settle ourselves in our hard fought-for security, we know (although we try so hard to forget it) that life can be as precarious as it has always been. Something can arrive out of the blue, and knock our carefully constructed house to rubble and we stand unprotected once more. We know we must secure ourselves; but at what cost, how much and when? And should we ever consider the possibilities of a breakdown of our security systems, so that we are prepared for it when it happens?

This collapse can also happen to a nation, or to a minority in a nation. It is happening at the moment in many parts of the world, and it happened to us during and after the Second World War.

There we were at the turn of the twentieth century, a German community in Bohemia as part of the Austro-Hungarian Empire, secure in the knowledge that the Kaiser reigned over us and the Czechs, Slovaks and others alike, only to wake up one morning to find that we had lost our nationality and were ultimately to lose our possessions, homes and homeland.

What does it feel like to be safe (as we had imagined) one day, only to feel the ground give way under our feet the next? And could this happen to anyone at any time, keeping in mind the present threat to us from global climate change, financial instability, bad health (often through interference with our water, food and air) and their consequences?

How safe are we really with all our possessions, monetary security, our deadly weapons and our advanced technology? How do we respond and what can save us, if these "securities" fail and we fall?

PROLOGUE

A Short History of Bohemia

The early history of Bohemia is, as with many other states in Europe, not easy to ascertain. The name *Bohemia* probably originates from the Celtic **Boii;** the inhabitants were the Boiis and also the teutonic Marcomans. Legend says that the name *cech* comes from Bohemia's first mythical leader, in the same way as Magyar is supposed to be the first mythical leader of Hungary.

The first settlements of Czechs in the land is dated at the beginning of 6th Century. In the late 8th Century arose a national Czech Dynasty of the Premysl family, which ruled for the next 500 years and made Bohemia one of the earliest National States in the region. The borders were indeterminate as in Europe as a whole. Princes and warlords reigned and soldier had to fight against soldier face to face, and mostly for an area which would later be exchanged for another patch of land. One gave something in order to get something else. The Slavs wanted to secure their realm through connections. In order to obtain advantages, they had to make deals with their Western neighbours.

Charles, the Great, could not conquer Bohemia as a whole, but he managed to make them obedient subjects, so that his son and successor Ludwig the Pious, could concentrate on the neigbouring Slavstate of Moravia.

In the 9th Century, Bohemia almost vanished from the map, and Moravia became more important under the rule of 2 heathen princes – Moojmir and Rostislav, who converted to Christianity in the 9th Century. The Eastern Emperor Michael had sent 2 missionaries, the brothers Constantine and Methodius, who knew the slav dialects. Constantine called himself Cyril and created a new Slav language, based on the Greek, from which we have the Cyrillic Alphabet, on which is built the modern Russian, Serbian and Bulgarian Orthography. Cyril died in 869 and his brother Methodius became archbishop of Moravia and received, after a long struggle, permission to read the liturgy in Slavonic. After his death, this was not allowed any more and Bohemia and Moravia were controlled by Rome. They were advantageously oriented towards the West whilst endeavouring to maintain contacts with the East.

When one looks at the World Atlas, one realizes that Bohemia, with its natural mountainous borders, looks like an arrow that penetrates deeply into Germany, and that Bohemia and Moravia have always represented a buffer zone between East and West and are also very important politically.

In the 10th Century, under the 17year old Wenceslas (Vacloa), Bohemia reached new heights. At the age of 22, he was murdered by his brother Boleslav, who succeeded him. In later years, he allied with the German king, Otto the Great and took part in one of the most decisive battles of the Middle Ages, the battle against the heathen Magyars at the river Lech near Augsburg-Bavaria in 955. He pushed back the Magyars from invading Germany and Italy and transformed them from a nomadic way of life to a settled one. In 1241, the Tartars invaded Hungary and pushed forward as far as Moravia.

Christianity went hand in hand with political development and after many years of war with Germans and Poles, Bohemia formed its natural borders at the beginning of the 11th Century, which were settled under Henry II in 1013. Bismarck later called Bohemia "a God formed fortress in the heart of the continent."

There were many internal conflicts in Bohemia, which were settled by the German Crown. Conversely, the Bohemian leadership interfered with internal German politics. Each kingdom in Europe was technically under the civil-rule of the Holy Roman Empire. Bohemia, at that time in the 12th Century, had to deal with the mightiest rulers of the Middle Ages – the Saxon, the Frankonian and the Hohenstauffen Emperors. The Bohemian princes often married German princesses and adopted German customs to their advantage. Czechs adhered to the Pope. The German Church influenced Bohemian life and more and more German colonists occupied the towns and opened the mining industry. They brought with them their own rule of law. It was the three mightiest rulers of the Czech Dynasty, who were responsible for the integration of the non-Slav elements in Bohemia.

1253 – 1318, Ottokar II specifically invited the Germans to open up Bohemia, as it has to this day many raw materials, i.e. coal, silver, ore, copper, healing wells, pewter, now also uranium, and the hops from Saaz are world-famous to this day. These Germans were given special rights and privileges. At the beginning of the 14th Century, the Premysl Dynasty died out, Bohemia and Hungary separated and Poland separated from Bohemia, so that the slavonic union broke up.

Ottokar had been crowned king of Bohemia in Mainz-Germany in 1198 at the same time as Philip von Hohenstauffen became king of the Romans. Frederick II was crowned in 1213 and was the last great Emperor of the Middle Ages.

Countries, at that time and much later, were acquired through marriage. The son of a king married the daughter of another sovereign, when there was no other successor to the throne, and in this way two countries were either allied or totally united.

Another Wenceslas confiscated Hungary for his son, and also through trade wars, borders were shifted. The Hungarians had received permission to occupy the Steiermark, but to leave the rest of Austria to Ottokar, who had conquered it in a war with Hungary in 1260. He had also taken other areas in 1269, so that Bohemia ruled from Silesia-Poland to as far as the Adriatic Sea; practically from there to the Baltic, and here Shakespeare mentions the sea in connection with Bohemia.

In 1273, Rudolf von Habsburg was crowned Emperor. He was in constant conflict with Ottokar, who marched against Vienna in 1278 and, with the help of Hungarian troops, was defeated and killed by Rudolf von Habsburg in Dürnkrut. The Habsburg Dynasty reigned from then on for hundreds of years, but Bohemia was still independent. Another Wenceslas was crowned as king of Bohemia and Poland in 1300 in Gnesen.

In this way, the dream of a united Slav state, stretching from the Danube to the Baltic Sea was achieved. Henry VII, who had power over all of Europe, was asked by Czech nobles to intervene when Henry of Carinthia worked mainly with the German population in Bohemia, which occupied the towns, whereas the Czech people were mainly landowners. They offered his eldest son John the Bohemian the crown and the youngest sister, Elizabeth, of the last Premyslide king, in marriage. This was accepted and so John became king of Bohemia in 1311. Eight years of Civil War followed between the Habsburgs and the Wittelsbachs, which was lost by Friedrich of Austria. John spent most of this time in France and had his son Charles educated there. His teacher later became Pope Clement VI in 1342. He had prophesied that Charles would one day become king of the Romans, to which the prince replied: *Before that happens, you will be Pope!*

Silesia, under John, was gradually annexed to Bohemia, and in 1335 this was legally accepted by the Polish king on condition that John made no hereditary claims to the Polish crown.

John's son, Charles, was extremely well educated. He spoke several languages and was an internationalist. He had spent his youth in France, Germany and Italy and now, when he was supposed to become ruler over Bohemia, he found that Bohemia had nothing to offer him. He built a new palace, so that he had a home there.

His father John was killed in battle in 1346. Charles was injured, but escaped from the battle at Crecy with difficulty. King Edward, the Black Prince, sent John's body to Germany for burial and took over the crest and insignia of his fallen enemy. In this way, the three ostrich feathers and the motto *Ich dien* became the first link between England and Bohemia. Charles then inherited two of the major crowns of Europe. He became Charles IV. In 1348, he built a German University in Prague after the Parisian model. It had 4 faculties – Theology (he was not just a good diplomat and very fair, but also very religious), Medicine, Art and Law for all neighbouring countries as far as Scandinavia. Up to then, there were only three such high places of learning – Bologna, Paris and Oxford. In Prague, there were also students from England, France etc, mainly children of aristocrats and clergy. Teachers were preferred to monks. Prague was full of intellectuals, artists and clergy. To this day, it has a unique architecture thanks to Charles, who brought in talented people from all over Europe. Charles married 4 times, each time adding to his kingdom. Not without difficulty and judicious bribes did he secure the election of this son Wenceslas as king of the Romans in 1376. In Charles' reign, there were four great German nations – Franconia, Swabia, Saxony and Bavaria. A united state of Germany did not exist until 1870.

Jan Hus became a priest in 1400 and was a follower of John Wycliffe, who rebelled against the views of clerics. Hus was the first Czech rector of Prague university. He started a religious war, and was a forerunner of Martin Luther a hundred years later. Hus was against the strict authority of the Roman Church and the Germanic rule over Bohemia and Moravia. His attempt to reform unleashed a national struggle between Czechs and Germans and a social one between the peasants and the landowners. He was asked to recant, but refused and was subsequently burned at the stake in 1415 at Constance. The religious conflict became a militaristic one, with the Hussite Army invading Silesia and Saxony in 1425-26 and by 1429 having reached Frankonia. Civil war followed. Eventually, some Hussites rejoined the Catholic Church, others, the Taborites rejected the Pope's Compactata. Peace was at last made in 1478, by which time, the conflict had nothing more to do with religion.

At the beginning of the 19th Century, Napoleon I tried several times to invade Austria and Bohemia. Franz II, who was the last Holy Roman Emperor, came to an agreement with Napoleon that, after the latter was crowned, he, Franz, would be crowned emperor of Austria and Bohemia, this time as Franz I, as he had hitherto only been emperor of Hungary.

In 1808, Austria had to give up Venice after having possessed it for 2 years, and also Tirol, which was annexed to Bavaria. This was the consequence of Napoleon having conquered Russia and Austria on Moravian territory at the battle of Austerlitz

Napoleon was finally defeated at the great battle of Leipzig, because he had failed to secure to himself the necessary control of the Bohemian natural borders. Thus, in the Napoleonic Wars, the strategic importance of Bohemia was again demonstrated as strikingly as ever. Napoleon's influence is felt to the present day in Bohemian cuisine and the German Bohemian language of yesteryear. We had many French words in our German vocabulary that did not exist in Germany itself.

At the beginning of the 19th Century, the *National Revival* movement started in order to bring back the Czech language, culture and national identity. The Czech language in schools was introduced, *The History of the Czech People* and a Czech-German Dictionary in five volumes was published from 1834-39. Also Czech institutions were established.
Industrialisation began with the opening of the railway link between Vienna and Prague in 1845. Czechs began to move from the countryside to the towns.

The power of the Habsburg Dynasty came to an end with the assassination of Prince Franz Ferdinand, which became the accepted reason for the start of the for First World War in 1914. Franz Joseph, emperor from 1848-1916, was succeeded by Karl, until his abdication with the collapse of the Autro-Hungarian Empire at the end of the First World War.

(Parts taken with acknowledgements from *The History of the Czechs and Slovaks*, by R. W. Seton-Watson, publ. by Hutchinson & Co. Ltd. in 1943.)

Introduction

Anyone who has had to leave their home as a child for political reasons will eventually come to ask him- or herself the question "Why?" The question seems to be asked more frequently and becomes more relevant to that person's life with age, or at least, that was my experience.

I never asked myself the question until I stumbled over it two or three years after I married. It was during the early sixties, and I was pushing my eldest daughter in her pram through an allotment in South Harrow, Middlesex, when some bonfire smoke drifting over me evoked such intense memories, it was as though a thunderbolt had crossed a cloudless blue sky. From then on my recollections have not left me alone, and I cannot help feeling that until I wrote everything down, they would continue to pursue me. I feel as if the real present-day situation cannot have my undivided attention until I have released my recurring memories. Nevertheless, they will never be a burden to me. If anything, I feel they help me see the present and future with greater clarity.

So, in this book, I shall try to write down everything I can remember myself, all the testimonies I have collected from my relatives and the information from the few books currently available on the subject of Bohemia and its history leading up to our abrupt departure. Every day, this task of recording everything seems more urgent to me, even if only for my children's sake and for people who want to understand the truth about that chapter in history, as they will rarely be able to find this information in history books.

I do not want to cast blame for what happened. Certain actions have certain consequences. However, it seems important to me to recall the events leading to the expulsion of millions of Germans from Eastern Europe situated near the West. The Allies signed and sealed this act in the conferences of Teheran in 1943 and at Potsdam in 1945. I am also aware that there are people all over the world thrown arbitrarily into similar situations and circumstances today.

To be honest, I have to admit that these frightening and bewildering experiences have made my life a lot richer and have taught me many valuable lessons, for which I am thankful. I can only speak for myself in this. Nevertheless, I feel that the fact of this mass-expulsion, up to now 'the missing link' in the picture, is somewhat unjust.

If it is fair to condemn the Bohemian Germans for everything they did and believed in, as happened in the post-war years, then it should be at least freely available knowledge that approximately 15 million

Germans, including the Sudeten Germans, who had lived in many East European countries for hundreds of years, had to leave their homes and fatherland from 1945 onwards, and that in the process of this murderous act 250,000 Sudeten Germans alone lost their lives, in addition to the 200,000 Sudeten Germans, who died during the six year war.

By 13th September 1950 the following picture is visible in West Germany:

States in West Germany	Germans deported from the East European countries to Germany	% of the indigenous population
Schleswig Holstein	856,943	33.0
Hamburg	115,981	7.2
Niedersachsen	1.851,472	27.2
Bremen	48,183	8. 6
Nordrhein-Westfalen	1.331,959	10.1
Hessen	720,583	16.7
Rheinland-Pfalz	152,267	5.1
Baden-Württemberg	861,526	13. 4
Bayern	1,937,297	21.1
Total:	**7,876,211**	

Let us not forget that by 1950 many "Heimatvertriebene", deportees and refugees, had already emigrated to America, Canada, Australia, New Zealand, etc., and many had died before, and some, after leaving their fatherland due to the disaster that had befallen them.

The number of deported and fleeing Germans to East Germany from the East is unknown to me, but it is known that there were over 2 million dead and missing during the deportation. When we were evicted from Saaz to East Germany, the place was swarming with people like us after a short while. There was chaos everywhere, and as the Russians were also exhausted after the war, their occupation of East Germany added to the desparate situation. All this has been pushed under the historical carpet.

It has been proven beyond a doubt that great numbers of Germans lived in Bohemia since time immemorial. German and Slavonic history in Bohemia had been intertwined until 1945. The quarter of a million Germans who were "allowed" to stay in 1945 (either because they had a German partner or their jobs made them indispensable) would eventually integrate and intermarry; in other words, leave their German roots well behind. My uncle Gustl, married to my father's sister Mina, was one of those people. He applied eight times during the 1950s to be allowed to go to West Germany as all his other relations were there. His wife, as a German, was sent down the mines and was treated like a slave in the first year or so after the war. On the ninth application, however, they were allowed to leave. They were taken to the railway station with some other people, where an official produced a list and ticked off the people present. Theirs was the last name to be ticked off, when they had nearly given up hope that their name was on that list.

There was a time when some Czech people changed their names to German ones, because German culture and craftsmanship were sought after. Then there were other times, when Germans adopted Czech names for good reasons. What is now the Czech Republic and Slovakia had previously been the home of many nationalities under the Austro-Hungarian Empire over hundreds of years. Czechs were good administrators. At the end of the First World War, the 6.7 million Czechs saw an opportunity to create their own country and formed, with reluctant Slovakia and the help of the Allies, the country of Czechoslovakia. With this, they dismissed an equal number of different nationalities, including German Jews, Sudeten Germans, Hungarians, Gypsies and others who claimed the same rights, having lived there for a long time and contributed considerably toward the wealth and progress of the country. They had never pushed themselves forward, nor spoken with one voice, but just got on with the task in hand, developing many areas that showed potential, experimenting with vine, hops and victuals, opening up rich mines until they were able to export many products and raw materials all over the world, as well as making the spas world-famous. Suddenly, the Czech Government was in charge of everything, although the other parties, theoretically, were also represented in parliament After 1945 and the expulsion of the Germans, 600,000 Czechs had moved into the Sudetenland in Czechoslovakia. This number was not sufficient to occupy every village and town and many German villages were left to go to rack and ruin.

CHAPTER 1
A Bohemian Childhood

My father, Ferdinand Schroll, was 10 years old when the Republic of Czechoslovakia was declared on 28th October 1918. The Austrian Empire and Monarchy had been disposed of along with all the German-speaking pockets and areas, known as Bohemia and Moravia (Böhmen and Mähren), all round the edges of Czechoslovakia.

Ferdinand was born in Gerten (in the Sudetenland, Bohemia), a.small village with one or two big farms, some smallholdings, a school, a church, and about 350 inhabitants. A brook trickled through the village, in the middle of which it became a pond, much to the delight of the village geese and ducks, and in the summer small naked girls and boys. In later years this brook was dyked through the whole village centre, but where my Grandfather's house stood (which he bought in 1921), it murmured quietly, but reassuringly alongside it.

Coming home from school, Ferdinand (nicknamed 'Nandl' or 'Ferdl') had reached the brook with the wooden plank laid across it. A kick with his strong shoe was enough to throw a shower of small stones into the water. He was a thin, but strong muscular boy with blond wavy hair, a soft, full mouth and penetrating, determined eyes. He jumped effortlessly onto the wooden plank, and looked up to the side of his father's house. A faint smile of pride and satisfaction widened his sensitive mouth. He read 'Stefan Schroll, Schuhmachermeister' (Master Shoemaker), im Gassel Number 69[*]. A lot of children at school had no shoes, but he and his brothers were fortunate in that their father was the village shoemaker. Ferdinand was proud of his father's house and garden and felt honoured when his parents asked him to help with the chores.

School hours were from 8 am -12 am and from 1-4 p.m except for Wednesday when there was no afternoon school. So after school he would take the five goats into the woods, a job requiring much patience, as the mischievous creatures , with their long, bent horns close to the ground, had a will of their own and would stop for anything they could swallow, from grass to paper or bits of old boots. The normal walking time to the nearest wood would be five minutes, but with the goats he walked to a different wood and this could take any amount of time. Coming home was different, particularly as they sensed their home was

---

[*] My father's youngest sister Waldtraud visited her old home with her daughter in the late 1970's and this inscription on the house was still visible.

near. He would be just in time for the evening meal, for which everyone
assembled at about 7 p.m..

'Everyone' being:-
Stefan Schroll, father   born 26.12.1868
Marie, nee Ulm, mother,   born 4.7.1880

Children:
Emil,   born 27.10.1899
Wilhelmina (Mina),   born 8.6.1901
Oskar,   born 10.8.1902
Josef,   born 22.7.1905
Ferdinand,   born 14.6.1908
Wilhelm,   born 2.9.1911
Franz,   born 3.9.1913
Maria,   born 12.5.1915
Karl,   born 5.7.1917
Waltraud,   born 7.8.1922

A big family, but not all were present. By 1922 the last child,
Waltraud, or short, Traudl, was born. By this time, Emil, Mina and Oskar
had left. Oskar was a painter and decorator in Scheles, a small place about
15 km. from Gerten. He walked home every weekend. By train it would
have meant a change in Pladen, which was too bothersome. Emil and
Josef learned their father's trade. But as there was no money to be made
in Gerten, Emil looked after the local tree-nursery where he met Aunt
Anna. They married, took over the local post-office and built their own
house. Emil was also in charge of the village steam-threshing machine, so
that he had three jobs. They had one child who was still-born.

Josef worked in the local quarry which was rich in granite. Willi
worked there too for a while after he had left school. Later he became a
stonemason. Mina, the oldest girl, had looked after her younger siblings
for many years until she left home and married a cheerful, clever
half-Czech who was called Joseph Peruth (she called him "Gustl",
another name for a   clown, due to his witty disposition). They had no
children. Willi always got on particularly well with Mina and her
husband. He visited and stayed with them in Brüx many times as a young
man until he died in the Second World War. He had been on short leave
from Russia, when he was ordered to Poland (not with his company),
where shortly afterwards he died of typhoid fever.

My grandmother was heart-broken. Until her death, she kept a
portrait of him (with his black wavy hair and eyes, and thick lips) hanging
in her room. The third-last girl, Maria, had also died of influenza, aged
just 6 months. When my grandmother told me about her, years later, her

eyes would fill with tears. She had loved all ten of her children with equal passion.

It was always a hard life. They were poor, and yet they had enough and managed to stay afloat. During the week there was no meat. But during the mushroom or berry season, 'Nandl' got up with his mother, and sometimes another brother, at 5 a.m. to go to the woods, so that by the time school started, piles of mushrooms would be cleaned, cut, and ready for drying on big sieves that father had made.

Father Stefan was a man of character. Honest and just, industrious and practical, he asked the same of his children. And woe betide them if they strayed even slightly! It began with black looks from beneath his spectacles and a mouthful of sarcastic witticism, but as he got older and these measures no longer sufficed, the stragglers at the end of the long line of children were introduced to a leather belt, commonly used in those days for sharpening the razor knife or "cut throat", or a long whip that reached every corner of the room. This ensured a fair measure of continuity in his shoemaking and repairing trade, so that he wouldn't have to jump up every few minutes to chase the little blighters around the house and garden, whilst losing his authority and temper in the process. It was most important to keep his "Master" image alive; he couldn't count on his wife Marie to enforce discipline, since she had the lowest status in the family.

She was an innocent girl who fell under his spell at a very young age. Her father, Josef Ulm, was the local policeman in Scheles. Stefan had made her pregnant, and married her in Schaar when she was 18 years old. They managed a public house in Podarsanka for a short time, then Stefan became a self-employed Master Shoemaker. The two older children were not born in Gerten. A photo existed of the young family, in which the children stand in a row like organ pipes next to their parents, who look very handsome indeed. Mother appears very slim, not to be compared with the figure she cut in later years, no wonder. And father, astute, with a proud moustache and a gleam in his eyes, his feet spread outward, sure of his ground. Marie complained sullenly about her husband's dictatorial behaviour throughout her life, but never dared to really challenge him. She had an air of kindly martyrdom about her. The children were buffeted by their parents' continuous squabbles and had to bear the brunt of it all. Their servile mother appealed to their sense of justice and fairplay, while their father made them feel his power over her by humiliating and mocking her. When they had an argument, it would always go back to when they were first married. Neither of them could forget what a rude awakening they had after the initial honeymoon period. My grandmother would say "I thought I would be happy after I married!" She would go back to when her husband was very young and avoided work by sitting around in pubs. He only had to have a laugh with a woman or crack a joke, and my grandmother would immediately be jealous. He would say she was stupid, that she couldn't even boil water when she got married, and that to this day did not know much about how to run a household. The arguments always returned to these issues. But before they reached a climax and grandmother ended up in tears, the children would persuade her to be quiet. Was it really worth it? Life seemed to centre around this bitterness that was harboured day in, day out.

"Has he swept the floor yet, as you told him?"

"No, he just had to go somewhere for a moment,"

"And where on earth would he have to go to when he's supposed to sweep the floor, and whose fault is it that he gets away with it?" he would boom down from the pedestal supporting his cobbler's stool, surrounded by old lasts and odd shoes all jumbled up. If looks could have killed, she would have dropped her sewing needle in that instant and collapsed on the floor.

The children's clothes were old, but never torn or dirty. With all the washing, mending and cooking there was little time for cleaning, tidying and washing up. So the children had to do these chores as best they could as well as jobs outside the house. The younger ones always tried to evade their pressing duties. There were always better things to do than cleaning the kitchen floor. Once a week, Father always baked seven enormous round loaves in the hall oven, which were the basis of their nourishment together with potatoes. At the weekend, mother would also bake treacle cake, when childrens' happy voices could be heard outside.

Karl, the second youngest, was supposed to take the goats out with Ferdl, so that he would get used to it, ready for when Ferdl would leave and start an apprenticeship. But Karl, although good-tempered and imaginative, never had the same strong will and drive behind him as Ferdl. Karl was more sociable, got on with everybody and was a great optimist. From very early on, he swore allegiance to his mother, who adored and spoiled him. "Mum, I don't have to take the goats out today, do I? Look how nice it is for playing outside. Robert and the others are out already. They're all waiting for me. P l e a s e. "Karl drawled the last word imploringly. Of course, mother couldn't be hard and adamant under such pleadings. Running her rough hand through his ginger curls, she would say: "Go on then, run along and enjoy yourself, but don't let your father see you".

Mother loved all her children and called Ferdl "Nandl". He was one of the best pupils at school and the teacher wanted him to go to a higher school when junior school had finished. Small for his age, but strong and willing, he was indispensable at home. When quite young, he would cut corn with a scythe and generally help both his father and mother with various jobs in and out of the house. But he loved school and would have preferred to continue his education.. Once the teacher asked his class what the difference between a cockerel and a hen was. One boy, who was well-known for his lack of intelligence decided to show how well he could speak High German and that he did know the answer to the question. *"Die wasn die langen Federn in Arsch han, das sin die Hannen,"* he said proudly, which can be summed up as "The ones that have the long feathers in their backside are the cockerels". Everybody fell about laughing. That statement became a school legend, and I am sure, the teacher never forgot that cryptic remark.

Ferdl never wasted time. Even as he enjoyed soaking up the atmosphere or contemplating a scene, his mind would be working away like a dynamo which would have no rest until it achieved something, however long it took. He pitied his mother, but also had great respect for his father.

When they first moved into the almost-new stone house, there had been no water. With a few friends, father had set to work and after digging a three metre deep hole in front of the house, the water was gushing out and they had struck gold, or as good as. They had taken over the house with Czech tenants, but the house was not big enough to accommodate the latter and all the children. It took some time before the tenants moved out. Father grew his own vegetables in the big garden to the left of the house. At the back of the garden was the manure heap and the little house with the heart carved out of the door. There were some noisy geese, goats, hens and ducks, which kept the two pigs company. They kept one for selling, and the other they slaughtered and ate themselves. They also kept about 25 rabbits, and Ferdl had some of his own as pets, which his father forced him to kill from time to time. It was a painful job and he hated to part from these beloved animals.

Ferdl was well liked, but he did not go out of his way to please his friends. The world was big and intricate, with many mysteries to be unravelled. Finding out how nature works and how man-made inventions came about was very important indeed. But what seemed even more fascinating were problems of an abstract nature. He needed time to consider these. Sitting on a tree stump in the woods one afternoon after school, deep in thought with the goats drifting away from him, he contemplated what it must be like to be a tree. Facing the elements, lightning threatening one's existence, gails, hail and frost inflicting injuries, but also snow and ice transforming and glorifying one's appearance with myriads of glittering crystals - a sight more uplifting than the best decorated Christmas tree. The crowns of the trees swayed gently in the breeze and touched each other. A bee buzzed round and round him, interrupting his thoughts, but not disturbing him. He became aware of another, and another still, a bit farther away, until he realised that there must be a swarm or some hives nearby. He jumped off the stump and started to explore his surroundings. Stumbling over bracken and heather, he found himself surrounded by bees. He began to walk slower and with great care. Suddenly he saw it: not very high on a tree, like a big brown growth subtly changing on the surface every few seconds - a queen bee in flight with her faithful workers; a swarm humming and buzzing in the cathedral-like stillness of the woods like a high voltage cable stretching over a pylon.

Ferdl regarded this spectacle with fascination, at the same time becoming aware that he was in a danger-zone. But suddenly a thought struck his mind, and in order to make it take shape, he would have to be quick. He headed home, running so fast that there was no time to look at the ground. Consequently he slipped and fell several times. He felt very hot and opened his shirt buttons, still running and panting. When he reached the village, it had taken him 15 minutes, a record time. Breathlessly, he told his father about his surprise-find who jumped up from his podium and ran to the headmaster of the local school to borrow a bee hive to capture the swarm in it.

This was the beginning of a nice little industry, which eventually extended to ten hives, situated in the vegetable garden. Father would proudly attend to this sizeable bee state, accepting their own law and order and protecting himself with only netting over his face and a cap on his balding head.

Father was also a verger, which meant ringing the church bells every morning at 5am, every midday and evening and every Friday at 3 p.m. (commemorating the Lord's death). In winter, it was bitterly cold at that hour of the morning, and sometimes mother would help out. In later years, she used to blame her ulcerated legs, constantly weeping, showing the raw flesh in places, to the times when she had to leave her bed a few days after the birth of a child, to ring the bells. "People told me it wouldn't do me any good, but he just used to laugh and say something sarcastic about "old wives' tales". Look at my poor legs. I'm over seventy, and they've been like this since the last few children were born. Just here (and she would point to it) the surface looks like white wax from old scars, can you see, here my leg looks as though it did not belong to me."

When young, she always had to go out into the fields with a big basket tied to her back. She would cut some grass with a sickle from the edges of the fields, put it into the basket and carry it home, ready for the goats' morning meal. Now, the physical work was even harder; also mentally her day was full of anxiety and tension. The everlasting war had to be fought with her husband, her children and circumstances. She was a simple, gullible, but loving woman, who was inclined to put up with trouble and feel sorry for herself, rather than try and change her lot if possible. On the whole, there was little she could do to improve her situation, but the feud between her and her husband made everything worse.

"I never thought marriage would be like this," she would moan, shaking her head and casting her eyes to the ground. "If anyone had warned me of this living hell, I wouldn't have married. But I thought life would be so much better being married, having children and a home. It didn't take me long to realise I was quite wrong. I used to sing this song: *Mariechen sass weinend im Garten* (young Marie sat in the garden crying), and as my name is the same as the girl's in the song and I felt as sad as her, it comforted me, but at the same time it made me cry." Fresh tears rolled down her lovely face at the thought of it.

Of course, father being responsible for the well-being of his large family and being an upright, honest and respected member of the village community, also had his work cut out. Being a sexton or verger, he was entitled to the crops of two fields. He borrowed a plough and some other simple machinery, also oxen from farmers, and in late summer he could reap the fruits of his labour, bringing home potatoes, corn and beets. The latter were for the goats. All in all, the family was nearly self-sufficient. They sold half the honey made, in order to buy the necessary sugar for the bees in winter.

Being a judicial and pious man of imposing stature in his Sunday clothes, father was well-respected and pursued for advice by his customers. This would lead to gossiping, a very amusing sight for anyone unaccustomed to it. His favourite partner in the art of political discussion and gossip of the local scene was his neighbour Worofka, who could be seen almost every day, walking round his house into his neighbour's sandy courtyard, past the well into the flagstoned hall with a swallow's nest over the oven, into the Schroll's living room.

Lifting his cap off his head for a fleeting moment, he would first turn to Frau Schroll: "Terrible weather again, don't you think? Reminds me of the war, you know." And over to the pedestal he would go. From then on, they might as well have been alone in the room, he and his good friend Stefan Schroll. They would expatiate on many different, equally important subjects, one leading to the other; father puffing great clouds of smoke from his porcelain pipe with the bent mouthpiece, occasionally looking sharply over his spectacles straight at Worofka, who sometimes looked obtuse or, at least, bewildered. The children, hanging on the two mens' lips, as if each spoken word was of the utmost importance and could not be missed in fear of the consequences, sat inert, their faces almost frowned with concentration.

"Go and tell Pepp (Josef) to stop practising the violin, will you?" one of the children would say to another. "They're talking about the war," he added meaningfully. This always explained any interruption in their normal life. Everything would come to a dead halt with this introductory word: War. A whole fascinating, new world opened up.

"It's a fact that we had better equipment, better weapons, better officers, better everything," father's voice was raised, but managed to maintain its equilibrium.

"But how can you fight a war with an empty belly and nothing to keep you warm, I ask you?", he continued, and, as if to emphasise his point, he would give the nail he was hammering such a bang that it just disappeared through the leather sole with just its flat head showing.

Worofka's face began to glow dangerously, from his neck up to his hairline. His eyeballs began to protrude and his voice pitched almost into a squeak.

"You think that's what it was, do you? You really think so? You really believe we would have given up because of that? I tell you, it wasn't the army that lost the war. It was the politicians! They are to blame and no one else. A stab in the back, that's what it was: All those thousands of soldiers slaughtered like cattle, not knowing what it was all about, just laying down their lives for the fatherland, trusting the politicians."

Worofka was beginning to shake all over and had to sit down. Mother wept silent tears on the socks that she was diligently darning, while father knocked the ashes of his pipe out and then proceeded to wipe his spectacles slowly and deliberately with eyes cast down, deep in concentration.

"We'll never know if that's so," he said slowly, still not looking up. "There's more to it than meets the eye in a big bloody war like that one, I grant you that, but I still say that you cannot fight properly with an empty stomach, lack of clothes and sleep. The whole thing was a horrendous power struggle between the existing superpowers and the up and coming ones, as far as I can see. Anyhow, don't let the memory of it all overwhelm you now, old chap. I have seen many a man not able to cope with their present lives because of the past. It refuses to lie still and be forgotten. You mustn't let it get on top of you, old friend," and he resumed his work, hammering the nails rhythmically and meticulously.

CHAPTER 2
Apprenticeship

F erdl became restless in his last year at school. His world was too narrow and restrictive and his duties weighed heavily on him. He could not get on with his father any longer. He became argumentative and felt frustrated. Although he loved school, he longed for the day when he could be his own master and leave his environment to look for new pastures. The house with the four rooms and big attic was becoming too small. The viewpoints attitudes of the people he knew were too onesided. He felt that a whole new world was waiting for him just outside his village. He had heard of Saaz to which Gerten and the whole province belonged. Saaz must be the ultimate goal, but he could not hope to reach this splendid town from a place like Gerten, this small village between two bigger ones - Jechnitz and Podersam. Being a quiet, conscientious and practical boy, it was decided he should learn a trade. The schoolmaster thought it a great waste that he should be deprived of a higher education, but there was no money available for this kind of luxury, especially with four younger children at home.

On a crisp, bitterly cold January day in 1923, he was frogmarched through the village by his father, who still needed him at home, but money was scarce and the older children had to leave one by one. The village people saw this, for his age, small boy with no winter coat, but one jacket on top of another, going down the road, accompanied by his father. He had never taken him anywhere before, so that Ferdl really felt the importance and gravity of the occasion, and the total helplessness with no say in his future. Yes, he wanted to get away. Yet, he had mixed feelings sitting in the train opposite his father with his bundle of clothes on his knees, getting ever closer to his unknown destination. What was it going to bring him – freedom, or more bondage, misunderstanding and lack of care?

It had been decided that he was going to be a blacksmith; Father had a brother also called Ferdinand, who owned a smithy in Saaz. He was also a most respected man and his brother Stefan consulted him on important matters. He asked his brother if he knew of a vacancy for his son. His brother answered that he knew of two available apprenticeships, one as a butcher, the other as a blacksmith in Reitschowes. His father had asked Ferdl, out of the blue: "What to you want to be? A butcher or a blacksmith?" For a fraction of a second, he was going to answer "neither", but then thought better of it and said "a blacksmith". He thought that he could never be a butcher, but that he might eventually work for his uncle in Saaz and inherit the smithy.

This busy smithy in Reitschowes, a village about 20 km. away from Saaz, looked after Count Czernin's 15 pairs of horses and 20 pairs of oxen, in other words 70 animals from one farm estate alone.

Count Czernin was said to have 99 estates in various places, one of them in Reitschowes. He had 99, because had he had 100 or more he would have had to keep a regiment, it was said.

Father introduced Ferdl to Herrn Stengl, the blacksmith, and his family with the words: "Make him work hard", and to his son before leaving: "If you decide to run away or if you are ever thrown out for bad behaviour, you cannot come over my doorstep again". (*Uber meine Schwelle kommst Du nicht mehr!*) On one of his last school photos, Ferdl looks small and undeveloped for his age. It couldn't have done him much good being in the hardest working trade there was. He was used to manual work, but this was too much. It's difficult to imagine the boy in the picture even lifting the hammer, let alone swinging it.

Ferdl was led up a rickety ladder to a rough attic which had a special addition on the right, just above the bellows, namely a brick floor with Ferdl's bed on it. This was to be his accommodation for the next three years. When he looked down from his "quarters", he could see the small, black pieces of coal in the fire amongst the ashes that were waiting to be cleaned out, so that the embers could glow once more throughout the day. On his first working-day there, a shout from downstairs woke him up in what he thought was the middle of the night. Ferdl felt for his shoes under his bed. They felt like dry bones and he dropped them like a frozen skeleton on the brick floor. The day seemed never-ending. He had completed one day of strenuous work there, but it already felt like a year. His whole body ached, not just from the work that he was not used to, but also from the cold. It was about -30°C in those winters.

Although he had worked hard at home for a boy of his age, there was no comparison to be made with this.

Swinging the big hammer through the smoky air towards the anvil, reshaping the softened red metal, so that sparks flew all around him and smutted his face and old clothes, he muttered: "You cannot ever come home again, never again, never." He repeated "never" with every hammering down on the anvil. He was only a child, moving quickly from the anvil to the bellows in the big, dark smithy, trying to do an adult's job, but he had understood. There was no way out for him, but to tow the line, to stick it out, to make the best of it.

The nearest water pump was about half a kilometre away in the village. Ferdl was to carry every drop of water for the household and smithy back from that distance. Herr and Frau Stengl had three children, for whom he was babysitter when the parents decided to go out at night. It was also his job to clean everyone's shoes every Sunday. All these tasks were considered to be part of his apprenticeship. His only 'free' day was Sunday; even then he had to attend *Gewerbeschule* (a kind of craftsman's college) in Michelob from 8am -12am. Every morning he was up at 5am; there was no pulling the covers over his head (the only items that reminded him of home) one more time before hauling himself out of bed.

He had to work for four hours before he saw a morsel of food at 9 am. This consisted of a piece of bread spread with margarine, the look and smell of which he could not bear after a while, so that he began to fling it out of window with automatic monotony. Although he was thin and small, his muscles that had been firm from work for many years now began to bulge and he felt himself growing into a man.

Sharpening ploughs, fixing new shoes on horses and oxen, maintaining and repairing farm machinery in the lunch hour, (spare parts had to be brought from a small place a few hours away), placing new metal hoops round big wheels, (which involved heating the hoops for half an hour and banging them into place on the wheel), were just some of the jobs that needed doing. There was never enough time to eat the midday meal properly. Work, work, work was the motto of the day, everyday for two years. After that, a *Geselle*, a qualified blacksmith was employed, and things began to ease a bit.

There was one small recreation Ferdl had enjoyed for some time. He had joined the *Deutsche Landjugend* (German Rural Youth) which met every Sunday afternoon (his only spare time), and found himself appointed secretary, which helped him acquire the badly needed self-confidence he lacked as a boy. He had always known what he wanted, but he had always been a quiet, polite boy and needed to come out of his shell and find his feet more.

With combined efforts, the last year of his apprenticeship was bearable and sometimes even fun. When the oxen were fed a lot of beet leaves, Ferdl and his partner shared jovial moments fixing oxen's shoes while trying to keep clear of the beasts' rear ends - only sometimes they did not manage to avoid the worst scenario. The oxen were suspended with the help of two chains, their hind legs tied to a post. Oxen as well as horses were used for transporting materials in the area at that time.

"Ferdl, untie his leg and we'll get this silly beast out of the way before he messes everything up around here… oh, boy, oh boy, sorry I'm laughing so much, but you really look a sight, Ferdl. If only you could see yourself. Is it stinging your eyes and can you still hear all right? You're absolutely plastered with it, mate. Dear me, I must stop this, otherwise I'll get tummy ache!"

   Ferdinand took his examination for the title of master at the end of his apprenticeship in Eger. One of his test-pieces was a small, silver-plated horse shoe.

   Long after his apprenticeship had ended, Ferdl could still see the image of Master Stengl standing next to the heavy pair of bellows (which Ferdl had to pull), moving up and down on his heels with his hands dug in his pockets, presenting a most carefree figure in his breeches and whistling a jolly tune to himself.

CHAPTER 3
Boy meets Girl

As soon as Ferdl was back in Gerten, he was working as a tool-maker for a short while (*Werkzeugschmied*) at Bokorny's quarry, where he was badly needed. He was not familiar with the work, but was willing to learn. Late in 1925, he had the chance to go to the town of his boyhood dreams - Saaz, where his uncle owned a big smithy. Here he was introduced to the finer and more varied ways of living. He got on all right with his uncle, but to his aunt he might just as well have been a foreigner.

   During the six years he was there until his uncle died in March 1931, he had joined the *Katholischer Gesellenverein* (Catholic Youth Club), which met each Wednesday night at the Drehscheib' (a junction in Saaz) at their local Gasthaus zur Glocke. This organisation had a junior section, of which Ferdl became the leader. They would go hiking on Sundays and generally enjoy each others company. It was at this time that father received a letter, and without telling anyone what it was all about, he travelled to Saaz to talk to his brother. A little later Ferdl was called to face a kind of cross-examination from the two men.

   "Did you sign these invoices from Kautzner & Neumann (all smithies bought their nails etc. from this firm) for all these nails over this period of time?"

   "No, I certainly did not."

   "But this is your signature, or are you denying that you signed these bills?"

   "I don't know anything about this. Someone must have forged my signature".

   "Well, who could have thought of buying nails in your name? I know you buy nails for uncle. Have you ever seen anyone there who knows you and could forge your signature?"

   "Come to think of it, there are two brothers who go there, I suppose, and who know me from the *Gewerbeschule* in Michelob. They must have looked up my signature from the *Landjugend* books from when I was secretary there," Ferdl answered after considering the matter.

Uncle decided to pay all those bills rather than make a fuss. He did not want his good name tarnished for the sake of a few nails.

Later, during Ferdl's stay at his uncle's firm, he became senior of the Gesellen - or Kolpingsverein. Kolping had been a Catholic priest who had founded this youth movement. Apart from "senior" there was *praeses* (president), who had to be a priest. It was at that time during Ferdl's *'Sturm und Drang'* years' that he met Josefine Soukup, 7 years his senior and very vivacious and popular wherever she went.

Every Sunday evening, the choir Liedertafel (of which she was an active member for 22 years) would meet up to sing and play. Ferdl and Josefine were always in the forefront of the activities. They performed plays in public and Josefine sang a lot of music hall solos and had good parts in popular plays (eg. *Froni in Der Meineidbauer*). Women, at that time, became very daring, dancing the Charleston in short skirts as well as wearing men's clothes at other times. Dressed up in a man's posh suit with a feathered hat cocked on her head, she would leap about the stage, singing: "*I bin der Schurl von Herr Nols, im schwarzen Viertel kennt mi olls...*" at the end of which she would give a piercing whistle through two fingers while swinging her walking-stick suavely with the other hand. She always was a great success playing this charming villain and many other characters. Dancing was another of her talents. She would go to balls, stay out all night (especially at carnival time), come home, have a bath and leave for work shortly after.

Josefine was a hairdresser by trade. She had learned how to master heated tongs and finger-waving, and all the other skills of this trade from her eldest sister Marie, who in, turn, had learned it from an Italian in Karlsbad, the world famous spa. After Marie married in 1918, she handed the job over to Josefine. When Pepi and Nand (Ferdinand and Josefine was too long a name for friends and family) got married on 18th October 1931, Nand wanted his wife to give up working. They had been going out together for nearly three years. Pepi did not want to marry at first; she was, after all 7 years older, but eventually conceded to the idea. Nand was badly in need of someone to attend to his clothes and food, and she felt that she wanted to care for him. So she only worked part-time after they married. But things began to turn against them from the start.

Nand had returned to Bokorny's Quarry in Gerten after his uncle's death (March 1931). So when he married, he could only visit Pepi at her mother's in Saaz over the weekend. He despised this arrangement, especially since he realized that Pepi could manage very well without him; she had always been an independent woman, and being 30 years old, was unlikely to change now. Not that she had done anything untoward.

Still, it grieved Nand that he could not really contribute much to this marriage; on the contrary, he could only bring his dirty washing into a flat which was made more crowded by his presence. When he became unemployed after a year at the quarry, he became angry and insecure. He was now nothing but a burden on Pepi and her mother, at least that was how he felt.

CHAPTER 4
Pepi and her family in Saaz

Pepi's father was Anton Soukup and her mother Rosa Langer, who came from Lauterbach in the Egerland before she married Anton. Rosa was full of life and very humorous. She had three sisters and one brother. She was a very practical, caring woman with a lot of common sense, but she often lacked sensitivity and tact. Pepi's sister Marie was thirty when she received a slap on the face from her mother; when Pepi laughed at this spectacle, she received the same treatment, despite her not much younger age than her sister.

Rosa knew the meaning of hardship. When her children were small, there were times when she got up at 4am to sew for other people (she made mainly women's vests for a Jewish textile firm called "Friedlaender") and made the clothes for her children. Pepi's family had spent the first years of Pepi's life in the Musch house (owner Herr Musch), mainly being looked after by an elderly, much loved lady, she called "Waawi", who lived in a small annexe overlooking the backyard of the house. Pepi used to sit on the stone doorstep and look all around the Lorettoplatz with the brewery and the Muttergotteshaus monastery on one end of the cobbled square and the main church and back of the town hall on the other. Directly opposite her, she could see a big, imposing house, called Husarenhaus, which made her wonder, which rich ladies and gentlemen could afford to live in a posh place like that.

One day, when Pepi was about 6, her father said to her: "Look, Peperl, you see the house over there. We are going to move there, quite soon". Pepi stared at her father in disbelief. She would soon be moving into the Husarenhaus, the house with the beautiful façade and a glass-covered verandah at the back of it. How lucky she was, but she was still uneasy about her acceptance in her family.

Years later, sitting around the dinner table, she complained to her family that she felt not really wanted or appreciated by them and expressed her desire to stay with Waawi for a few days. She wanted to test her family to see whether they would miss her, if she stayed with

Waawi for three solid days and nights. She waited every day, if someone would come and fetch her. Her disappointment grew from day to day. After three days, however, nobody had come to fetch her back as she had hoped they would. Bitterly disappointed and deeply wounded (with a scar for the rest of her life), she returned home by herself, humiliated.

Pepi was a challenging child to care for, but it nevertheless seemed harsh that not even her beloved father had claimed back his own after she had absconded. She had entered the world quite unexpectedly and it took her mother a long time to get over the shock of having her.

In those days, girls wore frilly, long underpants beneath their longish dresses. The frills were slightly longer than the dress, to show up. The pants were lily-white and had to be boiled and ironed laboriously. Pepi, a tomboy and always playing with the boys, would go sliding down a long coal chute, screaming, shouting, and laughing and never giving a thought to her mother who would have to somehow clean the now black knickers. Later she showed traces of remorse and tried to mitigate her crime. But to no avail. Black was black, white was white, and that was that.

Once Pepi nearly drowned in the millstream (*Mühlgraben* – a creek of the river Eger). Not being able to swim, she fell in whilst trying to fish something interesting out of the water, but thanks to her full clothes and, no doubt, the aforementioned knickers, which had trapped the air inside them, she floated on the stream's surface until she came to a tree branch which she grasped with all her might, pulling herself towards the bank. The problem once again was how to face her mother. Fortunately it was summer, so she decided to strip and spread the dripping clothes out on a meadow with fairly long grass in which she could hide. Meadows near the Mühlgraben were used for spreading out laundry to bleach in the sun. White clothes were soaked in soda water, boiled, washed by hand the next day, spread out on the meadows near the Mühlgraben or Eger (Bleichplätze),watered several times, then rinsed in the flowing rivers. When she arrived home, her mother was singing in a most melodious voice one of the many tunes she knew from her native village. The women there had met in each other's houses on dark, cold nights, passing the time spinning, weaving, embroidering, singing cheeky songs and especially bantering. Gossiping, but not in a vicious way, was also common. The whole thing was called *hutschen*. Rosa would often talk about those days, and the children found it fascinating and could not hear it often enough.

Hearing her mother sing was a good omen. It meant that she was not particularly worried about the long absence of her second daughter, but she would have to tread carefully, nevertheless. Mother's hand had a way of landing swiftly and painfully in the wrong places. It was always a shock, even when well anticipated.

"Where have you been so long?" she enquired, halting her song abruptly and giving Pepi a sharp sideways glance.

"Nowhere in particular, really. Sorry for being late, mother. I forgot to ask someone for the time."

Her mother had not even noticed. Pepi must have made a good job of drying her clothes without creasing them. She felt one of her rare triumphant moments which made her heart beat faster for a minute or two.There was no doubt love and hate within her with regard to her mother, coupled with admiration and a degree of fascination. The lurid stories of haunting premonitions and strange prophesies that eventually became realities were part and parcel of her mother's background and often followed Pepi into her dreams.

"And so he sat, lonely and forlorn, by the fireside. A gust of wind rattled the window and rickety door. The wood in the fire crackled and sang, sending him off to sleep with its warmth and tunefulness. But suddenly his head jerked up, his ears seemed to strain and his eyes followed the staircase that wound itself up to the attic. Soft, but distinct steps could be heard above; frighteningly, slowly and deliberately they moved towards the trapdoor. Then there was complete silence for a moment, only the gusts of wind could be heard outside. Then, as the trapdoor opened, creaking and heaving as if in slow motion, the man's frame froze to a statue. Nothing gave away his breath, his agony, or his thoughts. The door fell shut with a bang, instantaneously bringing the man alive and into action. He was now behind the chair, holding its back as though it could save him; gripping it, so that his knuckles looked white and dead like his face. His eyes followed the sound of the footsteps down the stairs one by one, as though he could see them. They nearly popped out of his head; the compulsion to scream and give up the ghost in exchange for peace became overwhelming, as the footsteps, firmly but ever so slowly, marched round him and up the stairs again. The door banged as before and an unearthly silence followed.

"The man collapsed next to the chair, panting and shaking from head to toe, and fell into a deep sleep of exhaustion. He heard later that his brother had been killed on exactly the same day and time as the terrifying unseen ghost had walked around him".

One can imagine this story in all its variations and similar other ones being passed on from house to house in Lauterbach and the whole Egerland, where Rosa grew up around 1875 after the Franco-Prussian War.

Pepi's father's stiff white shirt collar was seen rolling towards the door one day, after it had been placed in its usual position on the table where it had not been disturbed by human contact. Sure enough, bad news followed this ghostly occurrence - Uncle Julius, her father's brother, had died.

Although Pepi's mother was an imposing and sometimes "larger than life" figure, whose influence stayed with her children throughout their lives, it was her father whom Pepi loved and adored most. He was a most gentle, musically gifted man; a civil servant, first under the Austro-Hungarian Monarchy, to which the Sudetenland in Bohemia then belonged, and later in 1918 in the Czech Republic due to his knowledge of Czech. In fact, he was not only a Court official, noting down what was said in Court, but also translating it, as from 1918 onwards the official language in Czechoslovakia, (including its German regions) was Czech. Anyone who could not speak and write Czech in an official capacity (esp. civil servants) was out of a job. His German title was *Oberoffizial*.

In his spare time he gave music lessons, mostly to children, played the cello at home for his own amusement, was a member of the theatre-orchestra, and helped out when operas were performed.

Pepi liked to learn about her parents' background, i.e. that her father's father Anton had been a *Herrschaftskutscher* (coachman for an aristocratic family) and that he had died in 1873 in a smallpox epidemic when Anton was 4 years old, and his brother Julius died, aged 42. His mother was Anna Soukup, nee Frank, who had to bring the two boys up on her own after her husband's death, which was not easy in those days with no state benefits.

Pepi's father was originally a painter, who had worked his way up to office-clerk for the mayor of Saaz, and finally to working in the courts. He played several woodwind and string instruments in his youth, but when he was older, concentrated principally on the cello. When he was young, he went to Vienna and also played music on ships. His son Franz followed in his footsteps, wanting to see the world and taking a lively interest in anything and everything. Anton was never ill-tempered and always ready to entertain. So it was easy to forgive him almost anything. He would come home unusually jolly from some of the rehearsals, and although Rosa did not greet him with a rolling pin, she made sure that he did not take her reaction as one of approval. They were very fond of each other, but somehow, there was never any question who was the dominant figure in the Soukup household. It was not just the fact that Rosa was four years older than her husband; her more earthy approach with light and dark shades of character, her no-nonsense-stance and forthright, unequivocal approach made it a natural consequence.

A threat like: "Wait till your father gets home tonight!" would have been mystifying to the children, if not downright laughable. In fact, the only physical violence Anton ever used towards Pepi was a smack on the cheek, when he found out that she had given up learning French at the *Buergerschule* (high school) without asking his permission. He was still the master when it came to official matters like school, etc.

To demonstrate the no-nonsense approach: Pepi's mother had bought her a new hat for school. Pepi hated it and said so.

"You'll wear this hat till it's worn out. It cost me enough, my dear child," Rosa said with emphasis. "I'll show her and make it wear out", Pepi thought to herself. No sooner thought than done, she cut two large holes in the expensive monstrosity. Handing her mother the hat with a self-satisfied grin, she announced: "A gust of wind swept my hat right off my head today straight into a dog's path. You can't expect me to go to school like that now, can you?"

"Can't I? It might come as a surprise to you, but I do expect you to wear the hat like that, unless you can find a way of patching it up. What kind of dog was this then, one that had teeth like scissors?" There was the faintest of smiles on Rosa's face while she contemplated the consequences of her order.

Pepi's pet hates in terms of food were carrots and anchovy sauce, which were abhorrent to her. Once she came home late from school. They had kept her food warm. She was famished, and when she had finished eating said: "I really enjoyed that mushroom sauce." Everyone laughed, as they had been eyeing her secretly to see how she would like the anchovy sauce.

Another time carrots were served. Pepi refused to eat them. They were taken away and served again to her for the next meal until she was so hungry that she enjoyed every bit of it and never refused it again. As long as Grandmother Soukup lived in the same house, the children could afford to refuse certain dishes. They knew that grandma would always open her door and hand out a big slice of bread and dripping.

Sometimes,Pepi had to go shopping for her mother after school. Once her mother gave her a 10 kronen coin (Goldstückl) for the shopping and told her not to lose it. A few boys joined her as she walked up to the shop. They came to a grate in the pavement. Pepi suddenly bent down and tried to put the gold coin in between two bars."This grate has unusually small gaps between the bars" she explained to the boys. "I bet this coin won't go through." At that moment the door behind her opened, and a woman appeared with a dog, which jumped on Pepi's back as she was bending down. The gold coin fell out of her hand into the hole through the grate. Pepi could not believe her eyes. For hours she hid behind the statue of a saint to wait for her father who came home each day for his lunch. The lost money was supposed to pay for the midday meal. Every now and then, she saw her mother look out of the window. Once she shouted down to the children asking if they had seen Pepi, but "they knew nothing". At half past twelve, the beloved figure of her father appeared. Pepi ran up to him and told him about the catastrophe. "Peperl, how could you? That's a lot of money to lose," he said reproachfully, but it was exactly what she had expected him to say. The storm did not break until Anton had gone back to work again, although by then the temperature had cooled down a few degrees, so that the punishment was "just" kneeling in the corner. At other times, when Pepi was smaller, she was sometimes chained by her foot to a table or an object outside the door. Incredibly, no one was allowed to speak at the dinner table, only the parents, but this rule was very often broken.

Rosa might have seemed draconian at times, but she was always soft and open-handed to the needy. Nobody was sent away empty-handed, however short they were of food and money themselves.

After church on Sunday morning, she would return home with a middle-aged man, whom everyone called *Schguttl* (someone who plays about a lot to people's amusement and is lacking most of his mental faculties). He had studied theology in his youth. All the studying was too much for him and he consequently lost his mind. Everything he said and did was holy. He thanked Rosa every Sunday for the "holy watersoup" with a thousand holy blessings on the holy Sunday, etc.

An impoverished tailor from a nearby village visited just before Rosa's last child, Franz, was born and asked if they could accommodate his son while he did his apprenticeship in town. Again Rosa could not say "no". She and her husband were well known for their benevolence. Anton was guardian to several children he had come in contact with in court. He was not just a guardian on paper, but made concerted efforts to provide the best care for them.

The First World War disrupted most families. Tobacconists were nationalised and disabled war veterans put in charge of them. The children were sent to the *Volksküche* (soup kitchen) to get some vegetable soup made with dried vegetables. Anton sometimes brought a few potatoes home after a day's tramping around the countryside like so many others of his contemporaries. Schools shut down at times to save coal, and people began to look ragged and malnourished.

When the troops returned after the war, the soldiers were a pitiful sight. A lot of them had amputated limbs; all of them were starved, exhausted and filthy. What a contrast to the glorious Army that had set out to win. Never had life been so cheap and used as cannon fodder as in the aptly called Great War. Great in immeasurable losses of land, goods, food, prestige and especially lives. Ebert became first president of the Weimar Republic in the Reich after Kaiser Wilhelm II had gone to Holland.

The motto 'God, Emperor and Fatherland' began to sound a little hollow to men and women who had believed in it blindly. What was an important figure today, could be murdered tomorrow and no one dared ask any questions about him. One country might be partitioned overnight and the inhabitants there would suddenly find themselves belonging to another country. A soldier might be told that he should risk his life to defend his country, only to learn later that this bloodiest of wars could have been settled long before on paper. As strategists convinced their employers that the frontline never moved far and that they could win a few yards backwards/forwards, thousands were sacrificed senselessly.

What was there left to believe in when everything around one crumbled and disintegrated before one's very eyes? As the church had always played a leading role in politics, and had organised a welfare system which had given rise to education, Church and State seemed inseparable. Now that anything was possible in the political arena, the Church's credibility and inviolability was thrown into question.

The population of Bohemia adhered mainly to the Catholic religion. The decentralization of power had pushed ahead in the previous century, aspirations were for liberalism and democracy, but in Bohemia the Germans felt that this could never be a reality for them. They had initially been ruled by Austria and now by the Czechs, and Czech natives always had priority over Germans. Czech intelligentsia, which had always been Western-orientated had changed direction and found in the first world-war that they did not like fighting for the Austrian Monarchy and against other Slavs. For over 1000 years, Czechs and Germans had lived in fruitful cooperation for the benefit of the land, weathering the storms together. There had been ups and downs since the Hussite wars and in the 19th Century, Czech nationalism had grown stronger. They had seen other peoples seeking independence; and taking their chances, successfully followed suit. There were more than six nationalities now living in the so-called Czech-o-Slovakia: Czechs, Germans, Slovaks, Poles, Ukranians, Hungarians, (the latter two amounted to 1,6 million) Romanies and others.

On 28th October 1918 the Republic of Czechoslovakia had been declared and the Austro-Hungarian Empire with all its different countries was now part of history.

Johann Wolfgang von Goethe frequented Saaz, staying in der Goldenen Ride am Ringplatz Nr. 52, and visiting the theatre there. He wrote in 1810: "The market square with its patrician houses equals the most beautiful squares of Frankonian towns ….a truly wonderful town". In 1833 Kaiser Franz I and his wife Karoline visited Saaz on their way through Bohemia.

On 21st December 1918, the statue of the Emperor Joseph II was pulled down in Saaz and the area declared Czech. The statue had been erected in 1882, the same year that the German Prague University underwent a German-Czech partition, and the Hop Cultivation Society in Saaz celebrated its 50th anniversary the following year. Saaz was not only a lovely, well-preserved medieval town, situated on a hill with its ancient steeples and towers, but it was and is famous all over the world for the best hops.

In 1889 an attack was made on Jewish hop dealers in Saaz, entitled: 'The destructive influence of Jewry on the hop trade' by a hop merchant by the name of Danzer. It aired the antisemitic feeling that enabled a new party in Vienna, under the leadership of an MP called Georg Ritter von Schönerer, to openly declare their antipathy for Jews. Influential circles and the council in Saaz tried to prevent these divides in the town's economy, but as they spread across the nation, there was little they could do. In 1888, the man who had been mainly responsible for the abolition of "forced services" inflicted on farmers, was allowed to return to Saaz from Hoboken (America), to witness the laying of the foundation stone for his memorial (Hans Kudlich).

Germans all over Czechoslovakia protested and held demonstrations (many were Social Democrats) on 4th March 1919 relating to the 14 points of the American President Woodrow Wilson about the right of self-determination for even the smallest groups of peoples. The ruling Czechs had incorporated Slovakia into their territory and declared the newly formed Republic of Czecho-Slovakia. This had enabled the Czechs to seize power and now reign over the rest of the population. If these 14 points applied to the Czechs, then they must also apply to the Germans and Slovaks. Czechs accounted for 43% of the population, Slovaks for 22%, Germans for 23%, the remaining 12% taken up by other minority groups. At these demonstrations, 57 Germans died and several hundreds were injured.

Czech civil servants took over from Germans unless the latter had full command of the Czech language. Czech schools (in Saaz a teacher's training college) took over German schools and German classes were shut down.

A large school had been built in Saaz which occasioned the Austrian Teachers' Association in 1890 to hold their annual meeting there. In the same year, the price of hops per 50 kg sack reached the rare price of 200 fl. (Kronen).

In 1891 the population of Saaz had doubled in 50 years from 6600 to 13,234. In 1892 the currency was changed all over the country to Kronen and Heller.

In 1910, Josefine Ziegler, an author's widow, left Saaz one million Kronen for the poor. Every year 40,000 Kronen were distributed. In 1912, gas was replaced by electricity with the exception of street lighting. The arrangement with the British Continental-Gas-Association was maintained until 1920.

In 1920, elections took place and five German parties took their seats in parliament in Prague, which did not help the Germans, because they stood alone. Although the Slovaks voted with the Czechs, they did not like the way they were treated by them, a factor which was later to give Hitler a reason to take over the whole of Czechoslovakia, not just the German areas.

In 1918, on 29th October, (before the elections), the Germans in Bohemia declared themselves a provincial government with the aim to be part of Austria. Not surprisingly, the Czechs did not agree with this. In Saaz, people could not get accustomed to the fact that nearly every inscription and sign was in Czech, and every effort was made to wipe out any traces of the Austrian Empire. The Germans could do very little about this, but did what was possible. For instance, in 1922, they attempted to prove that Saaz had a long history of being a German town by unveiling a plaque at the town hall commemorating Johannes von Schüttwa, known as Johannes von Saaz; a town clerk who had written a major German work around the year 1400, which proved to be not only a masterpiece in German literature, but laid the foundations for a common German language, a forerunner of the first Bible translation by Martin Luther. Officially, a common German, bureaucratic language had existed for some time, created by Johann von Neumarkt and taken from Meissen in Saxony.

This work by Johannes von Saaz was the first work written in it, and when printing began a few decades later, 'Der Ackerman' was the first illustrated, as well as one of the most widely published books in Germany.

In this early literary jewel, entitled *Der Ackermann und der Tod* (Death and the Ploughman), Death separates Johannes from his beloved wife. As the ploughman, Johannes accuses Death of senselessly destroying all human efforts and aspirations. He wants to defend humanity, speak of the absolute value of life, and of man as God's most beautiful work of art. Death appears as an almost satanic figure, who insists on his unlimited power and points to the worthlessness and nonentity of human existence, which derives from a void, runs a short course of being, and seeps back into a void, forever yoked and coerced. After repeated reproaches made by Johannes, Death restrains his attacks and finally finds words of consolation for Johannes. The ploughman realizes the senselessness of his accusations and accepts his fate. In humility he bows before God the judge, the abode of the secret that reveals itself only in man's belief and trust, the mystery of the resurrection and the immortality of the soul.

Although the world that Pepi lived in seemed to have changed a lot, life, and especially youth, went on pursuing its carefree and hopeful course in enjoying and exploring the world. Pepi was now an attractive teenager with black hair and a tremendous sense of fun like her brother. The eldest sister was also good-looking with an eye-catching figure that did not diminish much with age, but both she and her younger sister Anni lacked Pepi's elan and buoyancy. Elegance they had, always; a feature usually absent in Pepi. Admittedly, as a teenager she did try to dress à la mode. As the first silk stockings made their victorious entry into the world of ladies and ladies-to-be, Pepi scraped her meagre earnings together and paraded a pair proudly through the town. The favourite walk for young people was "unter den Lauben", one of the most imposing streets in Bohemia, an arcade on one side of the town's square which prevented the stroller and window-shopper from coming in direct contact with the elements, whilst creating a pleasant atmosphere for eyeing and attracting the opposite sex and promoting his own qualities. Many a blushing maiden would promenade up and down this arcade with her silken stockings disintegrating slowly but surely. The grey, glass-like fabric embracing a shapely leg did not stretch much. Something had to give, and not the leg.. First one ladder, then a second would appear until one stocking looked entirely different from the other.

However much Pepi tried to be ladylike, her carefree temperament always got the better of her. Even aged 18, when her father played in the band which marched through the town during festivals, she would hop in front, conducting and making great, sweeping gestures with her hands.

Pepi's dream had always been to become a dressmaker. She was in fact an unwaged apprentice in a needlework shop for a while, where she just watched the girls at their work from 1916-1917, and if she wanted to sew anything, she had to bring her own materials and threads. Inflation was soaring (hops per cwt. were 7000 Kr. or more) and she needed to earn some money like her eldest sister Marie. The latter was getting married and needed someone to take over her customers in her hairdressing business. Thus, Pepi became a self-employed hairdresser with a string of faithful clients. She saw them in their own houses on certain days or every day, depending on their means. There was Frau Wurdinger, the rich wife of a doctor who owned a brewery; also director Luksch who was head of the local grammar school and could afford to have his wife groomed regularly. For over 20 years, an engineer's wife, whose husband worked in the sugarbeet factory, was another regular customer. Also Frau Bondy, a Hungarian hopdealer's wife, who asked Pepi to join her in Pystian, a Hungarian spa, where she hoped to cure her rheumatism. Pepi was not only her hairdresser, but also her companion for five weeks. There was lovely food, beautiful surroundings and the spa orchestra. Pepi felt spoilt and pampered by it all. All these ladies could not be seen by anyone till they had their hair coiffured early in the morning.

Pepi was admired by numerous young men. One of them, a good-looking, muscular lad, invited her on a boat trip on the river Eger that looked like a moat (Saaz being situated on top of a hill represented the castle). Pepi enjoyed the hardly audible dipping of the oars into the water, the stillness of the air, cut occasionally by the cry of a bird, the delightful view of the town with its old guard towers and new white houses, the big iron bridge (*Kettenbrücke*) leading into the hop fields with their long wires reaching up into the sky and the hop plants twisting around them, trying to outdo each other. What impressed her the most was the strength of this boy which she gauged by the ease with which he handled the oars and the speed they created with their smooth, forward movement. She stared at him admiringly. Suddenly, as her examining eye rested on his socks which peeped from beneath his loose trouser legs, she realized that one was a different colour from the other. The young man smiled at her, unaware that his fate was sealed, and nothing he did from then on would reawaken the tender feelings Pepi had felt for him just two seconds before. One could question whether these were indeed two socks from two different pairs. Could it not be that one had been put on inside out and thus looked entirely different? Through her mistake (not to mention her prejudice!), she may have missed the chance of a lifetime and changed her own fate dramatically.

On the other hand, one could speculate that this was puppy-love, for soon after she fell genuinely in love with a young barber who bought her an engagement ring, only to disappear shortly afterwards to Vienna without a word of explanation. She decided not to marry anyone, and for a long while it looked as though she would be true to her word. After her beloved father died early through hardening of the arteries in 1928, a gloom spread over her life that she had never known before.

At times, when she was quite young and particularly happy, she would try to imagine life without her parents, and her cheerfulness would turn to inconsolable sadness and dread. Now that her father was dead, she couldn't prevent herself becoming nostalgic about all the little and big events and incidents connected with him.

There was only one such event that she would have liked to forget, but the older she grew, the more she accepted it. Pepi and her sister Anni sang very sweetly together. One carnival time, they had been asked to sing, with a woman pianist accompanying them. They had something to eat and drink in a cellar bar beneath a large hall in which many balls and other entertainments were held. Anni wanted to show off a bit, lit a cigarette and ostentatiously blew the smoke as far away from herself as possible. The bar was called 'Hell', a befitting name for it as Pepi spotted her father coming down the steps from the hall during the interval. He wanted to refresh himself after playing in the band upstairs to which he would be returning in a few minutes. Sometimes he played in a trio in 'Hell'. Pepi signalled to her sister and pointed in the direction of 'father'. But at that precise moment, 'father' saw Anni with her cigarette between pouting lips and without hesitation, he came over and brought his hand sharply across her face. Nobody present could avoid hearing and seeing this spectacle; thus the girls were forced to leave right away, with Pepi blaming Anni for having spoiled a nice evening , and for having upset father. This behaviour was very out of character for him.

There was another incident which became engraved on Pepi's memory. Carnival times were mad occasions, but pleasantly so, and they were fondly recalled for the rest of the year. People threw themselves into a stream of bustling activities and pleasures. Every year, on the occasion of the Gherkin Ball (Saaz was also famous for its gherkins), a gherkin king was elected.

One day, a postal worker called Zulauf Pold came to the flat to ask if he could borrow a top hat. He knew that Pepi's father always had to wear one for work. Pepi told Pold that her father was currently wearing the hat.

"Hasn't he got another one at home?" he pressed.

"Yes, but it's a brand new one. He's only worn it a few times."

"I assure you; in fact, I swear to you that I'll bring it back in mint condition," he said in his broad local accent.

After some hesitation on Pepi's side, and constant assurances that he "only needed it for carnival" and "he won't know I've had it," Zulauf Pold made his exit with the hat. Not long afterwards, Pepi spent an evening with friends in a public house called *Die Herberge*, when the door opened and none other than Pold with entourage breezed in, whistling and more than a little tipsy, wearing a top hat with... No, it couldn't be. Pepi felt her heart miss a beat and the blood rush to her face with anger, as though a trigger had been pulled. She rushed over and nearly fell towards him, blocking his waving hands and swaying body at a stroke.

"How dare you cut two holes in my father's new hat just to put a stupid big feather through – are you completely stupid or something ?"

Pold's complacent smile faded instantly, but otherwise he didn't seem particularly bothered. Pepi blamed herself; she should have known better. Pold never went out with his wife. She suffered from headaches a lot, which was not surprising with a house full of canaries and budgerigars that he insisted on breeding. It was obvious that thoughtfulness and consideration were not Pold's forte. Pepi decided to go to Mentschek's where the hat had been bought. They had to order another one from Vienna, and fortunately, Anton never knew any better. When Pepi saw Pold clamber into his own window early one morning after a big carnival ball, she could not help laughing; he had a huge sun painted on his behind and just as he bent down and manoeuvered himself over the window ledge, it looked like the rising sun and rather funny in the circumstances.

Franz, the youngest and most cherished brother, was growing up. His trade was the construction and French-polishing of pianos. He had been a sickly child, but his health improved with time and his vivacity increased the older he got.

His father sent him to have piano lessons, and in summer Franz would arrive outside the teacher's house panting with thirst. So he took his felt hat off and from the long-handled iron pump pumped a good measure of water into it. While drinking from the hat, he would spill half the water over his face and nearly into his protruding ears, then he would shake himself and the hat (which he threw over the top of the pump to dry) and stride into the house with a grin. That was Franz.

When he came home from playing the accordion somewhere, he had to pass through Pepi's room to get to his own. Disregarding her tiredness, he would shake her vigorously from her sleep and tell her the latest gags. "This is no joke, waking me up so rudely in the middle of the night, when you know I have to get up early," she hissed at him. But after hearing the joke, delivered with deliberation and Franz's usual slow and good-natured way of talking, she would tell him to get lost in a monotonous tone that she could maintain only as long as she heard the door bang; then constrained chuckles would shake the feather bed for a good while after.

Once he came home from entertaining and found Pepi up scrubbing the floor. He was pleased. "Stand on this little footstool over here," he demanded. "Not me, mate," she grunted. "You're not making a fool of me again." He assured her that this was something really good and quite different from the usual tomfoolery. "You tap out a tune with this shoe-horn while standing on the stool and I have to tell you what tune it is," he said eagerly, bending down to look at her. She got up slowly, wiped her hands on her apron, got the shoe-horn and quickly mounted the stool. As she faced him, with her arms ready to conduct a large symphony orchestra, Franz had to fight an intense urge to break down into a fit of laughter. Instead he urged her:-

"Come on, tap on the wall with your shoe horn and I'll tell you what you're playing." Her face became tense with concentration and she banged out a tune deliberately and with great emphasis. He began to tap his foot to her rhythm and hummed quietly. "What have I been playing then?" she asked, her chin forward and arms relaxed again. "The fool. The fool again, my dear girl, as always."

Apart from listening to brass bands, (Pepi's favourite entertainment - she had walked behind many and always wanted to be in front, conducting), going dancing or seeing an operetta at the theatre, there was one innovation that never ceased to amaze her and most of her contemporaries - talking films as compared to silent movies; how the heroine would swoon, and flash her long, dark eyelashes towards her elegant and suave partner, and now, you could actually hear the very words they were saying with all these meaningful gestures.

The world had launched itself like a rocket and was gathering incredible pace and momentum – automobiles were taking over from horses, sewing machines from seamstresses and a variety of other intricate machinery was replacing man; women's legs could now be seen, canalisation took a large step forward, electricity had become a reality (and was to, partially, substitute gas) and the crowning glory of man's progress and achievement was a flying machine which made nonsense of the world's leading mathematician's prediction that it was a physical impossibility for such a machine to lift off: now or ever.

Households which had appreciated gas or petroleum lights, water from the pump outside and latrines either in or outside, now considered these 'mod-cons' outdated and established luxuries like flushing toilets inside their living quarters, electric light in all rooms and even cold water directly from a tap over a sink. What would grandma and pa say now, were they alive? At the same time, they would surely turn in their graves at the sight of the liberties that young people took these days. Not in awe of their elders any more, they smoked cigarettes in long holders while dancing the Charleston, a dance which would have been suitable for the uncivilized, but was wholly inappropriate for respectable people.

Marie had married a very handsome accountant, called Karl Stupka. They had a daughter Elli in 1918, a son Gerhard in 1919 and another son Erich in 1926. Marie and Karl were an eye-catching couple, and their children inherited their beauty. They all had very bright blue eyes like their father with one difference. Their father had steel-blue penetrating eyes and was very quick-witted and intelligent. That does not mean that his children lacked in these qualities, but his were outstanding. With his straight black hair, even features, firm mouth and enquiring eyes, he had an incredible effect on the opposite sex. He was naturally well aware of this, but although he enjoyed the attention showered on him by the fairer sex, he was equally interested in financial matters. He turned from accountant to tax adviser to estate-agent and later became a taxi-contractor (see taxis at Saaz market square). He was something of a gambler all round. If his wife needed him, she knew where to find him. He could usually be found playing cards in the most popular hotel of the town. Nevertheless, he had managed to buy a house and was a respected member of the Saaz bourgeoisie. He had borrowed money from various people, including Pepi's mother (insurance from Anton's death) and also from Franz, without ever repaying it and nearly ruining some of his own relatives financially.

Saaz had boomed in the two decades before the Great War. It was never the same afterwards, although its hops were as popular as ever, even abroad, and its vegetables (esp. cucumbers) were sought after throughout the region. (The inhabitants of Saaz were affectionately known as "Soozer Gorgenlootscher" which meant that they trod in cucumbers wherever they went.) Many guilds took endless opportunities for celebrations, in which brass bands had important roles to play. The life of the town was colourful, with many different associations, various music clubs and choirs. They had always been in the forefront of all social life. The two newspapers, the theatre and cinema, the weekly market,[1] etc., entertained, informed and supplied the citizens as best they could. Everyone was willing to contribute towards a common goal, and even now the people were prepared to give the President, Thomas Masaryk, a chance "to make the Czechoslovak Republic a kind of Switzerland, taking into consideration, of course, the special conditions in Bohemia." (This phrase was taken from a memorandum composed by the then Foreign Secretary Dr. Benes for the benefit of the Peace Conference in St. Germain in September 1919, in which the British and American delegations had expressed doubts concerning the newly-founded Republic). In 1926 the Czech government began to introduce a 'land-reform', under which large German estates were confiscated and Czech minions brought in, so that many German villages had strong Czech minority groups.

A certain independence in small matters was given to the Germans, so that they occasionally felt progress was being made. The Germans had worked hard over many centuries to develop the vital industries all round the peripheral areas, especially in Bohemia and Moravia, where the German communities lived. The rich, fertile land in the centre of the country was owned and cultivated by Czechs. When the depression struck at the end of the twenties, the Czech authorities were able to make good use of their position.

---

[1] It had been in existence for hundreds of years.

In the aforementioned memorandum III, Benes highlighted the assistance that the Czech government had given the Allies toward winning the First World War through withholding the delivery of agricultural produce to German areas. This strategy was now being repeated. When the Czechs mobilized in 1921 against Hungary, nearly all the Germans in Czechoslovakia, but not all Czechs, were conscripted. According to some estimates, of all the unemployed in Czechoslovakia (500,000), three quarters were Sudeten-Germans. Already in 1923, the Sudeten German Social Democrats had handed over a memorandum to the International Socialist Congress in Hamburg protesting against the treatment of the Germans in CSR.

Pepi's mother was able to draw a pension of 900 Kronen a month after her husband died in 1928. Pepi and Nand had married on 18th October 1931 (Church Dedication Sunday) in the Dekanatskirche in Saaz. Father had come and Emil, Nand's eldest brother, was Best Man. Marie, Nand's mother could not be present, but came later, to meet Pepi's mother just before Rosa died. Rosa was supporting Pepi and Nand financially, not just letting them stay in her flat, but in every way possible. Pepi had saved 10.000 kronen at the time of her marriage to Nand. She also had a considerable trousseau, put together over many years. She now bought a sewing machine, (a dream come true, as sewing had always been her passion) and was able to save a little more after her marriage, as they lived with Rosa in the Husarenhaus (which belonged to a Czech Jew, called Justiz. Franz also lived there until he was drafted into the Czech Army, where he was when Pepi and Nand married.)

Pepi's mother had tried in vain to prevent her daughter's marriage. "He's a child and a peasant, and you have nothing in common with him," she would say sorrowfully. "I wish you'd gone to America with that man, but who's to know..." she hinted about a previous friendship Pepi had renounced for the sake of her mother who was already ill at the time. She had not actually prevented Pepi from going to Bogota, but Pepi could not bring herself to leave her, old and infirm as she was.

Once the deed was done and they had married, however, Rosa never said another word about it, but went about helping as much as she could. On 31st October 1932 Pepi gave birth to a little girl with long, black, bushy hair and questioning eyes. They called her Elisabeth. Her arrival was hardly convenient, but they loved her dearly. Pepi breastfed the child exclusively and had to dash back from her customers every few hours, finding her mother was walking up and down the room with the screaming baby in her arms. Pepi was also a paid wet-nurse for another baby.

Dr. Heller, the Jewish house doctor attended to Rosa more frequently, and when Elisabeth was just five months old, Rosa died in hospital, on 29th March 1933.

CHAPTER 5
Hitler becomes Chancellor

Just a couple of months earlier, on 30th January 1933, Adolf Hitler, the power-hungry dreamer, who had renounced orthodox religion after the Great War and decided just to believe in himself, had become the leader of Germany. The Weimar Republic was now history.

With his Austrian charm he swashbuckled his way through many tricky situations and failing this, used lies, blackmail and brute force to materialise his dreams and plans. His path to absolute power was a remarkable and curious achievement (288 seats =44%) in the Reichstag elections on 5th March 1933, considering that on 6th November 1932 his party, the NSDAP (National Socialists German Workers Party), had lost 34 seats since July 1932 to a total of 196. The Socialists had 121 seats, the Communists 100 in November 1932. In the 1928 elections, the NSDAP had 12 seats, *and the Communists 54.[1]

Becoming aware of the gathering strength of the communist party in North Germany (in Berlin, they were the strongest party under the leadership of Ernst Thälmann), the industrialists and important people from abroad started financing Hitler to stem this menacing tide from the East. The Social Democrats were also seen as a threat. Both were para-military organisations,calling themselves *Reichsbanner* and *Rotfrontkämpferbund, respectively*. By 1930, Hitler's party was the second biggest after the Social Democrats. In that year, there were 3 million unemployed, by 1932 it was 6 million. On 10th April 1932, Hitler had tried to get the presidency, opposing Hindenburg, who was backed by the Social Democrats, the Centre Party and liberal groups in the Reichstag (Parliament). Hitler failed, but his NSDAP now had 230 out of 608 seats in parliament by 31st July 1932. His defeat made him realize that he could only achieve his aims by being the sheep in wolf's clothing. Hindenburg stood for democracy and the Weimar Constitution. So did his supporters. Hitler's para-military NSDAP, formed in 1920 from ex-soldiers and the SA-*Sturmabteilungen* (Stormtroopers), with ex-officers joining under Goering's and Hitler's leadership, had been banned several

---

[1] Reichspräsident Hindenburg and other powerful politicians thought they could use him as a tool and expediently dispose of him in due course, but he railroaded them instead. Germany needed to adapt from a Kaiserreich to an industrialised society which takes responsibility for itself.

times, but always resurged. Hindenburg had refused the appointment of Hitler as Chancellor in August 1932. But Hitler would not give up. After his unsuccessful coup in Munich in 1923, he was sentenced to 5 years imprisonment, in which time he wrote *Mein Kampf*. With the help of General Ludendorff, he was released from prison after only 8 months. He now had to convince the masses and the 'wounded' ex-military that Germany was still a great nation after the humiliating loss of land and the absolute defeat in the power struggle of the Great War and that, under his, Hitler's, leadership Germany would show the world how intrinsically pre-eminent it was. Calling his party '*Arbeiterpartei*' (Labour Party) ensured that all German classes were included in his plan for the future greatness of Germany. Important people like General Ludendorff, Heinrich Himmler, Rudolf Hess, Hermann Göring, Julius Streicher and, by now, leading figures at home and abroad, came to Hitler's aid and supported him in any way they could.

In 1926, Hitler had met Dr. Joseph Goebbels, one of the greatest propagantists of all times. It was he who opened the way to Hitler's victory in Berlin, the capital of Germany. It was he and Hitler, who fired the nation to keep their goal in view to the bitter end, brainwashing the people to hold to the Machiavellian belief that the end justifies the means. Goebbels became the supreme administrator, legislator and judge.

Hitler, being Austrian, had to take on German nationality to be eligible for election. From April 1932 to December of the same year, General von Schleicher and Hitler were involved in several intrigues, which weakened and confused von Papen's government to the point of collapse on 3rd December 1932 when Schleicher became Chancellor. The latter had the army behind him and was influential in German politics. He wanted to use Hitler to form a new government. But Hitler's NSDAP refused its support to Schleicher. Von Papen's suggestion to Hindenburg to withdraw Schleicher's mandate and ask Hitler to form a new government as Chancellor on 3rd January 1933 finally opened the door to Hitler's long-nurtured dream. After some conflicts with his opponents, his party became the only legitimate one in Germany and the ruthless dictatorship began. On the death of Hindenburg on 2nd August 1934 (he had been too old and weak to be an effective participant in decision-making at the point of Hitler's inauguration), Hitler took it upon himself to become Führer of the nation. Also, the army was bound by oath to his person. He replaced the Trade Unions with the DAF, *Deutsche Arbeitsfront* on 2nd May 1933.

The S.A.(*Sturmabteilung* – fighting Communism) under Röhm which had brutally and illegally attacked opponents of Hitler's party in arbitrary ways was now relegated. It had developed into a powerful organ independent of the army and consisting mainly of terrorizing thugs. Hitler was urged to have Röhm, Schleicher and other party friends shot in June 1934. Instead of the S.A, the SS-*Schutzstaffel* (originally Hitler's bodygard) became a highly regulated, disciplined elite under Heinrich Himmler. It has been argued that without him and his organisational skills and 'divide and rule' policies to create rivalries, the war would have ended much quicker.

In Germany, at the time of Hitler's 'take-over', there were 6 million unemployed. In 1932, Nand became one of them. There was no work for Germans in Bohemia. For the next 6 years, he was granted 10 Kronen a month due to Pepi's family's links with the mayor of Saaz. Occasionally, he would do odd jobs for some of Pepi's customers who took pity on him; shovelling coal into cellars, selling shoe polish door to door (an occupation incompatible with his nature as he was relatively shy and proud and could not sell much, so that he had supplies of shoe polish for the next few years), seasonal work, e.g. on a building site and some years in the local sugar beet factory, where one of Pepi's client's Czech husband worked as an engineer. Other times, he had no work at all, which created friction at home.

Pepi was working twice as hard now, taking in people's washing, attending to her clients, looking after her baby, husband and brother Franz as well as being a wet nurse, all minus her mother's support now.

It was at this time that Nand got to know a tailor and his wife who lived next to him "am Lorettoplatz". They had no children, and were political fanatics.

Once Pepi came to visit them, just to have a chat as neighbours. Herr Ehmig opened the door and there was Frau Ehmig, a hefty woman, standing on the table like an actress with a big piece of cloth draped around her, and with outstretched hands she boomed down: "*Germania, der grösste Feind bist Du*". (Germany, you are the greatest enemy.) How soon this exclamation would be reversed by them! Although people had tried to live a normal life, the nationalising of German property, the replacing of Germans by Czechs in the Civil Service and all official posts, the infiltration of many Czechs into the German-speaking areas of Bohemia, the general contempt with which the Germans were treated, and the subtle and not so subtle persuasion to become Czech had a slow but progressive influence on the German population. As the majority of them lived in Bohemia, which possessed most of the precious raw materials and industry, it was here where the pressure was most felt. A number of Germans had capitulated and become Czech. Some German shopkeepers, with the new influx of Czech customers, could do nothing if the latter refused to pay their debts. Some became Czech, others emigrated, many went bankrupt.

In the face of all this, the Jewish population must have felt at least bewilderment. They, too, felt the pressure. Some Jews also became Czechs as a consequence.

In 1930, when a new Rabbi began the temple ceremony in Czech, some impatient voices were heard in the ensuing tumult, shouting:- "German, we're German!" How the population of Saaz must have felt eight years later, when they remembered the loyalty the German Jews had always shown to them, even in difficult times and circumstances.

Throughout the ages, some Germans had became Czech and changed their name, while Czechs became Germans, even in name. The two nationalities had intermarried, and there must have been many who did not have the ancestors they assumed they had. But what could not be wiped out or weakened in any way was the German language, architecture, tradition and culture upheld through successive generations. Too much sweat, sacrifice and deprivation, but also comradeship and ingenuity had been invested, as the gold, coal, lignite, glass, silver, lumber, iron and steel, cotton and wool, paper, chemical and china industries (apart from the fruit and beer industries) now testified. The pioneers of all these industries were mainly Germans; they had made Bohemia famous, not just as a country of great geographical importance as the buffer between East and West. Their reward was now being taken away from them systematically and insidiously, approved internationally, and no protest could be made with any hope of being heard. The ground had been pulled from under their feet and replaced with sticks on which they balanced without noticing it. They only knew that something was fundamentally wrong and their agitation and frustration grew from year to year.

In 1933, *der Deutsche Turnverband*, an athletic association, held a big athletic festival in Saaz for eight days in which 40,000 athletes from all over Czechoslovakia participated. The highlight was the procession to the Ringplatz, the centre of the town, where Konrad Henlein, (a gymnastics teacher and head of the Deutsche Turnverband) who was to play a decisive role in the next few important years, read out a manifesto that urged the so-called Sudeten Germans (because of the Sudeten mountain range) to gather together and speak with one voice.

The *Sudetendeutsche Heimatfront* (home front) was consequently founded, which soon turned into a political party under the name of *Sudetendeutsche Partei*. The political fever that had gripped the German areas was thus directed into a particular direction, gathering momentum and being exploited to the full at the expense of desperate people who had had no experience in airing their voices as one.

Every year, Nand would ask if he could be employed at the sugar beet factory when the sugar beet season started which necessitated extra labour. One year a Czech administrator there told him: "We have no work for Germans." Nand was stunned and furious. He decided to join a political party that instant, one which would voice his view on the present outrageous situation. He had not been interested in politics before this incident. He was often seen with Ehmig, the tailor, and another man, a brewery worker called Haug. Ehmig had joined the Sudetendeutsche Heimatfront as soon as it was founded, and Nand was now a member too. He had plenty of time on his hands being out of work, so in 1936 he changed over from the Arbeitsfront, and soon became an organizer for meetings and was in charge of a *Hundertschaft* (a group of a hundred).

He still went home to Gerten from time to time to visit his family. His brothers worked away in neighbouring districts, but they all met up on special occasions or religious feast days. Franz and Karl had learned all about retailing as apprentices in Kriegern and felt a little superior to the rest of their brothers, as they did not have to soil their hands in their occupation. Their brother Wilhelm or 'Pepp' had married a nice local girl called Anna (or Antsch as they all called her as there already was an Anna in the family), and they lived with Nand's parents in their house in two rooms that had first been occupied by a Czech family who had been sitting tenants.

The house was no longer teeming with young children and only the sound of Father's hammering could be heard. Looking over his spectacles at Nand and sucking his pipe, he would talk in his deliberate tone of voice:

"I see you're smoking one of those coffin nails. That's what I call them, because that's what they are. Nails are driven into the coffin, one by one, till the coffin is ready and waiting for you. But you young folk won't listen. You know it all, like that hothead Hitler who was a nobody and is now the Führer of Germany. Mind you, I have to admit he has been seen to succeed where others have failed. I give him that. He wiped out the Communists good and proper, just when they thought they had Germany as good as in their pockets. In Prussia, they were already in control in some areas. But that doesn't mean he's any good for the country in other respects." He pulled out his checkered handkerchief and began to wipe his chin, because he had had his pipe in his mouth during this (for him) unusually long speech.

"Father, you have no idea how effective Herr Hitler really is. He has only been in office a short while, but already he has rectified a thousand things. He's given us back our self respect; even statesmen abroad look up to him and the ordinary German can start to save again, now they shall have work once more thanks to him, without being afraid of their money losing its value overnight. You'll see Father, Hitler will make Germany great. You read his book: *Mein Kampf*, and you'll see what a great man he is. He has vision, father. That's what Germany needs. When they were down and out, he came and saved them just before total chaos and the Communists getting the upper hand. He should have succeeded the first time he tried in 1923, but those stupid Bavarians are such blockheads. They even put him in prison." [1]Nand's eyes shone and his wavy, receding hair which he and most of his brothers had inherited from their bald father fell about his ears with his emphatic gestures. Father just shook his head with all this "boys talk."

Mother had a new worry. Since Antsch, who was a wonderful woman with lots of courage and wit, had come into the house, a lot of innocent joke-cracking and laughing was going on in the yard between her and Father. Once Mother could not restrain herself and during one of their never-ending marital quarrels she burst out: "You seem to think more of her than you do of me." Father looked blank for a moment, then he roared with laughter and made the most of this new situation. Another victory won.

After Rosa had died, the landlord, Herr Justiz, wanted her flat, but although the law protected tenants in Pepi's situation, in October 1936 they moved into a nearby old monastery; which belonged to the brewery next door, because Nand was, by that time, on the 'wanted list', collated by the Czech authorities of all Germans in an official, party-serving capacity in the 'Sudetendeutsche Partei'. He was also seen associating with Ehmig on a regular basis, which only served to arouse further suspicion.

CHAPTER 6
Politics and Religion

I was born in this very neglected, former monastery on 29th December, 1936, my mother's birthday. During my birth, my collar bones broke, which nobody seemed to have noticed. Fifteen minutes after my birth, a gypsy woman appeared and told my mother the exact content of her purse. All through my life, I have encountered gypsies and their prophesies.

---

[1] Rudolf Hess was wounded in the leg in the struggle to overthrow a Communist regime in Munich in May 1919.

The house was called Muttergotteshaus - The Madonna's House – because a long time ago, the order had dedicated it to the "Mother of God"; later a Czech woman had bought it from them, then it was known after her name as "Bubitschka". It had beautiful, religious images painted on its façade, but nothing could hide the fact that it was swarming with beetles of all shapes and sizes. Despite my parents valiant efforts to drive them away, the beetles had decided that they had a long-standing right to live there and stood their ground in the face of these fastidious newcomers. The house was rent-free for brewery workers and my father qualified as such a one at that time. In 1936 he was a volunteer stoker for three months, and after an examination in Karlsbad and three more months volunteering in the brewery, he qualified as an engine fitter (*Heizer* and *Maschinenwärter*). An exception had been made in his case, because my mother had a client whose husband was an important figure in the brewery and was finally responsible for employing my father on a paid basis. He had been without proper pay or a job for six years and the examinations had been costly. Work for smithies was running out fast as cars were replacing horses, and machines were doing the work of artisans.

It was an interesting process, changing barley into malt. With six others, my father, (who was 28 at the time), had to half fill three enormous concrete tanks with water at 3.30 in the morning. The barley, placed in the water, became soft and after a few days began to sprout. During this time it had to be turned, and its temperature regularly monitored. After the now white looking barley had dried on the concrete floor (*auf der Tenne*), the white shoots were removed from the swollen grains (whilst still checking the temperature), then it was ready. The smell of damp barley was everywhere, but it was not an unpleasant one.

In 1937 Thomas Masaryk died. He had been a Slovak professor of philosophy and first president of the republic. The Germans had respected him. In his years as a history teacher in Vienna, he had published a thesis, called 'finis austriae', in which he expressed his conviction that a multinational state was doomed from the start due to the explosive will for freedom of the different nationalities contained within it. "twenty years of peace at any one time is the most we can hope for."

Eduard Benes had already taken over from him in 1935, although the biggest Czech party, the Agrarians (who were anti-Communist) did not agree with his foreign policies, especially his alignment with France and Russia.

M. Beran was pro some kind of pact with Henlein and Hitler on the Polish model (German Polish agreement in 1934, there were Germans in Poland too, Danzig was wholly German, some parts of German Silesia belonged to Poland and some to Czechoslovakia). On the whole, Czech peasants were grateful to the Government for the Land Reform that gave most farmers their own land, and whether they liked Benes and his policies or not, they would have to support him.

In 1936 there was a debate as to whether Czechs and Slovaks were one nation or two. The Slovaks were disunited; they sympathised more with the Poles than the Czechs. They looked upon the Czechs as chauvinistic and small-minded who dominated them by putting their own people in charge of official positions everywhere.

Konrad Henlein, who had seemed a modest man with good intentions and who by 1938 had most of the Sudeten-Germans behind him, (representing the second largest party in Parliament, some having transferred to his party en masse from social or sports clubs, etc.) transpired later not to be what he had seemed to be. A faithful follower of Hitler, he became "the voice in the wilderness" that could be heard loud and clear across oceans and frontiers. No more helpless and hopeless frustration for the Germans who had suffered all these years. With blazing banner, united they stood, with Henlein as their spokesman. Czech pressure eased. They even started to put Germans into official places again. Henlein demanded autonomy and the right to self-defence. But there was hesitation in Prague. Then Henlein changed his pleas to nothing less than annexation to Germany.

The *Times* newspaper in England reported in September 1938 that 'the essentially German-speaking part of Czechoslovakia should be conceded to Hitler', and *The Statesman* thought that 'the strategical value of the Bohemian frontier should not be made the occasion of a world war'. Lord Runciman, in his report to the British Prime Minister (26th September 1938) mentions 'discrimination, lack of understanding, petty intolerance, empty promises, tactlessness, and obstinacy on the part of the Czech authorities towards the Sudeten Germans, which has led to a deep mistrust.' He said that although the Germans were represented in Parliament with 44 seats out of 300, they could be overruled at any time, so that they were powerless on a parliamentary basis. Czechs with little knowledge of German had been put in control everywhere in these German areas with the result of many Czech schools having been built for their children. Czech enterprises were being used a lot more for supply and services to the detriment of the German firms.

In the last days of his stay in Czechoslovakia, Lord Runciman had seen no willingness on the part of the Czech Government to try to remedy these bad conditions in any way, which were mainly responsible for the grossly ruinous effects that the depression had on the vital industries. It was not without reason that the Government had been made responsible for the ensuing impoverishment. The main complaint from the Sudeten Germans was their fear of being "swallowed up" by their former counterparts, the Czechs.

All these conditions were truthfully reported by Lord Runciman. But what reasons could a British delegate possibly have for pointing out and investigating the complaints of a 'minority in a faraway land of whom we know nothing,' as one politician had once put it? The last part of Lord Runciman's report gives an answer to this. He points out that Czechoslovakia would never be able to afford a confrontation with any of its neighbours, not just to maintain its existence, but for the preservation of European peace. This was the crux of the matter. To put it as simply as possible, Czechoslovakia, and to an extent Austria are the central points where East meets West and North meets South, when considering Europe and Asia as a whole. So many millions of Germans lived in these Eastern European countries (Czechoslovakia, Austria, Poland, Yugoslavia, Romania, Bulgaria, North Italy and even as far away as Estonia, Latvia and Lithuania). The latter had been given the German Memel land in the Treaty of Versailles. These areas had been acting as buffer-zones between East and West for as long as Germans had lived there, which was, as in the case of Bohemia, since time immemorial, but specially, according to existing records, since the 14th Century.

Austria had been competing with Prussia over who would rule over Germany. Austria's influence and power dwindled gradually and although Bismarck's reply to what his action would be if the German-Austrians wished to be annexed to Germany was: "Fight a war against them", he was well aware of the vital balance between East and West that the Austro-Hungarian Empire represented. In 1879, in Bismarck's arguments for a pact with the Empire of Austria, Bohemia was the main reason.

When I looked up "Bohemia" in my local library, one can find the following information: 'The first known inhabitants of Bohemia were the Boii who gave the country its name. By AD 400, both Slavs and Germans lived in the area. Bohemia was a German duchy during the 11th century, but became independent in 1198. During the 13th century, it was a powerful country. A period of civil wars followed the execution of John Huss in the early fourteenth century. These wars were called the Hussite wars and afterwards, the people of Bohemia followed a mildly Protestant form of religion, but in 1526 the country fell under the rule of the Catholic Habsburgs. Their repression of Protestantism caused the Thirty Years War.'

During those religious wars, Slavs and Germans had fought side by side, according to their religious beliefs. There was a common history, but as time went on, Czech voices could be heard that Slavonic traditions were being neglected and that there was a danger of becoming completely Westernised. Finally, the Slavs had to fight with the Austrians and Germans against Russia in the First World War. Their national pride stirred, and although they considered themselves as "Westerners", they did not want to lose their Slavonic heritage, the same, in fact, as the Sudeten Germans felt, after they had actually been 'swallowed up' in 1919.

The Church was caught in the middle of this conflict. The Protestant Church was proclaimed as German and many Sudeten Germans changed from being Catholics to Protestants.

My father was in the habit of going to church, being a good Catholic all his life. One Sunday morning, the priest warned and advised from the pulpit that "we have nothing to fear from Russia, only from our neighbouring country" (by which he meant Germany). This was too much for my father. How could this priest say that we had nothing to fear from Russia, when Germany, the neighbouring country, had nearly been overrun by Communism – hadn't Adolf Hitler crushed it?! He had rooted them out relentlessly, and those who did not like his punishments and necessary measures would have to be made to see things properly and face facts. What was the alternative? Poverty throughout the classes, shame and humiliation, not only for having lost the war, but for loss of territory, money, prestige and power, even the right to defend oneself or determine one's own future. Everything was ruined, and thus the Communists had achieved an easy victory in many places. People everywhere in Germany had lost all drive, initiative and incentive. Until recently, they had been bewildered, frightened and trusted nobody. Hitler had changed all that.

Everything was being built up - roads, factories and bridges, as well as people's minds and morale. The "Führer" knew that once you have persuaded and indoctrinated people with your aims and goals, shown your ability and strength, added the hatred of a minority as a driving force, kept them in check with 'carrot and stick' to make them feel safe, the people would give everything they had. Nand argued that we had nothing to fear from Germany; in fact, our help came from there. Our mother country Germany was being freed from being strangled by the victorious allies. They had cut it up and destroyed it. Hitler was seen to restore it – a true saviour.

It was not difficult to convince people that something had to be done. Their very existence depended on action at that crucial point, when Hitler was seen and heard to be doing something about it and doing it effectively.

"The little corporal," as Hindenburg had once called him, knew how the populace could be manoeuvred and made into a vehicle suited to his purpose. Not only had he read Freud, Schopenhauer and studied all the great politicians, generals and monarchs, he had also lived amongst many people in the trenches and as a waif in Vienna, where he had had ample opportunity to study each character in detail, getting a clear picture of what appealed to all of them and why.

In the Great War he had received six medals for bravery, including the First and Second Iron Cross. Then why had he never risen above the rank of corporal? He was intelligent, yet he had never been able to do something really constructive in a job or in the Arts which he loved. Why, on earth, had he not been accepted by the Art Academy in Vienna, when recent tests have shown that he had sufficient talent for it The world would have been saved from one of the greatest tragedies it had ever known.

He was able to memorize whole scores of Wagner, whose heroic themes had had an enormous impact on him since his early youth. There is no doubt that he was obsessed by power, and we can see now that the difference between him and other leaders throughout history is that they knew how far they could go (like Frederick the Great on whom he modelled himself) without creating utter chaos and desolation. Unfortunately, Hitler knew of no limitations or boundaries as many dictators before of after him.

So, my father told my mother that he was going to be a Protestant. My mother was shocked. She could not agree with the priest either, but she was not going to change her religion, her ancestors had held sacred, for the sake of a different political opinion. As my father started to walk across the big square Lorettoplatz in front of the house to go through with his plan, my mother, watching him through the window, felt a fierce conflict raging inside her. What was she going to do? As a Catholic it would be very difficult to raise her children in that faith with her husband being a Protestant. They would not be able to go to church together as a family, and what would the children say when she took them to the Catholic church while their father attended a service at the Protestant church? It was an impossible situation. She would have to put her personal, innermost feelings aside for the sake of the common good. She foresaw that everything personal would have to be sacrificed for the Führer and the party. They had got the Germans out of the mire, and the least one could do now, was to do exactly what one was told; indeed one should accept the decisions and doctrines like one embraces a religion, willingly, never minding the cost and denying oneself.

She opened the window and shouted down loudly and with determination: "Nand, it's all right. I don't want to be different." He nodded and went on his way. They had had their difficulties in the first few years of marriage, but now they had a common goal where personal differences could not be tolerated.

My mother had been the obedient wife during the first years of their marriage, as it was the culture of the day for the husband to be "the master" as the provider, leaving the wife the time and leisure to raise the children. My father was naturally very upset that his wife had been the provider. He had tried hard enough to find work, and a proper job, but all to no avail. In his pricked pride and frustration, his behaviour became quite bizarre.

One day he saw some plums that were going cheap in town and he had recommended them to her. He asked my mother for the price of the ones she had bought.They had been considerably dearer than the recommended ones, as my mother had bought them on her way home from work. She had no time to go to the market, combining all her commitments at home with her job. Not long after this, she received a letter from a solicitor telling her to see him on a certain day at a certain time. She felt perplexed and could not think of a reason for this summons. With shaky knees she appeared before the solicitor, only to learn that she had persistently disobeyed her husband. Why, for instance, had she not bought her fruit and vegetables at the cheaper establishment suggested by her husband? She stammered something and left as soon as she could, not quite believing her own ears for a while. She should not have married him, she thought bitterly - her mother had been right. She had a difficult life as it was without him making it completely impossible. But she had to admit that she cared for him, whatever happened.

Czech officials and the militia were looking for him, sometimes every night. (*Regierungskommisar* and Polizei). He and a few others hid mostly in a big barrel at the brewery (established in 1901) next to the old monastery where we lived. Sometimes it was possible for my father to slip into the house at night under the cover of darkness, and hide there. Most of the time he stayed hidden at the brewery at night until 4-5am. After that time, he would first try Haug's house, which was even closer than ours. The whole family (I was still a baby) had to be ready to leave at any time, day or night. We kept our clothes on, even in bed, in case someone alerted us of their approach. Eventually, my mother could stand it no longer. From one day to the next, we moved in with my Aunt Marie and Uncle Karl at Lange Gasse, not far away from our home, but nobody suspected my father being there.

Haug was arrested one night, just before he tried to jump out of the window. He had hesitated as he saw some Czech officials outside. "Too late," he thought. They burst in and asked where 'Schroll' (my father) was. Haug replied that he had no idea, which was true. They dragged him into a van and beat him all the way to the jail and court (Bezirksgericht) which was near the theatre. He was lucky. Some, amongst them Freiherr,'Edler Meier von Weinertsgrün', a rich aristocrat who owned an estate with hop fields and nine houses in town, were dragged to the 'Bori', the Czech prison near Prague.

The political atmosphere had by now reached boiling point, and a crisis was anticipated at any moment. Henlein and his cry of "*Wir wollen heim ins Reich*" (We want to return to the German Reich) was initially just a whisper, but now this demand was bellowed out with deafening force. How ironic it sounded in 1945.

The German Socialists in Czechoslovakia fell between two camps. They were neither for Hitler, nor for the suppression of German rights by the Czech Government They had people in London and Prague communicating with the two Governments there, but in 1945 the same fate befell them as the rest of the Sudeten Germans (in many cases even worse). Wenzel Jaksch was their spokesman, but Henlein occupied the platform now with his many more supporters who took every opportunity to steep themselves in the new religion. Adolf Hitler, their new God, was sweeping them off their feet in all major cities in Germany. He could be seen and heard in Nuremberg in September 1938, at an impressive party rally, which many Germans from Czechoslovakia attended. It was not far away, and the spectacle was never forgotten by anyone who attended it. The 'Führer' had marched through the streets, mostly without expression. When he addressed the masses, there was hatred and determination on his face and his thundering voice sounded raucous and menacing.[2] But he could also be a charming man who would bend down, smilingly, to his favourite members of the crowd, namely the children from whom he had nothing to fear.[1]

Hitler made most people believe that although he did not want war, he would be prepared to fight to resolve the Sudetenland question. Even diplomats and Foreign Correspondents were impressed by this great orator. An official of the American Embassy in Berlin, a Captain Truman Smith, who had been sent to assess the strength of the National Socialist Movement as far back as 1922, wrote in his diary after a Hitler meeting that he had attended: "...a marvellous demagogue. I have rarely listened to such a logical and fanatical man. His power over the mob must be immense". Coming from an educated and well-travelled man, this is very revealing. People today are surprised at the stupidity of the German people. "How could they fall for such a madman and the whole system that he created?" they ask. It does seem incredible now. But Hitler's so-called logic, especially when delivered in person, seemed very credible

---

[1] In 1978, I met a citizen of Nuremberg who had been a small boy at the time of the Rally. Hitler had gripped his hand and shaken it fervently. This hand was not washed for a week.

[2] Leni Riefenstahl, the official photographer, captured the moment showing row after row of uniformed people with banners in line and Hitler holding forth and hypnotizing the masses

and true. At the height of anti-semitism throughout the world, Hitler's warnings about the Jews and the elite of Marxism that controlled the global monetary system evoked nightmarish memories of the great crash. Now they knew whose fault it all was, and what these people had in mind.

His conclusions that contained 'eradication by severest measures' brought relief, and "expansion of Germany's frontiers to ensure self sufficiency and Lebensraum" created gratitude for the great man, on whose shoulders this tremendous task rested. There only remained to be said in his inimitable and compelling fashion that he would make Germany a very great country - the Third Reich would last a thousand years -, and the house would be brought down. Yes, Adolf Hitler had worked hard for many years to make Germany what it was now. A respected nation, a nation to be reckoned with, a happy nation.

Indeed, visitors from abroad could hardly believe their eyes. Everyone and everything was highly organized and teeming with vivacity, energy and enthusiasm. The young Germans in particular seemed so much more bronzed, bursting with strength and health, more confident and zealous than their own youth at home. They were trained in open-air youth camps all summer, taught and indoctrinated and kept fit by dedicated fervent supporters of the regime. Every young and fit person had to complete a year's *Arbeitsdienst* (labour service), mostly on farms, for reasons of manpower shortage in the country, but also for indoctrination purposes. If they worked hard, they would have to work harder, for the enemy knew no rest and lay in waiting; thus they were warned to "Be prepared." The enemy was anyone who was against them, so it might even be their own mother, father, sister or brother. "Be ready for anything" was their motto, and they were.

Visitors and holidaymakers did not see what happened to obstinate people who would 'not see the light'. They heard rumours about the SA, the brown-shirts, who had been invaluable to Hitler before and after becoming Chancellor. When they began to give him a bad name with their premature, radical measures, he got rid of them, and the SS and Gestapo (*Geheime Staatspolizei* – Secret Police) took their place. The typical Third Reich culture came into existence with everything *völkisch* (people-oriented, proletarian) being good and everything a little more sophisticated being condemned to the fire. Masterworks and Masterpieces were also destroyed or found their way to elitists' hideouts, and new artists and writers replaced the Old Masters. 'Straight lined and heroic' was now the motto for art, and everything else, including the family. All members of the family should be clean, simply dressed; women should have simple hairstyles, girls plaits; women who had more than six children were awarded the "Mothercross". The Führer obviously wanted as many 'hands' and men in uniform as possible for the future. Girl guides and Boy scouts were replaced by the Hitler Youth with a thoroughly programmed indoctrination plan. An abundance of sporting activities were practised everywhere.

Goebbels, the Propaganda Minister, preached the new religion and culture very effectively day in, day out. He had been a Communist sympathizer until he became enthralled with Hitler's oratory. He thought at first that Communists and National Socialists should unite as they were, more or less, the same. But Hitler did not agree. He had, after all, given the threat of Communism as a reason for all the measures he had taken up to now. This small, wiry man with a limp may have been lacking in physical attraction, but more than made up for it in mental agility and persuasiveness. He had studied at seven universities and obtained a PhD at the age of 24.

Rudolf Hess, who joined the party in 1920, and Hermann Göring had both studied economics at the University of Munich, and were now Deputy of the Führer and Minister of Aviation respectively. The newly created concentration camps were now in the hands of the SS with the infamous Heinrich Himmler at its head (he was also in charge of the Gestapo and German police). The concentration camps had no stigma attached to them as yet. They were small compared to what they were at the end of the war, when the Nazi regime and its policies were so desperate that their massive grinding wheels spun totally out of control. Nevertheless, they were already quite brutal from the start, acting mainly as a warning to anyone who had maintained a sense of proportion and had not been swept overboard into the sea of hysteria. 'Agitators' as they were called, "would be hanged for inciting speeches and holding meetings, forming cliques, loitering with others, smuggling true or false information out of the camps into the hands of foreign visitors, etc." These measures were taken after all else had failed and total submission was achieved. For years, the SA had done a most efficient job in blackmailing, harassing and bullying shopkeepers, professional people and anyone in the public eye into joining the party and attending the meetings in Germany. It was a kind of protection racket that brought terror to most small towns.

Hitler had broken the Treaty of Versailles time and again over many years, first insidiously, then more blatantly. The drastic fall of the currency, which had been the ruin of a lot of Germans, had helped him to pay off some of the reparations. Krupp in the Ruhr and other big concerns had all necessary arms and ordnance designs ready when it was needed, so that the production of weapons, planes and tanks, etc. could go ahead at short notice. The League of Nations set up after the First World War, which had seemed to be a safeguard against international conflicts anywhere in the world, had watched various unjustified aggressive attacks by one country against another without batting an eyelid.

The Western powers and many amongst the English aristocracy, grateful to Hitler for actively combatting Communism, had positively supported him, also financially, and closed both eyes whenever something 'indiscreet' happened. America was not going to be dragged into anything at this stage and everybody in Europe was, quite naturally, terrified of another war, like the first horrific one, only a few years previously. The peacemakers and keepers were busily at work and no one really believed that anyone in his right mind would breach the peace.

France, which had been made into a bloody slaughterhouse with so many wars being fought on its territory for generations, dared not put one foot in front of the other lest the ground should tremble conspicuously. They had been coaxed along by Britain, but signed a pact of mutual assistance with Russia quite spontaneously, who in turn also made one with Czechoslovakia.

Wherever Hitler went, he vouchsafed Peace in Europe. "Whoever lights the torch of war in Europe can wish for nothing but chaos ...." Words like these were taken seriously nearly everywhere abroad, and as the Germans had suffered monumental injustices by the Treaty of Versailles and Communism presented a real threat to the West, Hitler's demands were met one by one and his trespasses overlooked. It was true. He did not want to fight a war in Europe on all fronts, as his main objective was the vast expanse of Russia with its many raw materials, such as oil. As long as he was marching East, everyone in Europe would be fine; this must have been the general attitude of Western politicians until they realised that things were not as simple as that. The German armed forces had been building up, with evermore ships and submarines, etc. under construction.

His statement that "Germany's problems cannot be settled by war" was all the more credible after the inhabitants of the Saarland voted unanimously to return to the Reich in 1935, and Hitler gave up all claims to Alsace Lorraine. Nevertheless, Britain and France began to build up their own armaments, finally acknowledging Hitler's increasing boldness and developing a 'better safe than sorry' attitude.

Their decision was confirmed on 16th March 1935, when Hitler confronted the world with the fact that Germany had a military air force again and a 'peacetime' force of about half a million men. The Treaty of Versailles had apparently been forgotten. France and Britain protested, but no counter-measures were taken. It is perhaps true to say that many Germans must have felt a sense of relief, and even if they disliked Hitler, (which they were not allowed to show) they expressed gratitude.

In the Spanish Civil War, which broke out in 1936, the new German weapons and planes could be tested in anticipation of his own war, which no doubt gave Hitler a growing measure of confidence for his aims and achievements.

Another coup took place on 7th March 1936, when Hitler, against the advice of his generals, sent a small force of troops across the Rhine into the demilitarised zone just to 'test the waters'. With this move he broke the Locarno Treaty (which he had never liked anyway due to his intentions in the East). At the same time he proclaimed his plans for peace and understanding in Europe, which would allow him to concentrate on achieving his aims in the East. He was particularly fond of Britain, an Ayrian race[1]. In *Mein Kampf* he states that one of the emperor's (Wilhelm II) greatest mistakes had been his dislike of the British.

After several assurances that Germany would not meddle with Austria's internal affairs, after intrigues and even murder, Hitler annexed Austria to Germany in March 1938, driving through his native country, welcomed with open arms and hearts by the common people. The Bishops of Austria declared their support for the National Socialist Movement for this reason: "It warded off the threat of the destructive and atheistic doctrine of Bolshevism", as in the declaration on 18th March 1938. On the night before the annexation of Autria to Germany, Himmler had arrested 67,000 Austrians for reasons of security.

Everything had been carefully prepared, but it was still a big gamble, as there was still uncertainty as to how the Czech and Italian peoples would react. The Czechs were assured that they had nothing to fear, as the *Anschluss* (Annexation) was more or less a family affair. Although the Czechs had, by now, strengthened their most threatened borders and had an air force, they did not fully realize the existing danger. They had mobilised, enlisting resident Germans as well as their own men, which made the whole situation grotesque beyond belief.

Chamberlain knew, when he wrote to his sister that "...Nothing that France or we could do could possibly save Czechoslovakia from being overrun by the Germans if they wanted to do it". Stalin would only give aid to Czechoslovakia if France did, but the latter did not want to endanger itself unless their own land came under direct attack.

---

[1] The idea of Ayrian superiority was first proclaimed by a French Count, J.A. Gobineau (1816-82).

CHAPTER 7
The wild cat with a glint in its eyes

The Western powers suddenly recognised this once listless and near to death cat, last seen licking its wounds quite feebly, suddenly stretch to incredible proportions and start to show its powerful claws and splintersharp teeth. Now they only hoped somehow to appease it with a few tempting morsels.

Hitler had made everything much more complex than could ever have been foreseen initially. How could he have hoodwinked experienced politicians and ordinary people alike? Would he really start a war, if someone attempted to block his continuous quests?

My father wrote a postcard home to Gerten showing the market square and plague- memorial of Saaz, with the print and stamp all Czech. The date was 4th August 1938. "Dear Mum, dad, Traudl (this was the only child still permanently at home). This is to let you know that we'll collect Traudl on Saturday from the station. Please get her to bring some honey. We're sorry that she is in such pain; I'll call the doctor here. Today, we collected our Liesl from hospital; everything is all right so far. My head is still full of Breslau. All our love, Ferd."

At Breslau there had been another rally where all the stops were pulled out and the new Nazi culture and might were paraded in front of thousands. No doubt, Hitler was there proclaiming peace and asking the Czechs to give justice to the Sudeten Germans, otherwise Germany would have to intervene, as he had warned at the Nuremburg Rally. On 26th September 1938, Hitler had said the following: "…when the Czechs have come to terms with their other minorities, and that peacefully and not through oppression, then I have no further interest in the Czech state. And that is guaranteed to them. We want no Czechs at all!"

Whatever historians have said about the Czech-German situation, it does seem to be clear now that the Western Powers were confirmed in their belief that Hitler was right in wanting to correct the injustice against the Sudeten Germans, in the face of the Czech government's refusal to make any concrete move towards a better understanding with the other nationalities in Czechoslovakia. The one million Hungarians, half a million Ruthenians, three and a quarter million Sudeten Germans and nearly as many Slovaks seemed to count for little.

Benes had promised to reach an agreement with all sections of the newly formed Republic, and possibly create another Switzerland which could embrace all the ethnic groups. When he was reminded of this, throughout the twenties and thirties, the reply towards the Germans was always: 'We do not enter into negotiations with rebels" and the others were promptly ignored.

But now, the Czech Republic was surrounded on three sides, with Germany now boasting a further 7 million supporters in Austria, (practically overnight without a shot being fired) situated on their extended southern border; their western and northern borders surrounded by Germans. In early September 1938, President Benes asked the Sudeten leaders to make known all their demands, and a few days later a broadcast went out in which he urged people to be calm, and to have mutual trust and goodwill. By this time, Henlein had no more contact with the Czech government. Hitler had made it clear that Germany had a right to gather ill-treated Germans in the East into the fold. "We want no Czechs!" he shouted in a speech in Berlin. He was believed, for everyone knew by now that he only wanted Ayrian blood in the German Reich. If no one conceded, he would have to use force. Plenty of warning was given that he would wait no longer than 1st October 1938. His generals disagreed with his plan to use force (no one in Germany wanted war) and some planned to have him arrested if he started a war over the issue of Czechoslovakia.

With hindsight it is possible to see that the longer the Czech government procrastinated, the more Hitler demanded. Some people would say, had they created a state in which democracy was granted to the different nationalities, Hitler would have been seen in his true colours much earlier. It is untrue that only after 1933 did the Sudeten Germans become "obstinate" and create "trouble". Slovakian and other political prisoners had existed long before 1933. The Czech government did not want to hear of anyone demanding self-determination in their state. If they had granted it to one, all the others would have claimed it as well.They stuck by their all or nothing principle.

The Sudeten Germans and the German Moravians occupied the border areas of Czechoslovakia. Specially in the Sudetenland the Germans had a lot to lose with all the raw materials the world could offer, the mines of which their ancestors hundreds of years ago had opened and made use of for the good of the whole Austro-Hungarian Empire, Czechs included. The famous spas in Karlsbad, Marienbad, Teplitz and Franzensbad, visited by people from all over the world, were also in the Sudetenland. The Czech people did not want to lose any of these territories, although they had a textile, machine and cotton industry of their own in addition to the central plane of Czechoslovakia which had rich soil and made them more or less self-sufficient in terms of food. But it irked them understandably that, with their considerable population, they were under the Habsburg rule for so long. Nevertheless, in their new superior role, their uncompromising policies lacked foresight. The

Germans were prepared to recognize the   Czech Government, if they could preserve their ethnicity and be fairly treated. It soon became clear that this was unlikely to happen.

Had the Czech government granted ethnic self-determination and equal rights in Czechoslovakia, Hitler would have had no pretext to use the Sudeten Germans as pawns in his future plans. Czechoslovakia's defences were quite considerable together with their impenetrable forests surrounding the country. Even if Benes had granted more freedom as late as August 1938, the ground would have been pulled from under Hitler's feet; he would have been exposed for what he was. But with the Great War only 20 years behind, Chamberlain was not alone in hoping that this would be the last demand from Hitler where territory was concerned. What is hard to believe is that it came as a complete surprise to the Western Powers and even to Russia, when Hitler marched eastwards. They could not grasp that he was prepared to risk everything he had gained and plunge the world into another ghastly war.

Karl, my father's youngest brother, was supposed to join the Czech army by 1st October 1938. He was branch manager of a big food concern, Leopold Fischer in Luditz, Egerland, and intended to marry Ria, a relation of the boss in a few years time. He, along with many other German youths did not want to fight the Germans. A large number of them had joined the Sudeten Free Corps, fleeing across to Germany to escape conscription.

Karl kissed Ria for the last time, not telling her of his plans. He went home and found his mother sick with fear that she might lose her seven boys one by one in another bloody war like the first one, from which Emil, the eldest, had returned broken, half-starved and showered with abuse and shame. Karl and his friend Toni told their parents of their intention to cycle to some relatives across the border in Germany.

On 15th September 1938, they left Luditz for Brüx where Karl's sister Mina and her husband owned a shop.[1] They had lunch with them, then cycled towards the Erzgebirge, where they crossed the border with the help of friends at Rossbach, who knew that the Czech guards all left for tea at a certain time. Excitedly, they pedalled the packed bikes through no-man's- land and were amicably received by German police after customs officers had led them there. They put them up free of charge in a comfortable inn, from where they wrote home. The next day they were given complimentary train tickets to Berlin Neukölln with many Sudeten Germans (mostly Czech conscripted young Germans) who were disguised as farm labourers, mushroom pickers etc. Some of them,

---

[1] Mina's husband Gustl was half Czech, but was a German sympathizer as so many Czechs were.

including Karl and Toni stayed in the 'House of the German Youth', earning money by working in teams, shovelling potatoes into trucks, etc. They were given free tickets for the opera, theatre and other entertainment. This was the agreeable part; what then followed was not so pleasant for Karl. They were being trained by the S.A., which fortunately did not last long. To the accompaniment of music from the Egerland and the clapping of the Berliners, they were marched to Treptow station, from where they were transported to the Czech border and told, "You will be expected to be in combat any day now". Toni had stayed with the S.A., *Standarte Feldherrnhalle* in Berlin and later became a parachutist.

Meanwhile, our family stayed at my mother's eldest sister Marie's home. The Czechs did not suspect my father of hiding there, but as a precaution, a knocking sign had been agreed upon in case of danger. My father was being looked after in the attic as well as was possible. In his anxiety, he must have imagined hearing the knocking sign and subsequently climbed out onto the roof. It was raining heavily, so that his figure, drenched and incongruous, must have looked highly suspicious to the neighbours opposite. Sure enough, someone came to tell my mother that there was a Czech policeman in "plain clothes" on her sister's roof.

One thing was clear: something had to give. No one wanted a war, but that it was imminent was almost an inevitability.

CHAPTER 8
Prague concedes

On Saturday, October 1st 1938, newspapers proclaimed that "Prague accepts the Munich Agreement." A sigh of relief rippled through Europe and spread through the rest of the world. Mussolini had a hero's welcome when he returned to Italy from Munich. It was he who negotiated between Hitler and the relevant parties to sign "The Munich Agreement". The parties were Neville Chamberlain, Edouard Daladier, Benito Mussolini and Adolf Hitler. A major war had been avoided just minutes before the deadline. Adolf Hitler had done it again. This time, surely only the blind would refuse to see how great Adolf Hitler really was. How did he do it?

The *Prager Presse* carried the headlines: "The decisions of Munich - Acceptance under protest to the world; Decision achieved partially and without participation of Czechoslovakia."[1] Two members of the Czech

---

[1] The *Prager Presse* had a short, but memorable life from 1921-1939. They printed only 20-22000 copies a day, six times a week. It was run by private individuals from

government had been just outside the room in which the decision was taken (Munich 29th September). Army General Syrovy had broadcast to the Czech nation on 30th September 1938 'United into a new life'. Here are extracts from the *Prager Presse*, which published the broadcast:

"...In Munich the four European powers met and decided to urge us to accept the new borders, which will sever the German territory of our state. We had the choice between a despairing and desperate defence, which would not only mean the sacrifice of a whole mature generation, but also of the women and children, and between the acceptance of conditions that have no example in history as to their callousness and as they were demanded without a war and under pressure. We wanted to contribute towards peace and we would have done, but not in the way in which it was forced upon us. We have been deserted and remain alone. All European States, also our neighbours in the North and South, have been beleaguered. We are, in a certain sense, a fortress occupied by powers mightier than our own. In deep agitation, all our leaders together with the Army and the president of the republic have considered any possibilities that remain. They have recognized that in the choice between a diminution of frontiers and death of the nation, our sacred duty must be to preserve the life of our people as a nation, so that we do not emerge weakened from these horrific times and in order not to forget that our nation will take heart again, the same as it has done so often in her past.

...We shall be within narrower borders, but we shall be amongst ourselves. Many hindrances that stood in the way of a good and peaceful public administration will now fall away. The understanding between ourselves and our neighbours will also be made easier..."

On the second page, all the details of the Munich Agreement were laid out as well as the occupation that was to take place by the German Army of certain areas at a certain time.

The deed was done. In the German zones, the excitement and relief knew no bounds. When the German troops occupied the Sudetenland, most windows displayed the *Hakenkreuzfahne* (Swastika flag), which surprised most people, as they had previously believed themselves to be the sole possessors of that flag; all bells rang from all directions and people hugged and kissed each other in the streets.

After it had been publicised that Prague had accepted the Munich Agreement, my father gave a sigh of relief and left his hiding place. The next day, the Czech authorities were looking for him and the others again.

Prague, amongst them Civil Servants from the Czech Foreign Office, all of them well-informed people. The language used was German.

Consequently, when the big celebrations took place and people rejoiced in the streets, my father was nowhere to be seen. For a short while, they lived in a fool's paradise. The German areas of Czechoslovakia now belonged to Germany. The annexation was made easy due to the German geographic position. The Germans all lived on the periphery of the country, although in certain areas it was far more than border land, cutting deeper into the interior. Everything they now did was for the good of the country; the country now being Germany, and no longer the Republic of Czechoslovakia. No sacrifice was too great, no burden too heavy.

It had hardly been acknowledged that many of the Czechs who had lived in Saaz had now departed. Hitler had demanded in Bad Godesberg on 22nd September 1938 that all Czech citizens, including those who had been urged by the Czech government to move to the German occupied territories, when the Republic of Czechoslovakia had come into existence in 1919, should move back to the interior of the country where they had come from unless they obeyed the new German rules. Some stayed and were left in peace, following the rules. Czech people had settled and built up a good living in the German areas. Now, they felt like aliens and felt pressurised to leave, which was obviously an enormous upheaval in their lives. Many went temporarily to relations and then had to start a new life.

The NSDAP (National Socialist German Workers Party) worked day and night to slot everyone into some kind of function or youth work. Thugs were roaming the streets and a kind of lawlessness began, in which the Führer's voice was heard, full of hate and malice, encouraging these ruffians who had to be taken into account now. The Social Democrats had virtually disappeared overnight. Their dialogue with London and Prague aiming for autonomy had ceased, when Hitler put his first reasonable, then increasingly outrageous propositions forward, which ultimately amounted to blackmail and allowed no veto.

Gregor Strasser had made the "National Socialist German Freedom Movement" popular in the north of Germany with his extensive campaign, beginning in 1924, and backing it up with the publication of a newspaper, called *Berliner Arbeiter Zeitung*, which was edited by his brother, Otto, in Berlin. It was Gregor Strasser who introduced Joseph Goebbels onto the scene.

His brother,Otto Strasser, was a Social Democrat until 1925 when he joined the NSDAP and befriended Hitler. In 1930 he had become just as disenchanted with the whole system as with his good friend. In the 1970's he described how he felt like a mouse in a trap, when the German troops marched into Czechoslovakia on the morning of October 1st 1938. He was living in Prague at the time. Flying over Czechoslovakia or Germany was prohibited, so that it seemed impossible to escape.

Although Czechs between 18 and 60 years of age were not allowed to leave the country, Otto Strasser and Wenzel Jaksch found a young Czech pilot with a plane at Prague airport, ready to take them to Strassburg, high over a long colony of tanks, artillery and infantry, they emerged from the beautiful Bohemian Woods - and across Bavaria - Strasser's homeland.

CHAPTER 9
The German Conscience

Many more people besides the Social Democrats were escaping, and all of them had more to fear, as well as to lose. A lot of Jews had already left Saaz before the Germans took over, especially some dealers of the famous hops of Saaz.

On 8th November 1938, the SA (Sturmabteilung) stormed the synagogue and a notorious villain in Saaz set fire to it. The next morning, the remaining Jews were forced to assemble in front of the town hall and also next to the monastery wall. They were subjected to terrible humiliation, without being physically attacked. Dr. Heller, my mother's family doctor was amongst them. My mother never forgot this. How she had praised him all her life, and yet also tried so hard to overlook the injustices imposed on the Jews. The *Ariersierung* began. "Are you an Ayrian?" was now the first life or death question. Many people, whose mother or father had been Jewish or of any other non-Ayrian nationality, now had to be doubly fervent and demonstrate what good Hitler supporters they really were.[1]

On 9th November 1938, the Kristallnacht took place in Germany. The pretext for it was the murder of a German diplomat 'Ernst von Rath' in Paris by Herschl Grynszpan, a seventeen year old student, whose parents had recently been expelled from Germany. During that night, the real face of National Socialism showed itself in the systematic smashing of thousands of Jewish shop windows, the beatings and manhandling of Jews, lootings, the subsequent demand for The Star of David being displayed on their shops and their persons, so that Germans should boycott their businesses, and refain from supplying any kind of services to them. The Jewish people were subjected to never-ceasing humiliation. In January 1939, Heydrich was given the job of arranging the emigration and expulsion of those Jews, who were fortunate enough to have enough money to buy exit visas to leave this hell on earth. Many now fled in

---

[1] The Jewish people insisted that they were Germans with a different religion, but after 1941, they received no education nor ration cards any more.

terror, taking with them what they could, but having to leave property, land, businesses including stock and most other possessions behind. Some went into hiding, assisted by German friends at the risk of their lives. In Berlin alone, 5000 Jews survived the war with the help of secretly anti-Hitler Germans in leading positions, but also from ordinary Berlin citizens. Already in April 1933, Jews were expelled from the civil service, journalism and excluded from universities. In 1935, the Nuremberg laws and the Reich Citizenship Law outlawed marriage or extra-marital sexual intercourse between Jews and German gentiles and deprived Jews of their German citizenship.

In Saaz, this treatment of the Jewish population was less radical, but the humiliation was the same. Many of the millionaire hop dealers in Saaz had seen the writing on the wall and had left in good time. A few had no means to do so. For instance, Malvine Stein, a talented actress and singer, 'was allowed' to be the cleaning lady for the S.A. Isidor and Nathan, two well-known street sellers of small goods in Saaz now had to accept alms and sell their wares secretly to survive. Nathan was often seen putting little stones on a grave at the Jewish cemetery. Dr. Noel had gone into hiding. Many Jews still believed that the 'storm would pass' as so often before in their history. Worse was to come. With the ensuing deportations of remaining Jews, as we were told to work camps, over the next few years, together with anyone speaking out in any way about the 'new order' to unknown destinations, the scale of the German conscience slowly but surely began to sink on one side. On the surface, there was no sign of it. We had been told that all these people had been sent to work camps where they belonged. The unspeakable human misery this heinous crime caused was thus 'pushed under the carpet'and the German people, with the apparent acceptance of it demonstrated their complete submission and shedding of all moral responsibility to Hitler and his so-called friends. Some of them were people who saw an opportunity to boost their ego and further their career at the expense of others. Those who were beginning to see the dangerous road ahead opted out of the limelight if they were able to; some going underground, others following the example of the common man. All that was required was to close one's eyes and be carried away in the centre of the powerful stream by the general exultation, trying not to be pushed to the periphery where the deviants and martyrs alike were to be found.

On the other hand, was it not already too late now? What would have happened if large sections of the people had remonstrated openly? Apart from the Socialists, some Prussian aristocrats had negotiated with Britain. They did not like Hitler and needed support from abroad, but nobody trusted them enough to deal with them.

My mother and father had been brought up in devout Catholic families. They were severely punished as children if they did anything "wrong" ie. telling lies, stealing, being disrespectful, not keeping a promise, etc.

Now these things were occurring on a massive scale and on a daily basis, bringing their good names, their village, their town, and their fatherland into disrepute. It was a very high price to pay, which increased as time went on, until one lost count of the final astronomical cost.

My godmother Frau Guschl, a bank clerk, who had inherited a house from her parents, was married to a man who had worked for years in a jeweller's shop in the town square. The owner was Jewish. He left Saaz with his savings and handed over his business and stock to my godmother's husband. One Christmas, my sister and I were each given a propelling pencil by my godmother from this jeweller's shop. They looked like gold. Mine had strands of green silk hanging from the back. The colour of the silk on my sister's pencil was pink. I was extremely proud of mine and only used it on rare occasions. It was a pleasure just to gaze at it. I had never owned and handled anything so beautiful. The Jewish proprietor with such creative talent had no choice. He could take his money and try and reach England, or Switzerland and later, America, but his business had to be left behind. Those Jews who hesitated were even worse off as it became more and more difficult to leave the country. The one who escaped with their lives were never personally compensated by anyone for what they had lost, except indirectly through the reparations Germany paid to the state of Israel over the years after the Second World War.

A lot of people were on the move in those days; all of them having to make crucial decisions in a short space of time, desperately hoping that they had made the right ones. People felt persecuted and hunted down like animals for their race, religion, political opinion, and even for simply obeying their consciences.

Meanwhile Saaz was divided into four NSDAP sections. The leaders of these could be seen parading proudly round the market place (Ringplatz), their revolvers attached to their belts. They ensured that the people were taught all the new doctrines, and that their lives were filled with innovations and bustling activities. Some clubs and associations were closed or amalgamated, others opened, newspapers were shut down; schools were forced to adopt new, strange methods of teaching and administration. Propaganda was foremost on the curriculum. The youth had to serve a year's Arbeitsdienst (community service, including farming)[1]. Lots of men belonged to the S.A.(Sturmabteilung- ex and paramilitary). Then there were *Ortsgruppen*, Block-and-Zellenleiter, all of them proud of their 'important position'.

Streets and squares were renamed, so that ancient names and terms disappeared overnight. A lot of marching was heard in the streets. Boots echoed the sounds of officialdom and dictation from above. *Blockleiterinnen* (women in charge of street blocks) visited people day and night, investigating anything and everything. Many people were drafted into the intelligence service.

In January of 1939, after much cajoling on my mother's part, my father left the brewery, where he had actually earned a little money for a while) and joined the railways in Saaz. He did not want to show disloyalty to the brewery, as they had helped him through difficult times. But after the departure of about 200,000 Czechs from the German areas to the interior of the country from October 1938 onwards, many official positions were left unfilled and the railway had to close down for a while in Saaz until the Germans from Saxony (across the Ore mountains) came and helped out whilst more Sudeten Germans were trained. My father had been asked to join several times. I can only assume that he did not feel confident enough to accept initially, apart from not wanting to let the brewery down.

The Czechs, who stayed, were not treated badly. They were left alone for the most part, but had to tread carefully for fear of Nazi victimisation, the shoe now being firmly on the other foot. Everybody had to 'toe the line'.

The railway was now called the *Reichsbahn* and my father's work as a locksmith was to construct and maintain the necessary big tanks, pipes, and tubes, etc. There were mostly steam-engines, few electric ones, with 51 tubes. The heat through the tubes generated steam in the water, which escaped on two sides into the steam cylinders with pistons. The tubes eventually loosened. It was my father's job to tighten them. It was a good job, and he enjoyed being one with a massive, vital organisation, keeping the country on the move and linking his part of the world with Germany, with which it was now affiliated. He felt like a small cog ticking away in an intricate network of wheels; all of them necessary to keep the big machinery in motion.

---

[1] There were big Jewish farms in our neighbourhood, which were now deserted and needed attention.

CHAPTER 10
My private world

When I was two years old, we had moved from the Muttergotteshaus to the Trnovaner Strasse, so called as it led straight to the nearby village of Trnovan. Under the new regime, it became the Horst Wessel Strasse and our number was 1678/77. Opposite our two new identical blocks of flats, a wide meadow stretched back to the cemetery, which was surrounded by a high wall and a few cone-shaped poplar trees that looked like tall guards, ready for action. The meadow, lined on either side by small silver birch trees, represented a little paradise to me. My mother could let me play there with an easy conscience, as she was able to see me just across the road from her first floor windows at any time. I would lie in the fragrant grass, listening to the bees and birds and the rustling of the poplar- leaves in the wind, observing the changing of their colour from green to silver and back again, accompanied by the never-ending cacophony of sounds. Up above, blue skies stretched endlessly with occasional wispy clouds passing by for extra entertainment. The question always came up 'from where did they come and how did they just disintegrate into nothing?'

Walking into the town, after two blocks of flats came a street called Am Semmering; then the pavement widened, opening out onto a parade of shops with a general store on the corner. Farther along, amongst a few private houses was a large nursery with rows of flowers, healthy looking vegetables and a few greenhouses. All along, the street was lined by large trees and imposing villas on either side as far as the monastery wall. From there, the street curved to the right, the trees discontinued and the main street with shops on either side, including the cinema and a hotel, led to the town square with the before mentioned arcades and the plague monument in the lower half near the town hall.

Our residence - set back a little, with a lawn and two big granite stone spheres on either side of the path leading to the house – prided itself with a substantial porch, a number of granite stone steps leading up to the door, and two little brick platforms on either side of the steps. These two "benches" were favoured seats for resident children, who used to perch on them, their long, thin legs dangling down. My sister was particularly slender and generally called "beanpole". Our heels would be knocking against the bricks and we would be aware of the exciting danger, if we sat farther and farther away from the door and, daringly, even right by the "precipice."

Each of the two blocks consisted of twelve flats, four on each floor, the middle one privileged with a balcony. Each flat had an individual cellar and attic. The cellars stored bicycles, coal, sacks of potatoes for the winter, preserved fruit, gherkins and eggs, jams, bottles of wine, old furniture and anything else that could not be stored in the flat or attic. The atmosphere down there was warm and smelling musty, whereas the lofty attic compartments appeared stark and cold, almost unearthly, with a big open space in the middle. This was used for drying the laundry of the residents on wet, cold days, when it was not possible to dry it on washing lines in the yard behind the house. In the basement, there was also a big communal laundry and separate bathroom with a rota on the wall in the corridor, so that the tenants' intentions were known in advance. *Die Hausordnung* was another important task in the lives of the housewives, although they usually already knew whose turn it was to sweep and wash the stairs and landings of the building.

The flats themselves were bright and modern, consisting of two big rooms, a square hall with a built-in cupboard, leading out onto the balcony (ours was just above the porch) and a modern toilet. I stood on the balcony when we first moved there in 1938, before the takeover, and shout into the street below: "*Da dei deu = Saaz bleibt deutsch*," which translates into English and adult language as "Saaz remains German", a remarkable example of early political awareness or propaganda fired by my parents' friends! The hall led into the kitchen, which served also as a living and dining room. This room also served as a bathroom for us two girls every Saturday night when a big tin bath was brought down from the loft and placed next to the range with adjoining *Kachelofen*, a tiled high stove. My sister and I thoroughly enjoyed our splashing sessions in the lashings of warm water from the stove. But the biggest job for my mother was to get me out of that bath.. When I was finally dragged out of it and placed on a low wooden stool to dry [1], the skin of my fingers and feet had a white, wrinkled and detached appearance. This did not worry me at all, for I had been well compensated for it, and for everything else during the week I had not appreciated. My bath was definitely the highlight of the week, although Sunday always started well too, and held a few surprises in store on many occasions.

I can see my father now; dressed in a lily-white shirt, with braces to pull his trousers right up above his waist, he would stride about the room, the master of his own house. There was an atmosphere of expectancy and contentment in the room, with cocoa exuding its fragrance like perfume. We were only allowed this delicacy on Sundays. It seemed to me that this same scene and atmosphere had been repeated since time immemorial. It created a sense of security and well-being, never to be erased from my memory.

---

[1] I once had a nasty accident, slipping and banging one of the corners of the stool between my legs with blood all over the place

I also remember him taking his wet and dirty galoshes off, carefully unbuttoning these protectors of shoes until they fell away like an onion skin and exposing his dry and shiny shoes underneath. While my father tried to put his cufflinks on, awkwardly and deliberately with his big, rough fingers, my mother occupied herself with her usual household chores, but her movements and behaviour were different on Sundays. The top of the kitchen range consisted of just one big cast-iron hot-plate, usable even into the corners. It was an impressive monstrosity with all its polished rails, knobs, doors (including the oven door), shiny tiles and ever-crackling, sometimes roaring fire underneath.

"Don't hang on the rails. Go and play. And Liesl, darling, have a look at your Fibel (school reading book).We have visitors coming this afternoon."

"Who is it, Mama?" my sister asked inquisitively. "Is it the man with the dark skin and moles on his face and his wife, or is it Tante Marie and Onkel Karl? They haven't been here for ages."

"They were here a fortnight ago, child. No, it's the people with the Dachshund; you know the Wachtels, don't you?"

I left my place by the stove and started to dance around the table that stood in the middle of the room, carefully avoiding the four sharp corners.

"I like that dog. Is his name 'Hexl'? (little witch)." The way I spoke reminded the others that I was still a mere baby. My sentences were kept short and some words avoided for fear of not being able to pronounce them.

After a delicious meal that only I did not appreciate, my mother dressed us in pretty frocks, combed my sister's thick black hair thoroughly and adorned it with a mother-of-pearl band to keep it off her face, and gave me three strokes through my three thin, blond strands.

"Don't get yourselves dirty now, will you," she warned us, while stretching herself out on the sofa in anticipation of her daily siesta after lunch.

"We won't, Mama," my sister replied obediently. "But I don't know if Erika is going to be quiet enough for you to sleep."

My father picked me up, so that I could look out of the big window, quietly explaining the view outside.

" Can you see the trees to the right of the meadow? There, next to the cemetery warden's house is a big tree. It's very big, because it's many, many years old."

"Are the smaller ones the children of that big one?" I interrupted.

"No," my father said seriously, "they are not poplar trees, they are young birches, all along the meadow down to the road. Not many old birch trees keep their white bark. But the young ones look as though they had been painted white and wrapped in cellophane afterwards."

"I must go there and see" I thought to myself. One day I would go and take a closer look, also on the other side of the meadow, where there was a much bigger and denser wood. I knew there was a path leading into it.

"Papa, do you know what's past these houses here, going this way?" I flung my arm out pointing to the left and struck my father on the nose; he blinked, but remained unperturbed. "I know what's down this way", I swung half round on his arm and pointed to the right where there was nothing obstructing me, "because Mama takes me to town sometimes, but when she takes Liesl to school on her back, I stay with the neighbours, the Rauscher's."

My father nodded sympathetically. "Well, there isn't much past these blocks of flats on the left. There are a few private houses on the same side as ours, then nothing till the soldiers' barracks, then nothing again until the next village, called Trnovan. That's why this street used to be called Trnovaner Strasse."

"Why isn't it called that now?" I puzzled. "Is it because it was too hard to say?" I burst out, pleased with myself for knowing the answer to my own question.

"Probably," my father said whilst easing me to the ground. My sister and I began climbing on the chairs and jumping down to the floor simultaneously. Mama woke with a start and sprang with one leap over to Liesl.

"My God, Liesele," she screamed breathlessly, "what are you doing? You know you mustn't jump, or run or climb, you remember what Herr Doktor told you, don't you?" She was now kneeling on the floor, holding Liesl just where she had jumped down.

My sister looked a little surprised, but not for long. She said slowly:

"Yes, Mama, I know, I haven't forgotten. They told me at the hospital. I won't do it again."

The doorbell rang shrilly and my father went to open the door.

"Why didn't you stop her?" My mother reproached him. As he opened the door to the hall, he said over his shoulder: "There will be times when she won't want to move. So let her be sometimes!"

Our expected visitors were a corpulent lady, her undersized husband and their small, black Dachshund. After much welcoming and handshaking, the couple sat on the sofa with me in between, and the dog resting at the feet of his mistress.

"Well, Erika, whom do you like better, your mother or your father?" She looked down at me searchingly, so that the cumulative effect of her presence, voice and interrogation induced a kind of paralysis in me which could be compared to that experienced by a victim of a snake. Yet, as I pondered the question in order to understand it, a bright light appeared at the end of the tunnel. Beaming all over my face, I said "Papa," while gazing straight into her grey, piercing eyes.

"She always says that," my mother interrupted. "Everybody always asks her that question and each time she answers the same."

"I don't suppose she's forgotten how cross you were, Pepi, when her little baby feet trampled all over Liesl's toy piano till the very last strangled sound escaped from it!" The big woman shook like a jolly jelly and made the sofa vibrate so violently that, first I and then her husband were lifted from our seats for a fraction of a second.

"She knew what she was doing, I tell you," my mother said emphatically. "I know the piano was only small, but you could play all the little children's songs on it and Liesl loved it. I just couldn't believe my eyes when I entered the room and Little Miss Innocent - look at her now - dug her little heels into it with a crack and a thud. I shall never forget it. Poor Liesl couldn't stop crying."

I had slipped down from the sofa to examine 'Hexl's' shiny, black, short hair. A curious creature, I concluded, after studying the bitch's short crooked legs, her long, sad ears and her rat-like body and coat. Her best feature was definitely her soft black eyes.

Liesl began to do the rest of her homework with everybody commenting on her good progress in spite of all the setbacks caused by her illness. I concentrated on the general conversation as much as other thoughts flashing through my head allowed me.

"Well, you know how healthy she was as a baby, and even till she was five or six. That St Vitus Dance business wasn't really that bad, and even the diphtheria was mild, although she'd had it for some time before it was diagnosed. But what really did it was the Rheumatic Fever. You remember how her knees swelled up? Oh, and the scarlet fever, that was awful too. The poor child, how she has suffered already, and now we're told that all this has affected her heart valves. They don't function properly. That's why she looks blue, especially her lips and hands, and why she suffers from so many nosebleeds and fatigue." My mother wrung her hands in despair. "Some of those doctors have a lot to answer for. If they'd diagnosed all the symptoms in time, all or most of this could have been avoided. Now I have to tell her not to jump or run or exhaust herself in any way; not that she can do many normal activities anyway."

Looking past my sister's legs, I was focusing my eyes across the room onto our big kitchen cabinet. For a piece of furniture, it was nothing short of a masterpiece. Its beauty with its cream coloured French polishing made such an impression on me that everything else that I had seen before in my short life had to come up to that standard; unfortunately most things fell short of it. The sliding doors of the cabinet showed more lustre than ordinary glass, and the matching washing- up unit next to the sink could only be called ingenious. It had a brown, cork like work-top, and after opening the two smooth, gleaming doors, two shining stainless steel sinks appeared, one for washing, the other for drying the crockery. I did not know then that the kitchen furniture had been bought by my father on hire purchase under protest from my mother, because it was so expensive that it took them the entire war period to pay it off. There was never any need for dirty pots and pans standing around. They could all be stacked away in there ready for washing-up time, when a big pan of hot water was hoisted over from the stove and emptied into the washing- up bowl. Knives were meticulously rubbed with a white, sand-like mixture until they shone like blades of swords.The items in the larder, next to the impressive kitchen cabinet, stood like soldiers on parade, and even the profusion of begonia and pelargonium on our balcony, which trailed down over the wrought iron, looked orderly and were all growing in all the right directions.

I sneaked out of the door, just as my mother put the radio on (*Volksempfänger* – state issued radio, which only broadcast the state station and what they wanted us to hear, withholding what they did not want us to know). No doubt, there was going to be an important speech that no one could afford to miss. This radio, which everybody had been given, held an important position in every household. In ours, it was situated high up on a shelf next to the window and the sofa, like the eye of Zeus. Of course, everybody wanted to know in what situation we found ourselves; therefore it was regarded as the most precious possession in the house. As no other radio was allowed, we depended on this one to give us the answer to our many questions and we had to believe what we heard from this single source. There were people who hated Hitler and the regime, who treasured their own radio-sets, which was free of German propaganda and gave them an idea of what was happening outside Germany. They listened in anguish, not daring to breathe, to foreign stations - an offence that could cost them their lives.

I tiptoed through the corridor, opened the door and shut it as quietly as possible. Then, feeling freer, I stopped by the clean, cool stone stairs, undecided as to whom I should honour with my visit.

To the left of me lived the Hopps, an elderly couple and the wife's sister. They, obviously, did not like the present political situation and did not socialise much with anyone and their door was an enigma to me. Just as I turned to my right, Frau Schmidt, a big grey-haired lady of about fifty, thundered slowly down the stairs to where I stood.

"Well, what is our Erika doing here, I wonder!" She stopped to catch her breath. "Are you going to visit some of your numerous friends, then?"

"Ayah," I said sheepishly, pretending to be a baby. She descended the stairs and I could not help marvel at the structure and quality of the stone stairs beneath her, which could support her and enable her to reach the safer ground floor.

Two doors beckoned me. I dismissed the one next to ours after short consideration, for the owners were young, and at that stage, I was not really interested in their age group as a whole. The feeling may have been mutual, as I was always quick to detect how the wind blew on new territory.

I rang the doorbell next to the name- sign 'Rauscher', straining my eyes to look through the peephole, although I knew that I would not be able to tell who was going to open the door. Every flat in the house had one of those, with a shiny brass lid covering it.

Whoever looked through the Rauscher's door from the inside, probably could not see down to my level, but the door opened welcomingly nevertheless, and Herbert, with his dark, brown eyes and bushy eyebrows looked down at me. He was the Rauscher's only child, a lad of about ten at that time.

"Doing your rounds, eh? Come in and see your daddy number two". In the living and dining room, I found Herr Rauscher ironing, a skill which was to serve him well later when he was forced to join the Navy. He was a mechanic for a bicycle dealer (Heidler), Unter den Lauben, and later worked in the sugar beet factory.

He was a slight, pleasant man, whose countenance was somewhat disfigured by a blind eye which resembled a fried egg. It had a whitish film over it which made him look slightly grotesque. His manners and perpetual good humour endeared him to me, so that I did not even notice his physical handicap any more.

"How is Erika today?" He held the iron up and looked at me inquiringly. "Have you eaten all your dinner today?"

This was a sore point with me. If it had been up to me, I would never have eaten a proper lunch at home. My mother used to bring my dinners over to the Rauscher's in secret, sending me there a little later where I was spoon-fed, sitting on Herrn Rauscher's lap.

Every spoonful was consumed with relish. Little did I know that it was still my mother's food I was eating. Of course, it amused all the onlookers. This now explains why there was always a jolly atmosphere in the room while I tucked in, which, in turn, encouraged me to practically scrape the plate clean. "My mother can't cook half as well as you can," I would say to Frau Rauscher.

I did not need to look at Frau Rauscher. There was an image of her engraved on my mind, sitting on the sofa, tight-lipped and tense, knitting at the speed of light, so that you could not even see the stitches transferred from one needle to another. She was very kind, but seemed unable to relax for even a fraction of a second. Her bluish lips had been pressed relentlessly together for years, her worried, restless eyes could only be controlled whilst focusing on the job in hand, which was invariably knitting. She now stared at her husband mistrustfully. What was he up to now with his questions? He always smiled when he talked, and yet his words and deeds hurt her so much.

Herbert sat down at the table to continue his homework. He had just started at grammar school and was constantly reminded by his mother that if he were lazy, he would soon be expelled. His parents' relationship to each other affected him deeply. No doubt, he was also thinking about how he had beaten up Franz Hüttl, when self-same Neanderthaler had killed some wren babies in their nest.

Ignoring Herrn Rauscher's question, I scrambled up onto a chair. With my feet dangling and my body supported by my stick-like arms on the chair seat, I faced the room, studying everything and everyone in detail.

"Well, if you don't want to talk to us today, we might as well have the radio on. But it's not like you, not to talk, is it?" He flicked the radio on and continued his ironing.

The atmosphere in the room immediately changed, with the sound of march music overriding any uncertainty, any question in the air, any gloom that might have been lurking in the corners. It was, undoubtedly, the Horst Wessel song, the Nazi hero, after whom our road had been renamed. "*Die Fahne hoch, die Reihen fest geschlossen...* (The flag raised high, the rows of men united...)

My legs began to sway frantically to the music, and even when lying in my big cot at night, I was still mentally humming the lively and confident tune. My mother folded my hands together, and looking through the bars of the cot, she prayed:

Müde bin ich, geh' zur Ruh, schliesse meine Äuglein zu.
Vater, lass' die Augen Dein über meinem Bette sein.
Hab' ich Unrecht heut' getan, sieh es, lieber Gott, nicht an.
Deine Gnad' and Christi Blut, macht ja allen Schaden gut.

*Alle, die mir sind verwandt, **Herr, lass' ruhn** in Deiner Hand,*
Alle Menschen, gross und klein, sollen Dir befohlen sein,
Kranken Herzen sende Ruh, nasse Augen schliesse zu,
Lass Dein' Engel halten Wacht, gib uns eine gute Nacht.

This evening prayer always had a very calming effect on me. In fact, on many occasions, the end of the prayer faded away into deep breathing and sleep. As long as I heard my favourite passage in this prayer: *"Herr, lass' ruhn"*, I did not really mind not hearing the end. I had no idea what it meant, because I always imagined it to be one word. Not that I had any clue about a word being of grammatical significance; I had, however, grasped that a certain sound has a certain meaning, and although this enormously long sound meant nothing to me, it sounded absolutely splendid, especially with my mother's rolled "r's", the whole magnificence of the phrase, became apparent. There were more verses, all equally wonderful to me.

The translation of this prayer is something like this:
"Tired am I, go to rest, close my eyes. Father, let your eyes rest over my bed. If I have done wrong today, don't look at it, dear God. Your Grace and Christ's blood cleanse all sins.
All who are related to me, Lord, let them rest in your hand, all people, small and tall, are commended to you. Sick hearts send peace, close wet eyes, let your angels keep watch, give us a good night."

CHAPTER 11
Herr Lorenz, the blacksmith

Erika Lorenz was a very good friend of mine. Her father was a blacksmith, whose smithy sheltered and fascinated me on many an unfriendly day.

Nothing can erase the image of the hearth with the perpetual fire flickering under the big metal hood leading into the flue. I can see Herr Lorenz in his big leather apron, compressing the concertina-like bellows with the aid of a handle. Through the oxygen thus introduced, the fire sprang up like a sleeping lion suddenly stirred into action. A long metal rod stoked the small burning pieces of coal, sending sparks in all directions. After a while, the rod was removed, and its red glowing tip placed on the anvil, whose base rested on a wooden block made of oak or elm. The purpose of this wood was to give the hammer some spring as it struck the red hot metal.

I can still hear the bell-like sound of the hammer making contact with the anvil. I can see Herr Lorenz beat the red, soft metal and anvil alternately, creating a rhythmical, musical and visual spectacle all at the same time. If the metal looked white after being in the fire, hundreds of small white sparks, (metal particles) made a halo all round the anvil after the whiteness had been hit. "Thunder and lightening," I thought, "a direct hit." Sometimes he shaped a rod with the aid of various tools over the beak of the anvil into a round shape, putting it back into the fire when the metal had cooled a little, then beating it into the desired shape. Thick, short rods would be elongated and made thin by continuous hammering. I thought of how my mother rolled a piece of dough with her hands on a board achieving the same effect, only her working conditions were entirely different from those of Herrn Lorenz. He stood in a large, draughty room, his face hot and dirty, handling a roaring fire and heavy, cumbersome as well as hazardous tools and materials, while my mother stood in a spotless, temperate kitchen in her clean clothes and frilly apron, kneading her white, soft dough with her soft, white hands. Both had the same delicate job of preparing the material, so that it would withstand the vigorous treatment and come out perfect in the end. In the same way that my mother had to mix the right quantities of certain materials together and heat them correctly, Herr Lorenz had to know which heat was correct for which metal. If he were to sharpen some ploughshares, he had to heat them just enough to sharpen them, so that they would not be too soft or blunt again soon; at the same time, he had to ensure that they were not too hard, otherwise the first stone encountering them would have broken a piece out of the metal. Therefore a very important process of this business was the inserting of the material into water, which was contained in a trough near the hearth and anvil for the purpose of dousing the hot metals if they were too hot. The hissing sound this produced was another fascination for me. In a flash, the metal changed from red or white to dark again.

I never saw Herr Lorenz forging a horseshoe or shoeing a horse, but I did see it very occasionally when my mother went to the dentist's and took me with her. The dentist had his surgery at the Drehscheibe, on top of my great-uncle's smithy. I remember staying in the courtyard, where the horses were fixed with new shoes and having an occasional peep into the black, echoing smithy. The old nails and shoes were removed, a new shoe was tried after removing old parts of the hooves with the hoof parer, cleaned inside with a blade knife and smoothed with a rasp. After trying the new shoe, which had been made in advance for this particular horse (as there were not many horses left around Saaz, this one might have been from the Brewery), the farrier had to heat the new shoe and press it against the hoof to fit into place. I always thought how painful this must be for the horse as, invariably, the hoof would begin to smoke, although the horse never stirred. Cold, the shoe would then be fixed with the special nails, starting at the front and working all round, with the aid of a flat-headed shoeing hammer which was used on the other side to turn the outcoming nails over into the hoof. After that, they were clinched and smoothed with a rasp. The hoof was finally oiled. The hoof itself, dead as a human finger- or toenail, is only very thin and great care had to be taken to hammer the nails straight up and not into the foot, as used to be done with crippling effect on the horse.

Little did I know that the blacksmith and farrier were at that point beginning to die out as we had known them for thousands of years.

I suppose they must have existed since the Iron Age, but smithies with an open fire and anvil as the centre of any community down the ages (the smith must have been a most important man when handmade weapons and tools were used), were fast disappearing, just as the horse was being replaced by tractors and motor vehicles.

CHAPTER 12
From liberation to domination

On 15th March 1939 Hitler occupied Prague, and with this step changed 'liberation' to 'domination'. In Berlin, State president Emil Hacha of Czechoslovakia had been forced to "lay the fate of Czechoslovakian people in the hands of the Führer of the German Reich" (Quote from the treaty). It had been made easy for him, once again; this time his excuse for annexing the whole of Czechoslovakia, was to free Slovakia which had sought his help. The difference now was that people were still hearing Hitler's voice ringing in their ears: "We want no Czechs". Czechs were not Aryans, after all. So, what was Hitler up to now?

A thin stretch of Southern Slovakia had belonged to Hungary since 2nd October 1938, and a small area around Teschen in the North had been annexed by Poland on 1st November 1938, so that Czechoslovakia as a whole had been severely mutilated. Slovakia and Karpato-Ukrania were now able to declare themselves independent (14th March 1939) and made a *Schutzvertrag* (protection treaty) with Germany on 23rd March 1939, the same day that Germany signed a trade agreement with Romania. Now, Czechoslovakia had been completely taken over.

I had a photo of many Sudeten-Germans being led, their hands folded behind their heads, into concentration camps or KZs (as they were called in German) for opposing Hitler. There must have been many Czechs going the same way now. Britain and France congratulated themselves for having had the sense to speed up their rearmament programme since 1938, but feared that they would run out of time before the outbreak of war. Everybody still hoped it would not happen, but Hitler's seemingly arbitrary actions produced nightmares, even amongst many of his supporters. Had they been wrong about him? If so, what could they do about it now? Once committed to a cause that is steering in the wrong direction, there is no way out. It would be too dangerous to jump off the band-wagon. The answer was self-sacrifice, or nothing at all.

Adolf Hitler now presented an unprecedented display of cunning with his numerous treaties, pacts and agreements, which he signed with countries far and near. A conjuror, throwing twenty plates up in the air and catching them again, would have looked an amateur by comparison.

On 28th March 1939, the Spanish Civil War ended with victory for Franco and his Fascist Party. Hitler, in preparation for his own planned war, tested his newly manufactured aeroplanes in this conflict, in support of Franco. Three days later France and Britain, having anticipated Hitler's demand for Danzig, declared their support for Poland and gave a guarantee to defend it if the need arose. They now had to decide who was the most dangerous - Hitler or Stalin. Having come to the conclusion that Hitler was a far closer danger to them and now seemed the more menacing figure, they began negotiations with Russia as a potential Eastern ally. The Soviets demanded, amongst other things, the right to march through Poland and Romania. Poland certainly disliked this idea, as they mistrusted Stalin more than Hitler. While the Allies still searched for a solution to this dilemma, Hitler once again saw his chances, and ignoring and be-lying his anti-Comintern propaganda, signed a ten year non-aggression pact with Russia on 23rd August 1939, with clauses enabling the two countries to split Poland anew. Hitler now felt sure he could tackle the West first without being attacked from the East. Stalin presumed that Germany and the West would destroy each other once more, so that he could pick up the pieces and assemble them in his own way. The pact with Russia had been made only after Ribbentrop[1] suggested to the Poles in Warsaw a united attack against the East and was turned down.

In fact, Hitler attacked Poland from the north and south on 1st September 1939. This was not because of the German enclave of Danzig and the Corridor as had been anticipated, although at the last moment on 31st August 1939, Germany demanded from England and France the immediate handing over of Danzig and a referendum on the Corridor. With his attack on Poland, he had swept aside his non-aggression pact with Poland. This had been a clever move in January 1934, as it nullified Poland's alliance with France. Russian troops were ready on the other side of Poland. At six o'clock on that same day, Hitler attacked Warsaw from the air.

On 3rd September 1939, Britain and France declared war on Germany.

---

[1] German Foreign Minister since 1938.

It was ironic: the two countries which had tried the hardest to preserve peace, now had to declare war on a country whose spokesman had said in 1935: "Whoever raises the torch of war in Europe can only desire chaos." Hitler had hoped to avoid war in Europe by overrunning it. He did not want to attack Russia, and have to deal with an attack on the Western front at the same time.

No action was possible in Poland with Russian and German troops on either side of it, both ready to penetrate in order to divide it. Hitler had offered peace to the West, provided they returned the former German colonies and stopped intervening in his East European affairs. He had not expected Britain and France to act in such a way and was initially shocked.[2]

Hitler then only occupied half of Poland; Russia, coming in from the East, took the other half on 17th September 1939. 57 German Divisions faced 38 Polish Divisions. In the face of overwhelming German superiority, (a six week Blitzkrieg), Poland surrendered. The Polish Government went into exile in France and later in London. Polish intelligentsia and Jews were hunted down and many killed by mostly Russian commandos. After making a deal with Hitler, seizing Latvia, Lithuania and Estonia, the Russian forces withdrew, taking many Poles with them to Siberia as slave labourers, where most of them perished, but also endless columns of defeated Polish soldiers were marched into Germany as slave labourers. Russia, having made a pact with Hitler, even gave him economic and military assistance during the winter of 1939-1940. They gave protection to the German merchant navy, thus neutralising the economic consequences of the British blockade.

When Britain categorically refused to accept Hitler's suggestions and offer of peace, he was outraged, and would have set about defeating his Western opponents immediately, had his plans not fallen into their hands. Also, his advisers argued against it.

On 27th September 1939 Warsaw had capitulated. Hitler could not rest; he had to move on, although his generals continuously warned him of the disastrous consequences of his hasty actions. He would rant and rave, asking himself why he had surrounded himself with such cowards, men with no vision, sheep who did not deserve to be generals, advisers or have any rank whatsoever. Finally, he would recall his successful coups, his bloodless victories, the respect he had gained for Germany throughout the world. Should all this now be handed over on a silver platter? Did they not realise that their task had only just begun, and that the real struggle lay still ahead? Could they not see that in order to become great and take their glorified place in history, much had to be renounced, such

---

[2] 4th September 1939 French -Polish Pact.

as old, outdated ideas, consideration towards other races, sentimental feelings for people and ideas, which were obstructing their path? No time could be wasted on pity for themselves or others, or on wasteful, long drawn-out decisions. They would have to take their chances, and if an opening could be detected anywhere, no time should be lost over capitalising on it. Of course, plans would have to be made in advance, but if something better availed itself in the meantime, it would be no loss to abandon them.

Plans were drawn up for the occupation of Norway and Denmark just as Britain sent her fleet to Norway to get a foothold in Finland. Hitler beat them to it when he took over Denmark and Norway on 9th April 1940. In July 1940 Lithuania, Estonia and Latvia were integrated into the USSR as Socialist-Soviet Republics. They had been under German control. On 26th June 1940, Romania was split up, some parts going to the USSR on demand. On 30th August 1940, another part went to Hungary and in September a third to Bulgaria.

On 27th September 1940, a 10 year *Dreimächtepakt* (three nation pact) was struck between Germany, Italy and Japan, 'not aimed at the Soviet Union', but to create a 'new order' in Europe and East Asia. In November 1940, Hungary, Romania and Slovakia also joined, followed by Bulgaria in March of the following year.

France boasted an allegedly impenetrable defence - the Maginot line (stretching over 500 km from Switzerland to Luxembourg). Positioned parallel to the Rhine and thus facing Germany and the Siegfried line, it seemed impossible that any army could gain entry into France from the East.

On the day that Winston Churchill became England's Prime Minister (10th May 1940), the German army commenced their offensive move toward the West. On 15th May, Holland capitulated, followed by Belgium a week later (28th May 1940). Norway followed suit on 8th June 1940 and two days later, Italy entered the war on Germany's side with Mussolini (who was already well-established as a dictator, and had been one of Hitler's role models). In June 1940, Italian troops tried to penetrate the South of France after Mussolini had declared war on that nation, so that the enemy was now attacking France from the north-east and south.

On 14th June 1940, German troops marched into Paris from the North without encountering resistance, having by-passed the Maginot-line; thus reopening old wounds. The French people feared that their country would once more be turned into a bloody battlefield. They felt powerless against the aggressor; all their worst nightmares had been realised. The French Government under Marshal Petain created the Vichy collaboration regime, but the resistance movement under General Charles de Gaulle, driven by agony, despair and hatred ceaselessly worked throughout the war underground. But many innocent people lost their lives on both sides in the process. They, together with the resistance fighters were used as slave labourers in Germany or sent to concentration camps, or worse still, executed.

Although their country, up to that point, did not suffer the same scale of devastation as during the First World War, their country remained under German occupation until 1944. Mussolini had not succeeded in conquering the French mountainous defences in the South. It is alleged that 1,200 French sailors lost their lives when the British destroyed the French Fleet at Oran on 3rd July 1940. The reasons being that they had refused to defend England, and also that the Germans might have captured the ships and used them for their own purposes. After this drastic measure, diplomatic relations between the Vichy and British governments ceased. On 22nd June 1940 a Franco-German armistice had been signed.

Holland, a very liberal country, had harboured many German Jews. They were now trapped, since the Dutch forces had been quite unexpectedly steamrollered by Hitler, Rotterdam having been bombarded on 14th May 1940. Great heroism was shown by Germans, the Dutch (maybe one remembers the moving story of Anne Frank), Belgians, French and others, who sheltered some of the condemned refugees at the risk of losing their own lives. In Berlin alone, about 5000 Jews were sheltered, and survived the war, but 50000 had to leave Berlin, the most in any one place. Many German aristocrats, who were in leading positions under Hitler, sheltered and helped the persecuted, worked against him underground and risked their lives throughout the war. They and their families suffered agony every day, in case they were discovered.

I was blissfully unaware of all this back in Saaz. However, I knew that something extraordinary was taking place, because adults everywhere used to gather together whenever possible, to discuss (sometimes in whispers, at other times heatedly) the major political moves which were now overtaking the ordinary people, with no time to mentally digest the latest news, dramatically broadcast over the 'Volksempfänger.' No other radio channel was allowed. People were confused, but as they were powerless either way, some decided that they would obey orders and enjoy the 'progress' and victories going on all around them. They realised that this progress was made at their own expense, but at least the responsibility for the way this was being achieved had been completely taken out of their hands, and for this they were grateful. They probably had never heard or had forgotten what the British Prime Minister Lloyd George had said after the First World War's dust had settled and the harsh terms and reparations inflicted on Germany were spelled out, namely, "we shall have to fight another war all over again in 25 years at three times the cost". For many people, the humiliation, suffering and deprivations during and following the Great War were now over. The people were now on the band waggon, cajoled by hook or by crook. There was only one leader, who must be obeyed, otherwise the nation was lost.

CHAPTER 13
My introduction to the wider world

My cousin Elli fell in love with a man, named Anton Beran, who was considerably older than herself; in fact, he was a friend of her father's. Toni, as everyone called him, had grown up in the 'Vorstadt' (suburbia), in the Eger Valley, whereas the town itself was situated on the hill. His mother owned a house and grocer's shop. Toni and his brother Joseph were very different in nature and temperament. Toni was sent to the local Commercial School, after which he worked in a bank at the time when he met Elli. In true romantic fashion, she escaped from a convent school at the age of 17 to be near Toni. She managed his mother's shop while the latter underwent an operation, and took over the shop after Toni's mother died. Elli and Toni married in the January of 1939. Their first child, Wolfgang, was born in the same year. The shop had to be let. Toni looked for a better job to be able to afford a suitable flat for Elli and the children, as in 1940 Gerhard, their second child was born. Toni had a weak heart, but he could manage a civil servant's job at the Landratsamt, which involved distributing petrol rationing coupons.[1]

These posts, after Czechoslovakia had been created after 1919, had previously been held by Czechs. Toni disliked anything to do with National Socialism. Therefore he was determined not to join the party. Unfortunately, all civil servants were supposed to be party members. Toni got away with it until someone discovered that he had not, in fact, joined the Party and denounced him. In order to keep his post, which suited his physical condition so well due to his heart condition, he became a 'Nazi'. Many thousands of people found themselves in the same position. Although opposed to Hitler and Fascism, they were forced to join the hateful NSDAP just to keep their jobs, factories, firms, shops, etc.

---

[1] Who would have thought that the motor car, in front of which a man originally had to walk to alert people to its terrifying speed of 5 km per hour, would become so popular in the next fifty years?

Toni was an easy-going, placid character with a wonderful quiet sense of humour, which not even Elli's occasional outbursts could subdue. When she released the highly nervous energy that was constantly trying to pierce her thin crust of self-restraint, Toni would find himself in the position of a drowning man who, when coming up for air, still has the sense to look for something to grasp, instead of thrashing around wildly and wasting precious energy in the process.

Elli's blue eyes could look like diamonds ready to cut glass, her beautiful pearly teeth would show up even whiter and more perfect when her terrifying anger engulfed her environment like a deluge. Her voice could divide the sea and enable her to walk through it - no one could stop her. With eyebrows slightly raised, Toni, looking slightly uncertain at times, would nevertheless lose no opportunities - it must be admitted that there were only very few - to react in his own characteristic, but effective way. "Did you have a good day today, darling?" or "Have the plants been watered today?" The plants referred to were magnificent specimens of palms, vines and other leafy flora in the conservatory, which was filled to the roof with shiny, green chlorophyll in all shapes and sizes and created a trance-enducing atmosphere all of its own. To me, it was mysterious and awe-inspiring.

It was a complete contrast to visit Elli's mother and father, my aunt Marie and uncle Karl. By now they owned a house in the Lange Gasse, just around the corner from the market square. I remember walking with my mother, holding her hand and crying for some reason, past all the shops, past a house with a rockery in the front garden, spiralling up to the pinnacle of a model castle. At the foot of the rockery, some red-hatted garden gnomes languished like contortionists. We past the place where the trees on either side of the road had created a green canopy above, past the little milk shop, past the villas and the manor house and estate, which belonged to Liesl's school-friend Trude Meier von Weinertsgrün's grandparents.

We had arrived at the junction where the Klostermauer (monastery wall) and road curve sharply to the right, and I was still crying when I suddenly noticed that the ground had come dangerously near to my face. This discovery startled me considerably, so that I forgot all about crying and instead concentrated on why the ground had been raised so high in such a short space of time. I reasoned that I had either shrunk or there was something wrong with my eyes. There could be nothing unusual about the ground, as I was still walking normally on it. In an instant, everything was back to normal, just after two big tears had rolled down over my cheeks. They had obviously been hanging in my eyes, magnifying my view of everything for a moment. All the way to aunt Marie's house I tried to puzzle out the link between the tears and the diminishing distance between me and the pavement. I hardly saw the mainstreet with the shopping centre and there was no fluttering of heart-strings when we reached the cinema there, (usually the advertising pictures outside sufficed to induce great excitement in me), neither did I cast one glance at the Marktplatz with its Lauben (arcades) opening up before us as we descended the slight hill of the main street. Turning right from the market square into a small road, we could see the synagogue ahead. It was in fact already in the Lange Gasse, but was clearly visible from this small road. The sight of this church made me click back into reality. Each time we passed by it, I would bombard my mother with questions: "Why are there wooden boards across the door? Why does it look so shabby and neglected and blackened at the bottom? Churches usually look clean and inviting and open. What had happened here?" My mother would always drag me along round the corner as I strained to look back over my shoulder, and tell me that we were nearly there now, anyway.

Sure enough, next to a baker's shop, we opened a dark painted front door, made our way through a dark hall up some rickety stairs, where we were welcomed by aunt Marie who scolded my mother. "Where have you been so long? I've been sitting here worrying." Frowning all the while, she led us into the kitchen, which also served as the dining room. The best room next to it, was hardly used. I slipped into it, leaving the two women to their necessary, amiable 'arguments'. As I opened the door, the first object to catch my eye was the huge ebony grand piano, which uncle Karl had probably bought for his children from the firm Sieber, where my uncle Franz, his brother-in-law worked. It was impressive and beautiful, but very rarely played. As I approached it, fascinated, I noticed my uncle Karl standing by the window. He looked tall and elegant, as always, and the cigarette between his slim fingers had been elongated by a black cigarette holder. His severe expression changed as he turned towards me, and his voice carried the usual nonchalance in its tone. "Finally arrived, Kleine? When will your mother learn to be punctual, hm? Can you say your name properly now? You used to say Attata Loll, when you were asked what your name was, because your real name Erika Schroll was too hard to pronounce – that's a sure sign that you won't give up easily." He slapped me gently on the shoulder and went into the kitchen to greet my mother. While I tried tentatively to play a few notes on the awe-inspiring instrument, I half listened to the conversation next door. It was not difficult, as the living room door was wide open, and the three people in the kitchen all had penetrating voices, uncle Karl's being more sonorous than the two women's.

The notes C, D, E tinkled on the piano; and while my little fingers tried to reach the next octave, I could not help hearing aunt Marie's voice crying out: "If you had spent more time with your family when they needed you most, all this wouldn't have happened. How do you think I felt when I was ordered to go to the town hall? I racked my brains trying to think what I might have done wrong, but never once did it enter my head that it could have something to do with your son Erich."

"Isn't he your son too?" Uncle Karl's testy voice rose, and I visualised the corners of his mouth curling up in arrogant irony, very much like his daughter Elli's.

"Only Gerhard is like me, I'm afraid. Hardworking, responsible, reliable..."

"Have you got a list handy, you might run out of superlatives and impressive qualities," my Uncle quipped.

"Why don't you stop acting like children and think of what can be done now?" My mother sounded resolute and determined not to be dismissed by either of her relatives. "All right, he 's been playing truant for some time without you realising it. I suppose it all started when he began to be more interested in building boats than trying to cram some theoretical facts into his brain. That's when his work deteriorated and the teacher kept him in detention. The scallywag, climbing down the drainpipe of the school and making straight for the Eger to pursue his boat-building." My mother gave a short chuckle. "I would have liked to see that teacher's face when he saw nothing but the open window in that classroom and Toni's face when he discovered that his bicycle was missing. And your face when you were told at the town hall that your son hadn't been near that school for so long, when he had been leaving home dutifully each morning at the right time and returning home at the normal time; a bit dirty maybe, but happy."

"You can laugh!" Marie was now nearly hysterical and I shifted uncomfortably on the piano stool, "He's not your son, and- "

"Oh, come now," my Uncle interrupted her benignly, "He's just a young hothead with imagination who's finding his feet and forming his own ideas. Why make him look like a criminal? I had a talk with him just now and he tells me he wants to join the Merchant Navy."

An ominous silence followed that lively exchange of words. The shockwave could be felt through the wall. My mother, no doubt, realised that her brother-in-law had waited for our arrival to break the news to his wife.

"And why not, in time?" he continued.

I did not wait to hear the end of this heated discussion. Thinking that Erich must be somewhere in the dog-house, I clambered down from the stool and silently entered my cousin's bedroom. It was dark inside, but I could just make out his shapeless form in the bed. Without hesitation, I climbed into bed with him, just as I did at home with my father and mother after having nightmares or wetting my bed. He stirred and moved away a little. I got out of bed and moved round the other side, where I could now see his blond head dimly, as my eyes became accustomed to the darkness. He was my favourite cousin and I felt the urge to stroke his hair. I realise now that it must have been acutely embarrassing for a fourteen-year-old boy to be pitied by his four year-old cousin. While I stood there, he stretched out his hand, pressed mine and said quietly: "It's alright Eriker'll, go back to the others, I just need some sleep." I tiptoed out of the room and made my way to the back of the house where a door opened out onto a ballustrade leading to the toilet, from where there was a good view of the courtyard below. This side of the house was always bright, whereas the living quarters faced north and gave a sombre impression. I enjoyed soaking up the sunlight and being by myself.

The thought of Toni coming out of the toilet one day, whistling his favourite tune: '*Laut klingt das Telefon*' and looking relieved, made me smile; Tante Marie had been anxious that he had taken so long in there. "He's got haemorrhoids, you know," she'd once confided meaningfully to my mother. "He suffers agony each time, poor chap." We had all been there that afternoon, and although I wanted to ask what this dreadful affliction was, I had forgotten all about it on our way home. I sympathised with Toni, for I too suffered agonies during my 'toilet session' at home. While waiting between bouts of dreadful pain, I would demonstrate my singing ability totally uninhibited in that little closet, grateful that one bout of suffering was over and bracing myself for the next. This had earned me the nickname of 'Abortsängerin' (Lavatory Singer) by Herbert who had heard me through the little window leading onto the balcony. I must have thought that I was in a safe, sound and sight proof place, never realising that anyone walking past the house could hear me.

I definitely did not appreciate Herbert calling me that name. Inevitably, the more he knew I hated it, the more he would torment me with it.[1]

On my return to the kitchen, I found an idyllic scene - aunt Marie pouring out steaming coffee into translucent, flower-patterned cups with gold rims, while my mother and uncle Karl chatted convivially.

"Would you like a piece of cake?" aunt Marie turned to me, thus acknowledging my existence. "Has she been eating horse manure again? I meant to ask you a long time ago." She was now looking at my mother.

"No, never again," my mother replied. "I took her to the doctor for something else, and while I was there, I asked him why she was so mad on horse manure, and why she liked scratching the whitewash off walls and eating it. He said the reason must be lack of calcium. He gave me

---

[1] Years later, he told me that my singing had been the purest sound he had ever heard.

some tablets for her, which I gave her like sweets; and soon after there was no sign of her craving such unsavoury things. But now she does something equally weird – she rubs her forehead up and down walls – the sight of it makes you cringe. I dread to think what other kind of deficiency she might have now."

My aunt was about to say something, when my uncle stretched his legs across the room and sniggered quietly: "That girl has always been a bit of an eccentric. I remember how you used to put her outside the Muttergotteshaus in her playpen, and one day your neighbour saw her pushing this playpen right across the big square towards the townhall over all these big cobblestones. What a sight that must have been for you. The playpen was going humperdy-bumperdy and your Erika never faltered, forcing it vigorously forward in a straight line. I bet she couldn't even walk by herself then." They all laughed, and although I felt embarrassed, I could not help feeling proud of my infant achievement. Somehow, the smashing of my sister's toy piano did not seem quite as bad.

CHAPTER 14
The Blitz

Hitler admired the British and their success in ruling the world for so many years. With all the connections and support from important members of the British Establishment, he could not understand that Britain had declared war on Germany. He argued that Britain feared Communism as much as many people in Germany, where Communism was getting a steady foothold. Why could Britain not go with Germany against a common enemy, rather than against Germany? We shall never know, if Hitler sent Rudolf Hess over the Channel on 10th May 1941 to mediate between Germany and Britain, or if Hess himself decided to intervene and come over in a small plane. This last minute effort was not successful and Hess spent all of the war years under house arrest in Britain and the rest of his life in solitary confinement in Spandau prison, Berlin.[1]

France had surrendered on 22th June 1940. The British were trapped in Dunkirk and could have been bombed out of existence. They escaped across the Channel with the help of any big or small vessel that had come

---

[1] Rudolf Hess, son of a wealthy German merchant, was born in 1894 in Alexandria, Egypt, at 12 years old came to Germany, was severely wounded in WW1 at Verdun, attempted to overthrow the Bavarian Government with Hitler in Munich in August 1923, was subsequently imprisoned with Hitler in Landsberg, where Hitler wrote *Mein Kampf,* and became Hitler's private secretary when the latter became chancellor.

to rescue them from England. Their arms, they had to leave behind. Hitler could now attack London from as near as Calais, whereas the Royal Airforce had a long approach to Berlin, Germany's Capital. Hitler procrastinated until Churchill, who had become British Prime Minister on 11th May 1940, gave orders on the same night to bomb the streets and railways of Mönchengladbach with 35 Hampden and Whitley bombers. On 15th May 1940, British planes dropped bombs in the Ruhr area, including Münster, wherever they saw lights in settled places. Two bombs were dropped by twelve German aircraft on London docks on Saturday, 24th August 1940 with 'very minor damage' reported by the Times on Monday, 26th August.

Churchill, in retaliation, sent 89 bombers over Berlin straightaway, (according to Churchill's private secretary John Colville). It was indiscriminate bombing and Churchill had said over the telephone that he was 'averse to administering pin pricks.' The then Air Vice Marshal in Bomber Command Arthur Harris approved of the attack in saying that it was a unique opportunity for retribution that would not come again very soon. According to Goebbels diary, there had been several hours of air-raid alarms, that it was a majestic spectacle and that there was major flak barrage. Harris had been given the order to destroy, through incendiary bombs, the four largest cities in the Ruhr and 14 industrial cities in Germany.

Goebbels was pleased that Berlin had been attacked. Now, the real battle could begin. Churchill, in turn, told Air Chief Marshal Newall to try again as no major damage had been inflicted on Berlin the first time. "I want you to hit them hard. And Berlin is the place to hit them." British planes could attack day and night, whereas the German planes could only attack on clear nights. On 4th and 6th September more raids took place over Berlin.[1] London and other English cities, it was felt, would have to "stick it out" when Germany counter-attacked. Their attention would be taken off British airfields and other essential productions for the war. Dummy planes and tanks were produced en masse and placed all around the English coast.

1940 turned out to be a beautiful, dry summer, so that the fires caused by the British incendiary bombs, which were initially dropped to light up the targets, spread fast and devastation followed. Goering felt his Air force (Deutsche Luftwaffe) was not yet ready for a big counter attack, but Hitler could wait no longer and wanted the British 'out of the way'

---

[1] Britain spent almost half of its war expenses on the air force. There were 1,481 air operations by night and 1,089 by day over Germany during the Battle of Britain. By October 1940, the German Air force (Luftwaffe) had lost 1,733 planes since July, the RAF had lost 915. By December, there were 23,000 civilian casualties, 14,000 in London alone. But the people had to stick to their leader's decisions.

one way or another, so that he could concentrate on his ultimate objective, the East.

On 24th May 1940, Hitler had commanded a halt at the La-Bassée Canal, so that the ten British divisions (338,000 men) trapped there could retreat to the bridge-head of Dunkirk and, in an audacious venture, escape across the Channel.

Again in October, the German aircrew felt that their commanders had betrayed them by not counter-attacking by now. They felt the longer they waited, the stronger the enemy would become. Britain had not produced enough planes at the beginning of the war. Churchill did not think Britain was ready to have air superiority or the capability 'of great offensive operations on land against Germany until 1942'. He had already pioneered the concept of winning a war from the air, when he was minister of munitions in the First World War. It was then that he had planned 'a thousand bomber attack' on Berlin. In June 1940, he declared that he would 'make Germany a desert, yes a desert'. Churchill still hoped that Hitler would be making mistakes, which would vastly increase England's chances of winning the war.[2]

Hitler procrastinated and felt uneasy to go against the admired British Empire. After making definite plans to go East, he gave up the idea of invading England. Each side was feverishly working to manufacture every aspect of the war machine and perfect the most important, sophisticated aid in winning the battle in the air, namely "radar". The British stumbled across the principle of it in 1935. Initially, it was only intended to guide planes safely to the runways. In June 1940, something was retrieved from a shot-down German plane, which revealed the German capability of blind-landing. It took almost two years before the British GEE and OBOE radar could be used. GEE, like the German "Knickebein beam", roughly helped to find the target to be bombed. Each time the Germans found a new idea or technique to outmanoeuvre the British, they in turn would be putting their finest minds together in some isolated place to solve the puzzle and vice- versa. It became a battle of wits, in which Churchill outwitted the German High Command more than once. He would, for instance, sacrifice much, including ships, so that the other side would be unaware that Britain had cracked the German "Enigma Code". The de-coding of it was also made possible through German sabotage. For instance, a German captain of a torpedoed ship left the decoding book deliberately on board to be found by the British. Many

---

[2] This was certainly a hope that became a reality many times over in the future, as is often the case with all ruthless dictators, who will stop at nothing and will change their minds many times, due to their being reckless gamblers and opportunists. Churchill said in April 1941:"There are less than 70 million malignant Huns, some of them are curable and others killable.

German commanders did not believe in the leadership of Hitler and tried to bring the war to an end as soon as possible (also the Kreisau Circle).

Finally, after several British air-attacks on North Germany and Berlin, Göring gave the order to attack London docks and the city centre on 7th September 1940. But it was the East End that suffered the most. There were 1300 injured and 300 dead. The people began to protest and Churchill had to appear in person in the Eastend amongst the rubble to show his sympathy. 53% of the population was in favour of bombing civilians, 38% voted against it.

By now, the Germans could attack by night as well as by day. The raid continued throughout the night and the ensuing fires could be seen far away. The attacks continued for 57 nights and sometimes during the day as well. Londoners were told to shelter in the underground stations, and the evacuation of the children to rural areas began. It became a tit for tat campaign with the concentration being on Berlin and London first. But more and more German planes were shot down over London by the RAF, so that Goering decided to bomb other important cities like Plymouth, Portsmouth, Southampton, Liverpool and Coventry. The latter lost 568 people in one night. So, Operation *Seelöwe* (Sealion, the invasion of England, which was never one of Hitler's favourite plans) was called off; Hitler's first defeat and of his own making. He thought that an invasion was not necessary as he could defeat England from the air. As it turned out, this was not possible and Hitler ultimately had to fight his war on all fronts; in Africa, thanks to Mussolini, who had started a war in Africa. German towns and cities were being systematically destroyed throughout the war, culminating, at the end of the war, in the total destruction of Berlin, Hamburg, the Ruhr and most German cities.

The Battle of Britain, which Churchill encouraged, to draw the Germans out of their stagnant position as far as Britain was concerned, became very expensive for the Germans; for when they most needed the air force shortly after the attacks in the East, they were so depleted of vital equipment and aircrew that the outcome in the East was almost a foregone conclusion..

The German population had no inkling of their leader's ultimate plans and their outcome, unless they were directly affected, as in the air-raids. Amongst others, Spitfires and Hurricanes were sent up to intercept the Junkers, Stukas, Messerschmitts, Focke-Wolfs and Heinkels which approached at a speed of 160-180 mph and a height of 25- 30,000 feet. Many of the pilots and crew of the British planes were manned by British, French, Polish, Czech and Canadian pilots as well as by men from other Commonwealth countries, who experienced a sense of exhiliaration after such a tedious waiting period during which the arrival time of the German 'visitors' was calculated. The British were sent on their missions five to seven times a day and also at night. Initially Hitler bombed strategic targets such as docks. When Churchill decided to attack Berlin with its population in mind, the scene escalated and indiscriminate bombing took place on both sides. In the months to come, the art of navigation turned into a science.

The first big raids were on the Ruhr, Hamburg, Leipzig and Berlin. The one on Hamburg lasted only 40 minutes, but the ensuing devastating fire spread very fast and claimed 40-50,000 lives. Berlin, to the regret of Churchill and Harris, did not burn so well in spite of 363 attempts to wipe it off the face of the earth.

Now the German people knew what Warsaw civilians must have felt in October 1939 when Hitler destroyed great parts of it in the first heavy air attack on a city in this conflict. Attacks and victories were always publicised to the exclusion of all else unless the loss was too great to ignore.

By 1941, German voices could be heard openly criticising Goering for his pledge made in 1940: "If any British plane flies over Germany, I should be called Meier."

"Meier is up to his tricks again," my mother nodded over to Frau Schmidt from upstairs who sometimes called in for a chat. "He says a lot of impressive things, but you can't believe any of them."

"Not like our Führer," Frau Schmidt said enthusiastically, "you can always trust him. Your neighbour, Frau Lava, doesn't seem to think so, nor does that woman up the road in one of those private houses. She listens to foreign stations on her wireless, you know."

"Actually I didn't know that," my mother answered nonchalantly. She never was one for gossip, and disliked vulgar people, although no one could have used more vulgar expressions than her brother Franz, and she herself did not mince her words at times! However, she only ever swore when she was incensed. She would reprimand Franz for his colourful language, but it never made the slightest difference. She once told us about an argument she'd had with a woman, who began to attack her physically. My mother had pushed her away, saying: "*Ich fühle mich zu Höherem geboren.* (I was born for higher things.)

When I was a little older and allowed to go out by myself, I used to stand and stare at the woman's house who supposedly listened to foreign stations. I speculated how she must have looked - like an old evil witch despised by all. Why would she be doing a wicked thing like that? My mind simply could not grasp it.

Meanwhile I continued to admire Herbert. He was undoubtedly my hero. With his square face, dark hair and bushy black eyebrows, his peculiar way of talking, so that every word stood out and sank into your consciousness, he epitomised the youth of the time and place - confused, idealistic, ready for action. He was often the leader of a small group of boys who liked to play outdoors opposite the house on the big meadow or in the little wood next to it, at the back of which was the Jewish cemetery. Sitting on our balcony, I often saw Frau Rauscher standing beneath me just by the steps, using a fierce whistle to call her wayward son back home from his fun and games. With face moist and dirty, his hair in disarray, he would breathlessly appear from nowhere. Her feeble, reproachful voice seemed to have little effect on him, unlike her orders, reinforced by the formidable whistle, which never failed to work.

Sometimes he was put in charge of me when he played outside after school. "Keep an eye on her, won't you, Herbert," my mother asked him the first few times. But he invariably disappeared with the older children and occasionally with my sister, so that I was left to fend for myself, which I quite enjoyed. Being timid, but wanting to meet people, I soon made friends with a flaxen-haired, round faced girl called Irene Luft, who lived in one of those mysterious private houses next to the 'traitor.' Further down the road, near the shops adjacent to the fascinating nursery, I noticed a quick-witted girl of about the same age as myself and Irene, whose name was the same as mine, but her surname I found rather amusing, Erika Hühner (hens). I cannot remember ever playing with the two of them at the same time. It could be that they both belonged to separate 'gangs' of children and never mixed, whereas I was quite at home with both.

In the morning I went to the Kindergarten further down the road. The first time I went, I was rather apprehensive about the whole venture. The Tante showed me my peg which had two cherries underneath to identify where my clothes were to be hung. Other children had a doll, spade, bucket, flower etc as their sign, but I was quite pleased with my cherries. I liked playschool on the whole, but on the odd occasion I felt that I would rather be at home. There was an ironing board and a little toy iron that rather took my fancy, but they were never available to me. No matter how many times I went to look, there was always another child happily pressing dolls clothes on it. It never occurred to me that I could ask to participate as well. Still, it was better than playing at home. There were more toys and I did not have to clear them away afterwards. At home, I had some treasures like a celluloid baby bath with green and white stripes, (a present from Uncle Franz), and a doll's toilet which actually flushed, if you had not forgotten to fill the tiny cistern with water. I had dolls of all shapes and sizes, and even a kaleidoscope. The trouble was that I had to put everything neatly away afterwards into their appropriate places. Somehow, this made the otherwise enjoyable playtime a tedious task and hardly worth the effort.

Enviously I would glance at my sister's dolls house, which stood majestically in a corner of the bedroom, displaying its three luxurious floors, each one better than the next. To own a house like this, every room a model of perfection right down to the Persian carpets on the immaculate parquet floors, would be the realisation of a dream. Of course, I frequently begged my sister to let me play with it, which I sometimes did behind her back, guiltily, until one day she softened and asked my mother if she would allow it. As soon as it was mine, I lost interest due to the weekly dusting nonsense. My sister had little time for playing now. She took her homework and all academic matters very seriously, and as she had to miss a lot of school through her illness, she was always catching up with her work. She had an inexhaustible appetite for more and more knowledge, which she believed I should also strive for. It was not always easy for me to make her understand that I did not share her view on this, at least, not for the time being.

I was more concerned with people and nature. To lie in the long, fragrant grass of "our" meadow on a warm, glorious summer's day, listening to the crickets and the songs of birds. Watching them glide graciously under a clear blue sky was my idea of a stage, on which there was continuous, fascinating action. I could never tire of it. The pulsating earth and its forthcoming life, held safely by the firmament, made me hold my breath.. A miracle in front of my very eyes, which I felt in every waking minute. I could not, of course, put it in so many words, but this is how it felt.

Sometimes, I would not even follow the call of nature. It was too much trouble to go home for this. I would remain where I was and then hang my underclothes up in the bushes to dry. Meanwhile, there was a lot to do. Looking for different coloured pieces of glass on the gravel path or a four-leafed clover - everything was a unique experience. I remember the exaltation I felt when I managed to climb up a fairly accessible lilac-tree opposite our house; my mother was always telling everybody what a tomboy my sister had been before she became ill.

"I used to dress her in a pair of smart Lederhosen (leather shorts)", my mother would say to friends, "and she would go and climb anything she saw in the neighbourhood. Nothing was too high for her. She gave me some frights sometimes, I can tell you. She would just shout: 'Mama, where do you think I am ?' I could hear her, but there was no sign of her anywhere. "Liesele", I would say, "don't be silly. Come down from wherever you are, quickly. But she would play a game with me, giving me some nasty moments, till in the end, she would just appear right next to me, laughing. I would just take her in my arms and squeeze her with tears in my eyes. But it's all different with Erika. She can't even jump over two sticks, let alone climb a tree."

This time it was the Szöny's my mother was talking to. They were good friends of my parents. He was Hungarian, and she came from Saaz and was Czech. They had two girls, who attended the German school. He was a dark-haired man with kind brown eyes and numerous moles dotting his face. They spoke German quite well, but it was obvious that it was not their mother tongue. He worked at Skoda's, the big Bohemian concern. His work place was about 50 km away from Saaz and he often did nightshifts making trucks, munitions and tanks for the Germans.

"We went to see my in-laws recently," my mother told the Szöny's in confidence. "Nand's youngest brother was there. You know I told you that he'd joined the infantry (pioneers) in '39 at the Stengelkaserne in Germersheim. He told us all about the Frankreich-Feldzug (he had to fight in France) and how optimistic he'd been at first. They reckoned the war would be over in a year and that they were lucky to be in it. They didn't actually have to fight, but were occupied with temporary bridge-building, mine-removal and just marching. The longest march in a day was 75 km. He was in the infantry, which was quite foot sore at times. He'd thought it would be a cheap way to see other countries and meet other people, but it didn't take long for him to change his mind. They pay with their own blood, and people aren't the same in war. He did tell us a funny story, though. He was in the 4th division (Bayerisch Württembergisch), as a Meldefahrer (motorcycle messenger) whilst in France. It was January, the roads were iced up, and *Kolonnenfahrt* (transporting of troops) was on the agenda. On the return trip his motorcycle-clutch broke, so that when he arrived at the barracks, he began to encircle the arriving company like a sheep dog, just missing a guard, to top it all. Everybody laughed at him; he lost his nerve, feeling the blood rush to his head, until the unbearable situation was saved by a friend who shouted 'turn the ignition off!' Consequently he was given a job as a clerk in the *Schirrmeisterei* (supply office) and as an ad-hoc petrol attendant. He was sent home on leave (he hadn't seen his mother for two years). So he bought his girlfriend Ria a watch, and some pink silk lingerie; for my mother-in-law some woollen material for a dress, for my father-in-law some tobacco and some presents for Traudl and Mina. He had sent Ria a telegram, so she was already waiting for him in Karlsbad. He knew straightaway that there was something wrong, but later, walking through the lovely Karlsbad Spa gardens, he forgot his doubts and thought he had imagined them all."

My mother hesitated and looked sad. Frau Szöny wanted to hear the end of the story, now that it was getting interesting for her. "Go on", she said, "what happened next?"

"They went by bus to Luditz. Ria's mother seemed very pleased to see him. A large picture of him hung in the lounge, but the idea of enlarging his photo and adorning the wall with it had been Ria's mother's idea. He now asked Ria directly if she had met someone else, as he had intended to get engaged to her while on leave. But she dismissed the question flippantly, saying: 'What thoughts! Why do you want to spoil your leave?' He remained suspicious as he told her about his experiences in France. He had heard that there were soldiers in town, and one of them was staying at Ria's house."

"Well, to cut a long story short, he lost her, and his dreams are shattered. He'd found his time in France bearable, thinking of her and their future life together. Now he's on his way to Russia with this tremendous disappointment still tearing him up inside."

Szöny looked sad. "There'll be many in the same situation, I'm afraid," he said slowly, and his kind eyes lowered to the ground. "War brings a lot of unnecessary unhappiness. I wouldn't want to know how many brides have lost their loved ones by now, on either side. He's lucky. He's alive and can start again, if he survives the war, that is."

"What do you think about the attack on Russia?" my father now asked, gently easing me off his lap. (In November 1940, Molotov, who was Foreign Minister of Soviet Russia, came to Berlin for talks, but no agreement was possible on mutual demands in Middle Eastern Europe).

Herr and Frau Szöny were not keen to answer that question. Finally Szöny commented in his deliberate, benevolent way that it seemed a bit unreasonable to wage a war on virtually all fronts. At that point, my father interjected that Mussolini, after appearing rather feeble in France, which was already conquered, must have been trying to improve on this state of affairs in Africa. He failed as Churchill defeated him in defence of the Suez Canal. At the same time, Mussolini lost Abyssinia, which he had taken so brazenly in 1935 whilst the League of Nations had looked on.

"Before these defeats he'd marched into Greece (28th Oct 1940), and what do you think? He was just as unsuccessful there," Szöny shook his head, smiling to himself. "I hope Herr Hitler didn't take over from Mussolini in those places just to help him out. He doesn't usually care about people; if an objective is high enough or when he favours a certain person, he doesn't mind how many people he sacrifices for it."

"I don't think he intervened there for that reason," my father interrupted, a little annoyed. "He probably wants to get rid of the British, they've been dominating the Mediterranean for a long time and they'll be a danger to him sooner or later. The only thing is that Mussolini forced him to start there prematurely, and at a very awkward moment, in fact, just when he must have started his preparations for the *Balkanfeldzug* (invasion of Russia) in April. He had to send troops to Africa at the beginning of this year (1941) when he should have been concentrating on

Russia. Even the Balkanfeldzug (Russian invasion) wasn't planned at the time it started. I think he wanted to attack Russia first and foremost, although he signed a pact with them in January this year for the Baltic Germans to be evacuated into the Reich. Who knows what's on his mind. Let's hope he knows best. Franco owes him a lot, but he let him down good and proper, don't you think? He refused our Führer's request to take Gibraltar from inland." (23rd October 1940)

My father paused. Then his eyes lit up. "What do you think about Hess going to England?"

Szöny looked at his wife who had started talking to my mother. They must have found more entertaining topics to talk about than politics and current affairs and were happy to let others discuss them without getting involved. Szöny looked as if he wouldn't have minded joining the women in their comfortable small talk.

"The trouble is," he now looked straight at my father as he wrung his hands as if in dispair, "you only ever hear snatches here and there on the radio - reading the newspaper is no good – and you have to put two and two together. Even then we know very little and we're kept in the dark most of the time. I should think Hitler sent Hess over to warn the British of the forthcoming battle against Russia and ask for their support, so that they could concentrate on that alone and not be needled by the British everywhere they go."[1]

On 22nd June 1941, Hitler started the attack on Soviet Russia. The decision to grab the oilfields in the South first, moved the major attack back by months, making it impossible from the start to overcome the well prepared and well-kitted-out Russian Army in winter. Like Napoleon, Hitler underestimated the severe Russian winter and threw his brave army into the abyss. He had set out to destroy Russia (*Vernichtungskrieg*), but Russia was the beginning of the end for him and Germany.

At the same time, the *Endlösung* – the "final solution" or the systematic murder of Jews and 'undesirables' had begun. Most of the German population knew nothing of this. It was carried out by the S.S. in complete secrecy; with the extermination camps situated in isolated places, some of the worst ones in Poland. Although Hitler had never given the order in writing, he had dropped enough hints as to what his wishes were. All these useless millions, now in the East, were a hindrance. They had to be 'disposed of' like the Slavs who counted for nothing. Hitler had told Göring to empower Heydrich to arrange the total evacuation of European Jews. While Hitler talked about social ideals, moral values of humanity and *Endziel* (final solution), an estimated ten

---

[1] On the German side were Romania, Hungary, Slovakia, Finland and some Italian troops.

million people were annihilated, including six million Jews. As these people counted for nothing in Hitlers's and his brainwashed elitists' eyes, they became subject to indescribable experiments and misery, supposedly for the good of the German people. These experiments were made for scientific reasons, looking ahead to the defence of the thousand year German Empire. [2]

Szöny continued: "But when the attempt failed, Hitler obviously had to deny all knowledge of the plot and pass the buck to poor old Hess. It was just another big gamble, which didn't come off this time."

"You think that?" my father exclaimed in astonishment. He pondered this for a moment. "I thought he'd just defected. There could be several reasons for doing that, but your idea would never have entered my head."

My mother interrupted the dialogue. "Guess what I found in my kitchen-cabinet the other day? I was taking everything out to clean when I found a whole load of pebbles, stones, coloured glass etc. hidden inside the cups at the back. I couldn't believe my eyes. Of course I threw the lot out. I have a good idea who put them there, although it's pointless asking her about it. She really is a little so-and-so. She kept interfering with Liesl's doll's house, so Liesl gave it to her. But do you think she wants to keep it clean now and dust it once a week? No, she'd rather not play with it anymore."

Later on, when the visitors had gone, and my father was resting on the sofa I crept over to him and kissed him. He blew 'a raspberry' on my cheek which tickled, and then he drew his knees up, perched me on top of them, then straightened his legs abruptly, so that I fell down onto them with a delighted shriek, still holding his hands.

I loved my father, despite the fact he kept three different-sized bamboo sticks on the cupboard by the door. Sometimes, when he came home from work, my mother would relate all the sins I had committed during the day, and he would have to work himself up into a rage and threaten to punish me according to the severity of my crime. Sometimes he used the small stick, other times the middle one, but only once did he use the thickest of the three. I don't recall being hit, but only threatened by the two smaller ones, whereas I shall never forget being at the receiving end of the most dreaded one. I don't think my father hit me more than three times. What hurt the most was the humiliation and endless accusations my mother hurled in my direction. She must have been subject to the same treatment in her own childhood and now saw fit

---

[2] After the war, the Americans used the results of these experiments for their space explorations.

to pass it on to me, maybe out of a sense of duty or obligation to a 'decent' upbringing.

As I had no brother, I wanted to know what boys of my own age looked like. I was always interested in anything and everything, and this was just another quest of mine. My parents could not comprehend that kind of curiosity. They thought I was wicked and dirty, and were horrified that I had been found in the graveyard opposite our house (Antoniusfriedhof, a spacious 'playground for the children of the vicinity) with a boy engaged in a kind of mutual peepshow.

The boy, called Bruno, was quite repulsive, with his perpetual stream of mucus making its way towards his mouth. With his round head, long straight blond hair and squint, his expression was mostly placid to the point of stupidity - in contrast to his uncle's face, Herr Seifert, who always looked as though each breath could be his last. Bruno must have been on holiday there every now and then, and each time he came, he followed me around like a dog. I presume he was an only child and only gradually got to know the other children in his uncle's neighbourhood. He was very generous and I remember him offering me the best-tasting pear I'd ever had. Every bit of it was a treat, with the sweet juice dripping down my hand and forearm, forever wasted. It was a case of Adam tempting Eve with a pear.

Sobbing on my potty after being hit with the biggest stick, with my parents looking on reproachfully and still scolding, a feeling of guilt flooded over me. What had I done? How could I have done it? I must have known that it was wrong. My sister would never have done such a thing. She always did everything right. What would my parents have said if they had known about Willi Blecher? He was a boy about my age who lived Am Semmering behind us in a villa with an orchard, in which he had a tent in the summer. He invited me through the fence to play with him one day. His parents were always pleased to see me when I came down the Semmering to his house. We tried to climb trees, but without success. Eventually we entered his tent; he sat on one side and I on the other as far apart as possible. Playing with toys in silence, we had begun this secret, dangerous game which Bruno and I continued and which led to my downfall.

My father was now a *Wagenmeister* (inspecting goods-trains) at the railway station. He belonged to a group of men responsible for the maintenance of the freight trains. Sometimes, coming home from work, he would bring home some pale ale, best Saazer Lager[1], especially when

---

[1] Saazer hops, which is seedless and produces a delicate, dry flavour, is one of the best in the world to this day, but it is now too precious to brew Saazer Beer with. It is now mainly exported.

he worked for the brewery. However, we girls preferred our 'lemonade', made from two square tablets wrapped in paper; the white one contained citric acid, the other was orange and provided the fruit flavour. We would throw them into a glass of water and watch the amazing transformation take place. You could also suck them as sweets.

In the summer, my father would cycle home while it was still light and I was allowed to play outside with the other children. It was a delight to spot him from afar and run up to him. He would sit me on the crossbar until we reached our house.

One night, my sister and I were already asleep when some men brought my father home in an awful state. He had a small hole in his head, as well as a large bump, and each time they moved him, he screamed. He had to sit up in bed and the slightest move would produce an agonizing moan. Apparently, some men had removed a heavy, damaged iron door from one of the waggons. It became too heavy. They all let go, but my father was still holding on when it crashed down on him. Apart from his head injury, he had a few bent ribs, which caused the excruciating pain. The doctor was worried about the danger of concussion, but as soon as my father's ribs felt better, he went back to work.

Nevertheless, it was a shock to me to be woken by my father's expression of pain, which I had never heard before. To me, he was invincible - strong, kind, self-disciplined, sensitive, yet thick-skinned and inflexible on occasions.

Uncle Karl, Aunt Marie's husband, who had already served in the First World War, was now an officer in the Rhineland and held an administrative post. He used to come home on odd weekends. Sometimes he came to see us on a Sunday afternoon in his spotless uniform with a long sword, in First World War fashion, hanging impressively by his side; his hair, buttons and shoes gleaming, and his muscles like coiled springs straining to burst through his clothes. Even the lines around his mouth, with jaw muscles flexing rhythmically, were symmetrical, and the cigarette between his lips seemed a fitting punctuation in a perfect composition.

His eldest son Gerhard was already playing the saxophone and clarinet in a café (Hotel Am Löwen and also in a youth club) in his spare time. Around 1938, he and his best friend Otto Girge formed a band "The Canons" with Otto playing the piano, Gerhard the double bass or other instruments. Fred Lang played the trumpet and trombone and Hans Schleh percussion. Onkel Franz gave his name for it as he had a licence. Their emblem was a black velvet pennant. As a boy, he'd wanted to be an artist and paint with oils. When he was told that this would not be possible, he became a painter of furniture. "I'll be a painter, nevertheless,"

he determined. He joined Lackierer Luft and as his apprenticeship piece
he painted my parents' bedroom furniture (from Rosa) which had been
modernized by Herrn Wellisch' master, Herrn Gröschl. Gerhard then
painted the bedframes, so that they resembled Swedish birch wood
covered with varnish. I remember admiring the smoothness of the texture
and fluency of design. Now they had only to buy a new dressing table
like the kitchen furniture, the cost of which took years to pay off. The
cabinet alone cost 1020 Kronen or 350 RM (Reichsmark). My mother
thought this outrageous extravagance and wastefulness. But my father
insisted on throwing out my grandmother's old things and replacing them
with new ones.

Herr Wellisch was a friend from the social club for men
(*Gesellenverein*), who lived in the block of flats next to ours. My mother
had also been a member of The Liedertafel, a mixed choir, for over two
decades. I used to wander over to the Wellisch' about once a week and
have a chat with Frau Wellisch. I preferred her company to that of her
two children Gerold and Edith. Gerold was a wild young fellow, with
whom I had nothing in common, and Edith was too young to play with.
Frau Wellisch, a very nervous, restless person, who seemed to hover over
one place or person like a dragonfly, and then suddenly appear
somewhere else, would invariably finish our dialogue with a monologue
about her young and beautiful sister, who had died suddenly from a brain
tumour. She would show me a little wooden box, which had belonged to
her sister, and which she now treasured like a shrine. I sat in awe and took
in every word she uttered until it was embedded in my mind forever.
Little did I know that I would have a similar story to tell in just a few
years time. How much misery I could have saved myself, if I had ever
considered this possibility; but it never entered my mind, although Liesl
was sufficiently ill to be rushed off to hospital on more than one occasion.
She had frequent nosebleeds which seemed to be never-ending. It usually
relieved her condition of faulty heartvalves. Her lips and fingernails
appeared dark blue or purple, her breathing was laboured, and her
calmness only served to exacerbate my mother's panic. Once, my parents
had to take the risk of bringing her home from Bad Elster in an
ambulance. The attempts made to improve her complaint had failed
miserably.

All this made the particular concern and preference bestowed on
Liesl (including the purchase of special fruit/food) natural to my mother.
I could only see this when it was too late; at the time, all I could see was
that she preferred my sister to me, and that nothing could ever change
this. I began wetting the bed again and coughing my lungs out.

After a recurring dream of sitting on the toilet, I would feel the sheet
beneath me grow wet and warm, wake up, stop my 'misdeed' and sneak

into my mother's bed. I would lie close to her and try to synchronise my breathing with hers, which in the end, always proved impossible. However hard I tried to breathe as slowly and evenly as my mother, I could never keep it up for longer than a few seconds. Nevertheless, I always felt a deep peace, which induced contentment and a desire for this feeling to be permanent. When my mother had her customary siesta, after having banished me to my cot, with the multicoloured, striped towelling blanket, I would stand at the bottom of the bed, make myself as stiff as a board and let myself fall down onto the mattress. It was an entertaining little exercise for a while until I tired of it. After that, I would resort to a less socially accepted occupation which only served to make me feel guilty.

After coughing for a few months, with the doctor finding no cause for it, my neck began to bulge visibly, and my mother pointed this out to me. I was vain and felt disturbed by the prospect of growing up with a great, thick neck with protruding blue veins. In order to combat this, I tied a long scarf around my neck, so that I could hardly breathe. When this did not help, my mother got her inhaler out which hissed and spluttered and frightened me more than my sister's stories. One of which was about the little man, who came every midnight to get his little liver (das kleine Leberle) back, which had apparently been taken from him - a kind of organ transplant-nightmare.

This inhaler was a small glass container with a top like a blow-lamp, with the same forceful ejection, not of gas, but of steam mixed with camphorous substances, the smell of which filled the whole place. As soon as I heard the odious sound, my mind was made up that it was a nice day outside, either for soaking up the sunshine like the birds, the trees, crickets, etc. or, if there was no sun, for exploration. If it was really too unpleasant outside, I could always go and visit people. Herr Seifert and his twins downstairs were interesting, especially because of his 'pet fish' in their green- shimmering aquariums. However, he was a socialist, and therefore a communist, and could not be trusted, or so I had heard.

I could go downstairs to the Wollnheits, the Meiers, the Pescheks, or upstairs to the Schmidt's, the Gotthardts, the Krals, the Steigenhöfers (he was also a socialist), or next door to the Rauscher's, or to the next block or to Erika Hühner, Irene Luft or Erika Lorenz. I felt that everybody was my friend, but some were friendlier and more interesting than others. Only very few were somewhat 'scary', not in a violent, but rather unpredictable sense. Frau Schmidt, who was very fond of Herbert, certainly was an overpowering figure, whose ego consumed her on occasion, and this disturbing fact did nothing to desire her company.

CHAPTER 15

Pain and happiness

W hen I returned home again from my jaunt, the dreaded lamp appeared again from nowhere. This time, Frau Schmidt happened to be present, so that my mother's idea found reinforcement and there was no chance to escape anymore. They dragged me, kicking and screaming, to the table and hoisted me up onto a chair, directing my face toward the steam. I felt the vapour on my tongue and nose, and the foul smell penetrating my sensitive nostrils until I felt it overwhelming my brain. After what seemed an eternity, the two women tired of my yelling and let me climb down. I threw a devastating look at them, which failed to produce the desired result.

Finally, the doctor told my mother to buy a black, round radish, the size of a large egg; she was to cut the top off and the middle out and fill it with an egg yolk mixed with candy-sugar (I occasionally bought the latter from Frau Smolik's grocer's shop as a treat after having received a few pennies from my parents' friends). She then was to replace the top and leave the whole mysterious concoction on top of our tiled stove to keep warm. Every few hours my mother had to give me a spoonful of this mixture - a procedure which I never allowed her to forget. I am sure that this doctor was a clever psychologist, who knew that my psychosomatic phenomenon could only be cured by giving sufficient attention to the patient, and he was absolutely right in his diognosis and prognosis. The hacking, body-shaking cough disappeared, when, in my estimation, I had received sufficient attention from my mother.

Lacking iron, I was also made to eat a recommended spoon of raw, scraped liver, not to speak of the boiled carrots or sour lung for dinner. Of course, times were becoming hard and food far less plentiful, with everything going toward the war effort.

Collections took place time and again (*Hilfswerk*), complete with colourful souvenir badges and trophies to show off with in return for what was donated.. Posters went up everywhere to warn of thieves stealing the precious coal needed for the war. I can still picture them now - a man called Kohlenklau, (coal thief) as black as coal, his shape at one with a sackful of coal draped over his shoulder.

Captured Poles helped on farms and in hop gardens; later Frenchmen in berets came to decorate the flats and buildings. I remember two in our home. They were painting the walls of our flat, using rollers to imprint a pattern on top of the paint. They hardly talked, just got on with their work. They were, in all probability, resistance fighters from France. They also painted the Rauscher's flat just as they had wanted it. Herbert told us of some foreign workers, who had painted blue roses (at that time unknown in the natural world) on someone's walls to get their own back.

A call for help went out to housewives to accommodate some children evacuated from Berlin to protect them from the terrible air attacks there. There had already been many, but the Battle of Berlin was still in the future. It took place, in 19 major raids, from August 1943 to March 1944 killing 9,390 civilians and 2,690 airmen. 10,813 bombers dropped 17,000 tons of high-explosive bombs and 16,000 tons of incendiaries. In the final assault and conquest of Berlin by the Russians, 1.8 million shells were dropped on it. Hamburg was also a major target and as in other ancient, medieval towns and cities of Germany, different to Berlin, the ensuing firestorms caused through the incendiary bombs finished the destruction for the Allies. A stream of bombers, often 90 miles long, would approach a city and drop its load one by one into the inferno. All in all, 70,000 children were killed in Germany during the war.

These Berlin children were at a school near Saaz station, waiting to be collected by anyone who took pity on them - no previous arrangements had been made. Frau Rauscher told us all about it. We promptly took in Manfred, a pale boy with a longish face, who spoke 'strangely' and who told us about a hole in his kitchen where beetles crawled in and out to their hearts content. Frau Rauscher also took in a boy, Jürgen by name, from Berlin. Endless exchanges of views and comments were made about these two boys, which made life more interesting, and preferable to being secretly frightened by overwhelming events.

One day, Frau Rauscher announced that Jürgen was going back to Berlin after a year's stay in Saaz. Manfred, who had shown no sign of homesickness up until then, immediately wanted to go home too. His tales of Bobbo, his mother's friend, who once had fallen into a hole in a drunken stupour had subsided, so that my mother felt it was now a good time to intersperse the mundane with the divine. She started to say a short prayer with him at bedtime. The first few times he merely looked surprised, then he began to think about the words:-

"Lieber Gott, mach' mich fromm, dass ich in den Himmel komm". ("Dear God, make me trust you that I may go to Heaven." The word *Himmel* in German means both, Heaven and Sky, in English.)

One night, after they had finished praying, he burst out: "But Mama, how would I get back down again?"

It had been traumatic in Berlin with air-raids and the war routine, but as soon as people began to somehow cope, the parents wanted their children back. Far from giving up, they became resigned to the destruction and death all around them and showed a stoic determination. At the end of 1943, 500000 Berliners had been made homeless. Manfred's mother wrote to say that when her son returned, she had paced up and down the platform several times before she recognised him. He had grown substantially, and his face, formerly pale and drawn, now looked full and rosy.

The story of how my father started to work for the railway is a curious one. While he worked in the brewery with very little return, he was asked to become a fireman for the railway. After one year's service, firemen could take an exam and become engine drivers - every schoolboy's dream in those days. These were urgently needed now that a lot of Czech workers had left. My mother had repeatedly urged him to apply for a job there. He had always declined, saying that it would seem ungrateful to leave the brewery after having received so much goodwill and support from them. He finally accepted. After a short period working on freight trains as a fireman, facing the blasting heat, then looking out of the window to watch the signals, my father's stomach began to complain. My mother walked through the town to bring his lunch to the station most days when he was not far away. She never shied away from any arduous task, in the same way she had carried my sister on her back to school for three weeks when the latter was too ill to walk. Liesl was very conscientious and had insisted that she could not afford to miss school.

However, my father was found to be colourblind after just seven months of being a fireman. If you cannot distinguish the different coloured signal lights, you cannot become an engine driver on the railway. He therefore became a Wagenmeister on the railway for the rest of his working life. [1]

He also became a member of the town council around this time, for which he was honoured with an expensive wrist watch. Under different circumstances, nobody would have asked this 'newcomer' to assume such a responsible position, but because my father showed political initiative, he seemed the right man. He could not enjoy this task for very long, because 'his service at the front was requested.'

About all this, I knew nothing. It was winter 1942; my sister felt a little better, the snow lay thick on the ground and looked like yet another adventure. Equipped with a sledge, Liesl and I stomped through the snow, past Aunt Marie's house to the Schiesshausberg; a steep, long slope, which had to be laboriously conquered before each thrilling slide down. Nevertheless, it was always worth the effort; the long, fast sledge ride downhill brought colour to our cheeks and produced immediate anti-cipation again, the moment the joy-ride was over. Many children scrambled, sometimes on all fours, up the icy slippery slope wet and cold, but nothing could dampen their spirits. Loud screams of joy and elation

---

[1] Climbing to the top of the ladder in his career, he eventually became a civil servant.

pierced the exhilarating air, and I for one did not want to budge until it began to grow dark.

Liesl had been collected by my mother long before. She had only been able to stay a short while, and my mother had come from aunt Marie's house to pull her up the hill a few times, so that she could enjoy the thrill of the ride along with the other children.

Another delight in winter presented itself in the shape of the little slope outside our house. The 'paradise-meadow', now covered with pure, white snow sloped down to the street, and offered a unique opportunity for sliding down and right across the road. Several mirror-like slope tracks appeared within hours of sufficient snow and frost. I surprised myself with the heroic courage I showed, standing up straight, one leg forward and slightly bent, following the other children in their pursuit of happiness and abandonment. There were few cars, and I was always extra careful in any case.

However, one day I did have quite a surprise. Coming from the 'green roof' past the shops, rode three beautiful, proud horses with their equally proud and beautiful riders on top of them - two officers in riding-breeches and one slender, elegant lady with immaculate poise. They disappeared down the Semmering, the horses slipping and carefully redressing their balance on the icy surface. I thought of running after them, wanting to find out their destination. Down the Semmering, the houses came to an end and the hopfields started next to the meandering river Eger. I ran down a little way, but was stopped by a boy on skates. I asked him to let me have a go on them. They had to be fixed with a little handle. I found it hard enough just to balance on them, let alone skate down the hill without sprawling about in all directions.

I had forgotten all about the officers when suddenly a riderless horse came galloping towards us from the bottom of the hill followed by one of the officers. This time, he looked distinctly bewildered, dishevelled and agitated. We doubted his chances of catching up with the wild creature. A little later, the other horse appeared ridden by the lady and led by the other officer. All of them had lost their former confidence, which had bordered on arrogance. They were, in fact, a sorry sight. Limping and sliding about, the lady's hair in disarray, they looked nervous and disappointed.

One afternoon we visited Elli, my much older married cousin. On the way, we had to pass an open-air skating rink, the sight of which was so entertaining, I could not tear myself away from it. Never before had I seen such harmony of movement and rhythm, graceful balancing and energetic vehemence. The surface of the ice showed the circular movements of the skaters like beautiful patterns engraved on crystal glass. Not everyone, of course, managed to float and glide on the slippery, yet beckoning attraction. A few times I laughed out aloud at the learners' repeated attempts to imitate the accomplished skaters, each time with the same result – their wavering limbs folded up and collapsed with a thud on the inflexible ice like my toy puppet August with lax strings. An odd leg or arm would stick out, and screams of pain and delight could be heard every now and then.

My mother kept pulling me away, but she had a hard job. At Elli's, we found Tante Marie and Onkel Karl present and also a most beautiful young girl, called Trixi, shortened from Beatrice. She turned out to be Gerhard's fiancée, an exotic looking, dark-haired Czech girl, whom he had met in Mährisch-Ostrau where he was stationed when first conscripted. She had been a conductress on a tram-line, engaged to Gerhard's best friend, who had told him to look after her, if anything happened to him, shortly before he died in combat. Gerhard found this no obligation, although he found it hard to face his friend's death. He got her transferred to Saaz, because large families were entitled to a help in the home, and Gerhard knew that she would become one of the family. All young people had to do a year's national service (*Arbeitsdienst*).

In spite of initial doubts aired by certain family members as to how Elli would get on with a help in her house, the two women turned out to compliment each other. Trixi was a cool and collected person at all times. When she got under Elli's feet at times, she would take the baby out in the pram and promenade around the Stadtpark or wherever she liked. I often saw her push the pram in the streets, a content, smooth-skinned, fascinating woman, usually wearing the fashionable turban of the era, wound artistically round her beautifully black hair, her eyes dark and full of lustre. Trixi might have joined the Beran family much later, as help was only granted for families with more than four or five children.

Gerhard played his instruments so well that he became a popular musician in the Army. They had a special music badge or sign on their epaulettes. He made one or two records and was heard to play on the wireless. Music seemed to be in his veins. Small wonder; his mother's and my mother's cousin was a professor of music in Prague and a concert-pianist. His name was Franz Langer, whose father had also been a gifted musician like Gerhard's grandfather Anton.

CHAPTER 16
Christmas 1942

Although, in certain ways the Czech people were better off than others (they had enough to eat, living in the mainly rural centre of Czechoslovakia unless they had decided to stay in the German areas, and they were not conscripted), they had to be in constant dread of the German tyranny, if they did anything wrong in the eyes of the occupying forces. They worked in ammunition factories and were forced to help the war-effort like other occupied nations. As soon as any partisan and underground activities stirred, and there were plenty, Heydrich, who was governor in the Protectorate of Böhmen, Mähren and Schlesien (Bohemia, Moravia and Silesia) and who had been instructed by Göring in July 1941 to draw up plans for the distruction of European Jewry, would appear on the scene with his collective punitive measures, so that he soon became an object of hate, a bete noire, to the Czech population.

Consequently, Heydrich was killed by British-trained Czechs on 26th May 1942. As a form of retribution, the Czech village of Lidice near Prague, which seemed to have been implicated in this plot, was razed to the ground, and all its male adults from 16 years on (172 in all) were shot on 10th June 1942. The 198 women were taken to the women's concentration camp of Ravensbruck, in which 143 of them survived their ordeal. 98 children were taken to a concentration camp in Gneisenau, of whom some were taken to German orphanages, if they looked German or for 'Germanisation'.

Hitler was furious and wanted thousands of people to suffer for this outrageous murder. There were rumours that he had intended to make Reinhard Heydrich his successor. He called him "the man with the iron heart". A wave of retribution, affecting nearly a thousand people, was unleashed, although Hitler's orders of eliminating thousands for this assassination were mitigated by Heydrich's successor Karl Frank with the argument that the Czech labour force was essential. They had the same rights as the Germans (earnings, pensions etc.), but also the same duties. If they were coerced to go somewhere and do a specific job, they, like the Germans, had to obey. Thousands of Czechs collaborated, and thousands belonged to the Underground Movement with predictable consequences.

These measures were repeated in other countries (e.g. Oradour in France) until the end of the war, as Hitler's sycophants realised that conquered people did not welcome their visitors, even if they let them live their lives as normally as possible under the circumstances. They expected them to cooperate and be glad that the all-embracing new religion had reached their land also, but found instead that people had to be forced to understand their doctrines and goals.

By now, it was obvious to most Germans that they had 'backed the wrong horse', but they could not admit it. It had taken them long enough to persuade their conscience that every action taken by the Führer was for the best - the ultimate goal before consideration of the individual and his qualms and sacrifices. Most-- people like following a strong leader, a person who knows what they want and strongly pursues his or her goals.

This person is then solely responsible for the consequences, and all that has to be done by the citizens is to follow. Whom else can they follow in dangerous situations? Whatever doubts existed, were buried deep, otherwise the burden of guilt would have become unbearable.

In June of 1941, three million German soldiers were making their way to Russia (eight times as many as Napoleon had against Russia) advancing about 300 km in one month. The front is extensive. They capture the Romanian oilfields, but the objective is the Ukranian ones. Due to this delay, winter has set in on arriving at Moscow. They occupy the Donez-Becken and the Crimea (not Sevastopol), but Leningrad is isolated from September 1941 until January 1943. Thousands of Russians fall and an estimated 300,000 are taken prisoner. In the whole campaign, about 600,000 Russian soldiers are taken prisoner, (a lot of non-Russians from the USSR, who were not fond of being governed by Russia, wanted to be captured by the Germans – and in the end, over one million subsequently fought for the Germans).[1]

In October they reached Moscow, but the freezing temperatures had set in, and troops from the Far East came to help defend the city. They had been stationed there for the possibility of an attack by Japan. The German Army was now threatened from behind by guerrillas and partisans, and ahead by the Red Army, as well as the severe winter (-40°C) for which it was not prepared. Hitler could not have imagined the enormity of the Russian expanse and how long it would take his army to reach and take Moscow, especially as he had taken the oilfields "on the way" there.

On 19th October 1942, the entire sixth Army under General-feldmarschall Paulus (parts of the 4th Panzer armee, Romanians included) was surrounded outside Stalingrad by the Russians. The battle of Stalingrad raged from July to October 1942, in the course of which most of Stalingrad was destroyed. By the beginning of October, 90% of the city was in German hands. Stalin was equally as determined as Hitler to keep Stalingrad. One million Russian soldiers who came from the North and South were sent to fight. Snow and ice set in and German planes could supply just 100 tons instead of 300 tons of supplies needed in one day. The German Army had been fighting on all fronts. There were few planes and less and less of all essentials for such a massive offensive.

In the face of this impossible situation, Hitler's command was to fight on. This was to be the pattern throughout the war. *"Es ist mein unbeugsamer Wille"* (it is my unrelenting will) preceded many of his speeches and was followed by "If the German nation proves to be too

---

[1] About 1 million Russian civilians died of cold, hunger, disease and attacks from German and Russian Government forces.

weak to win this war, then it does not deserve to survive." This mind that had to convince itself that it was unique in order to quash its feeling of inadequacy haunting it all its life, was now, more than ever, obsessed with the idea that others were responsible for the hitherto successful coups now threatening to turn into nightmares and destroy everything in their wake

On 31st Jan 1943, Paulus capitulated. Some sources state that in the Battle of Stalingrad 160,000 Germans died and 6,000 returned to Germany. Hitler ordered three days of official mourning, after which Sahra Leander with her penetrating voice was allowed to entertain again. She was the forces sweetheart, the German equivalent of Vera Lynn.[1]

In the fight for Stalingrad, 91,000 German soldiers were taken into Russian captivity on 2nd February 1943 where, in Siberia, they probably suffered the same fate as the Russian soldiers and Cossacks who were sent back in their millions by the Western Allies after the war. A few survived, including a German doctor of medicine who had been treating and operating on German soldiers in the city without proper medical facilities. This man, Dr. Ottmar Kohler, operated with a penknife and once sewed up wounds in Siberia using threads from a scarf (He was offered to be sent home in 1951, but refused to leave his companions without medical attention. Three years later, in 1954, he returned to Germany, where he was presented with the Grosse Verdienstkrenz by the first president after the war, Theodor Heuss. Dr. Kohler did not care for honours of that kind. To him it was not only a doctor's duty to save life, but a human duty in general. He died in 1979 at the age of 71, after being the main character in a book *Der Arzt von Stalingrad* (the doctor of Stalingrad), in which the author, Konsalik, emphasises the caring of the

---

[1] August 1941. Atlantic Charter (Roosevelt and Churchill), from which the conquered were excluded. The US had declared their neutrality at the beginning of the war. But the attack on Pearl Harbour on 7.12.41. forced the nation to declare war on Japan.

8th December. 1941: USA and Britain declare war on Japan.

11th December 1941: Germany and Italy declare war on the US.

21st December 1941: Hitler assumes the role of commander-in-chief.

1st January 1942: Beginning of the United Nations.

6th January 1942: "The four liberties" declared for everybody by Roosevelt – – freedom of speech, of religion, from poverty, from fear.

26th May 1942: Soviet Russian-British treaty. May/July continuation of German offensive in North-Africa as far as El-Alamein.

June - Germans capture Sabastopol.

. 23rd October 1942 beginning of British offensive under General Montgomery in Africa.

December 1942, First V2 rocket developed (V = *Vernichtungs* or *Vergeltungswaffe* (revenge weapon)

individual by the individual. From the fall of Stalingrad 30th January 1943, there was a slow, but steady retreat on the German side. The suffering of both sides in the deprivation, unimaginable cold and lack of the basics to sustain life occupies a large chapter in human history.

Christmas was always an exciting and mysterious time. For many weeks in advance, my mother would be working on something at night when we were in bed. I remember getting a cushion one year in the shape of a cat with green trousers on, which did not exactly enthrall me, but in order not to seem ungrateful, I hugged the lifeless, beautifully stitched form with the necessary affection in my eyes. I usually knew beforehand what we were going to get, if it was something handmade. A careless mistake, and the surprise was unmasked. But I always pretended that I had never seen it before in my life. My mother loved sewing and needlework of any kind. Used garments would be transformed into dainty, frilly girls' dresses with white collars and mother-of-pearl buttons and useful, warm children's coats, and if possible, with a scarf to match. As previously mentioned, I was in the habit of leaving my clothes on the grass or on branches of trees to dry. One day, my mother saw two women carrying a coat very similar to mine as they passed our house, where she had been attending to our rabbits, which were kept in a big trunk-like box on the balcony. She leaned over the window boxes and shouted, "Excuse me, is that your coat? I'm only asking, because it looks just like my daughter's". One of the women held the coat up after a moment's hesitation, exchanging surprised glances with her friend.

"We found it lying on the meadow over there and thought it didn't belong to anyone. But we 're glad you saw us and recognised it as your daughter's coat."

These clothes had their usefulness, no doubt, but getting them for Christmas was like giving a pet a mirror, through which it could see something to eat. There was a lot of speculation amongst my friends as to what presents they might be getting as soon as December came around. I preferred to be carried by the atmosphere and think of nothing in particular. I forgot from year to year that Father Christmas (Ruprecht) and 'Krampus' might come on 6th December. The first notion we had of the latter was when the most hair-raising sounds of hand-bells and rattling of chains could be heard from the ground-floor. Krampus was no doubt with Heinz and Margit and was on his way up with his fearful gang. How could I have forgotten? Should I hide, and if so, where? How was my sister behaving? Where was my mother? Krampus was the helper of Father Christmas. They carried large sacks of presents and torture implements, and came to "sort you out" before Christmas. This was to avoid the danger of rewarding a naughty child for a year's mischief-making.

The rowdy rebels rumbled up the stairs, and by this time, my heart seemed to beat from the lobes of my ears down to my little toes. I looked at my sister. Even she looked apprehensive, although my mother was talking quietly and reassuringly to her. My father was still at work, so that the only thing I could do was cling to my mother's skirt and ask her what Krampus was going to do to me. My conscience had obviously pricked me.

"If you've been good, he won't do anything to you," she said sternly. I never had time to ponder this annihilating verdict. My mother had already opened the door to the apparently marauding posse, leading them directly to the two little figures huddled together on the sofa. The nerveshredding din of the bells and chains blotted out every thought in my head until I heard my sister say quietly and yet audibly through it all: "I don't think I've been too bad." I seized this unique opportunity to defend myself. "Neither have I!"

Krampus was ready to shake his chains again to make me change my mind about this, which I would have done in an instant. I could feel the tears well up in my eyes. Just then, my mother whispered something in his ear, which made Krampus turn on his heels (after Father Christmas having left two small gifts) and disappear, taking his whole entourage and awe-inspiring equipment with him. The door shut behind them, and it seemed as if they were falling down the stairs higgledy-piggledy, as we sat rooted to the spot, straining our eardrums until the world seemed as empty as a desert.

Christmas Eve began with an afternoon atmosphere all of its own. Every minor event seemed to hold a secret. My eyes, ears and nostrils were tuned to the hilt. Nothing escaped me, and the flat was transformed from a place of domestic security to a kind of celestial corridor, whose doors open and shut, offering fleeting moments to glimpse Heaven, if you stayed alert enough to catch them. Anything was possible. My mother had told me that, in the evening, the 'Christkind' (Baby Jesus) would come flying in angel-form into the room with the presents, when my mother would immediately ring the bell to give us the chance to see the heavenly creature, if we were quick enough. Of course, the angel never appeared while we were in the room, which is why we had to wait outside; but we lived in hope of catching a glimpse of the apparition floating out of the window one day. However, no matter how hard we tried, we never managed to see her, and this remained a great source of frustration every year.

The 'Christmas-room' with the big tree was our bedroom. We would hover around the door all afternoon and early evening, so that my mother would be fairly irate by about 7.30pm. Whenever she opened the door, we would be right there trying to catch a glimpse of any new development in the magical room. Naturally, it would have spoiled her story, which she maintained for years, if we had seen any presents beforehand, or if the tree had gradually accumulated more decorations each time we were able to peep into the room as she emerged from it.

The tension had always reached fever-pitch by the time the bell tinkled like no other bell in the world. My sister and I fell over each other after thrusting the door open, looking spellbound at the enchanting and breathtaking scene. The only light radiating from the candles on the Christmas tree imbued the room with such mystery that the embellishment of each object was indescribable. We stood and gazed open-mouthed, trying to take it all in, and secretly wishing that this moment would never pass. We dared not advance any farther into the room for fear of somehow disturbing this sanctum.

"Did you see the Christkindl?", my mother enquired, her face shining in the half-light, whilst her figure retreated into the background. We came to with a jump as the spell was broken. "Oh bother, we missed her again, we'll have to wait another year now." We stumbled toward our presents and regarded them in wonder. One year, I was given a tiny baby doll which I treasured more than any other toy for the next 35 years, when I reluctantly threw it in the dustbin; its face had been too badly damaged by then. It almost physically hurt me to get rid of it.

Another Christmas, a big, beautiful doll with wonderful clothes stood under the tree, staring at me with piercing blue eyes. She had cost my parents a lot and I could tell by the way they looked at me that they were anticipating nothing short of my total elation on receiving her. So I made believe I was overjoyed and very grateful, but subsequently played very little with her, so that she was able to keep a clean and tidy existence in her box. One day, my mother asked me what her name was. I had not expected this question, but didn't intend to be stumped.

"Is it Rosalinde?" my mother said.

"Yes, that's right," I confirmed with relief.[1]

On some evenings my mother would light the candles of the tree next to my cot, which illuminated not only our faces as we sang Christmas carols, but also that of Adolf Hitler, whose picture hung suitably framed next to the window and my bed. In subsequent years, however, he was removed for the duration that the tree was up (24th Dec – 6th January) because, as my mother said, there was not enough room for him and the tree. In retrospect, I suspect the reason may have been that the image of Hitler and a Christian Festival did not mix, and my mother must have felt as if his beady eyes were watching the peaceful scene

---

[1] Strangely enough, my husband to be, years later, gave our second daughter Marion this as a middle name .

disapprovingly. After the First World War, he was alleged to have said that he did not need religion any more. Indeed, he tried to replace all religious practices and sacraments with his own. Confirmation for the youngsters now meant confirming their faith in their Führer and swearing an oath of allegiance to him.

In a local newspaper, an article appeared asking the readers for their suggestions on what was to replace the parish church, the Stadtkirche, if it was to be pulled down. Of course, this was a tentative measure to probe the atmosphere for bold actions to commence. Nothing more was heard about it in the future. Many party members preferred to be buried without a clergyman conducting the funeral, but with plenty of flags and badges and medals on display instead, and a 'Zeitgeistiger' delivering an eloquent speech about the merits of the deceased in the light of the Third Reich. People became quieter and more demure, especially since the situation on the front lines and at sea became less certain, and Wagner's fanfare introducing an announcement of victory was heard far less frequently now. The Propaganda Minister and his men had to work overtime to make up for the loss of natural stimuli required to evoke euphoria. Eulogies and euphemisms abounded.

It was now Christmas 1942, and things were not too bad as yet in my world. I lay in bed, contemplating the authenticity of the Christmas tree decorations. There was supposed to be chocolate inside the silver and gold wrappers. I hesitated many times before actually opening a little Father Christmas one night. To my surprise, I did find chocolate, but it looked as though it had woodworm. Should I try some? The taste was discouraging, so I concluded that for lack of new supply, the decorations must be at least several years old. Even fruit was now a luxury, and only my sister was allowed some occasionally, at great expense. Fortunately I was not very partial to fruit. My favourite treat was chocolate.

We spent nearly every Christmas holiday in Gerten, my father's birthplace. As food was already scarce, it made a welcome change to go to such a small village, where there was enough space and grassland for livestock, (even as a village cobbler, as my grandfather was) and indulge in roast goose at Christmas and other special festivals with the family. The simple room changed into a banqueting hall with several tables pushed together to form a central point, at which the meal of the year was to be ceremoniously enjoyed.

My grandfather, sitting mostly mute at the head of the banquet - looks sufficed - was the focal-point of this family gathering. Whenever he cracked a joke or smiled benevolently, the atmosphere relaxed and lost some of its severity, but the moment his eyebrows rose and deep creases began to appear on his forehead, the air became too dense for easy breathing and the food more difficult to swallow. I suspect his reputation went before him, and in reality, he was not as awe-inspiring as we imagined, but he certainly made the most of it. Occasionally he would come home inebriated (for example on his birthday which was Boxing Day). One night, Stefan Schroll, one of the most respected men in Gerten, actually threw his family out in a drunken stupor, so that they had to take refuge at their neighbour's. The only person who took no notice of grandfather's facial expressions was Tante Antsch, in whose rooms the dinner usually took place. She was always cheerful, but also very honest and outspoken, though not without tact.

Grandmother was happy to have everyone assembled under her roof - the entire brood gathered under her wings - and an uneasy truce prevailed over Christmas in the everlasting war of her marriage.

Wiping some goose fat off his chin, grandfather turned round to my father after dinner and said: "Well, what do you think of Adolf Hitler taking over command from the generals?"

My father winced a little. "It's difficult for him, because of all the partisans in the East and South-East attacking the troops from behind. Nothing is safe from them. Also, the harsh Russian winters have to be taken into consideration. We don't know anything like it here. It's a good thing our army is strengthened by thousands of non-Russian volunteers." (white Russians of the USSR who joined them due to their disillusionment with the Russian Government and what it stood for).

My cousins came to talk and play with me. I obliged, although I had enjoyed listening to the men. Not that I had understood their conversation, but I liked to tune into discussions and see the way they turned. Sometimes, a simple dialogue could culminate in a screaming match, at other times, the opponent simply fizzled out. The observation of calm faces and manners, which changed within minutes to aggravation and explosion for no reason apparent to me, held a never ending fascination for me. After playing for a little while, I felt rather sick, as happened every year. Not being able to eat a lot even at the best of times, I was certainly not used to eating fatty food like goose.

"Come on, girl, have a bit more. This is no good. You won't grow into a big healthy girl if you don't eat. Especially this dinner, it's not every day you get a feast like this."

So, a little more went down my reluctant oesophagus with regrettable results later on.

I was never very healthy. If I did not suffer from a hacking cough, I had tonsilitis, or inflammation of the middle ear, or flu, or one of the infectious childrens'diseases doing the rounds at the time. I was a sorry sight after having been sick. With hindsight, I should have had my tonsils removed to improve my appetite. A lot of my ills could be attributed to psychological upsets or poor diet, but after my tonsils were removed much later at the age of thirteen, my appetite improved dramatically.

We played happily outside for a while, fooling around by the brook and getting a little cart going, ready for pulling my cousins Helmut, Irma and myself in it; this job fell to Josef (Peppi). He was the eldest and always very sensible. (Tragically, he died after the war in a motorcycle accident while very young). I did not want him to run too near the garden where the bees and the toilet were. The bees represented no danger in winter, but I still had a healthy respect for them. The toilet was disagreeable in all seasons. In summer it emitted a nauseating smell, in winter it was nearly as bad as exposing your bare backside to the North Pole. Although there was an endearing little heart carved out of the door, it was fairly dark and grim inside that wooden box with the 'holy throne' as it was called.

Our hands became blue and stiff after a while, so we quickly scuttled back into the cramped house, where grandmother's dark treacle cake had just come out of the oven, along with various other delicacies. None for me, though, I could not face any more food until later the following day. My sister was also sick, to the amusement of our cousins who thought themselves much tougher and indeed they were. Usually, they admired us for our fine skin, manners and clothes, but at times like this, they felt superior to us.

On our way home in the train, I could not help wondering - as always - why the telegraph wires went up and down as I was looking out of the window. Between the two telegraph poles the wire plummeted, but as they reached another pole, they rose again. It took me years to find out why.

Dr. Schally from Teplitz, the famous spa town, continued to come and examine my sister once a month for 50 Reichsmark. There was not really a great deal anyone could do for Liesl, but my parents felt more confident that nothing would go drastically wrong as long as such an eminent doctor was attending to her.

Ration cards made it possible for everyone to have just enough to eat, although the *Kraft durch Freude* theme (strength through joy, an organisation that gave the worker the illusion that his luck had changed and he could enjoy some of the rich man's luxuries) sounded a little hollow at times. Anyone who dared to overtly criticize and oppose the new order/ work /discipline/unity/brotherhood,/final goal, etc, was sent to a work camp.

I used to walk down the road oblivious to all this, past Smolik, the grocer; Seemann, the shoemaker; Dirschmied, the butcher; Hoffmann's dairy, and Krimmer, the baker's, to buy some cheaper milk from a tiny shop near my kindergarten. It was usually *Magermilch* (fat-free), which had a bluish tint and tasted like water. It fascinated me how some children, who had been given the same errand, could swing their full milk-cans (no lids) around by the handle over and over again like a Catherine wheel without a drop being spilled. I pondered on how this could be possible. The can I carried had a lid, so after long deliberations of certain possibilities (unfortunately not all) I dared to throw the can up in the air one day with the intention of swinging it right round, but found that it got stuck upside down in the air, and more than half the milk spilled onto the ground. The can, of course, did not falter of its own accord. It was obvious that my confidence had wavered half way, at a crucial stage of my bold experiment. I simply could not believe that I could make it work and that was the only reason why it didn't. I was lucky not to get drenched. Careful as I was, I must have held my arm a fair distance away from me. My mother would never consider this when I arrived home. What hurt me far more than my mother's scolding was the laughter of the other children in front of whom I had boasted about my exploit, and having made such a fool of myself, being obliged to retreat with my tail between my legs and prepare to face the music at home.

CHAPTER 17
Conscription

My father was conscripted at the end of January 1943. He was 35 years old. He had been given his *Wehrpass* (Service Record Book) as early as 17th November 1939 in Kaaden, but was apparently not needed until early 1943 on account of his work for the railway. He never left his job there, only his duty in it changed.

Frau Rauscher insisted on taking his heavy case on her bike down to the station and walked back with my mother, pushing the bike. This bike had been very useful. Herr Rauscher used it to fetch the doctor when I could not breathe one night after going to bed. My cot had to be brought into the kitchen for two days. The doctor diagnosed a kind of diphtheria. Frau Rauscher also used the bike to go to a neighbouring village, Jeraditch, where her brother owned a pub and her sister a milk shop; in fact most of her family lived there. It was her birthplace. She had 17 other sisters and brothers. She had to do her homework on the stable door on a piece of paper torn from a sugar bag. On Sundays, she was sent to get a heavy load of beer for her father from a long way away. In order to save her shoes, which were precious, she walked on the badly made road barefoot, even in winter.

From Hanover, where my father was not even medically examined (only his papers), and where he was given a gas mask, two blankets, a rucksack, but no rifle (due to insufficient supplies), he found his way via Krakau in Poland(where the new recruits had to swear the oath of allegiance to Hitler and were shown all the different Russian mines and how to handle them) to Charkow in Russia, which, in the course of time, was to be taken two or three times by the Germans.

My father and his colleagues wore ordinary green uniforms, although they still worked for the railway. There was no difference any more, they all worked for Hitler now. Their work consisted of supervising Ukranian rail maintenance workers, including a woman whose husband was a Russian pilot. As soon as my father took in the scene near and at the front, he knew that the war was lost. Naturally, he kept this to himself, which was hard, because of his bitter disillusionment.

How he had taken every word that came forth from the Führer's lips as the ultimate truth! He realized for the first time that the people at home, sitting in front of their wireless, knew nothing of the stark reality that was impossible to face. What course was open to him, now that the idealistic notions of Strength through Joy, knowing what you are working for and enjoying the fruits of your labour, no more class or age difference – all these things were in danger of disappearing like a spider's web in a cloudburst. Feelings surged through him which, at normal times, he would have suppressed. Now he felt unable to ignore them. Questions flashed through his mind, which shook the foundations of his very existence. How could he justify his position here? He had been brought up according to a strict moral code, by which bounderies were clearly set. Although his work was with the railway, he saw things that made him question how he could look these indigenous people in the eye without trembling at the outcome of this tyrannical behaviour toward them.

Faint images of the Jews in Saaz, forced to stand in humiliation by the monastery wall floated into his conscience, but he would not let them take over, ever. He knew that he would not be able to go on, if he faced them honestly.

The German air force was almost non-existent now. The thinking common soldier could now (like the generals and the elite who felt some kind of responsibility) see for himself on which bandwagon he had willingly or forcibly jumped, without being able to envisage "jumping off" this rolling monster-vehicle, heading for certain disaster.

My father decided to play it by ear, to live and let live. Some of his colleagues did not agree with these mottoes. There was a small fat, witty man from Cologne, who liked to think he was boss and acted accordingly. My father felt pity for the Ukranians working under him. They had little food and no say in how they wanted to live, rather like himself. He sometimes shared his food with them, and through being sympathetic to them, managed to gain their confidence and sometimes even affection. A certain number of them lived in a small village outside Charkow. It was run as a collective enterprise with the commissary in total control of them, as far as their domestic life was concerned.

The other half of them had had their working life taken over by the Germans. As so often happens in circumstances beyond our control, we tend to find our own tiny, private corner, detached from events and people imposing themselves on us. It enables us to look at a fraction of blue in an otherwise grey and stormy sky, which feeds our hopes and inspirations at certain times and prevents us from becoming bitter and inhuman. The only danger with this is becoming obsessed with our corner and indulging in it, some to the point of self-destruction.

My father was invited by one of his Ukranian workers to visit his family. This had to take place under cover of night, but the moonlight reflecting on the snow-covered ground made it possible to discern an enormous manure heap in the middle of the village, above which hung a loudspeaker used to transmit instructions from the commissary. Nobody possessed a wireless. The communal manure heap for fertilizing was never used, mainly because the soil there was so rich that it needed no improvement, but probably also on account of a lack of labour.

They almost tiptoed across the frozen whiteness, which had in places been smudged with dirty footmarks and traces of manure. At times the temperature dropped to minus 40 degrees centigrade. The Germans were grateful for having the luxury of sleeping in a proper building at night.

The man led him to a low building which breathed hospitality as they stepped inside. The diminutive woman of the house was ready to serve the few scraps of food she had saved up to prepare something 'special'. Her husband urged his friend to eat, and gave the impression that he wanted to show him something urgently. In the end he could stand it no longer and told my father that he would show him his 'distillery' as soon as he had eaten something. My father could not bring himself to eat from the precious scraps of their food, but his friend repeated "You must eat first, before you can drink."

Although nothing was further from his friend's thoughts than alcohol, it seemed difficult to convey this to the Ukranian. Eventually, he was to learn that alcohol was a way of life for many Russian men; a way to drown your feeling of ineffectiveness, a way to numb your senses to the stupidity of yourself and others, or to brave the cold of the murderous Russian winters (a fallacy, because alcohol expands the blood vessels leaving you more vulnerable to hypothermia).

They descended some rickety stairs to the cellar, where the host had found his little 'private corner', in which he produced Schnapps from potatoes. Proudly, he exhibited all his 'treasures', including all the various receptacles for the different stages of the distilling process. In whispers, he disclosed the tremendous risk he took in this secret enterprise - the death penalty for producing alcohol illegally threatened himself and his colleagues every day.

One strong, burly man fixed a tap to a freight-train, expecting something like alcohol in one of the trucks. It turned out to be methylated spirits, which turned his body black after consumption, killing him within a very short time.

The Germans had reached the outskirts of Moscow, but were beaten back by the Red Army with the help of climatic conditions, which the German soldiers were not used to nor sufficiently prepared for.

At the station was also an explosion squad. When the German Army was in retreat, which was nearly all the time now, the railway men (my father's troop) had the job of loading onto the train all useable materials and equipment and send it back to Germany. The explosion squad connected tracks, telephone masts etc. and blew them up, all in one instance, so that the incoming Russian troops could not use these vital installations.

By this time, a large number of generals and officers (including some Prussian aristocrats) had formed a clandestine clique against Hitler and his accomplices. Some communicated with certain British circles, but made little progress in this area.

On 13th March 1943, a time bomb disguised as a champagne bottle and placed in Hitler's plane failed to explode, so that Henning von Treschkow and Fabian von Schlabrendorff had sweated blood in vain. Eight days later, on 21st March 1943, a plan to throw a grenade at Hitler at the Zeughaus never materialized, because the Führer shortened his visit. From this time on, he disliked committing himself to a set timetable. A plan for a visit would either be cancelled, the visit shortened or the route changed at short notice, so that any assassination plots had to be cancelled too. Hitler talked ever more frequently about 'Providence'. What he meant by this is anybody's guess. He certainly did not believe in a God; but probably believed that he was God. At the same time, he felt that something or somebody was keeping him safe. He, Hitler, could not possibly be killed. Only when he himself had decided to die, was the time right. He instinctively smelled any 'proverbial rats' and naturally avoided them. Frustration, uncertainty and desperation grew from week to week as these freedom fighters in their important positions had to make vital decisions and give orders against their will, which they knew would have disastrous consequences.

In January 1943, Roosevelt and Churchill met at Casablanca. Their talk centred around the possible Allied Invasion of Sicily in the summer, and the invasion of France scheduled for early summer 1944. Taking into account great German losses in Russia and Africa by now, they agreed to demand unconditional surrender from the Germans. Goebbels whipped up his propaganda to shout from the roof tops:- '*Wir werden niemals kapitulieren; niemals, niemals, niemals.* (We shall never, never, never surrender). The Führer with entourage were seen attending grand operas, listening to concerts, shaking hands with conductors and important party members, a perpetual Buddha-like smile frozen onto Hitler's face.

The intensified bombing of the whole of Germany by the British and Americans and the increasing news of the retreating German Army made the German population more than ever determined not to give in to depression, resignation and disintegration of public morale, but instead to show a stubborn defiance to the last. Goebbels' scathing remarks and the knowledge that things were getting out of control, created a paralyzing fear in the German people, which made up their minds to throw themselves into the ever widening gap with dying breath.

CHAPTER 18
Fairy Tales

I had started school by now, but after a year, the alarm sirens soon put an end to being able to attend school on a regular basis. We had initially found shelter in the nearby monastery cellars, but later there was no time to go there, when the alarm was heard. On my way there, I sometimes saw a long column of PoWs with crew cuts, shiny metal-rings on their fingers, showing us hand-carved figures and birds behind the guards' backs. I could not figure out the meaning of all this. I asked my mother, who they were, and why they behaved in such a strange way.

"Who gave them those toys and why are they showing them to passers-by?" I asked. My mother hesitated. "They're Russians and they want bread for their rings and toys," - that was all I could extract from her. I knew that Herr Meier von Weinertsgrün, (Trude's grandfather) had a few Poles working for him; and those two French men with their berets, who had decorated our flat, were not inclined to talk to me. I liked chatting to people and they usually responded. There was a mystery somewhere, which could not be solved, in spite of all my efforts.

It had been fun, singing all those soldiers' songs. When my mother went hop-picking for Herr Weinertsgrün, down the hill from our house, I was supposed to stay with Frau Rauscher, but I slipped out of the house and ran down to the fields near the Eger, where the women were bent over their baskets, feverishly picking the hop flowers off the long leafy stalks, which had been pulled down with a hook from the wood or wire construction before the picking began. My mother wanted me to go home as the women were afraid I might knock their baskets and they would have to pick more to refill them. So I began to sing all the songs I had learned from 'Zeus'; or, as most people called it, the wireless. There was: *Heute wollen wir marschieren* (Today we want to march), which ended with the refrain: '*O du schöner Westerwald*' (O you lovely Westerwoods) - a stirring song, and a great favourite with the ladies. Then I sang a tune with the line: '*Freiheit ist das Feuer*', (freedom is the fire), which, for some reason, I had changed to '*Freiheit ist das Fräulein*' (freedom is the maiden). This welcome change from the ordinary, sung with such spontaneity, caused some of the women to nearly fall off their stools in a fit of laughter. I could not see the reason for this general peal of amusement and began to start on: '*Die Wolken zieh'n dahin, daher, sie zieh'n wohl übers Meer, der Mensch lebt nur einmal and dann nicht mehr*', (the clouds move this and that way, they move across the sea, humans live only once and then no more), an altogether more sombre perspective on life, which was quickly followed by '*Ich hatt'einen Kameraden*' (I had a comrade), at the sound of which many hands flew up, begging me to stop, because the words were too painful to hear. So I registered that one as a complete failure and began *Lilli Marlen* - a sure winner, making its way halfway through Europe in due course. '*Brüder zur Sonne der Freiheit*' (Brothers to the sun of freedom) was followed by '*Auf der Heide steht ein kleines Blümelein, and das heisst Erika*' (In the heather grows a little flower, which is called Erika). I sang this last one shamefacedly due to my name being mentioned in it. Whenever one of my family heard it on the radio, they would call me "Come and listen to your song, Erika." This embarrassed as much as it delighted me, but I wanted to hide my inward blushing. So I pretended not to like the tune at all.

It had been some time now since my parents had taken us to the Magic Lantern Panorama down town, to see the wonders of technology and curiosities of the world, through a kind of projector. Viewers stood round a big cylinder, looking through small glass windows, which revealed ever-changing, amazing transparencies. Instead, my mother took us, now and again, to the local cinema when there was a suitable film for children. *Dick and Doof* (Laurel and Hardy) were her favourites. Whenever they advertised a forthcoming event outside their entrance doors, which caught my mother's imagination, she would announce to us: "I'll take you to see that film. You'll love it." She did not have to add this last sentence. Of course we'd love it. The treat factor and the atmosphere of suspense enthralled us. Our minds were eager to absorb anything presented to us. Our senses, already sharp, now felt like catapults, ready to shoot in all directions. We gaped at newsreels that showed 'our Führer' as the real hero of the war. Yes, our soldiers were brave, defiant, reliable, but Adolf Hitler was more than that. He was not only the masterbrain behind all the previous brilliant victories, no indeed, he bore our burdens, made our decisions and still had enough strength to shake hands, talk encouragingly to old and young, important and unimportant people alike. No wonder everybody loved him. Those who didn't must be bizarre folk indeed.

I remember three films very well. Each time, I thought that seeing a film was even better than the Magic Lantern or looking through my wonderful kaleidoscope, which showed beautifully intricate patterns with bits of green like the deep river down in our valley and shapes of red, reminiscent of wine, dark and mysterious.

One was a funny film in which a man (most probably Charlie Chaplin) is placed in a mechanical chair, which begins to feed him with a spoon. The man reclines indulgently, enjoying the luxury of being spoonfed with the most delicate morsels imaginable. His eyes are half shut and his tastebuds are working overtime. Suddenly, the mechanism of the chair malfunctions and the arm holding the spoon starts to gather momentum. The man opens his eyes wide, sits up and tries to keep pace with the onslaught of the swinging robotic arm that now looks threatening. Alas, all is in vain, the trusting man in his ignorance is now bombarded with food not only in his face, but all over his head, and suit, until he looks a very sorry sight in his utter bewilderment and soiled from head to foot. But even while I laughed, I felt a little uneasy. Was there an underlying message?

Another film was the fairy tale of the *Süsse Brei* - the story of the poor man and his family, who were granted a wish. They wished for a bowl of hot, sweet porridge that would never end. First they were greatly relieved that their worries about where the next meal was coming from were over. But to their horror, they found that the quicker they ate it up, the quicker it appeared, until their whole house and finally village were engulfed in gooey, revolting porridge, which no one could escape. I remember vividly the thick mass of gruel oozing along the road towards me, silently, menacingly. It could not have been a coincidence that such films were made at that time. I never saw the deeper significance until recently, when I marvelled at the courage of those film makers. How did they get away with it? Of course, the films were for children, but most children went with their mothers.

The third film which stuck in my memory was the fairy tale *Rumpelstiltskin*, in which a tiny, evil goblin grants a young despairing girl a wish, which enables her to marry a prince. As a reward, he requests their first child. She sees no other way out and promises to oblige, but soon forgets. The goblin turns up true to his word and demands her child. She offers him everything money can buy, but he says he prefers something alive and warm. She pleads with him to let her keep her child until he agrees, on condition that she finds out what his own name is. She is temporarily relieved, and sends a messenger all over the country to enquire about different names. But each time the goblin calls, he shakes his head triumphantly as she guesses yet another wrong name. Finally, he gives her an ultimatum, at which the young woman's heart sinks. The case is hopeless, she will have to give her child away. Her messenger returns once more from his mission, despondent, and mentions in passing that he came across a little man in a wood, who was dancing around a fire, singing: *"Ach wie gut, dass niemand weiss, dass ich Rumpelstiltskin heiss!"* (O how good that noone knows that I am called Rumpelstiltskin). When the goblin calls to collect 'his' child, the mother, after mentioning several other names, asks him: "Your name couldn't be Rumpelstiltskin, could it?" at which the dwarf, in rage, stamps his foot right into the ground and tears himself apart by tugging hard at his other leg. The analogy is obvious. How easily, beset people promise anything to their rescuer under pressure. Also, what the consequence can be, and how hard it is to find the truth. Another oddity is the fact that truth is very often concealed under many layers of make-believe and self-deception. To peel back the layers and face the honest facts is always a terrible blow to the psyche. It either collapses or grows stronger and learns from the experience.

CHAPTER 19
Realities

An incident, which my mother is loathed to recall occurred just before the last Jews were deported to the camps. Frau Glaser, a former client of my mother's, came to our flat and asked for a haircut. Of course, no one dared to be seen with a Jew, however close they might have been prior to what was called the *Umsturz* (lit. "overthrow"). My mother, feeling very nervous and frightened, asked Frau Glaser in, (an act of heroic courage in itself) but asked her to excuse her impotence in this matter. She had given up her job as a hairdresser, and got rid of nearly all her tools of the trade. She then ushered Frau Glaser out, uncomfortably aware of the possibility that someone like Frau Schmidt had seen her.

Heinrich Himmler, head of the SS, made a speech to some of his men on 4th October 1943 "…When somebody comes to me and says: 'I cannot dig the anti-tank ditch with women and children, it is inhuman for it would kill them,' then I have to say: ' You are the murderer of your own blood, because if the anti-tank ditch is not dug, German soldiers will die, and they are the sons of German mothers, they are our own blood ... Our concern, our duty is to our people and our blood. We can be indifferent to everything else. I wish the SS to adopt this attitude to the problem of all foreign, non-Germanic peoples, especially Russians. I mean the evacuation of the Jews, the liquidation of the Jewish race. This is one of those things that is easily said. Every Party member says 'We will liquidate the Jewish race. Naturally: it is in the Party programme. We will eliminate them, liquidate them. Easily done.' Then your eighty million good German citizens turn up and each one has his decent Jew. Of course, all the others are pigs, but this one is a splendid Jew. None of those who talked like this has watched, none of them has stuck it out. Most of you know what it means when a hundred corpses are lying side by side, or five hundred, or a thousand. To have stuck it out, and at the same time - apart from exceptions caused by human weakness - to have remained decent fellows, that is what has made us hard. This is a page of glory in our history, which has never been written and is never to be written..." Just before, in the middle of this speech, he said: "We shall never be rough and heartless when it is not necessary, that is clear..."

This speech, discovered after the war, shows the real situation of the German people, particularly those who had 'the privilege to purify the German race'. It epitomizes Hitler's religion, which commanded that you must make yourself strong to reach, and not lose sight of the goal. What differentiated it from the old religion was that only fit Aryans could inherit 'the kingdom' here on earth (Darwinian-style), if they proved worthy of it. And, Machiavellian style, the end justifies the means. "Inferiors" were of no consequence and could be discounted. Some of them could do the 'mundane, necessary jobs' with this new religion in mind.

Strangely enough, Stalin had the same sentiments. He said that he wanted to see a strong Germany and, like Hitler, thought that Britain would remain passive. The German Foreign Minister J. von Ribbentrop had been sent to London in 1936 to secure an alliance, without success, but the Ruhr had been re-occupied and re-militarized by Hitler and no one had said a word against it. This was the turning point for Hitler. He began to push the bounderies of the Versailles Treaty until it did not exist anymore. Although Stalin and Hitler despised each other, they recognized similar character traits in each others personality. They had not just signed a pact on 24th August 1939, but were Allies.[1]

---

[1] They carved up Poland between them, Russia occupying the East (formerly under the Austro-Hungarian Empire) with Stalin's mind on other territories, incl. the Romanian oilfields. Stalin deported over 21,000 members of the Polish elite to Russia, whom he systematically murdered, 250 a night, over several weeks. In October 1940, a few remaining Polish collaborators, who knew nothing of the

The disturbing fact was that the mighty tower had begun to sway, first imperceptibly, then visibly, at which point many Germans decided to dig their heels in and keep the tower steady, even at the cost of losing their lives. What option did they have, at that point?

Unbelievably, Germany had declared war on the United States of America on 11th December 1941. They wanted to keep out of the war as long as possible to the chagrin of Winston Churchill, but they supplied Britain with much necessary equipment 'through the backdoor'. Russia also wanted to be seen as neutral as time went on.

The Battle of the Atlantic had been lost. Hitler tried to force the British to surrender by stopping their supply ships from reaching their destiny. From 1942 onwards, convoys with the help of the US and of radar protection by the airforce won this battle, and more than 300 German U-boats were torpedoed. The Germans could do little damage under water now. . Rome was freed on 5th July 1943 by the Allies.

There were still the odd German victories, such as the taking of Tobruk, in which 30,000 British soldiers were captured. Each time, the German population were jubilant and their hopes and spirit rose, if only temporarily.

The threat of German U-boats near the coast of America most likely determined the government's course of action, as did the attack on Pearl Harbour on 7th December 1941, which acted as a catalyst.

The war in North Africa was over, with General Rommel having fought valiantly, foxing the British by playing hide and seek with them and always covering and taking care of his men in the process, until Field marshal Montgomery defeated the German Army at El Alamein in October 1942, by securing a preponderance of men and equipment at his disposal (two thirds more than his opponent). Rommel had been awarded the Marshallstab, (marshall's baton) but knew even then that the war was lost. After capitulation on 13th May 1943 in Tunis (with 252,000 Germans and Italians taken prisoner) Rommel, like many other generals associated with the German Underground Movement had to continue supporting the Führer. He was involved in designing defensive devices in Northern France. In January 1943 the Russians reclaimed Leningrad, the Germans surrendered at Stalingrad (40,000 died in one day) and in July the Russians took Kursk.

The Allies also captured Italy during this month. Mussolini was arrested and exiled to a lonely mountain called Gran Sasso, from where Hitler had him rescued in a dare-devil raid in September with the aid of a Fieseler Storch (a special plane), and a troop of rescue experts. The

elimination of their compatriots, suggested a unification of their numbers with the Soviet Forces to make them stronger.

Italians changed allegiance in favour of the Allies in September 1943. Hitler had persuaded Mussolini to form a Republic, which eventually amounted to nothing. Mussolini hunted down defecting fascist leaders and even had his own son-in-law shot. Il Duce had never fought for Germany, but alongside it. The Italians had been roped in by their arrogant leader and were glad that this chapter in history was nearly over. In their desperation, the German population's hopes were raised by the daring rescue of Mussolini by Hitler.

A sigh of relief rippled through the country. Hitler had done it again. "We must trust our Führer, Frau Rauscher, what else can we do?" my mother tried to reassure Agnes. She now made frequent visits to the Rauschers, and the two women, alone with their children, comforted each other with long conversations about dreams and their meanings (Frau Rauscher had a thick book on dream interpretations). My mother was not superstitious, but preferred the dream conversation to discussing the present situation, with Agnes usually finishing up, saying: "Frau Schroll, what's going to happen? It doesn't bear thinking about," and wringing her hands in despair.

She had once confided to me that she had tried to gas herself by putting her head in the oven one day. Luckily, Herbert had arrived just in time to save her. I could not fathom this out at the time. I remember thinking "Why would she do a thing like that?" and "Herbert really is a hero, there's no doubt about it now."

I thought of the day we children were playing on 'our meadow', when suddenly thousands of silvery objects flying in symmetrical order against the blue sky passed over our heads. The air hummed and filled our brains until Herbert shouted: "They're either British or American planes!" He was right, of course. In spite of pledges by the Allies that only industrial areas in Germany should be bombed, the first airraid on Berlin, the capital of Germany, took place as early as May 1940 and 362 attacks on civilians in that city alone occurred during the war years. The systematic bombardment of industrial areas, like the Ruhr, dams and cities[1] had started early in 1943. The allied planes were now bombing Germany, approaching from the East over Bohemia. No one had expected them there.We had heard of the destruction of historic city centers with their own distinctive character, cathedrals, churches, castles, mansions, museums, Bürgerhouses etc. in Berlin, Frankfurt/Main, Köln, Nürnberg, Würzburg, Hildesheim, Braunscheig etc., but as always, people tend to feel pity whilst secretly thinking 'Good thing it didn't happen to us.' Only

---

[1] The Battle of Berlin started at that time in earnest. "Bomber" Harris believed that, once the head of the giant was severed, the body would be dead and the war was won. This wrong assumption has continued ever since Tens of thousands of civilians lost their lives in Berlin alone.

when the danger is creeping nearer our comfort zone, the full horror becomes apparent. We were prepared to pay a high price, yes - but this was too high, especially now that it was descending on us literally out of the blue.

Heinz Wollnheit, a sweet little boy of three from the ground floor of our house, called the condensation trail of the planes *Kredenzstreifen* instead of *Kondenzstreifen* (in Bohemia, Kredenz is a kitchen cabinet), which created general amusement amongst the tenants. Gradually, everyone got used to the regular 'traffic' of the many gleaming toy-like objects overhead; after all, they were doing *us* no harm.

CHAPTER 20
School and home

School was interesting, although I was always afraid of the other children. They might laugh at my clothes, for instance, or many other things that seemed incongruous to them. I was used to wearing anything that my mother had made for me from old clothes, except for any material containing wool, especially scratchy woollen stockings. I hated those. Nevertheless, in spite of my vehement protests, I had to wear them. Although I disliked my mother and showed my feelings at those times, I could not hold it against her for long. For one thing, my skin usually got used to the irritation and the initial redness settled down. For another, although my mother drove me mad over many things, I knew that I depended on her. What would I do without her, especially now my father had gone? I was surprised really that I did not miss my father more. Occasionally, something would remind me of him, and I would feel sad, but on the whole, life was still interesting and enjoyable as far as I was concerned.

So what if we had garlic-bread for tea sometimes. I disliked meals at the best of times, but could be tempted with a piece of toast, which my mother prepared on the cast-iron hotplate on top of the boiler. After she had spread it with margarine, she rubbed a clove of garlic over it, which I initially detested, but then grew to like. So what if I fell asleep on the sofa at night while my mother chatted with Frau Schmidt (or anyone else who 'dropped in') and was later rudely woken up by a loud voice, telling me to get washed and go to bed. I must admit that it did annoy me immensely. Her voice would seem twice as loud as it really was and would go right through me. My limbs were heavy, I wanted to go back to sleep, but the voice bellowed on relentlessly until I dragged myself to the washbasin. I often had to be undressed because I was too tired to bother with that on top of washing myself, brushing my teeth with a little pink toothbrush and hauling myself off to bed. These were minor irritations compared to the overall daily enjoyment of life.

Threadworms were another sore point. They would insist on appearing every evening (for their daily dose of fresh air, or so I assumed). The itching was so unbearable at times that I would have scratched myself to pieces had my mother not stopped me in time.

My sister was the only person who could rile me enough to hit her. Many a time, an argument would finish up in physical battle with my sister's long black hair coming undone, so that she looked like a long-maned angry lion. The fact was that Liesl occasionally had a sharp tongue, which would flick out in my direction and I could not bear it. It was always me, who initiated the violence, never the reverse. So when my mother came to 'sort us out', tearing the two twisted, panting figures apart, it was always me she focused on.

"Now look what you've done. Sit down, Liesele, let me get you a drink", she cooed. Then her voice became shrill and punitive: "You do that again and you'll see what you get." Her pointed forefinger wagged dangerously near my face, so that I sensed the need to retreat, but usually I secretly felt it had been well worth the risk. I suppose my jealousy could only contain itself up to a point, after which the slightest provocation provided the ignition spark. My sister was not the kind of person, who enjoyed arguments and warmongery, but she was four years older and wiser than me and liked to remind me of this fact.

Since I had started school, she had always offered her support, but I only let her help me with arithmetic, which was like a black hole in my head; in every other subject I was top of the class. I can remember receiving the long anticipated enticement that every German child still gets to this day on their first day of school, namely, a long cone-shaped bag full of sweets – most likely sugar-coated pills to mask the bitter fact of freedom lost until your retirement. No longer was it possible to find out about life in your own way, in your own time; rather then playing with your friends or just enjoying the nice weather, you were forcefed seemingly useless and unplalatable information. The thought occurred to me that Erich was right to play truant.

Nevertheless, I loved the bag of sweets in all its splendour (the cardboard was always hidden by colourful, shiny paper, and the opening decorated with white lace paper) and I also enjoyed belonging to a 'more important' class in society - I had come one step up on the social ladder and would therefore be taken more seriously.

The first few weeks I felt excited each time I slung my satchel over my shoulder. It smelled of new leather and revealed a string with a sponge and a cloth dangling down by the side. Both were attached to a new black slate, framed by beautiful wood. But my real pride and joy was my pencil case full of brand-new pencils, penholders, nibs, and one brand new rubber. When my mind wandered during certain lessons, I would quietly slide the pencil case lid open and eye my treasures.

My teacher was called Frau Wildgatsch, which seems a pure Jewish name. She must have somehow been able to conclusively prove her Aryan origin to be a teacher at that time. Her hair was grey, her expression kind. I gave her no trouble, although when it came to arithmetic, my mind would simply draw a blank. I can honestly say that nobody frightened me in the early stages of Maths, and yet I was scared by it from the beginning. If my sister did my homework with me and asked me a mathematical question, my brain was not available to help me find the answer. She never got cross, but announced: "We don't seem to be making any progress, Mama. She'll have to do her writing exercises instead."

Out came my slate and in next to no time, I had produced a string of joined up c's on one line, a's on the next, etc..

To balance the sedentary monotony of theoretical learning, we had singing and physical exercise-lessons, but no amount of coaxing, threats or promise of reward could persuade me to jump over those benches in the gymnasium. Some children even managed two at a time, but even when they took me by the hand and ran, I would always come to a dead halt in front of the formidable wooden monster.

The singing lesson was very enjoyable, although the teacher seemed more than a little deranged. While we stood behind our desks, he would conduct and shout at us from the front as though he were a sergeant major bawling at his soldiers.

"Wrong, wrong, wrong!" With each yell, his baton came down on the desk. "Repeat after me." His tenor voice was hardly flawless, but his wiry figure and nervous gestures induced a nervous response from us, so that soon the room echoed with lively children's voices. One song was particularly popular. It was *Jetzt fahr'n wir über'n See, über'n See* (now we are crossing the lake, the lake), which was not only a good tune, but also a mental exercise. More and more words had to be left out, with the correct beats kept silently. Strict counting and alertness were essential, otherwise we were 'out', and how embarrassing it was to blurt out a word by mistake, when everyone else was quiet.

One day, our *Schulrat* (a district school-inspector) visited our school[1] on some official occasion, most likely the Führer's birthday, which took place outside. The atmosphere was serious and heavy while a lot of flag-raising and speech-making took place. My eyes strained over a few shoulders to glimpse part of the Schulrat's slight figure. To meet the

---

[1] the most impressive school building due to so many multi-millionaires living in Saaz

required *völkische,* traditional standards where attire was concerned, he wore a pair of Lederhosen, which showed his spindly legs rather pitifully. As if this were not enough, his underpants proved to be about half an inch too long for the shorts, which in turn proved too much for me. Uncontrollable laughter suddenly shook my whole body, but I managed to convert it into one of my (now rare) coughing fits. Feeling the purple colour in my face, I looked round to see if anyone else had found this sight amusing, and found that no one had.

As I was walking home from school one day, uncomfortably aware of my 'concertina' stockings, a boy of my own age came running towards me from a portico-boasting villa. The boy, breathless and without a word, pressed a small white box into my hand, then turned and ran off again. I had never seen him before, whereas he seemed to know me. I opened the box, and to my surprise found a large, succulent-looking strawberry nestled in some cotton-wool. My mouth watered as I stared at it.

I was so pleased that I ran all the way home to tell my family and friends about this unexpected pleasure. Erika Hühner, my neighbourhood friend said:

"Well, so what, it's only a strawberry?" whereas Irene Luft, another local friend, shared my delight.

Still, I liked going to Erika's house. Her mother had just had a baby, and I am certain that I was more enthralled with this little girl than her sister was. I could not wait to go and see her as often as possible; Erika and her other friends would play in the garden shed, but I could always be found admiring the baby. Naturally, she was asleep most of the time, but this did not deter me in the least. With her tiny limbs perfectly still, it was easier to observe the minute fingernails, the delicate nose and chin, and contemplate the wonder of this little creature.

I had seen baby rabbits at home, diminutive bundles huddled together under bits of fur pulled out by the mother of her own coat to provide a warm bed for these little furry balls. But one morning, I found she had mauled them into a lifeless, nasty mess. It had upset me greatly. Nevertheless, when it was the mother rabbit's turn to be killed for our Sunday meal[1], I protested fervently.

"Don't kill her please, let her be," I pleaded with my mother.

"Don't be silly, what do you think we've been keeping her for?" my mother scolded, "the meat will be as tough as old boots already."

Herr Rauscher was on leave at the time. He offered to perform 'the murder' (as I saw it). He had kept lots of rabbits in hutches on his allotment near the SS camp. He used to take me on his bike to attend to

---

[1] Parts of the rabbit were preserved in a Kilner Jar, my mother's speciality, which turned out to be of special significance later.

his 'brutes'. "Don't you worry, Frau Schroll," he said confidently, "she won't suffer. It will be over and done with in a jiffy." Within seconds of taking the old rabbit out of its hutch, it had escaped from his grip and was seen leaping wildly around the kitchen, jumping over the table onto the sofa with her executioner in hot pursuit.

"Well, I never," he exclaimed, trying on all fours to retrieve the headstrong animal from under Liesl's, formerly Herbert's, writing desk. I returned to the balcony, refusing to watch the gruesome spectacle. The rabbit was eventually captured and slaughtered, with Herr Rauscher showing visible signs of the embittered struggle between him and the pet, that had refused to turn into meat. I sulked for days and refused to eat one bit of it.

CHAPTER 21
Herbert

The story about Herbert's desk, which finished up in our flat, is an interesting one. Frau Rauscher had threatened to 'turf Herbert out' if he did not pass his final school examinations. His school work had gradually deteriorated until anyone could see that only a miracle could save him. Being an only child, all his actions, work, and lack of work at school could easily be checked. But he had reached the critical age of fourteen and his parents' situation and relationship added to the complexity of his adolescence. He found it increasingly difficult to hide his rebellious feelings so as not to upset his mother. His square face seemed squarer, his dark-brown, penetrating eyes seemed to flash more often now, his sharp nose was more pointed, and his words more sharply pronounced than ever. Still, his regular white teeth and the dimple in one of his cheeks were reassuring signs of his charm and quick wit.

On the day the certificates were handed out, Herbert did not return home. Poor, kind Frau Rauscher! Mild irritation, gradual worry and final panic gave rise to a complete lack of self-control. Floods of tears followed, and later in the evening, one of Herbert's friends came, explaining that he and Herbert had intended to leave home together until he had lost courage at the last minute and Herbert had left on his own, who knows where.

The next day, after the police had been informed, a quiet voice, occasionally distorted by sobs, was heard to say: "I shouldn't have threatened to throw him out, of course, I could never have done it anyway. Why do children always take everything so literally?" My mother patted her shoulder.

"He'll be back soon, when his money runs out."

Frau Rauscher suddenly sat up straight.

"That little beast, fancy taking my money. He had it all planned out, das Luder (the wretch), how could he do this to me?" and the tears began to flow again.

Herbert stuck it out for three weeks. It was now the Spring of 1944. He was caught in Germany at the point of being penniless. The police picked him up on a platform at Regensburg station (a town on the Danube in Bavaria, which was to play a significant role in my later life) and sent him back to Saaz on the next train. His adventure was over. Everybody now knew what a hero he was, but from then on, he did not need his writing desk anymore.

One of his uncles, Hans Beutner, worked in nearby Eger, in a factory, manufacturing aircraft and aviation equipment. He was a very versatile young man, who could drive all kinds of motorised vehicles and was an excellent organiser and mediator, a skill which saved him his life in later years in Russia. He was very popular wherever he went and managed to get Herbert to work in the same plant as himself.

Herbert was to train as an aircraft mechanic with four other boys. They were still in the compulsory Hitler Youth Movement (HJ), following on from Jungvolk. They were taught how to fight in combat with knives and revolvers and seeing everyone as a potential enemy. Herbert, being an impressionable boy, was deeply disturbed by this, together with his home insecurity and by later life-threatening events, which were closer then anyone could have ever thought of.

The boys found hundreds of cigarettes stacked away under the eves of a low building. Herbert had to be seen to smoke them, otherwise he could not have sold or exchanged them for the things he wanted. When, after nine months, the training camp was bombed with two of the boys being killed and one injured, Herbert was sent home with the order to return on completion of the rebuilt training camp. Frau Rauscher did not want him to go back to Eger, so that, officially he was still in Eger and did not qualify for ration cards in Saaz. He had gone "underground" as the saying goes.

Herbert's father had at first wholeheartedly embraced the ideas of National Socialism. He was actively engaged in furthering its aims in Saaz. All leaders were regularly sent the Schulungsbrief, a document they had to carefully study and adhere to. In some of the meetings, Herr Rauscher voiced his discontent with what he saw and heard, which did not harmonize with the ideals of the Schulungsbrief, according to which he was a true "Nazi" and they were not. For this and now being seen as a Socialist, he was punished by being sent to Reichenberg with other Socialists and later to factory work in Kolberg. When he still could not

control his tongue, he was expelled from the party and sent to join the
Marines on the Baltic Island of Fehmann, although there were no more
boats. He was fifty now and had served in the First World War. His wife
was very cross with him, especially as the situation in the country was so
threatening and uncertain and she was an exceptionally nervous person,
having been one of sixteen children. She believed that, when he should
have been a support for herself and Herbert, he was absent from them for
years, due to his outspokenness.

Herbert, with millions of other children, had been brainwashed by
the Jungvolk for boys and the Jungmädel for girls since the age of ten, to
obey the teaching and commands of the Führer. Herbert's mother had
been a good catholic all her life and gave to the church from the little she
had all through her life. She had wanted Herbert to stay at school once a
week to be taught by Katechet Kunze, protestants and catholics alike.
Parents had to sign a form, if they wanted that "peculiarity". On Sundays,
at the same time as services were held at the church, the HJ would march
past the town church[1] with drums and fanfares to lead the boys to the
cinema to see a war film. What young man did not like that? There was
no choice anyway, otherwise the parents were suspect, and pressure and
chicanery were used to make them "toe the line".

Herbert had to pray every day of his school life with his class mates:
Du lieber Gott, ich bitte Dich, ein gutes Kind lass werden mich,
Schenk mir Gesundheit und Verstand,

u
und schütze unser deutsches Land, schütz' Adolf Hitler jeden Tag, dass
ihn kein Unglück treffen mag,
Du hast gesandt ihn in der Not, erhalt uns ihn, du lieber Gott
Translated:

"Dear God, I ask you to let me become a good child, give me health
and understanding and protect our German homeland. Protect Adolf
Hitler every day, so that no harm will come to him. You have sent him in
adversity, keep him for us, dear God. Amen."

Although I had never actually been in Herbert's 'gang', being six
years younger and a girl, nor played in their area (the Jewish cemetery
and the little wood in front of it), I missed him. He was like an older
brother to me, having a friendly, teasing chat with me now and then, and
helping me whenever I needed it.

"Can you show me how to spin this top, Herbert?," I would say
outside our house. I did not want to make a fool of myself in front of the

other children further down the road; I had done that often enough in the past. Herbert was always very patient and funny.

"You put the string in the groove of the top and wind it round, follow the grooves till there's no more string, then you put it down and pull the string hard and fast like this." He gave an energetic jerk, so that the top was left spinning beautifully.

"You do it." It was easy enough up to the point of the swift tug. My movements just weren't quick enough. "You've got to be faster. Also, you must choose a smooth surface."

Playing with marbles was another popular game where lots of children joined in. It was more fun this way, and even Herbert would sometimes participate when he passed.

He could not resist it, whereas writing in the sand or playing hopscotch held no interest for him. Neither was he moved by throwing a ball onto a wall, turning round, and catching it again and other ball-games we enjoyed.

I admired his astute mind, his decisiveness, his agility, his wit and his strong stance in the face of adversity. Now he had gone, I could not share my thoughts with him. This I missed the most. Although he hardly commented, he was happy to listen to my childish opinions, whereas he talked to my sister quite seriously on occasions.

I recalled an incident when I had been able to borrow a bicycle from someone. I had never ridden one before. The bicycle was too big for me, and I could not even sit on the saddle. But this was fun till I wanted to stop, but the two wheels had a mind of their own. I careered across the road and crashed headlong into a fence, which brought the thing to an abrupt halt.

While I was going round in circles on the bike near Erika Hühner's house under the lofty, green canopy, I smiled to myself, thinking about those first feeble attempts at riding a bike. It had been fun then, but now I could control it in addition to enjoying it; I could be proud of my achievement, confidently keeping in step with the other children of my age.

I recollected another event that had taken place before Herbert had gone to Eger. One day, a little haggard, middle-aged man had come up from the centre of the town, and walked past us towards the meadow opposite our house. I thought it strange that he did not use the pavement opposite after he passed us, for there were no more houses on the cemetery side of the road. He did not seem to be a person who intended to visit a grave. Such a person would bring flowers, a bag with a scrubbing brush and a cloth, with which to clean the stone, as I had observed a few times in the past. It wasn't long before I forgot this desperate, hopeless-looking man, and concentrated on enjoying myself again.

A few days later, Frau Rauscher came to see us; her wide eyes, and the fact that she had actually come to us, which did not happen very often, indicated that something was wrong.

"Did you know, a man hanged himself in the woods by the Jewish cemetery?"

My mother pushed a chair towards her. "No I didn't. Oh dear, the poor man; who found him and when?" she said, quite shocked. Frau Rauscher's anxious face took on an even more serious expression and her tight lips looked more blue and white-checkered than ever. "Herbert and his friends found him an hour ago;" her voice tried to be firm, which was not always successful. "He's been taken away now. He must have been there a few days."

While the two women talked together, I went to see Herbert next door. He looked pale and disturbed. I asked him what the man had looked like, and when he began to describe his clothes, I realized that it had been the same person I had noticed walking in that direction the day I was enjoying myself on the borrowed bicycle.

"We were playing soldiers in combat", Herbert said sadly, "and looking for enemy hideouts, when Walter saw this figure in the bushes. He went closer and started screaming. When we arrived, we saw this man hanging from a tree among the bushes. There was dead silence for a while till I said there was nothing we could do but cut him down, which we did. Actually, that was nastier than seeing him hanging in the first place." Herbert swallowed hard and continued to look haunted. "I've seen several like that now," he said quietly. "One was even kneeling when we found him; God knows how long it must have taken him to die."

A few weeks later, I asked some of my friends to come with me to the little wood, where I would show them the site of the 'incident'. We ventured out with courage, but slowed down more and more the nearer we got to the place Herbert had described to me. I never had liked this wood and now I liked it even less.

Herbert experienced something else that moved him almost to tears. With some friends, he was running in the market square after a load of hop-containers, ready to be sold. The boys wanted to snip off the lead-seals of the sacks and use the lead to make patterns to foresee the future on New Year's Eve. Someone spotted them doing this and started shouting and running towards them. The boys dispersed and Herbert found himself in a pub, where he tried to hide behind a curtain. Peeping out, he saw that there were a number of German soldiers or officers in the big room. They were urging Malvine Stein, the well-known singer of the town, to sing them a song. She was one of the few Jewish people who had been allowed to stay in Saaz, but was now denigrated to cleaning and doing menial jobs in this pub. They kept on at her until she positioned herself in the middle of the room, supported herself on her broom handle and started singing in her melodious, beautiful voice: *Ich bete an die Macht der Liebe* (I worship the power of love), a much-loved hymn that everybody knew and loved. As soon as the first notes reverberated in the room, everybody stopped in their tracks and listened with devout reverie to the words and inspired music, interpreted by a woman who had experienced humiliation, suffering and danger. Everybody realized that she sang from the heart. With this song and her rendition of it, she had touched something in the soul of these proud, self-confident men of which they had been unaware until now. Herbert stayed just to hear the last line of one verse and used the opportunity of the men's deep concentration and reverence to slip out as unnoticed as he had slipped in: *Ich will, anstatt an mich zu denken, ins Meer der Liebe mich versenken* (I want, instead of thinking of myself, to immerse myself into the sea of love).

CHAPTER 22
Truth

By now, some of the Stab (headquarters personnel) and generals had attempted several unsuccessful assassinations on Hitler. In the autumn of 1943, plans for a new Government had been made. In December, seven officers of Hitler's headquarters collaborated to kill him, but he failed to attend the designated conference. In December, Graf von-Stauffenberg smuggled a bomb into headquarters. This time, the meeting was cancelled. In January 1944, Stieffs plan to kill Hitler while he inspected new uniforms was jeopardized due to an air raid. On February 11th, another bomb plot failed when Himmler did not turn up. It must have been suspected by now that even if the head were severed from the body, some limbs might still function for some time and give trouble. Himmler and Eichmann must have been known to the elite as the men who had trained themselves harder than anyone else to kill their conscience 'for the good of the country'. They had gone all the way and stopped at nothing. The Führer had told his people that this was what was expected of them and he tried to set a good example. But, as far as was we know, Hitler was never seen inspecting 'their work' or personally bloodying his hands.

Slave labour, people being dragged away from their families and homelands (about four and a half million by the end of 1944) was to make up for the millions, who were fighting on all fronts and for those who had been killed by then, at home (Germany was now being systematically bombed into the ground[1]) and on the fronts. Defence was now paramount. Money and raw materials were needed to keep the war industries going, and to nourish and clothe the fighting nation. The rest of the people were regarded as useless and seen as parasites. Euthanasia, and the systematic killing of Jews and 'undesirables', (including the badly disabled) in concentration camps were kept secret from the public, but those at or near the top were obviously aware of it.[2]

Just as feverishly as the 'butchers' tried to carry out their task of eliminating 'all these useless millions' as discreetly as possible (most of these so-called labour camps, where millions died of disease and were murdered, were situated away from inhabited areas), the Resistance now tried to stop all this destructive madness at a stroke. It was a very dangerous undertaking.

Meanwhile, the Jews in the Warsaw Ghetto had just bled to death after having risen in one massive, heroic fight against their aggressors who had set out to starve them to death after their refusal to leave. Hollow bundles, huddled together; children with eyes of old men and women, wrapped in rags that had once been adult's clothes, were preserved in photographs, to be shown to all of us after the war. For now, however, we had no inkling of the gruesome nightmarish life and death of these innocent human beings.

'They' had successfully eliminated all 50,000 of 'them'. But for many more, it was only the beginning of the end. For some people, the end came the moment they entered the gates of some concentration camp. Those destined for extermination were shown to one side, the rest, (who might still be of use) to the other, where they were allocated to the hell of camp dormitories. The large barracks, filled with hundreds of bunk beds riddled with lice and flees, lacked all essential facilities, including sufficient water and toilets, not to mention privacy. Anne Frank and her family, except her father, died of typhoid fever with her sister in March 1945, just before the end of the war. Her father had been fighting with the German Army before going into hiding in Holland. He came out alive.

Thousands died of malnutrition, disease, and general neglect, but also of seeing no purpose to live in such misery, having lost everything including family and friends. One of the very few ways of escaping death early was to stay close to the dying in the barracks, so that they would be 'on the spot' and ready to take their clothes, rations and the few possessions the dead no longer needed. In other words, if the will to live was strong enough, they would search incessantly for a way out and

---

[1] Also, Churchill had given the order to use chemicals to destroy all of Germany, but this order had been disobeyed

[2] The euthanasia program of the disabled had to be quietly dropped at the end of 1941 due to mounting public hostility.

preserve a kind of order,   justification, and even morale in such a
wilderness. They would start over and over again after many setbacks and
with the help of others; also with luck, they might struggle through to the
day when freedom seemed a plausible thought and not a word, which had
lost its meaning forever. It was an important business to keep the spirit
and soul alive as well as the body. In fact, it was essential to come to
terms with the unspeakable brutality of these people, once the suffering
was over; some were able to see them as originating in a desire to wipe
out everything obstructing an 'ideal state, - extension of territory, purity
of the race and accumulation of wealth - nothing must stand in the way of
these goals. They, the victims, had apparently been in the way, because
they had not met the required standard set by the regime. For others it
was impossible to see anything but the screaming injustice of it all, which
demanded revenge. They wanted to kill the first German they met on the
way out of the concentration camp. Some of them soon realized that they
would then sink to the same level as their torturers, with blood on their
hands.

Unfortunately, many found it impossible to fit back into normal
society. Some victims would live like outcasts in the midst of a bustling
community, and never talk to anyone for twenty five years, as long as no
one cared enough to rescue them. Some were strengthened in their
religious beliefs, because they had always known that uninspired human
kind seeks its own truth, which can be interpreted in various and devious
ways, whereas the real truth cannot be changed and thus presents an
annoying obstacle for all those desiring to insert their own version in its
place. They had learned the lesson that a fruit-bearing tree needs careful
attention and nurturing, lest all kinds of diseases and pests creep up on it
and pervert its natural course of growth. This tree is the individual who
lives according to the truth of his conscience, which is the same in
everyone.

Bishop George Bell of Chichester, England, who knew Bonhöffer,
was an outspoken opponent of Churchill's obliteration policy of
Germany, which cost him his future position as Archbishop. He had said,
on 9th February 1944, in the House of Lords "…it is of extreme
importance that we, who with our Allies, are the Liberators of Europe
should so use power that it is always under the control of law. It is
because the bombing of enemy towns – this area bombing – raises this
issue of bombing unlimited and exclusive that such immense importance
is bound to attach to the policy and action of His Majesty's Government"

The British Press was totally against him and he stood alone with his
protest. Belsen, Auschwitz, Flossenbürg (where Bonhöffer had been
killed just before the end of the war), Dachau, Theresienstadt, etc. were
full of people whose consciences had been first on their list of priorities.

Parents, children, friends, principles (which have to be changed sometimes), were to be left and sacrificed for this. These were outspoken people, church ministers, political opponents, or just ordinary people who found the injustice of it all completely overwhelming. People who had sheltered or generally aided and abetted the innocent hunted-down victims of this nationalistic, twisted regime (jeopardizing their family or their friends in the process) were treated no better than those they had helped, if their deed was discovered. One family member might denounce another. Friend might turn against friend, son against father or vice versa, depending on whether their conscience had been swamped by the new religion.

"What is truth, and what is light?" people had asked through the ages. Now this question was asked more often, but rarely in the high and mighty places where it could be answered correctly, but in places where painful situations and despair were testing grounds. What was to appear in the crucible? Genuine gold or useless material, fit only to be discarded?

CHAPTER 23
The Mighty tower begins to sway

In the East, the terrifying battle continued. The Poles' suffering was immense since the beginning of the war. Young Poles had to dig trenches for the German Army, as there were not many older ones left. Many had been killed by German and Russian forces. Some were pilots in the British Royal Air force and fighting the Germans in other ways. Many had been deported to Siberia by the Russians. Now the Russians had to face Hitler's determination to win the lost territory back - a belief he upheld until the Russians were practically on his doorstep. Huge losses on either side, including Russian civilians in the villages of the vast Russian steppe, were the consequence. His transference of more and more troops from West to East made it easier for the Western Allies to work out an Invasion plan for France. In October 1943 at Tehran, Stalin had insisted on a broad front in Western Europe by early summer 1944. Churchill suggested the Balkans instead, probably with the intention of preventing the Russians from 'flooding' middle Europe. Finally the US decided on the French Channel coast.

Soviet troops pushed relentlessly towards Germany. General von Mannstein begged Hitler for permission to retreat, but to no avail. Ultimately, two million German soldiers were lost and Hitler ordered the complete destruction of the land. Only a desert should be left. The post-war estimation of Soviet Russian civilian casualties through hunger and homicide lies between 6.5. and 17 million; that of Soviet military casualties, dead and missing 8.5 million; death through injuries 2.5 million; and prisoners of war casualties 2.6 million, not to mention Stalin's destruction of his own people, even after the war. The figures are factual and bleak. Only the individual people who make up these numbers could tell us the terrible stories culminating in their death.

Of all this I knew nothing. My father had been writing as regularly as was possible, but by now I was beginning to miss our chats, stories and games we once enjoyed together. Sometimes he sent us long poems about the proximity of the front and the booms and rumblings of the big cannons, which spelt doom for the flat, empty steppe which stretched mile after mile without a single human soul to be seen.

One morning in Spring 1944, we received a letter from my father after a considerably long silence from him. "Thank God", my mother gave a sigh of relief as she ripped the envelope open. The letter began to tremble and shake in her hand as her restless eyes flew over the hastily scribbled lines. My father had nearly been killed by a mine near the front. After Charkow they had had the job of clearing the debris from the exploded trains (destroyed by mines) to keep the track open. The Russians usually planted the mines just outside the stations, where the engine or the whole supply train would tumble down a steep embankment with no hope of recovery. Another German platoon repaired the track after it had been cleared. On this particular day, a German transport train had to be cleared away, another victim of a mine, about 6 km from where my father's colleagues had spent the night. There was a small station, but they thought it safer to sleep inside the train. It consisted of a truck full of stones, the engine, and behind it a carriage full of tools used in conjunction with the little workshop there, and a living-quarter carriage. They had left very early in the morning when suddenly an explosion shook them to the core. All of them knew immediately what had finally caught up with them and could hardly believe they were still alive. My father's description of it was: "*Heute früh bin ich nahe am Himmelreich vorbeigegangen.*" (This morning, I was very close to heaven). Whenever I heard this in the next few weeks (of course, my mother told all our relatives and friends), I imagined my father flying through the air as a consequence of the explosion. In actual fact, nobody had been injured, but the tool truck and tender were ruined. Strangely, the tools were still intact, as were the stones intended to take the blow in the event of a mine explosion. It was bad enough being a sitting target day and night for an invisible enemy (my father did once see a partisan sitting in a tree). But now they had to exchange their engine, try and clear the transport train away, and expect to be shot at from all directions.

Early one morning, the field gendarmerie came to hang three Russians on gallows, which stood less than twenty metres away from the carriages of the eight man platoon, exposing them even more to partisan attacks. These three partisans had created havoc for some time by cutting the irreplaceable air cable brakes, so that the trains were piling up, practically waiting to be blown up by the enemy, instead of being sent to Germany for further use.

The ordinary German soldier must have been in a terrible predicament. If there was sabotage, either by the enemy or by his own people (the latter was increasing from month to month), he found himself in a more precarious position than he was in already; on the other hand, it was clear to most people now that the war could not be won and anyone who believed otherwise was fooling himself. The soldiers could hardly wait for the day the war was over, but feared they might be killed just beforehand, because their Führer was adamant that they should fight to their last breath.

Stalin, who now was overall commander of his army like Hitler, had given precisely the same order to his own army.

On 26th April 1944 my uncle Willi (my father's three years younger brother) with the black, wavy hair and full lips, died from typhoid fever (Fleckfieber) 'für Volk und Vaterland'. My grandmother was heart-broken. She cried every day for months. The phrase 'Ein Volk, ein Reich, ein Führer' sounded more hollow every day. Almost every family had one deceased member by now, some two or three. My cousin Erich's older brother Gerhard, Tante Marie's son, was soon to to be among them.[1]

We shuddered as we thought of all the others in our family 'out there.' It became obvious that most of the dead would not even be found, let alone buried. The same standard letter and cause of death were sent to the bereaved.

CHAPTER 24
At Elli's

All through 1943 and 1944, the indiscriminate and increased heavy bombings in Germany were met with decreased resistance due to lack of planes or pilots for the defence of the civilians.[1] Young girls and boys manned the anti-aircraft posts and were willing to die for their Führer.

---

[1] Tante Antsch in Gerten had 8 sisters and one brother, who was heir to their farm. He was killed like so many others, who were supposed to inherit their father's farm.
[1] From Spring 1943 to the end of April 1944, RAF Bomber Command lost 2824 aircraft in attacks on Germany, which meant that 20,000 aircrew were killed or missing – RAF Official History.

Gerhard, my cousin, engaged to Trixi, the beautiful Czech girl, had very little leave. Trixi loved Elli's brother Gerhard and missed him. She was still helping Elli with all her children as they continued to appear. They were a happy crowd, even if Elli lost her temper more than was necessary. She cared a great deal for her children and worked very hard to look after them, including making clothes for them, so that they always looked clean and smart.

I was there one day, scooting up and down the long corridor with Wolfgang, the oldest son, when I overheard Elli complain to her father that the Czech tenants upstairs were a blasted nuisance and she could not put up with them any more.

"They've written again, but I haven't opened the letter." She handed it to him. The black pencil-line, representing her eyebrows, twitched, but her smile showed her white, symmetrical teeth as always. He went upstairs with the letter in his hand and I followed. He rang the doorbell several times, but there was no sign of life behind the door. We came down again.

"I know they're in," Elli said in a vitriolic voice. He went through the conservatory into the garden. I followed him there as well, curious as to what he could possibly do about this matter out in the garden. He positioned himself on some stones which fortified the sloping ground, swung the letter up and down in his hand, and looking directly up at their window shouted: "*Kommen Sie nur 'raus aus Ihr'm Hasenhöhler!*" which loosely translated means something like: "Come out of your rabbit-warren!" I was flabbergasted. Never before had I heard an adult address another adult in this way. I reasoned that they must have behaved very badly for Onkel Karl to be so hostile. They might have complained about the noise downstairs in an uncivilized way, but even if Onkel Karl was justified in talking this way, I thought he was extremely brave. I would never have dared to do such a thing. Noone answered him, although I had expected the window to be opened quickly and angrily, with an equally irritated voice replying with equally insulting words. But everything remained still, so that we could do little else but return to the house and go our own ways - my uncle continuing his conversation with Elli and I resuming my attempts to master Wolfi's various vehicles.

The scooter was quite easy, but the fourwheeler managed to defeat me time after time. It had a long handle instead of a steering wheel, which had to be thrust back an forth to ensure a forward movement. But try as I may, I could only achieve a backward and forward movement on the seat of the 'machine.' Steering it would have been easy. The soles of ones feet rested on the axles in the front, which could be changed easily with a slight pressure applied by the foot. Wolfi laughed at me and I felt very inadequate. Although he was two and a half years my junior, he had no difficulties with any of his contraptions.

I thought shamefully of the time when my 'friends' had waited a few yards away from the school to beat me up. Erika Hühner was the gangleader, who had come up with the idea. The first time it happened, I thought they were waiting to go home with me, as most of them took the same route. I smiled at them as I approached and got a terrible shock when they all fell over me and beat me for all they were worth. I was puzzled and went to see Erika later on to find out the reason for this vicious and entirely unprovoked attack. My bewilderment increased when she behaved as if nothing unusual had happened. In the days that followed, her gang was waiting for me in the same spot and mercilessly thrashed me again.

I said nothing to my mother, or anyone else. I forget exactly how many times they beat me up, but Erika and I continued to play together with some other girls, who visited her parents' shed adorned with curtains, giving the impression that this was our own little house, where no adult had the right to enter. Secrecy was the password, and my face burned while I pressed a doll to my stuffed bosom in order to 'breastfeed' her. The others did the same and laughed, but I looked to the floor and blushed, although I enjoyed it as much as my friends. We had seen Erika's mother breastfeed the baby; our motherly instincts must have been aroused as a consequence.

To avoid further bashings, I decided to avoid the scene of violence near the school. Instead of going up the hill towards Weinertsgrün's, I went straight into town to the Buchstädtl, which was a kind of park. This way, I practically journeyed home in a semi-circle, rather than a straight line, so that I was half an hour late. This went on for days, until my mother finally questioned me about it.

"What's been going on, Erika? You're not usually late." Hesitatingly I told her the whole story. Nothing would be more embarrassing than a confrontation between my mother and my friends; at the same time, I felt that I needed help in my predicament. She decided to have a talk to Frau Wildgatsch, my teacher, who must have had a talk with my friends, unless they had given up through my decision to choose a roundabout way home.

CHAPTER 25
The End in Sight

The wardens, or civil defence men (none of whom were now able and competent men as these had been drafted or killed) began to paint white, intricate symmetrical lines on the house walls. I spent a lot of time studying these lines without deducing any meaning from them.

"Oh, they're shelter plans for the cellars of the houses," the adults said knowingly.

With all these planes roaring over our heads almost daily now, precautions had to be taken. One plane had actually swooped down like a formidable bird of prey with talons drawn, and dropped a bomb somewhere on the slope of the town, down to the Eger, so that dozens of windows had shattered all around.

We children had been playing the amusing game of pretending to be a *Stukka-Sturzkampfflugzeug* (a dive bomber) that approaches at an alarming speed and with an earsplitting din, terrifying its victims.

"Achtung Stukka!" someone would suddenly shout, and everyone else would fall to the ground at this prompt. This game eventually fizzled out with the increasing air raids, which announced themselves with the long tone-waves of the sirens warning everyone of an approaching attack. As the enemy planes approached with the sound of millions of giant locusts filling the air, so that the vibration in the air could be physically felt, the siren would start howling, like something from another planet, a fast, undulating sound :- "Too late, too late for help, we're being attacked and no one cares. Woe, woe!" This was true, of course, although our situation was hardly comparable with that of the towns-people in Germany, who were now dying like flies, squashed under the ruins of their houses or burnt to death.

Between 24th and 30th July 1943, Hamburg had been attacked leaving at least 30,000 dead and 277,000 residences totally demolished. Berlin met with the same fate from 18th November to 3rd December 1943, when 27,000 people had died and 250,000 were made homeless.

Still, the Hitler-youth marched with flying Swastika banners (*Hakenkreuzfahne*) and unrelenting drive and enthusiasm. Compared to them, the little rectangle of SS men that marched past our house almost every day seemed pitifully insignificant. One man always caught my eye, because of the stoic expression on his face. While the others threw their arms and legs up vigorously whilst singing their hearts out, he just walked briskly enough for the others not to fall over him and without opening his mouth. He was not a pretty sight from any angle. His ruddy complexion matched his receding ginger hair and bushy eyebrows; his stubby arms and legs went well with his small eyes, and his large nose reflected the bulkiness of his body. This man seemed to possess none of the right attributes, on the contrary. I had heard that SS men were required to have a certain height, good health and an 'idealistic' outlook. There were about 350000 non-German volunteers from 16 occupied countries in the Waffen- SS from 1940-1945. They were all supposed to be Aryans. They had been trained in Adolf Hitler schools, where strict discipline was hammered into them and brainwashing took place. Their blood group was tatooed on their arms. The less strong and determined men became Waffen SS. This whole idea was portrayed as an ideal, but many men realized only too late what they had let themselves in for. [1]

One day, I could hardly believe my eyes. Tante Anni, my mother's youngest sister, turned up at our flat with this same man. I stared at him with blatant curiosity, which was undiminished even after an hour's silence on his part. The only words he uttered were "yes" and "no" and occasionally a short sentence, which faintly indicated a joke.

Open-mouthed, I watched him squeeze some toothpaste out of a tube and eat it. Plucking up courage, I asked him: "Do you like toothpaste?"

"Yes," came the laconic answer.

"What does the SS camp look like from the inside?" was my next question.

He thought for a moment, then said in his heavy Swabian dialect: "I might be able to take you there one day if you're interested."

"Oh, yes!" I answered quickly, "I'd like that very much. When can I go?"

"I have to ask first, of course," he said, dampening my spirit.

My Aunt Anni, (who had lived with her sister Marie for some years now after her divorce from her dentist husband in Freiwaldau) opened a small bottle of perfume and carefully dabbed a little of it on her beautiful white hand.

"Eugen bought me this today, Pepi," she said in her melodic alto - voice. "He's so thoughtful and knows just what my tastes are."' I admired her immensely; she cared little for shopping, cleaning and other housewifely activities, but devoted her life entirely to aestheticism -

---

[1] The letters SS mean *Schutzstaffel* (which had many branches) – men, who originally were Hitler's bodyguard, but later also monitored the army and were used to massacre the 'undesirables'. Amongst their 900,000 in number were 350,000 non-German volunteers.

beauty in the arts, clothes, underclothes, perfumes, soaps, hats, or wherever there were sensuous pleasures to be found.

"Stop washing the coffee cups and come and sing one of our duets with me," she said to her sister, putting the lid back on the bottle, having transformed our humble abode into the intoxicating scent of the Hanging Gardens of Babylon. The two women started singing one of the songs they had sung together when still quite young. They had stood on platforms and stages together, entertained the public and enjoyed it without monetory benefits. The room was filled with music and lyrics that evoked many sentiments, from the joyous, via the dramatic to the tragic. My mother's soprano sounded pleasing, except for the very high notes, which were produced under strain. She always said that this was the result of her goitre operation, whose stitches resembled a white necklace around her neck. But my aunt's voice came over to me like a day in Spring, or the fragrant air after a thunderstorm, soft and mind-filling. The dark notes stirred something inside me that was indefinable and yet had a wonderous resonance.

Eugen seemed to share my sentiments, for the admiration in his eyes altered his entire expression. The bond between the two lovers was tangible, like a bridge of love that would span any distance, not just the few steps that were between them now. Even when his beloved gave more than a hint that he was tone deaf, Eugen's mouth still showed signs of emotion.

"I may not be able to sing, but I can and do appreciate music," he said and now sounded more like a learned music critic than an eccentric SS man.

"Eugen says that Hitler is a murderer," Aunt Anni said laughingly to my mother. He had looked at a large picture of Hitler at Anni's and said: "Get that mass murderer out of my sight!" He also said similar things in public until he was imprisoned for six weeks and reduced in rank. He was one of 13 children. He used to work for the Post Office and later became SS Post Escort, first in Berlin, then in Holland.

"Please don't say anything like that in my house," my mother said angrily, and her face grew pale and pointed. "I'm loyal to him come what may, otherwise all the sacrifices we have to make will have been in vain. Think of all our loved ones killed and maimed so far, and all those killed in air raids. Thousands have lost all their possessions and homes. Should all this be for nothing? No, I believe we'll be victorious yet." Her eyes sparkled, and her manner showed that she was ready to take on anyone or anything opposing her views.

I was reminded of my father as soon as she had said 'loved ones.' It was Summer now. In Spring, she had bought a few primuli –'*Himmel-schlüssel*' in German - which means 'key to heaven.' I had studied them carefully. Each colour was perfect, and no artist could have painted their intensity quite like it.

On a sudden whim, I had sat down in front of the flowers and had written my first letter to my father. The letters were big and awkward and it took me some time to finish the composition. The image of my father was in my mind as I stared at the perfect shapes and colours of the flowers on the table.

I concluded my letter with the words *"Du bist mein liebster Himmelschlüssel and wirst es immer bleiben,"*(you are my dearest key to heaven and always will be). I felt intuitively at that moment that although we were all frail like those flowers, here today and gone tomorrow, our lives should at least have some shape and colour just like them. Intensity in everything that could be held up in the light for everyone to see at any cost, was the issue. Drabness and shapelessness would never do. The air-bubbles in the transparent vase reminded me of beauty, daring clarity and timelessness.

I felt an affinity stronger than blood with my aunt (although she seemed frivolous on the surface) because she was looking for light, rather than darkness, for beauty instead of uncommitted uniformity. This required strength and nobility of character.

But what did she see in this man Eugen, I wondered? Was she merely basking in his admiration? Was she really all out for self-glorification, or was she just lonely in a confused world she did not understand? As a child, she had suffered from St. Vitus dance, like my sister. Was this world too much for her, and had she opted out of it in her own way? These were sentiments I felt without being able to put them into words, or conscious thoughts at the time.

I had observed her getting ready to go out for the evening in front of my Aunt Marie's big mirror. It struck me then what good taste she had. At that time she wore a small, coquettish hat with a feather that whipped up and down as she moved. This gave her a flamboyant look and it seemed as if her appearance would have been incomplete without it.

A few days later, Eugen came to collect me for 'inspection' of his abode. We walked the few yards from our house to the SS camp, which had no houses around it. The guard at the gate allowed us to go in without much formality. As soon as I entered the compound, the prevailing atmosphere struck me as sombre and oppressive. Hardly anyone talked, and everything in sight was grey in grey. The barracks consisted of the ground and first floor. Eugen's bed was upstairs, and in the whole overcrowded dormitory there was not one single superfluous object. Everything looked neat, bleak and characterless.

As I stood at the bottom of Eugen's bed, I wondered why I had come to this place. I felt no fear, only an uncertainty that made me wish I had been less curious about his accommodation. The marching SS men had been an enigma, but now I wished that they had remained one.

Whenever I enter a room, I always look out of the window to see the view, or just to reassure myself that Nature is not far away. But as I stood at the bottom of that bed, I knew that it was pointless to look out of the little rectangular window with strange brown meshing next to the glass. What would I see? Maybe a few miserable figures walking around the yard, going about their business. Little did I know that I would be standing in that room again in the not so distant future.

There was nothing particularly sinister about this scene, but these men seemed to have no personal belongings at all, and they did not talk to each other, let alone joke, as soldiers sometimes do. They left Saaz for Macedonia after 20th July 1944, a fateful day.

Herr Szöny and his family came to visit us again one Thursday afternoon. He worked on shifts at Maltheuern at the time. My mother wore a beautiful multi-coloured crepe dress with a belt. She was no dedicated follower of fashion unlike her sisters, but she usually managed to look smart, wearing clothes that suited her. She chatted to Frau Szöny, and Liesl and I with her daughters, while Herr Szöny listened to the news on the wireless before they left.

After switching it off, he said quietly: "There was another attempt on Hitler's life today. They are not saying, if it was successful."

At this, my mother flew over to switch the radio back on again. "Why did you turn it off?" she hissed at Szöny, without waiting for an answer. Sad music came over the airwaves and we feared the worst. What would we do without our leader? We would be swallowed up by the abyss. We children could feel my mother's dread and anxiety and wanted to stay up until there was some more news. It was around midnight that Hitler's voice was heard loud and clear, telling the nation of his narrow escape.

"Today, on 20th July 1944, your Führer miraculously escaped a most vicious assassination plot, that only the basest murderers could have contemplated. But Providence has once more protected me from even the slightest wounds to my body. It is now clear to friend and foe alike that I have been chosen to lead the German people to their final victory, whatever the cost might be. But the traitors will be dealt with as they deserve. There is no room for such criminals or their families in a decent society, which has sacrificed so much."

Words to this effect, Hitler spoke in a voice that betrayed shock and fear and which, at the same time, was strengthened and upheld through his *'unbeugsame Wille'* (unrelenting will) that transferred itself to the people thus addressed.

"The swines, the bastards!" my mother burst out. "What depths can human beings sink to? Thank goodness he's safe," she sighed, and collapsed on the sofa.

We said nothing, but stood silently and awkwardly till my sister rushed toward my mother and I followed. She was leaning on her elbow now, her eyes empty and searching.

I remembered what she had looked like in January 1944. Christmas 1943 had been a sad occasion without my father. We had spent it in the cellar due to an air raid. In the New Year, we had been told that he would soon have a few days leave. We had not seen him for a year, so naturally there was great excitement.

When, on the expected day, he had not arrived at my bedtime, I was determined to wake and get up, if I heard the door bell ring. I cannot remember if I actually fell asleep. What I do remember vividly is the sound of the doorbell, my jumping out of bed and rushing to the kitchen and dining-room, where I stopped dead in my tracks. Through the door leading to the hall, I saw my mother rush into the arms of my father as if nothing else on earth mattered. They stood there under the light, which illuminated my mother's black hair on my father's uniformed shoulder. I looked at the two silent, entwined figures, alone in their world and sneaked back to bed, in happy anticipation of the coming day. My father was only allowed to stay at home for a few days.

Looking at my mother now, she was hardly the same person. There was fear and desperation in her eyes, and she seemed unaware of our presence. Herr Szöny, on the other hand, probably went home, switched his radio on and rung his hands in despair that Hitler had not been removed, never to return.

Very soon, my mother composed herself, told my sister and me to go to bed quickly as it was very late by now.

What had in fact happened, was that Oberst Graf Schenk von Stauffenberg had this time managed to ignite a bomb in a briefcase beneath the infamous map-table around which Hitler and his staff debated and assessed the present situation at his headquarters in Wolfsschanze, near Rastenburg, East Prussia. Stauffenberg was a member of this elite and had been able to place the briefcase containing the bomb directly under the heavy oak table where Hitler sat. Colonel Brandt nearby had pushed it with his foot away from Hitler as not to inconvenience him.

On this unforgettable day of 20th July 1944, everything had been prepared on all fronts for a new provisional government after Hitler's death. It was a conspiracy on a grand scale with many generals and officers involved.

The great force of the explosion, in which people were blown out of the building (four died), left no doubt in Stauffenberg's mind that Hitler had been killed. He returned to Berlin to establish a centre for the new Government and to inform everyone who was awaiting confirmation of the plot that it had been successful.

Hitler's eyebrows had been singed, and his clothes were in rags, but he had not even been slightly injured on account of the heavy tabletop and tableleg, which had protected him. He later showed off his clothes to Mussolini, who came to see him the next day as planned beforehand. Mussolini had been arrested and replaced by Marshal Pietre Badoglio in July 1943. In a daring "Gran Sosso" raid, he was rescued from prison by German paratroopers on 12th September 1943 and under pressure from Hitler reinstated as leader of a puppet regime The Italian Socialist Republic in the North of Italy. There were now two leaders in Italy and until Italy declared war on Germany on 13th October 1943, the Italian army had split loyalties.

Following this unsuccessful attempt on Hitler's life, SS and SD leaders were arrested in Paris and Vienna. Many leading military, political and religious leaders (four hundred Lutheran pastors had resisted the regime and were murdered at Buchenwald concentration camp) as well as many remaining members of the Kreisauer Circle, founded surreptitiously by Graf Moltke on his estate in Kreisau in 1940[1], had come out to take over the leadership. They were now exposed. For hours, and for people, who had not heard Hitler's broadcast, for days, there were conflicting reports about Hitler's death or survival, which created an agonizing suspense for everyone. Colonel Count von Stauffenberg and a few other high-ranking military men were shot in the Ministry of War courtyard just hours after the blast. For them it must have been the longest, terrible hours of their lives. They could not even be sure if Hitler was really dead. These men, especially the generals on the front, must have agonized every time the Führer gave a command contrary to their conscience. Some disobeyed orders that would have sacrificed their men uselessly.

Five thousand others, from the top to the bottom ranks of the society, faced an agonizing death for weeks and months until the end of the war. Some were hanged on meat hooks, others killed in the last days of the war, having been imprisoned just after 20th July 1944. The Lutheran pastor Dietrich Bonhoeffer was already arrested in 1943 for calling Hitler the "Anti-Christ". Being indirectly implicated in Stauffenberg's assassination plot, he was tried in Regensburg, incarcerated in Flossenbürg concentration camp and hanged just a few

---

[1] The circle had been smashed in January 1944, when Count Moltke was arrested by the Gestapo and executed a year later.

days before the war ended. Pastor Niemöller was imprisoned, but escaped death.

Many generals committed suicide of their own accord or were forced into it by others. Field Marshal Rommel was forced to swallow cyanide within 15 minutes after being lead away from his family. Hitler dared not expose him as a 'traitor' after having hailed him as a hero. The game had to be played properly to the end. It was announced that Rommel had had a brain seizure or apoplexy, and in due course, one of the greatest state funerals of the time took place. Only very few people knew that it was in fact one of the foulest murders executed under the unsuspecting public eye.

Fieldmarshal Kluge, who knew of the conspiracy against Hitler, but had not complied in Paris, killed himself. He would have been tortured and killed in the notorious Freisler trials (which continued until judge Freisler was killed in an air raid in February 1945) for having knowledge of the conspiracy. A great number of generals on all fronts followed suit. Hitler ordered that the Gestapo now had power over even the Forces, and that any soldier could shoot his superior, if he knew of his involvement in the assassination plot. The hunt for Jewish victims was increased, especially in Hungary.

It was ironic that exactly ten years earlier, on July 20th 1934, the SS had become an independent organisation, putting a stop to the SA which had become too powerful and uncontrollable, even for Hitler. So after killing several hundred of them, including the chief of staff (Stabschef) Ernst Röhm, Hitler had set about organizing men, who would act as robots without their own will or conscience, subordinate only to him. There would be no more danger from 'his' own men, who did all the dirty work necessary to keep the system going.

CHAPTER 26
Guilt

To me, 20th July was a shock due to being associated with my mother's short, but sudden collapse.

A date which was also impressed on me was 4.4.44. We used to write the date in our books at school and this one just sprang out at me. I thought to myself: "I'll always remember this date." I knew that this peculiarity occurred once in every decade, but I probably wanted to remember it for the importance of the times. We had a reading book called *Fibel* at school, which showed illustrations of ugly-looking Jewish children standing on walls, spitting down on nice-looking German children. Little did we know about the possibility of brainwashing a whole nation in this way, which has always been very effective and has devastating effects. This illustrated book had been written by a 20year old and had a wide circulation in schools.

By now, I could read quite well, although I had suffered a never-ending spell of childhood diseases on top of all the other inflictions including earache, digestive trouble, feverish colds and hacking coughs, lack of appetite and frequent attacks of tonsillitis and toothache.[1] All this kept me in bed a good deal. When I had measles, the blinds were drawn for a fortnight even during the day, but I discovered that if I lifted them just a little bit, I could see enough to browse through all the books on the shelves in the bedroom. I can't remember a lot about them, but one impressed me a great deal.

It was a story about a freedom fighter, Andreas Hofer, who had fought a heroic underground fight for his country's freedom, the Tyrol against Napoleon. The pictures illustrating the story were particularly horrific at the start of the 19th century. I can see one now - Andreas Hofer chained and led along a snowy mountain slope in bare feet, leaving bloody footprints behind in the snow.

I could now read all the fairy tales by myself, as well as a book called *Der Struwwelpeter* and an equally popular children's book, *Max and Moritz*, instead of pestering adults to read them to me. I never tired of any of them; most of the gruesome stories in the two books, written in verse-form, I knew by heart by the time I could read them myself. At times, I wished that they had sunk less deeply into my memory. The consequences of misdeeds committed by these children always led to a terrible end. There were self-indulgent, thumbsucking children, whose thumbs were cut off by a man with an enormous pair of scissors. One poor lad shrank to the size of a match stick and died after refusing to eat his food over a period of time. Another fell into the river and drowned on account of his absentmindedness. Someone else was told not to play with fire while left at home alone. But when mother and father returned, there was just a small heap of ash in the front parlour instead of their inquisitive young infant.

And so it went on, until the guilt of all those children seemed synonymous with my own, and I wished that my fate would be that of a boy who, despite warnings, had gone out in a great hurricane and was ultimately swept up into the sky, becoming smaller and smaller with only his open umbrella still visible to the horrified earthbound onlookers. I sometimes wondered if these two books were so popular with children on account of the many tricks Max and Moritz played on adults while they

---

[1] Our dentist insisted that milk teeth could not be repaired, but he never pulled the culprit out either. When I was twelve, there was only the thin edge of one left.

watched gleefully around the corner the cruel outcome of their carefully planned ideas, until the consequences of it all consumed them. They also seemed to have been written for parents, who found them indispensable in their syllabus of how to raise their offspring.

"Und Miez and Mauz, die Katzen, erhoben ihre Tatzen and drohen mit den Pfoten: Der Vater hat's verboten..." (and Miez and Mauz, the cats, raised their paws and warned – father has forbidden it!).

In my mind, one line followed the other, involuntarily. In *Max and Moritz* each misdeed was concluded with: '*Dieses war der erste Streich, doch der zweite folgt sogleich.*' (this was the first misdeed/trick and the second follows immediately).

There was never any pause in between, the wickedness went on and on mercilessly. Oh, it was exhilarating while the forbidden deed was being done; what fervour, what support, what rapture went into it. Yet, you knew all the time that a heavy price would have to be paid for it. It was different with the fairy tales.

While I suffered in silence with chickenpox, occasionally scratching when I was not supposed to, I read most of the Grimm's stories. I had always liked them, but now I adored them. I read them over and over again. Yes, wickedness would be found out and punished severely as night follows day, but goodness would be rewarded with the highest prize - usually the princess as wife and the kingdom into the bargain. And they lived happily ever after. What was needed to gain these prizes were courage, righteousness, versatility, humility, mental alertness and charity.

Something else was very important to oneself and other people - humour and a faith which accepts the unavoidable, but also the miraculous. You also had to face the fact that the world was a cruel, violent, dangerous place and you needed your wits about you all the time - yet, all in all, it was one big exciting challenge.

I sometimes wonder now if fairy tales go back to pre-historic times, something dragged out of the subconscious like the idea that dinosaurs and worldwide volcanic activity combined made up the stories of a community, which sent brave young men to the top of a mountain to fight a huge, fire-spewing dragon. From fairy tales I learned that you do not need great brainpower to lead a happy, exciting life. Compassion in conjunction with a never-ending search for Truth will do.

It had been my aunt Traudl's (my father's youngest sister) wedding on 1st July 1944. Her new husband was uncle Otto from Berlin, a very good-looking, clever young man. They made an attractive couple together. The ceremony meant nothing to me. The little details that surrounded it were far more interesting; for instance, the whispering when the bride first appeared. Hardly anyone wore make-up in our family, so that Tante Traudl, heavily made up, became a definite object of disapproval on her greatest day, but only for this day.

Tante Hilde (my uncle Franz's wife) gave the wedding reception in Komotau, where they lived. She was an attractive black-haired young woman, in whose favour it spoke that she took on such a heavy task in the trying war years, when food was in short supply and rations only just met the minimum demand. She was not merely good-looking, but an equally enterprising and kind woman. She had a daughter from her first husband, whom (everybody thought at the time) Franz was courting. But it was in fact her mother, many years older than himself, he married. This caused a lot of bad feeling, and even shock at home. Grandmother said:

"But, my boy, what's wrong with her daughter? She's alright, whereas we've heard a few things about her mother."

Later, they all grew to love Hilde. They had a daughter called Eva, who looked the image of her mother with her big black eyes, thick, black curls and ivory skin. Eva was nearly three years younger than me, a mischievous, chubby little girl, whom I liked very much, and who got us into trouble on many occasions. I must say that her mother was very strict with her and I thanked my lucky stars that my own was not half as draconian.

Sometimes I complained about my hair being pulled when my mother combed it, but watching Eva's hair being accosted with a wire brush and listening to her cries of pain, I was grateful that my hair was fine and wavy, rather than thick and curly. Once on holiday in Domina, where Eva's father was stationmaster for a while, Eva and I had to kneel in two corners of a room (each on a rough log of wood) as punishment for (as far as I remember) climbing into a garden and 'trespassing'.

My aunt Hilde came with Eva several times, always bringing things that we could not obtain ourselves.

"Men fall over themselves to please me, you know", she said confidentially to my mother. "If I wanted, I could have anything I liked." My mother looked a bit taken aback at this. "Well, what would I do with it all anyway?" She laughed and continued her unpacking. My mother looked reassured and their good relationship continued.

The only thing I remember about Szöny's death was my mother telling all our relatives and neighbours that he had been killed in the first air raid on Maltheuern. It had been a huge scale attack aimed at the hydrogenation plant there, just as the shifts changed in order to have maximum effect. Szöny had just come off the shift. The bodies were mutilated beyond recognition. After they were arranged in some kind of order, the relatives had to identify them. Frau Szöny was obliged to pass row after row of bloody bundles of burnt flesh and examine each one carefully, so as not to miss her husband's body, or what was left of it.

Each time my mother reached this point of the tragedy, the tears began to flow.

"There were over 300 bodies, and Szöny's was one of the last. She only recognized him by a tattoo on his left arm and a ring."

He was buried at the Antonie cemetery in Saaz, opposite our house, where his Czech wife and children remained.

I had hardly ever listened to what Szöny had to say, because I was more interested in the tone of his soft, foreign tongue, and observing his mannerisms and general behaviour which were gentle, yet firm; also his appearance, which struck you the minute you looked into his soft, brown eyes. An epitaph which might befit him would be: 'Gentle giant, you will live forever.'

Gigantic he was, for he was great enough to see the truth and face it, not cringe and hide his face, however painful it was. He saw the big glass tower, filled with odious filth, the smell of which reeked to high heaven, even though it had a carefully painted exterior and looked impressive to those who refused to look closely, or not at all for various reasons. He could not possibly see the extent of the catastrophe, but he knew that the outcome of this systematic hardening and breaking of individuals could only be disastrous. He knew them for what they were - those who strove for the German nation to sit on the chair of the High Judge, from whom nothing is hidden and whose laws are written with the blood of millions of individuals, which never suffices to produce the perfect state for the next 1000 years. He had heard them promising the earth - literally - and this is what the German nation's fate would be – the legacy of burnt earth. The victories had swept them clean off their feet until their vision was blurred. There was still hope.

Hitler had occupied Hungary in March 1944. My father was sent there from 29rd March 1944 to 28th May 1944. At the same time, on 1st April 1944, he became an *Obersoldat* (probably one grade up from 'Private' what he had been), which meant that slightly more money was sent to our bank in Saaz from where my mother collected it (RM 234,-).

In Yugoslavia at Neusatz (Novi sad), the entire company, 120 men, had met up again. From there they went into Hungary. My father had lost them after returning from home. In Warsaw, all those who had lost their company, had to report each day at a collecting centre. He slept in a monastery on the floor, from where he wrote home: "*Die Barmherzigen Brüder waren aber garnicht so barmherzig*" (the Merciful Brothers weren't so merciful at all – they must have been anti-Nazi). All those who were to report each day were sent to near the front as one company. In Krakau they saw a disturbing sight; something they had never seen before and would never see again. Just outside a small factory, a huge mound of bodies and earth filled a mass grave, which must have been dug by the

Jewish workers of the factory before they were shot. My father was shocked and horrified, and never forgot it. He peeped inside the factory. Everything looked as if the workers had left in a hurry. The sewing machines were strewn with half finished German uniforms, scissors and other sewing accessories. [1]One more weight, together with Putten in Holland (another Lidice) in 1944 and the Volksgericht which, under Freisler, condemned more and more people of all ranks, who had had anything to do with the big *Verschwörung* (conspiracy) of 20th July 1944 to add to the scale that had begun to dip without any hope of ever being rebalanced.

In Romania, their Hauptmann (captain) heard on the radio that the Russians had broken through at Lithuania. The rail staff in blue uniforms had fled, so that my father's green uniformed company had to leave for Kaunas, (Litauen) within the hour. In the rush my father lost his watch. In his service record book (Wehrpass) the entry reads: '*Verwendung im Operationsgebiet der Heeresgruppe Nord* (used in the operational area of the army group North) from 9th July 1944 - 20th August 1944', and above it, (protection of the G.G.railway-lines) '*Sicherung des General Gouvernements (Eisenbahnstrecken)* 16th February-17th March 1944 and 3rd June to 8th August 1944.

Whenever Poles were responsible for the death of German soldiers, ten Poles were shot in reprisal for each soldier. Soldiers were no longer permitted to venture out on their own. Two would go, armed with rifles, ready to fire.

My sister's friend Trude Maier von Weinertsgrün was now an orphan. Her mother had died of TB (contracted after being imprisoned in the early 30s by the Czechs while pregnant with Trude). Trude's father who served in Poland in the war, must have been in the SS. He was shot by the SS in 1941, as rumour had it, for dating a Polish girl. No one in the SS was allowed to go out or associate with a foreigner. Trude was brought up by her grandparents, who engaged a governess for her, but Trude went, together with her friend, my sister, to the imposing building, the normal school, situated at the bottom of their estate.

My father was now stationed at the Hungarian-Yugoslavian border. There, some rich German farmers had fled in great haste, leaving all their livestock behind. Everywhere in the East European countries, the German population was getting restless and fearful of the oncoming Russian front which was rolling West, North-West and South-West, slowly but surely.

---

[1] It could have been Oskar Schindler's factory, whose Jewish workforce he saved, even out of the concentration camps (see Film: *Schindler's List*). Schindler was a Sudetengerman, who benefitted from the cheap Jewish workforce in collaboration with the German army, but who, later in the war, risked his life to save as many of his workers as he could.

My father's group was given the order to save as many pigs from these German farms as possible. Some animals were already dead. The live ones were loaded onto trains and sent to Germany. The soldiers asked the Hauptmann (captain) if they could have just one for themselves. At first, he flatly refused, but the men were so outraged at this that he finally gave in; not because he feared a mutiny; he simply did not want his popularity to suffer. In the cellars of the farms, the soldiers waded knee deep in wine. The farmers did not want the Russians to be met by cellars full of the best wines, so all barrels and bottles were spilled and wasted.

Almost at the same time as the Allied invasion of northern France began [1] in June 1944 (D-day), Hitler played one his few remaining trump cards. The V1 was launched against England; a fast plane without a pilot designed to frighten the British population and cause local damage from the bombs it dropped. The Germans felt that they had some hope left with this final assault. Some even began to sing again the song ending with the refrain: '*Und wir fahren, and wir fahren, and wir fahren gegen England*'(and we go, and we go, and we go against England). They had lost the *Graf Spee*, the *Great Bismarck*, the *Scharnhorst*, nearly all their U-boats, and the *Tirpitz* was yet to be sunk in November 1944. Germany was beginning to look battered and bruised, surrounded by its enemies on all sides, its population killed, injured, deprived, helpless, hungry and fearful. Yet, some were singing in the dark, depressing days, hoping that a miracle would pull them out of the quicksand and save them at the eleventh hour.

Gerhard Lava, our neighbour's boy, who played a lot downstairs at the Meier's, had a baby brother who had been born in our air raid cellar during an air raid. When she screamed during the contractions, I asked my mother why she was so frightened of the planes ahead.

Herr Lava, a *Feldwebel* (lance-corporal) was at home a lot these days, much to the annoyance of all the tenants, especially Frau Meier. Her son-in-law and most other men were never (or hardly ever) seen at home. 'Leave' was a dirty word on the front. So why was Herr Lava allowed home so often? Their baby was a great attraction to me. The atmosphere of boiling napkins, baby clothes, dummies, cuddly toys and the baby in its awe-inspiring, respect-commanding majesty represented as strong a power as a magnetic field. But, as usual, the answer to my greetings of the mandatary "Heil Hitler" was "Good morning" or "Goodbye" and never "Heil Hitler," as was the normal reply.

---

[1] In preparation for this, 76,000 tons of bombs had been dropped by the Allies over North West France; three American and two British divisions faced eight German ones.

CHAPTER 27
Gerhard

In view of the now frequent air alarms, (during which my sister and I sheltered in a wooden trough under the cellar stairs) my mother had forbidden all visits into town. I had previously gone on my own to see my great-cousins. After endless begging, she finally gave in and allowed me to go to Elli's, after instructing me about where to shelter on my way there if the need should arise.

I found Elli in a state of agitation, which was on the whole nothing unusual, but this time she seemed genuinely concerned about a letter she had received from the town hall telling her to call in on account of her mother's absence from town. For some unknown reason, she took me with her. As we walked along, we talked about her brothers. Erich had been torpedoed in Norwegian waters. I remembered what he looked like when he appeared at our place - young, carefree, good looking with his blue eyes, blond hair and dainty nose, wearing his navy uniform. Bernhard, one of his friends, was with him in Saaz. He told us the most hair-raising adventures about the British colliding with their convoy on the pitch-black surface of the North Sea one night and the resulting hole in the bow that could be repaired and about how their ship had to be abandoned after being torpedoed in a fjord. His friend, who had been burned by the hot oil in the engine room, had to be carried out on Erich's back, but later died. On another occasion, when his ship sank, Erich escaped because he was on duty on deck and jumped overboard as soon as possible. He swam towards a solitary light in the darkness, which engulfed the tragedy of most of the ship's crew drowning. Only Erich and Bernhard from Hamburg (who later died) reached safety in the shape of a wooden house, whose owner gave them dry clothes and rum to revive them.

How much of all these stories could be believed, and how much was a nicely spun sailor's yarn, could never be found out. The only evidence was Erich's watch, which he showed us with great pride. It was encrusted with salt inside, so that the hands were embedded in it. I admired Erich profoundly, especially in view of my own hang-ups concerning water.

I was reminded of the day when some older, taller children had taken me swimming in the River Eger. As we approached the middle of the river, the water reached my mouth, stretching endlessly before my eyes, and I began to free myself from the hands of the other children. From then on, my fear of water was profound. It gradually changed to a deep mistrust. I still liked water, if it came no farther than my waist. I suspect I was already a little suspicious of deep water, since my sister

.Anna Soukup, nee Frank with her grandchildren in 1913.
From left to right: Josefine, Marie, Franz and Annie.

Anton Soukup, Anna Soukup's son, with his wife Rosa Soukup, nee Langer in 1922.

3. Stefan Schroll, father of Ferdinand, with wife Marie, nee Ulm in 1949

4. Josefine Schroll with cousin Karl Schimmer in the 1920's.

5. Anni Soukup, Josefine's sister, Easter 1925.

6. Ferdinand and Josefine Schroll's wedding in Saaz on 18.10.1931.

7. Marie, Josefine's eldest sister with her husband Karl Stupka in August 1940.

8. Marie Stupka's daughter Elli with her husband Anton and their children in 1950.

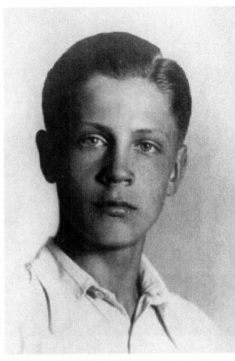

9. Erika, one year-old and sister Elizabeth on the right, Christmas 1937

10. Erika's cousin Erich, 13 years old

11. Outside the Schroll family house in Saaz. From left to right, cousin Eva, Erika and Elisabeth.

12. Ferdinand and Josefine, Elisabeth, Manfred (evacuee from Berlin) and Erika (on the right), Saaz 1940.

. Loretto Square in Saaz where Josefine lived as a child.
onastery Muttergotteshaus in the middle where Erika was born.
brewery was at the back of the monastery

15. Tante Antsch second from the right
with three of her children and her daugh-
ter-in-law on her left. Regensburg 1958.

. From left to right, Erika, Herbert,
au Rauscher and Josefine in Bad
auheim, 1954

16. Onkel Franz sitting in front of the piano with his band in Günzburg, 1949.

18. Erika, cousin Peppi and Onkel Karl (on right), New Year's Eve 1955.

17. Onkel Karl, in Munich, August 1951.

19. From left to right, Tante Traudl with children Dieter and Otti, Elisabeth, Grandma Schroll, Emil, Grandpa Schroll, Josefine, Ferdinand and Erika in Unter-Ühring in September 1949.

20. Left to right: Tante Anni, Ferdinand, Josefine and Tante Anni's husband Eugen Mannheim, 1954.

21. Erika and cousin Eva in Regensburg, 1956.

22. Tante Mina, Ferdinand's eldest sister, in Regensburg, 1976.

23. Onkel Gustl, Tante Mina's husband in Regensburg, March 1976.

24. At cousin Helmut's wedding in August 1961, Josefine entertains.

25. Left to right, Ferdinand, Josefine and Ferdinand;s youngest brother Franz in 1956.

26. The three siblings: Anni, Franz and Josefine at Easter in Regensburg 1969.

27. Erika and Josefine in the centre with cousin Pepi (second from right) and her family in Regensburg, August 1958.

28. Saaz town-hall in the 1930's with market-place and taxis in front of the arcades. The church is to the left of the town-hall.

29. Saaz from the west-side with the hop-gardens in the forefront.

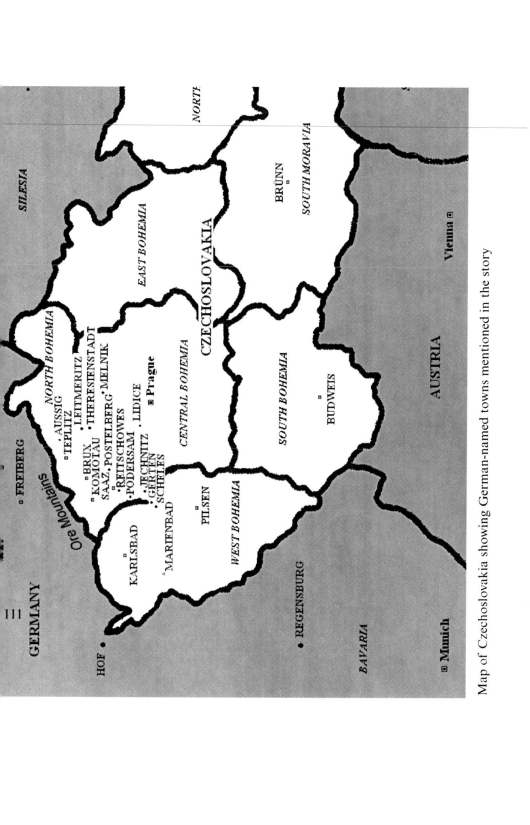

111

Map of Czechoslovakia showing German-named towns mentioned in the story

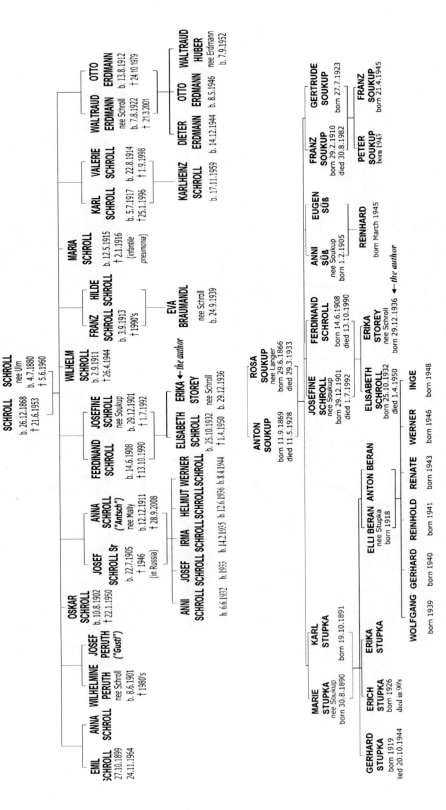

Family Tree of the Author

nearly drowned in a swimming pool in Niemes, where my mother visited a friend with us. Our journey home really crowned this distressing trip. My mother went to the lavatory with me at the railway station. On hearing the train approach, she rushed out and her dress got caught in the door. She saw me run onto the platform towards the oncoming train and gave an earsplitting scream. I stopped and looked behind me long enough for my mother to get her dress out of the door. She came running towards me, scolding as always, but I noticed that her hand trembled as she took mine in hers.

I was telling Elli how handsome I found her brothers. Gerhard had just been home on leave, because he was getting over a middle ear infection, which left him thin and haggard-looking. All musicians seemed to have a much easier life than the ordinary soldier. But when the partisan clashes in the Mährisch-Ostrau region began, the music corps was dissolved and Gerhard found himself in combat. He had been a member of the town's youth orchestra and gymnastics association, did not join the war voluntarily, was a peace-loving man with no interest in politics, only music. He played the violin, the clarinet, the double-bass and the saxophone. Before the war, Gerhard had played in cafes and hotels in Saaz and its neighbouring villages (ironically, in a band called 'The Canons.') When the war began, he was sent to France and then trained to be a pilot, but the Luftwaffe (air force) was not worth mentioning any more. Now he had to keep the army and the whole population amused with his performances on the radio while serving in a Grenadier-Infantry Battalion in Slovakia.

"They're supposed to fight the partisans there," Elli said, her face looked unusually grave and worried. "I just can't imagine Gerhard fighting anyone, let alone partisans!" she burst out.

We reached the town hall, where Elli received a very official-looking envelope. She excused herself and ran to the lavatory. After what seemed an eternity, she returned a changed woman. Her smile, which she always retained even whilst arguing, had left her and her eyes looked red and sore. Her expression was grief-stricken, her usually buoyant gait had gone, and her voice was passionless: "I knew, I knew straight away why they wanted to see us." She broke down, hiding her eyes behind a handkerchief. I led her down the stairs and back home.

Elli now had the job of telling Trixi and the whole family. Trixi understood everything very well by now. Her command of German was good, although she still had a strong Czech accent of which Elli used to make fun. Now the two women just sobbed together to the bewilderment of all the children who stood about gaping for a while.

Trixi eventually took me home. She just pushed me through the door of our house and left, unprepared as she was for a confrontation with my mother. I walked towards the granite stairs as the latter came up from the cellar with a bucketful of coal.

"Where have you been so late, I've been so worried?" she said breathlessly.

"Please don't tell me off, Mama," I pleaded, "I had to go with Elli to the Town-hall." I began to tell her the terrible news. Gerhard had died on 20th October 1944 in Slovakia during his first partisan encounter. He was buried at a soldier's cemetery in Waag Neustadt

Apparently, when Tante Marie came home, no one wanted to tell her of Gerhard's death. She came to Elli's flat one day, and little Gerhard (now four years old) greeted her with: "Oma, Uncle Gerhard has been killed!"

The obituary in the newspaper showed the swastika with the following words:

"We announce with indescribable sadness the heroic death of our beloved Son, Obergefreiter Gerhard Stupka, MG gunner in a Grenadier Regiment on 20th October 1944 at the age of 25. He died dutifully for his country and its leader in the partisan conflicts in the East. He was put to rest with military honour in a military cemetery. His sacrifice means our commitment. Karl Eduard and Marie Stupka, parents; Elfriede Beran, sister; Erich Stupka (marines), brother; Triti Kubitza, fiancee. Saaz, November 1944."

A few weeks later, while riding Wolfi's bikes with him up and down the long corridor, we heard the grown-ups scream and wail in the living room as they listened to records on which Gerhard could be heard playing the saxophone. The radio company had sent them on.

CHAPTER 28
Who is it going to be?

O ne day, I was walking up and down the pavement with my hands cupped, occasionally peeping into them when Irene Luft approached me hesitantly.

"What have you got there?" she said, bursting with curiosity.

"A bird," I replied laconically.

"Really?" She came closer and tried to look into my hands. We had had an argument and not talked to each other for a few days - a situation I found unbearable. I had racked my brains how I could make up with her without losing too much dignity.

"You weren't really angry with me, were you?" I said, giving her a sidelong glance. Her round, red face changed expression.

"Not really."

I dropped my hands to my sides and laughed. A feeling of triumph swelled my breast - I had succeeded with a simple idea, since curiosity is innate in most creatures.

She flung her flaxen hair round and looked at me angrily. But I knew already that she didn't mean it. We began to run down the road when a man with a briefcase stopped us.

"Kleine, can you tell me where the Kaserne (SS Camp) is? It's somewhere round here, isn't it?" He looked piercingly at us.

"Yes, it's just there on the left." We pointed to it. 'I'm sure he has nothing to do with the SS," I thought to myself as he made his way towards the camp.

We had a game of hopscotch, after which I remembered the suspicious-looking stranger and ran home. I told my mother about it and she immediately took me up to the SS camp to report the incident. Not long afterwards, an SS man called and told us that the man had been captured at   the back of the camp which slopes down towards the hop gardens. The neighbours congratulated my mother for her quick thinking.

"He would have described the exact site of the camp to our enemies and we would have been wiped off the map by these low flying surprise attackers. It was a question of who struck first."

There had been several American planes swooping down with no forewarning, only the attack siren.

Tante Antsch's youngest sister Ritsch was supposed to visit us one day. I can't recall if it was before or after Christmas 1944. The festive season had come and gone without any real excitement. Everyone was too afraid of the present and future. The young girl wanted a change of scenery and came to see the 'big town' of Saaz. She had not wanted to be collected from the station, in order to appear grown up and independent.

Suddenly, a Mustang appeared from nowhere, approaching one of our railway stations from an acute angle, and dropped a bomb directly on it. Ritsch arrived at our house shortly after, shaken and covered in plaster. Even her hair looked grey and sticky and she was in need of a bath. I don't remember the details, but the train and station were shot at and later the station had collapsed while she was near it, killing many people inside. There was no doubt now that particular buildings were targeted and destroyed. The attack on the other station in Saaz had failed later on, but a train was hit.

Bags of earth were piled up and placed in frames in front of the cellar windows for protection, and massive beams were erected to support the cellar ceiling. All these measures added to the anxiety of the people.

I thought, "if they believed in our Führer, they wouldn't be in such a state."[1] This was now the beginning of 1945 and people did not share my personal sentiments any more. Many now dreaded what was to come.

Another preventative measure was the removal of the tenants' attic cubicles in case of fire caused by bombs. The tenants were asked to clear their section, so that the wooden partitions could be removed.

My mother was in the process of sorting things out up there, when she came across a bundle of books and pictures glorifying Adolf Hitler, probably *Mein Kampf* being amonst it. Someone must have pushed this now dangerous material through the latticed door in order to relegate the incriminating evidence on someone else's doorstep. My mother was furious. Who could have done such a thing? She leafed through the books until the owner's name stared her in the face: 'Schmidt', it said unequivocally.

"I see," she muttered, rising from her crouched position. She took the bundle to Frau Schmidt's doorstep, where she deposited it with sufficient force to combat the temptation to ring the bell and tell Frau Schmidt what she thought of her.

Not only had the wind changed; it was also a question of "Who will it be, you or me?"

CHAPTER 29
Games

My ability to lose a game with dignity had never been outstanding. Usually, I would stalk out of the room, crying with anger and frustration. Why should I be the loser? I had planned my moves, I had concentrated well, I had taken risks, and I was generally flexible. All I needed was a bit of luck. Why was it not forthcoming?

The others laughed and made jokes at my expense. "Don't be silly, someone's got to lose. It was me last time, remember, and I didn't leave the room sulking, did I?"

My grandmother in Gerten was like me in this respect. A grim face with a sulky expression was nothing uncommon after she had lost at a game of cards. She had taught me several card games, which we played together whenever we visited her.

---

[1] Years later, I was to learn that an Englishman in London had exactly the same sentiments at the beginning of the war. As the German planes approached and everyone ran for shelter, this adult looked through the window of his attic at the oncoming planes, raised his hand in salute, and said solemnly: "Heil Hitler". "Hitler wasn't going to shoot at one of his most fervent followers, was he?" he said fourteen years after the war.

The last time we had come to the village square, where Tante Traudl now lived (she was expecting a baby), we walked past a farm, where big posters warned that *Maul- und Klauen-Seuche* (foot and mouth disease) raged. Then we passed two more corners to arrive at the old familiar brook and house, where my father had played and worked as a boy.

The atmosphere was sombre. Gerten had lost many fathers, brothers, husbands and sons, but a new one had just been born. Tante Antsch had given birth to a boy called Werner, whom his father, Onkel Pepp, had not even seen yet, and was never to see. There were five children now, all small. Little Irma had just swallowed some paraffin, but was none the worse for it. Grandmother had a little cry now and then, lamenting the unfairness of life as she looked at Willi's picture on the wall. Grandfather still made shoes and repaired them, while he and Worufka discussed world affairs.

As always, our arrival brought a welcome change, and interchange of thoughts for all concerned. The village children stood around us, staring us out, but our cousins played games with us outside in a carefree way that was no longer possible in Saaz. Although it was much sadder now, village life had hardly been affected by air raids, and restriction of movement.

We walked down to the end of the village where my Uncle Emil (my father's eldest brother) had built himself an impressive little house which he used, with the help of his wife Anna, as the village post office. As they had no children, Tante Anna had the time to read a great deal, mostly romantic novels, which bore no resemblance to any real life situations or characters. Onkel Emil possessed a quiet, but strong sense of humour and a confidence in life, which nothing seemed to be able to undermine. Their cuckoo clock in the front room attracted me the minute I saw it. This was magic indeed, like the ear, nose and throat specialist, whose stainless steel bin opened even before he bent down to open it. He was the same man who, on first seeing my mother, said: "Do you have a brother called Franz Soukup?" Onkel Franz was one of his patients, and the resemblance between him and his sister must have been obvious.

My mother told funny stories at grandfather's house to cheer everybody up. Usually she was quite successful; this time however, she only managed to produce faint smiles when she depicted a scene in Niemes, where aunt Mina and uncle Gustl lived, from a few years earlier.

'Gustl was holding Erika, ready to put her on the bus. She was facing this mountain, something she'd never seen before, and she said; "Haven't you got a big manure heap here?" He almost dropped her with laughter. You know, they had the finest food there for lunch. They told me they'd bought a goose on the black market from some Czechs. The

Czechs have better and more plentiful food than you have here, although you're still better off than us in the urban districts."

When we left Gerten, we felt that even there, the big shadow was stretching across the sky, ready to blot out the sun.

In January and February of 1945 in freezing conditions, waggon trains, an endless convoy of canvassed wagons drawn by horses, passed our house. Silently, yet shouting at us louder than any words, their message said: 'The big tower has fallen. Look at us. We've lost everything but our lives.'

These were landowners and farmers, refugees fleeing from Silesia, Pommerania and East Prussia. Their German identity had been signed away on a piece of paper even before the war ended. Hundreds of people had died whilst trying to flee from the approaching Russians in the Baltic areas. They had ventured out on the frozen sea with their wagon trains and sank into the icy waters. All these people had now been made 'stateless', being Germans in parts of Poland. We were Germans in parts of the newly created Czechoslovakia. Would we have to flee too? When would our turn come, or was there still a chance somewhere?

Some of the refugees stayed in Saaz. They had had enough. They had been travelling for weeks, their horses exhausted and thin, their children and old people ill and dying, their own spirits low and near despair. Saaz now counted about 40,000 inhabitants.

Frau Rauscher took a family in, whose relatives were sheltered by someone upstairs. We also took some, at first just a few, but as time went on, there were so many people in the flat that at night, there was no room to walk from the bedroom to the lavatory. They were all lying on the floor on blankets like sardines.[1]

Hitler had apparently given the order to use bigger towns in East Prussia, Poland, etc. as fortresses which the German Army were supposed to 'man' with boys of 14 - 16 as well as the few regular soldiers still left in the East in that area. The Führer was seen in the cinemas on the newsreel, patting these poor, bewildered boys on the shoulders, whispering encouraging words into their ears - the wolf who sent thousands of lambs to the slaughter in order to bridge the gap and prolong his own life by a few more days. His enemies were arriving from all sides now. The game of hide and seek was being played on the highest scale.

---

[1] I met a woman many years later who was on one of these treks as a child. Her parents had been rich landowners with livestock in Silesia. They fled from the marauding Russians, who had taken over their estate, slaughtered their animals, terrified the Germans living there and raping the women day and night. Her mother had been raped 23 times in one day. She had 8 children and lost her only son and a girl on the way to the West. They found no way to stay, so returned, only to be deported to Germany later on.

They were closing in on Berlin, where it would be hardest to get him. 22,000 Russian guns surrounded two million civilians in Berlin, but he would make sure that he had plenty of men to defend him. Berlin was a big place with many solid ruins standing, which could be used as fortifications. The Germans had proved to be too weak to meet his noble and worthy standards. This was not his fault. So why should he die? They deserved to die, every one of them, so that he might live. Schukow's front, 300 km in width, was rolling slowly but surely towards the West from the East.

The big luxury ship, the *Wilhelm Gustloff*[2], had been used as a hospital ship in the early years of the war, later as barracks ship for U-boats and now, at the beginning of 1945, together with some other ships, as a naval rescue vessel for two million refugees (mainly women and children fleeing from the incoming Russians) and wounded German soldiers, coming back from the fronts. On 30th January 1945, the Wilhelm Gustloff carried nearly 10,000 such people in the Baltic, when it was hit by a Russian U-boat with 3 torpedoes and sank in 50 minutes. 1,239 people were saved by other rescuing ships. There were other such rescue ships sunk at that time till the end of the war (the *Goya,* for instance, was sunk on 16th April 1945, with over 15,000 dead). It was the biggest naval rescue operation of all times and between 25–30,000 lives were lost.

Now Hitler's enemies were calling his bluff. They had met once more at Yalta in February 1945 to discuss the conclusion of the war, and the measures they were going to take against Germany. They had already agreed on the occupied zones, including Berlin, on 12th September 1944 in London. In Jalta, Roosevelt was already very ill. France was let in on the Occupation from parts of the American and British zones, although France was not actually represented at Yalta. Roosevelt, Churchill and Stalin gave each other many rights which all turned out to be in favour of Stalin's demands, and for which he, in turn, only gave the assurance of recognizing Tschiang Kai-schek. Of course, the Russian Army had the biggest assault to face in the East - alone. For this sacrifice and also for the terrible losses in terms of land, goods and people, they had to be rewarded. Nevertheless, the Western powers recognized the Curzon Line as the Eastern Border of Poland, and the Oder Line as the Western one, while the Soviets insisted on the Oder-and Neisse-Line. Stalin had the Lubliner Committee installed in Warsaw, which he proclaimed as the provisional government of Poland. Five Woiwodschaften were created in March, which stretched as far as the Oder-Neisse-Line.

---

[2] the *Wilhelm Gustloff,* a 208m long passenger ship had been launched in 1938 for 1463 passengers and 650 crew to enable workers' vacations.

Obviously, there was now no room for any Germans in those areas. For this reason, the refugees began to flood in, with Schleswig-Holstein in Germany to their left and nearest to them (some went farther West on to the Rhineland), and Czechoslovakia to the South. They did not intend to stay there, however. It was only those who were too weak, ill, had lost a member of the family or their horses who stayed behind. The others went on, like an army of ants, determined to stay on the march headed for I do not know where. Later, they trekked home, only to be deported for good.

Hitler's 'red earth policy', to burn Germany, if there was no victory, had fortunately fallen on deaf ears. Dönitz, Hitler's appointed successor for a short while forbade this policy, at least as far as Germany was concerned. Germany was already bombed into the ground. If all orders of the Führer in those last days had been carried out, especially those stipulating that **one** big disaster area must be left wherever there is a retreat, things would have looked even more gruesome than they did, if that was imaginable. It is only a pity that so few orders were disobeyed right to the bitter end. Thousands of people on both sides could have been saved. But such was the construction of Hitler's system that individualism and independent thought was stamped out at all cost. The machine rolled on, trampling and squashing everything under foot.

'Your orders are...' and the robot complied. It was easier than thinking, and if you did dare to think, where might it lead you? Disobeying was still punished with execution until the last day of the war.

Many now famous people, such as Dietrich von Bonhoeffer lost their lives in the closing phases of the war.

Some Western statesmen thought that the expulsion of the Germans, who lived in Eastern Europe (at least 16 Million of them), including the Sudeten Germans, would become a necessity. On 15th December 1944 Churchill had spoken in the House of Commons about "making a clean sweep."

Warsaw had been flattened on Himmler's orders (there had been an uprising), but now it was Dresden's turn. On 13th and 14th February 1945, British bombers launched three attacks on Dresden[1], which was filled with thousands of refugees from the East. No one knows how many people died in this most horrific raid. The estimations vary from 60,000 to 135,000. There were so many incendiary devices (which created a raging fire storm, in which inflammable material like curtains just burst

---

[1] The Americans bombed only in daytime. Their bombers arrived in the morning of 14th February, but the only targets left was the odd farmer ploughing his field outside Dresden. The 'job' had been thoroughly accomplished.

into flame) and blasting bombs dropped that the ensuing fire could be seen 300 km away.

We were standing at the back of our house facing North. Darkness had descended; yet, the horizon in the North was so bright red and reaching high into the night sky that we could read the newspaper by its glow. Saaz was situated in a different country, across the Ore mountain range hundreds of kilometres away, and yet it was not difficult to imagine the hell Dresden was enduring, and how many innocent women and children, including many refugees, (most men were at the front) and old people were dying an agonising death. I met a woman years later who had been on a train going through Dresden as a refugee at the time. She had suffered such severe burns that she had to have plastic surgery on her face in later years. How anyone could have emerged alive from this inferno is a miracle. Germany's houses have subterranean cellars, which saved many people. In Dresden, some streets had underground connections from house to house in anticipation of an attack.. Some more had to be made during that night for some of the people to be lead to safety.

The old city and the Eastern and Southern suburbs for three kilometers towards the East were totally destroyed. The people who did not actually burn, died from the heat. In the raging fire, 1,000 degrees Centigrade would be no exaggeration. Dresden had been a cultural centre of Europe.

Another estimation is that 750,000 civilians died in air raids on Germany during the war; half of that number in the last few months of the war. But life continued to go on, even the manufacturing of weapons and ammunition. Often, hundreds of tons of incendiaries were dropped in one attack on Germany. The usual route for the bomber planes was via Holland to the Ruhr.

In September 1944, Hitler's final trump card had been played. His hopes that the V2 would bring about a dramatic change of direction in the war had been dashed. The V2 was the first rocket ever to be launched and there was no anti-aircraft defence. It was used on England with no devastating effects, but, nevertheless, caused enough damage and panic to the population. The British soldiers did not come home any more and say: "We pity you, we have a much better life abroad," now they actually fought battles to get into Germany. British civilians and the Home Guard had shown singular solidarity; men and women alike worked for the war effort, being on fire watch, guarding the beaches and clearing the rubble, especially early on in the war, when London was under attack and hundreds were killed. It would have been many more, if the underground stations had not sheltered the Londoners from the bombs and ensuing fires. Those united efforts linger nostalgically in the older generations' minds, how the common danger united the population and made them face the hardship as one man.

In Germany, and of course, also in Saaz, any social activities and gatherings had come to an end. No more operas, concerts and operettas in the town's theatre. No more Anni Kuttner, the dream of all young men, trilling: *Die Julitschka, die Julitschka aus Buda-Budapest, die hat ein Herz aus Paprika, das keine Ruhe läßt ...* a song from the *Gypsy Baron*. Everything was shut down, and every effort went into the war right up to the last moment. The *Blockleiter, Zellenleiter, Ortsgruppenleiter*, etc., almost went on tiptoes now.

The glorious Wagnerian fanfare that introduced a victory was never to be heard again on the wireless, only ever more defeats and losses. Hanna Reitsch had stopped testing planes. But still the voice thundered and reverberated: "We shall never capitulate, never, never, never."

One evening, when it was announced that the Russian Army was practically on our doorstep, my mother began to lament and cry. When my sister and I saw this, we began to cry with her, for the first time realizing that nothing could save us now. The struggle was over.

CHAPTER 30
The Tower falls

The news that Franklin Delano Roosevelt had died on 12th April 1945 breathed new vigour into the exhausted, hopeless masses.

"This is it!" my mother shouted. "The miracle we've been hoping for has actually happened. Tear down the ugly tank obstruction down there." She pointed out of the window into the road where some people had gathered a fantastic array of old mattresses, kitchen cabinets, armchairs, in short, anything big and useless - decorated with barbed wire all round. There was only a small gap on the side for people to walk through.

The SS men had disappeared, including 'Onkel Eugen,' whose son had just been born to Tante Anni. They were not married, but Tante Anni was convinced that Eugen would return to her as soon as it was safe to do so.

Down at the Jahnstrasse, at Elli's, two Dutchmen were convalescing. They had been discharged from hospital, but were in no fit state to travel back to their homeland. For months they had spent a pleasant time in the hospitable care of Elli, who replaced Toni with one of them for the time of Toni's absence. This Dutchman was a young, handsome fellow; long wars and imprisonments do not further relationships.

Toni had had to join the Army just before the end of the war in spite of his weak heart. He spent some time in Deggendorf, Bavaria, then in Holland. Elli subsequently became pregnant in the last few days of the war. Herr Hitler had given his blessing too, he needed children, who grew into able-bodied men.

Heinzi Wollnheit's mother had just had a baby, but there was no news of her husband. She was a short, stout, dark-haired woman with a big gap in the middle of her upper front teeth. She was very quiet and friendly, but most of all, everybody loved her son Heinz.

I came into the house one day, and my eyes were immediately caught by a huge, compact bulk protruding between a pair of solid legs belonging to Frau Wollnheit. Her dress was short, and as she bent down, all I could see was her pregnant abdomen. It was a sight I never forgot. She was in the process of washing the polished granite stairs, which was part of her weekly 'Hausordnung' (tenants' house-cleaning rota). She now had two small children to look after, and no husband or friends, nor relatives to assist her or keep her company. Nevertheless, Heinzi was so sweet and talkative with his funny little ways that no one really thought of her as being lonely.

Frau Lava was in the same position, of course. But when her husband was not 'on leave', she would occasionally 'take off' to her mother's. Frau Rauscher did the same, visiting her birthplace of Ceradicz or her sister, who now lived with a retired navy captain downtown. She also worked in vegetable gardens. Where Herr Rauscher was, she did not know, but imagined at times that he was feeling fine - in the arms of another woman. She was kind, but her superstitious and suspicious mind found it hard to see anything in perspective. She had told Herbert that people who tell lies would have their hand showing through their grave, and other similar stories.

Herbert was back. The aviation factory had been bombed and he had used the opportunity to return home. No one was supposed to know of his return, but soon everyone knew and he ventured out once more, aside from taking part in the Hitler Youth marches.

"The HJ do nothing but march up and down town. I know they look impressive the first few times you see them, but after that, the whole thing is old hat," he would say contemptuously. He knew, of course, that they taught you plenty in the HJ, for instance how to kill someone with a knife in combat, which shocked and frightened him. His mother would shake her head and say: "Herbert, don't say things like that, you'll get into trouble."

One day, I went over to the Rauschers on my round of visits. There was only Herbert in. Suddenly, just as I was succeeding in drawing Herbert into a conversation, a low-flying plane approached without any warning, and as Herbert threw me on the floor beneath the window, I saw the nose of the plane come into view just above me. I could not think for a moment and was surprised to find Herbert protecting me like a vault, or tent. In a second, as the roaring noise subsided, he was on his feet again, pushing me out of the door.

"Run along!" he said, and then less hastily:- "That was a close one, don't you think?"

"Yes," I answered, my feet and legs aiming for our flat, but somehow not managing. Herbert saw that I was shaking like a leaf. He took me over to our door and handed me to my mother.

"I thought she'd want to see you, Frau Schroll. You never know when they might turn up now." He turned and disappeared through his door.

"Mama, Herbert put himself between me and the plane to protect me. He threw me under the window so quickly. He told me once that the best place in an air raid is there, because the window panes shatter all over the room from the blast."

My mother moved shakily into the bedroom, where she had been spring-cleaning. The refugees had all gone out, so that the place looked quite deserted. Here was a golden opportunity to forget everything and immerse herself in the hustle and bustle of daily necessities. Take down the curtains, wash the pelmet and curtains, and fix the little one across the pelmet with drawing pins after cleaning the windows. The dressing table (in front of which I had sat many times, brushing my lips hard for lack of a lipstick) gleamed in the sunlight; the neatly folded packs of bedlinen, tied with pink ribbons, could be seen through the open wardrobe doors as in a shop window, attracting the customers with their perfect whiteness and smoothness. The French polish of the furniture resembled the surface of an untouched ice rink, and the stand containing hundreds of old and new family photographs boasted a sparkling glass top. Barefoot, I ran over to take a look at the photos and stopped in my tracks. A sharp pain had shot up my leg through the sole of my foot. When I lifted my foot to investigate, a drawing pin could be seen flat against my skin. I showed it to my mother. She looked alarmed, but without much hesitation pulled it deftly out of my flesh.

"One shock after another, but this is nothing compared to what's coming," she muttered under her breath, getting absorbed again in her cleaning activities.

The same afternoon we went to see somebody. Our route did not take us through the main streets of our town, but through some back-quarters, through which we usually reached the town centre. Near where the enchanted house hid, behind a whole forest of fir trees, some children played outside a bungalow surrounded by a garden. The scene was idyllic. I stopped my mother and begged her to go in there. She protested, but I insisted, so that she followed me in with great reluctance. Everything had been so depressing; an atmosphere of gloom hung over everything and everybody and an ominous, queer silence prevailed with an unusual heaviness that could be felt on a physical level.

And here was sunshine, happy laughter, a carefree and playful atmosphere that sucked you in the minute you set eyes on it. The garden was strewn with the most wonderful toys I had ever seen. The woman of the house came out and chatted with my mother while I delved into all these treasures, which, I personally, would have hidden away and not left lying around for anyone to play with. It was sacrilege.

My mother urged me to come along and not waste her time any longer. In desperation, I took a small toy and put it in my pocket. I was glad I had taken it, but as the day went on, it seemed to burn a hole in my pocket. I did not hide it at home, but simply left it where it was, and sure enough, my mother found it and all hell broke loose. Now my father was not here to hit me 'on order', she could not face doing it herself (although her hand very often 'slipped' when I annoyed her). This required a '*Tracht Prügel*') a heavy thrashing, as they say in German. But there was no one to administer the 'medicine.' A barrage of well-targeted words came down on me, so that I was glad when, at the end of her wholesome monologue, she suggested that I give the toy back the next day. I could not have played with it anyway. Why had I wanted to take it in the first place, I wondered. All I knew was that this sudden impulse had totally wiped out any reasonable thought. Even afterwards, I had triumphed over having got away with it.

The next day, my mother made me hand the toy back and apologise.

The woman laughed and said: "I wouldn't have known there was anything missing if you hadn't come now. There are so many toys lying around. Let her keep it."

My mother, of course, would not have it. "What? Being rewarded for stealing? No, never. She has to learn that she cannot just take someone else's things. Where would we be, if everyone behaved like that?"[1]

Rumours that the Russians had actually entered Germany and Czechoslovakia, began to spread like wildfire. Grim stories of thousands of suicides taking place alternated with gruesome accounts of Russian soldiers and their behaviour towards the German population.

The tank-barricade was partially opened because the people felt they did not want to ask for more retribution. There would be plenty as it was. Life seemed to come to a complete standstill.

---

[1] What an ironic remark, seen on a world scale!

One afternoon, there was the most vicious thunderstorm we had ever had. The sky looked black and threatening, making the rooms so dark that hardly anything was distinguishable. My mother lit some candles, just as her mother had always done during a storm. She always did whatever her mother had done, down to the last detail. She also shared her fear of storms and assumed that Liesl and I felt the same.

I usually looked forward to the end of a thunderstorm, not because I was particularly scared of it and wanted it to end, but because, after the crashing and flashing and pouring, the sun would appear, the air would be mild and filled with heavenly perfume, the water drops on flowers and leaves would look like pearls and the puddles would be plentiful and warm, just right for our feet to wade around in.

This one, though, looked different. Nobody could imagine the outcome of this foreboding sky. One flash of lightning followed another, the thunder shaking the house almost instantaneously. My mother told us to put our heads under the feather beds which we duly did.

But after a while, I found it boring and came out of my hideout. Most of the time, the room was bathed in a ghastly light and my sister's thin long figure was seen crouching by the bed, with her head under the bedclothes. My mother could be heard every few seconds, crying out as though in pain: "*Jesus, Maria and Joseph, O Gott, O Gott!*" etc. This was nothing new to me. My mother easily panicked. Then she would utter words like these, no doubt, as her mother had done.

She was silenced as her words were swallowed up by the world-filling noise and force of the thunder, so that her mouth moved without a sound and her horror-stricken eyes screamed for help in the artificial brightness.

The minutes dragged on. There was no 'ceasefire.' Now and again a boom could be heard that indicated a direct hit of something big and resistant, which was finally dragged into this voracious vortex against its will.

"It's right above us!" My mother had not meant us to hear this, but just as she said it, the thunder and lightning subsided and her voice was clearly audible. I crept over to the window, past the candle whose flame began to flicker. Through the window, the high, flood-lit poplars across 'our meadow', brutally whipped, flinched to one side and bent over as much as they could until there was a short reprieve, only to bend sideways again with their silver leaves rustling like a waterfall.

Crash!

An ear-deafening roar enveloped us; the black sky became a transcendental whiteness, and the world stood still. My mother screamed and pulled me away from the window. We all huddled together on the floor, prepared for anything. The raindrops began to fall, slowly at first –

pit –a- pat-a - every swollen drop distinct and impressive until the
heavens finally opened and the drops became a deluge, covering the
precious bit of earth in minutes. It was as if the storm yelled:

"You wait! We'll get you in the end. You surround yourselves with
an `impregnable' wall, which you fortify all the time. You fools, how long
are you going to deceive yourselves!"

The next day, we saw that lightning had struck the big round poplar
next to the cemetery-warden's house. It had been completely destroyed,
split in half and blackened. Now we knew what the almighty crash had
been.

Tante Mina and Onkel Gustl came to stay with us. They did not
want to stay by themselves during these precarious times. They were
surprised at the multitude of people in our flat.

Not long after that, I woke up one morning quite late to find that the
Russians had finally arrived. It was 10th May 1945.

CHAPTER 31
The Verdict

By now, there were rumours that the Americans had entered
Bohemia, and had been just a few kilometres away from us, but
that they had to retreat South to Bavaria to make room for the
Russians. As a consequence, there were even more suicides. These
rumours turned out to be facts. The Americans had actually taken South
Germany, crossed the Czech border as far as the Karlsbad-Budweis line,
had continued into Austria and had reached the Brenner Pass on 3rd May
1945. As the Russians pressed in from the East, the Americans made way
for them. They had overestimated the German strength, once they had
crossed the Rhine, and conceded to Russian demands readily. Stalin
wanted a big slice of the cake and took as much as he could, coming in
from the East. Even we knew that the Russians must have suffered heavy
losses, from looking at our own losses in the East. Two million German
soldiers had been lost in Russia. General von Mannstein had asked Hitler
for permission to capitulate in order to save lives, but as always, Hitler
had refused.

Now, Adolf Hitler was dead. Reduced to a quivering silent mass of
human misery in his massive concrete underground bunker in Berlin,[1]

---

[1] Where he was, allegedly, still reading Thomas Carlisle as throughout his life. One
can imagine that he read his book *Heroes, Hero-Worship and the Heroic in History*,
published in 1897, first published in 1841. On the frontispiece was a picture of
William Shakespeare, whom he also loved. Hitler was known as an avid reader. He
would read most nights and was drawn to British literature.

having sent all but women to his defence, his *'unbeugsamer'Wille'* had finally given way and he had killed himself on 30th April 1945. Eva Braun, whom he had married just before committing suicide, felt obliged to commit suicide with him. This unfortunate woman had felt privileged to be the mistress of the giant who stopped Communism from conquering Europe, but finally saw her hero as he really was - a totally immature man, whose misfortune it had been to be rejected by the Academy of Art in Vienna as a young man. He was artistic and intelligent, but neurotic in all his thoughts, power having destroyed his reason, when his risky and often arbitary decisions could only lead to ruin. He had said on 19th March 1945:-

"If the war is to be lost, the nation also will perish. This fate is inevitable. There is no need to consider the basis even of a most primitive existence any longer. On the contrary, it is better to destroy even that, and to destroy it ourselves. The nation has proved itself weak, and the future belongs solely to the stronger Eastern nation. Besides, those who remain after the battle are of little value; for the good have fallen."

Goebbels, the propaganda minister, killed his six small children, then he and his wife killed themselves. He had deceived many empty hearts and filled them with Hitler's idealism, preaching the purification of the German nation and their supreme reign over other 'inferior' nations for the next thousand years. How painful and unbearable the truth was now. We shall never know if they actually faced up to it, or whether they believed to their last breath that the German nation was too weak and ineffective to be worthy of their leader's tremendous efforts, sacrifice and ruthlessness - all in aid of the common good of the German people.

But Germany had capitulated. On 2nd May 1945, Berlin capitulated to the Red Army. On 4th May, German troops capitulated to the British, on 5th May, Himmler had been 'released from his posts' and had committed suicide on 23rd May 1945. 7th May saw the capitulation of the entire German Army through Generaloberst Jodl, Generaladmiral v. Friedeburg, Generalmajor Oxenius at General Eisenhower's headquarters in Reims and the day after at the Soviet Russian headquarters in Karlshorst near Berlin.

On 9th May 1945, at one minute after midnight, the six long miserable years of war officially ended. For us it seemed the end, for millions the beginning of a new life. It was our turn to tremble, and not just we Germans, but thousands of Czechs who had spied for the Nazis.

We did not know at the time that my Onkel Gustl had actively sided with the Germans. I am not certain if both his parents were Czech, but I am sure that one of them was. One has to consider that he was married to a German as so many Czechs were, just as so many Germans were married to Czechs.

With this in mind, it was not surprising that Tante Mina and Onkel Gustl were even more scared than we ourselves were.

It soon became clear that these Soviet troops from Mongolia had never encountered civilization before. Mongolia had just been incorporated into the Soviet Union. They had never seen a watch or clock, water from a tap, indeed, any mechanism of any kind. They were just like wild creatures, in the sense that they acted instinctively and did not use their reason very much. On the other hand, if they had come across a concentration camp like Auschwitz, and witnessed the awful destruction through bombing, they probably would have wondered what the so called 'civilization' was all about.

On the first days of the occupation, no one left the relative safety of their house. The beautiful meadow opposite our house was soon the scene of roaming horses, campfires, drinking Mongols, who played the harmonica and danced, Cossack-style, all night; and litter strewn everywhere.

As far as I recall, only the commanders and officers who were Russians, not Mongolians, drove jeeps and lorries for transportation. The others were at home on horseback. There had also been tanks for which the Germans had to clear the barricades.

Day and night, they simply barged in. A bang with a machine gun on the door, impatient shouting and rumbustious noises everywhere. Hesitation to oblige could result in a hail of bullets through the door, or if a soldier was particularly drunk, through yourself. They walked through every room, inspecting everything, delighting in a toilet water cistern; watches, clocks, and even water taps were taken away, as was jewellery and anything that looked appealing, including every drop of alcohol that could be found from the cellar to the attic.

Some people tried to hide their treasures in the coal, but the Mongols soon found out. They ordered us to turn the coal over and helped by poking their ever-present machine guns into it.

At night, there was no thought of sleep. They came and went, and nothing was safe, especially not the women. This was bad enough in the day, but at night it was worse. No woman or young girl over twelve and under seventy wanted to be seen. Women would either try and hide, or dress and make up in such a way that an ordinary man would shudder and turn away in disgust. The Mongols and Russian soldiers were not easily deterred, but if there happened to be a nice looking, young girl in the house, they obviously preferred her to an older woman with a wrinkled face.

Herrn Seifert's twin daughters downstairs, who were in their twenties, were renowned objects of their desire and in great demand all round the clock. Whether some frightened woman had revealed their beauty and abode to some 'oncoming' soldiers or whether they had been seen somewhere was unknown. The fact was that the whole Russian Army seemed to be looking for these two slim, shy-looking girls.

One night, things came to a head. The twins had come to us in desperation to hide amongst the many people in our flat. My mother's eyes searched every nook and cranny for a possible hideout. Her gaze fastened on my cot in the corner by the bedroom door. A gap was visible between the wall and the bed, into which she squeezed the two terror-stricken figures, pulling my feather bed, as if being aired, over them. They just had time to tell us that their father usually sat with a poker by the door, ready to attack anyone who dared lay a finger on his daughters. By this time, they were as scared of their father's grim determination as of being raped by some Mongols. They might all be shot, through his anger and acrimony which grew daily. He had been a secret Communist and now proclaimed it from the roof tops. These stupid Mongols did not understand. Why did they insist on behaving in such a primitive, bestial manner, when he was their friend?

Day and night he sat by the window, hidden by the emerald beauty of his aquariums, his emaciated body and skull-like face heaving with breathlessness from his chronic asthma, his long opium-filled pipe dangling down as a constant companion. Nothing escaped him.

Heavy boots could be heard outside our door, immediately followed by a bang on the door. My mother resolutely opened it. She had her long, dark hair draped over her face and an old headscarf hanging down one side of her head. All the refugees were stretched out on the floor. They had to make way for the four hefty boots that marched directly to the bedroom. Before the two drunken soldiers reached the door, one of them stopped by the sofa, on which my sister lay alone (her bed was occupied by several children). She had been asleep, but was now leaning on her elbow, her long black hair covering part of her white face.

My sister was now nearly thirteen, and although she had not yet started to mature physically, my mother looked with growing alarm and dismay at the developing situation. One of the soldiers stooped down quickly and bit my sister's big toe so hard that she emitted a piercing scream. It can only be assumed that this ferocious act was the nearest sign of affection he could muster, for he smiled benevolently and continued his hunt. If the whole scene had not been so tragic, one might have been inclined to say: "Tally-ho, happy hunting, it's only the middle of the night, everyone wants to sleep as well as is possible on the floor, we're all tired from previous disturbed, ghastly nights and constant harassment during the day. But go ahead and take your pick, you gallant knights on horseback from the East!"

My mother stumbled in front of them. She had not turned the light on in the bedroom and they did not know where the switch was and how to operate it. As far as they were concerned, it was magic. They all carried torches, which, to their eyes, were little miracles in themselves. My mother made signs with her folded hands on which she rested her head, indicating sleep, in a desperate attempt to persuade them to leave before they found the twins. She was pushed out of the way by their machine guns, so that they could look under the beds, in the wardrobe, under the bedclothes; finally, they reached the corner where the twins hardly dared to breathe.

Everyone was transformed into a statue. My mother's eyes betrayed panic for just a fraction of a second, then she began to shout and scream that we had had just about enough now. She would not tolerate any more. Could they not see that the twins were definitely not here. Her voice was distorted and frightening. She grabbed one of the soldier's arms, and pushed both intruders through the kitchen, shouting all the while. Then she opened the door with one hand and pushed them through with the other, so that they nearly fell over each other. Just as she was about to shut the door violently, a machine gun pointed at her, but she was past caring and banged the door shut as loudly as she could.

A murmur of admiration went through the rooms. I sat in my big cot, the scene of unspeakable tension only a moment before, and witnessed the twin's reappearance, relieved and grateful to my mother for the courage and sense she had displayed in the face of impossible odds and two mighty guns pointed at her. Everybody admired and praised her. She looked exhausted now. "Let's hope they're not going to come back in a minute," she said quietly. My mother's natural acting ability and newfound courage in the face of looming disaster had saved the situation.

We collapsed and fell into a restless slumber, but at least we were able to sleep for once.

The next morning we were amazed to see that some mothers had allowed their children (mostly boys) to go out and beg for chocolate from the soldiers. There was Gerold Wellisch from the next block of flats, standing right next to the dancing soldiers on the meadow, who generously threw the odd bar of chocolate over to him.

These soldiers had not stopped dancing, drinking, marauding and raping since they had arrived. It seemed incredible that an army of soldiers, travelling thousands of kilometres from the East after having fought a bloody battle, could keep up this knee-bent dancing, let alone all their other strenuous activities.

Suddenly, a shot was heard and a little boy sank into the grass simultaneously. My mother screamed and turned away. "We won't look out of the window any more. It wasn't Gerold, but I daren't look who it was," she said sorrowfully.

A few days after this incident, the Hopp family next door to us gassed themselves. Herr Hopp had been sent home from the war with a massive carbuncle on the back of his neck. He and his wife and her sister were very quiet people who never mixed with anyone. All three bodies, but especially Herr Hopp, had looked blue in the face. He must have been in terrible agony, judging by his twisted features and expression. How could they have done this so quietly and without any hint of suggestion as to what was in their minds, right next to our kitchen wall?

Tante Mina and Onkel Gustl left straight after this and made their way to Tante (my father's aunt), the smith's wife down town.

Stories of hundreds of people (including entire families) committing suicide, reached our ears. Later, statistics showed that they accounted for about 3% of all Germans in Czechoslovakia in the months of May and June 1945. These thousands either had suffered enough or dreaded what was to come now or both. This gruesome record was repeated in all different areas wherever Eastern European Germans were fleeing or were expelled from their homeland.[1] All Germans were to wear a white armband and show a white flag in one of their windows.

My mother packed a few bags and left the gruesome scene, also leaving Frau Wellisch and the Krimmers (owners of the nearby café) in our flat. Their flat had been confiscated by the Russians, who ordered the refugees in our flat to leave. Frau Lava had gone to her parents.

In the twilight, we reached Stupka's house. Everything seemed quieter there and we breathed a sigh of relief. Onkel Karl, now looking humbler without his uniform and sabre, had already come home from the war.

Tante Marie, Tante Anni (her son Reinhard had just been born 6th March 1945) and my mother immediately dived into a stream of exchanged information, which went on for some time.

"I really didn't know what I would find here. It's been absolute hell up our way." My mother described the events that had led to our sudden

---

[1] In Demmin, a town in Pommerania near the Baltic, 900 people (whole families) killed themselves when the marauding Russian army destroyed the town and raped the women several times a day. They tied themselves together and went in the river, where they drowned. One woman, who had been raped ten times in one day, took her screaming children to the river to drown herself and them. The grandmother ran after them and stopped them from doing it. When Russian troops entered Berlin in April 1945, 6,000 people committed suicide.

escape from home. "I've been thinking about Elli, Trixi and the children. Have you had any news?"

"Yes," Tante Marie explained excitedly, "you'll never guess what happened. The Dutchman took Elli and the children to Holland, and Trixi has gone back home. There was a lot of crying going on before they parted from Trixi, and she was very upset, too. Of course, it's anyone's guess if they got safely to Holland. We don't know where Erich or Toni are. And you don't know where Nand is, do you?"

"No, I don't. But yesterday morning, about 5 o'clock, I heard the sound of hundreds of marching boots. I jumped up and ran to the window where I saw columns and columns of German soldiers guarded by Russians. Suddenly a face looked up to my window. It was Pepp (Tante Antsch's husband, my father's brother). I put my slippers and dressing-gown on and ran as fast as I could down to him. The Russians guarded their German prisoners on every side, every few yards, so it was very difficult to talk to him. I asked him where they were going and he answered 'They promised us, home.' Well, you know it's not far to Gerten from Saaz. I'm so glad that he , at least, will be home with his wife and five children. He told me to go away quickly, as they had apparently taken a number of relatives prisoner after they'd enquired after the fate of these POWs. I ran upstairs again and watched for a long while, more and more soldiers walking past. I also saw a number of civilians who had seen their son or husband amidst the prisoners, and as soon as they asked questions, they were forced to march with them." My mother turned to Tante Anni. "How's the baby?"

"He's fine. Elli gave me her beautiful pram before she left. But I'm so worried about Eugen. I don't know where he is or what's happened to him."[1]

They went into the bedroom to have a look at the baby while I sat at the table and ate some soup. It wasn't salty enough for me. After I'd added a considerable amount, the soup was inedible. There was a basin of sugar on the table. This gave me the idea that the sugar would somehow neutralise the salt. With this in mind, I added a good spoon of sugar and stirred vigorously. The soup tasted even more revolting now. Just playing around with the spoon in the soup, my eyes caught sight of a picture on the wall, straight in front of me. It was a poem which ended: '*Wir kapitulieren niemals, niemals, niemals*' (we shall never capitulate, never, never, never).

---

[1] He and the other SS men from Saaz, who used to practise shooting, go swimming and generally keep fit, had been sent to Macedonia after the assassination attempt on Hitler on 20th July 1944. The SS camp was now empty, but before Christmas 1944, he had, fleetingly, visited Anni from Belgrade with two geese and packs of cigarettes, very useful for bartering. No one in Saaz really liked the SS.

CHAPTER 32
Chaos

My father's company were in Deutschbrot at the end of 1944. From there, it was virtually impossible to go farther into the then Yugoslavia on account of the hundreds of different groups of partisans. Every day, the railway tracks were blown up. German soldiers worked their way through, so that my father's company on their trains could follow on to Sarajevo. Not one of the people who worked under him (he was a Wagenmeister – keeping the trains in working order) spoke German. They were White Russians who hated Communism. This was the reason why they worked so hard for the Germans. Some of them were more fanatical than the Germans, even now. They had had a taste of the Soviet regime and could think of nothing worse, even compared with Hitler's or Mussolini's fascism.

My father could therefore talk to no one. He let everyone get on with their duties and never interfered or even watched, but kept his eyes and ears open all the time. There was very little food by now and no money had been paid.

One day, he took courage and entered a German bakery for soldiers. He begged for a piece of bread, but they shook their heads and regretted that, without money in exchange, this was impossible.

The reason my father's company had to be in Sarajevo was because it used to receive everything from the German army that came from Greece, including hospital trains with wounded Germans (which were the main targets of the partisans) and send it to Germany. It was now crystal clear that Greece was lost to the Germans, and to remain in Yugoslavia longer than absolutely necessary, would be nothing short of suicide.

He spent Christmas 1944 in Sarajevo, and from then on, every day was the same. There was hardly any food, cigarettes, nor proper coats or shoes, and on top of their day duties, each soldier had to guard their company two hours a night. On top of that, he started having terrible toothache. There was no qualified dentist either. Someone in the company who had some medical knowledge offered to take the hurting tooth out. My father knew his teeth and their structure. It had never been easy to extract one. With no numbing injections at hand and no proper dental tools, the procedure was a complete nightmare. The roots had to be removed with hammer and chisel. My father had always had enormous self-discipline, which, later on, saved his life.

One Sunday morning at daybreak, he went to work along the tree-lined avenue. He could hardly take in the gruesome spectacle before him. There, for all to see, hung a partisan (including some women) on every tree. My father felt, by this time, that there was no German soldier, apart from himself, left in Sarajevo, probably not in the whole of Yugoslavia. He, a single German railway man, was seen walking through a city teeming with partisans, some hanging dead on trees, killed by Germans. As always, his company were sitting targets.

A few Italians had suddenly joined their company of 120 men. Another day, on his way to work, a scraggy horse lay dead. Being resourceful, the Italians soon saw the opportunity for a meal.

Eventually, it dawned on the leadership that it was high time to leave Sarajevo, where the partisans conglomerated to such a degree that fighting them seemed a useless exercise. The situation was not good for the Germans and they had to get out of it somehow. Their company was followed by the demolition squad who were last of all. Outside of Sarajevo, a wood stretched alongside the tracks. The men stood in the open doors of the freight train with rifles, expecting to be ambushed from the wood, but nothing happened.

As they pulled into the next station, full of trains, there was just enough room for their train to pull in. In the midst of it all stood a commissary train with food tins, Schnapps, chocolate, cigarettes and all the goodies they had not been able to get hold of for months. It had two guards who threatened anyone who came too close. Everybody wanted something, but the guards were adamant.

Soon all hell broke loose.[1] The partisans began to shoot at the thirty men from different companies from every angle imaginable, but especially from the woods nearby. After they had returned fire with their 8cm cannon, silence reigned supreme for three days. They were informed that a 50m long bridge had been blown up by partisans, and that the army was in the process of 'repairing' it. It was for this reason that the station was congested with trains. As far as my father was concerned, the army was something one heard about, but seemed to be invisible.

Shortly before they were able to leave the station, the shooting resumed. This time they did not retaliate. The order had been given to leave the commissary train to the partisans. It had to be obeyed, although it seemed patently obvious that they would never return there. The big war machinery still rumbled on in spite of the breakdown of everything else. 'All systems go' had been a powerful command and it still rang in

---

[1] The partisans had been reinforced by a contingent of SOS people and supplies from Britain, because the partisans were the ones achieving the best results in fighting the Germans. The Italians were giving up, so that the Allies tried to get a foothold there and in Greece. The partisans under Tito, (a nickname), had widespread support from the population, because of their Communist motto that 'nothing was too much for the common cause and the Communist regime, no sacrifice too great'; they engaged the enemy heavily and inflicted heavy losses on him. The Westminster line of thinking was, as everywhere else: 'The enemy must be beaten first and then we shall see.'

the ears of many, even without the forceful voice behind it. People were shot by some of their superiors, by no means all, for deserting at this godforsaken hour.

As they approached the bridge, my father began to feel terribly afraid. He had been in many tight spots before, but always kept a reasonably level head. Perhaps the accumulation of so many narrow escapes had begun to tell on his nerves, and to crown it all, the sight of the bridge pier with only beams and tracks on top, was more than he could stand. The trains rolled, as in slow motion, across the unseen makeshift-bridge underneath. Beneath it, the river had swollen to a dangerous level, with the waters gurgling and whirling and the beams creaking and bending alarmingly. They never thought for one moment they would make it across. They could already see themselves struggling in the dirty, fast flowing river, or crushed in the carriages of the train.

Miraculously, they reached the safety of the opposite river bank and continued their journey until they reached Stein, which was supposed to be on the Austrian border. There, they looked after more trains for a short while until it slowly dawned on them that it was now up to the individual to decide what the next step would be. Nobody knew what was going on, but they assumed that the war had ended and that it must be March 1945. They got on a train to Austria, which moved a little out of the station, then stopped on a steep incline. They left the train and scrambled down with their rucksacks into a meadow.

It was a beautiful day. They stood about in groups, not knowing what to do or where to go. For two and a half years, my father had done his rail and carriage servicing under restrictive and difficult conditions, never knowing where he would be next, not being able to talk freely to anyone, sometimes seemingly isolated in the vast areas of Russia, vulnerable to any attack from any quarters at any time, worrying about his family and friends - and now he was in limbo. It was impossible to imagine what was to come. Had the German Reich just crumbled away, were they going to step into a black abyss, in which so many before them had been swallowed up? What would the immediate future be like? Was there going to be a future at all? They were all talking openly together for the first time, airing their hopes, fears, and desperate insecurities. Most of them had lost relatives and nobody knew the fate of their families; they were utterly bewildered.

After half an hour, they started walking towards the next small road which meandered through the countryside. They had heard that the next station was occupied by partisans who were preventing any train from passing through.

The group of seventy men (officers carrying revolvers, soldiers rifles) walked six to seven hundred metres to a very small village. At a junction, stood a man with a machine gun. As the men walked past him, they had to surrender their weapons. Only a major and a captain in front of my father refused, saying that the last bullet would be for themselves.

They came to a bigger junction, where some German soldiers had already been made prisoners, but no one bothered about the newcomers.

The question now was, which road led to Austria, into freedom? Which one was right and which was wrong ? My father had been friends with an Austrian from Linz for some time. Now their ways parted. The Austrian accompanied two of his compatriots to try his luck by taking the other road.

The other group, including my father, came to some houses in front of a wood. The house-owners told them to avoid the partisans in the wood. So they went back to the junction, where those who wanted to be picked up by a waiting lorry, could do so; my father scrambled onto the connection with a trailer. The dust on the road was a foot deep, so that the cloud behind them blotted out the landscape. After a short time, they reached a small village. The lorry left and they were herded into a garden, through a narrow door. Behind the garden was a mansion. The garden had a locked, big gate, so that it represented a prison, undetected from the outside. Two partisans told them to put all their possessions into a corner and informed them that they would be released into Austria soon, which was just a few yards away.

An hour later, the two men returned, demanding jewellery, fountain pens etc. The penalty for not obliging would be a bullet in the head. Towards evening they were led through the village to a small camp. "You won't need any food now," they were assured, "you'll be in Austria soon." The partisans pointed across forests surrounding them. But the soldiers began to be more than doubtful about anything they said by now.

CHAPTER 33
Franz in Adversity

Onkel Franz, my mother's only brother, had been in the infantry in France (Argonnes) like my father's brother Karl, where he had been shot in the leg. His convalescence was to last a whole year; he married the pretty seventeen-year-old daughter (whom I came to love as my aunt Trude) of a Socialist market gardener, who had built himself a house in the fertile river valley of Saaz amidst rows of gherkins, tomatoes, potatoes, cauliflowers, pumpkins and a multitude of other vegetables.

I remember going to that house with my mother one day. At that time, being brand new, it had a few feet of water in the basement and we had to balance on some boards to walk to and fro in the lower rooms above the water, which was great fun. The owners were called Herr and Frau Kühnl, but our family simply called them "the Communists".

Onkel Franz, being a musician and natural entertainer, and now having a permanent disability (he limped slightly and his right foot felt numb), was never again sent to the front, but spent the rest of the war in Bayreuth (1.5 years), Bamberg and Regensburg, where he spent his time either playing music, or with girls and helping the paymaster a little in his spare time.

While stationed in Regensburg, he met a very nice girl, who was an employee of the Fürst von Thurn and Taxis (the heir fell at Stalingrad), a millionaire, aristocrat and descendant of the one, who had the original idea of transporting mail on post-coaches, drawn by several fast horses, thus bringing the postal service into being. (The word 'Taxi' probably originates from this family name.)

This girl was less clever, for she lost a big bunch of keys to the castle in the bushes surrounding the estate while making love and losing her heart to Franz, who was married and was to have several illegitimate children before the war was over. It must be said in his defence that he paid for these children's upkeep until they were eighteen, in other words, he paid enough maintenance to last him nearly a lifetime. It was a good thing that he never drank, smoked or gambled. And in all fairness to the girl concerned, many a young intelligent girl had done exactly the same, as love makes blind, so they say.

In the last year of the war, Franz had been trained as an accountant in charge of pay and maintenance. He received the soldiers' pay from the paymaster and handed it to the recipients, which could not have been a very demanding task. For this, his wife received 120 Reichsmarks. She lived with her parents and had her first child in 1943.

In May 1945, at the end of the war, Franz found himself in a mill in Swabia, listening to the last news bulletin of the German Reich. The Americans had reached Würzburg. Nearly every city and town had been reduced to rubble. He had lost his company and tried to be one step ahead of the American army. The mill-owner's wife still believed in victory. Franz laughed at her.

"Dear lady, the Americans are only minutes away from here, that's why I have to fly. Good luck!" he shouted as he ran out of the mill. The woman went on about her husband, missing in the East.

It was dark, except for the silent illumination in the sky which resembled fireworks, and which the Germans called Christbäume (Christmas trees). His plan had been to be in a different troop each day and work his way away from the Americans. It was usually during the night that he wandered through the forests. He was making his way back to the village as best he could, when suddenly a voice right next to him spoke in a heavy Swabian dialect.

"Well, would you believe it? There's still a Landser (soldier) about. Don't you know there's a big American tank up there?" He pointed up a slope to the village road.

"Thanks, friend," Franz said, pushing on between gardens and houses and taking a different direction, away from the Americans.

"A soldier on a stroll without a rifle or belt? I should shoot you on the spot." An SS man appeared from nowhere the next morning, after Franz had slept a few hours in a field that night.

"Do you belong to the 13th company? ... yes, I thought so, clear out then." Franz thanked his lucky stars, but considered that the ground of that area was getting too hot for his liking. So when an open lorry with soldiers came along, Franz waved to the driver to give him a lift. He was in such a hurry that he didn't stop, but merely slowed down a little, so that Franz could just grab hold of the packed lorry and cling to it for all he was worth. Within minutes, he felt a piercing pain in his calf. He was forced to let go. At the same time, it seemed to him that someone had strafed his leg. He rolled down an embankment and realized what had caused the pain in his leg. A herd of cows just vanished from view. "It must have been one of the horns," he thought to himself.

There was a farm nearby. Franz had been sleeping in the fields, eating leaves and stealing water, and whatever he could lay his hands on, for several days. As he became more careless, he was detected by a farmer's wife (there were no farmers anywhere) who told her two Polish farm hands to bring Franz over to her. They advised him to hide in the hay barn, as American soldiers now patrolled the two ends of the village and checked each farm every night. The farmer's wife gave him an old suit and felt hat from her husband, a rake and leather strap. Thus equipped, he faced the patrol without any trouble. He actually walked past several patrols in this outfit, until one stopped him with: "What are you doing?" Again Franz decided that it was time to quit walking on foot.

A car pulled up with screeching brakes. "What's your destination, brother? I'm from Munich and that's where I'm headed," a voice was heard from the cab.

"Thanks, mate. I don't care where you take me, as long as it's away from the Americans. I probably won't go right down to Munich. I really want to go to Saaz in Bohemia, but thanks anyway."

They had just passed Günzburg, near Ulm, (which was to be of special significance for him and his family in later years), when they ran out of petrol. There was nothing else they could do, but abandon the car and walk their different ways. He came to a camp where Rommel's troops must have been stationed. From there, he took two or three pairs of blue shorts and some mouldy bread.

Considering his situation, he could see no way of getting to Bohemia. He remembered a woman he had met, casually, during the war in Bayreuth. She had given him her address in Neuburg; he had never forgotten it. She might be able to help him! He was starving and longing to sleep in a proper bed. He knew that her husband was an officer; he could be home already. Yet, it was worth a try.

He made his way to Neuburg along the Danube. But first he came to Donauwörth, which was just across the river. The bridge had been blown up. There was only a military pontoon bridge, which the Americans had built, with no access for civilians. It was here that he decided - being surrounded by Americans - not to avoid them any more. After all, he looked like a farmer now, not like a soldier anymore. He saw the old bridge sticking out of the water and found himself balancing across it like a tightrope walker to the amusement of the onlooking American soldiers. He found Donauwörth extremely rewarding in respect of something to eat.

As he passed a Nestle's factory there, he saw some Poles raiding the stock. He managed to grab a packet of milk powder from which he ate a little whenever the feeling of hunger overwhelmed him. Someone suggested going to the town hall. The Americans had taken over the place. He saw that there was no shortage of food. Following his instinct, he went up to a piano and began to play. Within minutes, the soldiers surrounded him, applauding, and urging him to play more and more. He had an uneasy feeling playing for the 'enemy', who could have arrested him and done what they liked with him, now that the boot was on the other foot. Also, he could not communicate with these so-called soldiers, who put their feet up on the tables and generally behaved in a fairly 'unsoldierly' manner. He excused himself and went out into the town again, looking around and drawing the fresh air into his lungs.

He noticed a Pole leaning a bicycle against a house before disappearing inside. "I bet he stole that bike," he thought to himself. Quickly he swung himself on it and pedalled as fast as his weak legs would allow to Neuburg on the Danube (Donau).

The woman whose address he'd recalled, welcomed him warmly and told him that she did not know anything about her husband. It was the usual story. Her mother was staying with her to keep her company and to benefit herself. He had a bath and something to eat, and went to bed after weeks of sleeping rough in fields and barns. In the middle of the night, the door creaked. A white figure came towards his bed and sat down on it. He called her name and pulled her into his arms.

CHAPTER 34
Karl

From France, Karl, (my father's youngest brother) was suddenly and quickly trained as an ambulance man in a field hospital. He then took part with "mountain pioneers 94", on the Hungarian-Slovakian border, in the so-called Boer position on the edge of a wood. There was no mistake about it being "the front". The wood was bombarded all day. Nine men were shelled on the first day, although there were no serious injuries. On the second day, with nowhere to hide, there were two dead and one badly injured.

Karl was shocked. He was a country boy, but he had always hated the sight of blood and death in connection with animals, let alone human beings. In the night, when all was quiet, they dug a few trenches and covered them with oakwood. As soon as dawn broke, the murderous attack began again, this time worse than on previous days. All day, Karl's arms were covered in blood up to his elbows. He thought of the mothers and relatives of the dead, also of his best friend Tony Gossak, who had been wounded twice, and was now dead. His death meant as much to him as his own brother Oskar's death. One injury had deformed Toni's face slightly. The doctors had done their best. Shrapnel had penetrated his jaw and knocked his teeth out while he was involved in a street battle after parachuting over Rotterdam. It had all been in vain. Karl could see how this terrible war was going to finish. If he had wanted to, he could have attended an officer's training centre. He was well liked, even as a Stabsgefreiter. He had declined the offer.

So time went on and the cards were on the table for all who dared to look at them. The company's boss, an Oberleutnant, ordered Karl to take the wounded to a retreated position, Mährisch Weisskirchen, 30 km away to the battalion's doctor. The latter told Karl that the war would soon be over. For this reason he should make his way home as quickly as he could to avoid the Russians.

"I, myself, don't fancy being captured and maybe having to go to Russia, I'd rather kill myself. I'm obliged to stay here for the wounded, but they are no longer your responsibility. You can speak Czech, can't you? Put some decent clothes on and get out while the going's good. I saw the end of World War I, so I know what I'm talking about," the older man told Karl in a whisper.

From his Slovakian landlady, Karl obtained an old knickerbocker suit, a cap and an old black raincoat in exchange for some of his less suitable clothes. He changed in a forest, burnt his uniform (almost forgetting to burn his identity marker), so that nothing reminded him of the grey-green association he'd belonged to for five and a half years. He had imagined his exit somewhat differently. After having risked his neck almost every day, he now had to sneak away from the horrible scene in which he had, involuntarily, played a part, his life still endangered. He cycled to the next small town, where field police called `Kettenhunde' (chained, fierce dogs) checked cars for deserters. With his crooked cap, Karl looked typically Czech, so that no one stopped him.

It was May now; cycling through Czechoslovakia would have been a pleasant experience, if this deep hatred of everything German had not prevailed. However, some people did take risks by selling him food or even inviting him for a meal. The Czech population seemed to be split between German sympathizers or active collaborators, and those who despised even a picture of a German.

At most bridges and junctions there were Czech guards (militia). Karl's knowledge of Czech was not good enough to get through these check points. So he threw his bicycle away and started on a long, tedious march through woods and fields, avoiding human contact and habitation; day after day, up and downhill, hungry and tired, trusting only his compass, and hoping that he was making his way home in a more or less straight line.

One day, he saw a small, solitary signal house by a railway track. Smoke emerged from the chimney, suggesting food. He opened the door. A man in his fifties sat at a table, drinking coffee and helping himself to a mountain of cakes and biscuits. As soon as he saw Karl, he got up and asked kindly what he wanted. Karl's lips looked dry and cracked. He simply said: "A drink," and the man made him a large mug of sweet, white coffee and offered him a plate full of yeast buns and poppy seed cake, a speciality known in all the former Hungarian-Austrian empire countries.

"I'm sorry that the cake is from yesterday. Here's some bread if you're still hungry. You're German, aren't you? I know how our people are hunting the Germans down now. I think it's all wrong. How do you know Czech so well?"

"I'm a Sudeten German. The war is over, and all I want is to get home. Can you tell me if the trains are operating again? I have to cross the Moldau river ten kilometers from here."

"You'll have no chance of crossing it on account of the guards. Also, if you're found in the woods or fields, you could be shot, and no one would ever be any the wiser."

"Many thanks, but I'm going to risk taking the train." Karl felt immense gratitude toward the Czech. Continuing his march, he tried to bypass the next place by walking alongside its outlying cemetery wall.

Suddenly a gun was pointed at him over the wall and he heard a voice, shouting:

"Stay right where you are!"

At the same time, another man in a red shirt came running out of the cemetery with a gun at his side, ordering him to put his hands up, searching his pockets and the small case he had been carrying.

"Where are your papers?"

"I haven't got any."

"So you're a German soldier who obviously conveniently 'lost' them." (They knew, of course, that every able-bodied man would be a soldier).

"What on earth do you want from me? I just want to go home."

Now two more men with guns appeared and ordered him to take his case and follow them into the cemetery. They came to an empty, freshly dug mass grave, which four men were just completing. From time to time, these four exchanged places with four others from a group of a dozen or so men who stood in two rows next to the grave. Someone in a red shirt shouted: "Shirt off, stand here with the others!"

Karl smelt the moist earth and shuddered. He had survived the war with a minor injury, and now he would be murdered here and no one would ever know. Here he was, shovelling his own grave.

His brain worked feverishly. From past experience he knew that he could always trust himself to avoid an unpleasant task or tricky situation, but now he really could not think of a way out and his life depended on it. The victims were not allowed to speak to each other, so he said a prayer and submitted himself to God. A vicious mob had gathered by the wall, screaming and pointing to their necks and shouting "Heads off!" It was obvious that no mercy could be expected from those quarters. The grave was ready, except for the odd shovelful of soil here and there protruding at the bottom of it, for which the men were reprimanded. The half-naked figures were marched in pairs to the Totenhaus (mortuary). The first two were led in. Everyone expected some shots to be heard at any moment. They held their breath. The door opened and the two came out, carrying a dead Flaksoldier[1] over to the mass grave. Many bodies, it seemed, were awaiting burial. When one layer in the grave was complete, some lime was scattered on top. In the end, after they had dropped several layers of bodies in the grave and the grave was full, it was covered with earth.

Before the last bodies were covered, two women from the crowd by the wall rushed into the mortuary. One emerged with a brush and pan, the contents of which she emptied over the grave, the other approached with

---

[1] Flak was a defence gun, used against enemy attack. It is probably an acronym, meaning *Flugabwehrkanone* = flight defence canon.

a pail of dirty water and threw it over the motionless figures in the grave. Karl thought to himself. If these people hated these dead Germans to that degree, although they had probably never seen them before, just what would they like to do with the living?

CHAPTER 35
The Penalty[3]

Time passed slowly at Tante Marie's. The adults crept out to hunt for food. Several times, they brought home meat from the dead horses lying around. They had been taken to butchers and cut up. I had wondered why everyone muttered about its taste.

"Hmm, a bit sweet but otherwise quite palatable, almost like beef."

By the time I eventually found out that it was horsemeat, something happened that was to be a preamble to a drama in which we found ourselves playing the main characters. We had already obeyed and played our part, but now, we had a different master. The role we were to play was not to an audience, only to the director and the stage hands, who made sure that only they knew about it.

The Germans in the Reich had already suffered a lot during the war, having lost their accommodations and belongings and many had paid with their lives in air raids. We, like them, had lost many loved ones in combat, but our real misery was only just beginning. We obviously had an idea of the kind of losses and deprivations we, as a nation, had inflicted on our so-called enemies, but many felt that we had sacrificed enough ourselves for that, not realizing to what extent we had made the "enemy of the state" suffer. If we had known everything, some of us would probably have felt less despair, bitterness and hopelessness about our misfortune. The tremendous guilt followed later and to this day, although the injustice done to us can also not be forgotten.

The fate of the victims in the big extermination camps had been such a closely guarded secret that only a few at the top, the SS and the Sonderkommando, (those who had to do the dirty work and who themselves were carefully selected prisoners), knew about it. It is said that the Sonderkommando were always killed themselves after only a few months of relative luxury, imprisoned in the compound where the crematoriums and so-called 'disinfection centres' lay, which they had to keep going. Their job was, apparently, to usher the herded masses that had been sorted out at the gate into black and white sheep (these were the

---

[3] Parts of this chapter are a re-published translation from *Dokumente zur Austreibung der Sudentendeutschen*, section 29.

black ones) into the big disinfection hall after they had stripped off clothes, valuables, food, in fact, everything they had. Some SS men would then jump off a van, pour some crystals from a few containers down the shafts, and within twenty minutes, in which a human pyramid of distorted and twisted bodies had formed, the Sonderkommando could continue their macabre, feverish activity by pulling down the strongest from the top of the pyramid, disentangling the bodies down to where the weakest lay, extracting gold teeth and plates, pulling rings off fingers, then burning the bodies in huge ovens. Everything had to be done quickly and efficiently, especially the cleaning of the 'bath house' where the next load would soon, unsuspectingly, strip and expect to be cleansed. Sometimes the Sonderkommando had to work overtime, for instance, if an epidemic threatened to attack a section of the camp. The whole section would have to go on to the path of no return. Everything had to be kept under control at all times, clean and in good working order. The system must never break down, cost it what it may. The Sonderkommando eventually came to realize what fate was to befall them - and not in the distant future. Nerves would increasingly fray, until drink or depression took over completely. Death would then be a relief.

****

Not very many Russians came to the Stupka's. If they came, they usually went straight to the bathroom, where my uncle had some alcohol hidden. Somehow, they knew and had a nose for it. Sometimes, Russian women came. They were not Mongols. Armed with machine guns, they stepped over bodies, as if they had done nothing else all their lives (which was probably true). Strangely enough, I cannot remember anything about my new born cousin Reinhard, Tante Anni's son, born 6th March 1945, while staying at the Stupka's. He must have been there, too. Neither can I remember the fateful Sunday of 3rd June 1945.

On Saturday, 2nd June, the Russians had faded from the scene, which we acknowledged with huge relief. At the end of May, president Benes had issued an edict that the entire German assets of the whole country had come under Czech administration. Immediately after the Russians had left and the Czechs were in command, about 150 German men from Saaz were imprisoned and tortured in the local prison.

The next morning, Sunday 3rd at 6 o'clock, all men and boys from 14-65 years of age were drummed out of their houses by Czech police and soldiers banging their machine guns on their doors to assemble at the Ringplatz (town square) in front of the town hall. Quite a few had by now returned from the war. All these people were ordered to stand in several columns, five in a row, in the town square. Some men were still in their pyjamas and dressing gowns.

Fate had finally caught up with Herbert. He found himself amongst the men, although he was only 15. He wanted to be in the first row as taught in the Hitler Youth (HJ). You had to face danger without fear, assess the situation and then either act or disappear. When one straggler, arriving late at the town square, was shot dead point blank, the older men asked Herbert and the other boys to "hide" in their midst. They had now been warned of what was awaiting them, if they did not follow every command of General Swoboda's troops. Uncle Karl, my aunt Marie's husband, was amongst the men as well. He was dragged away and had no time to finish shaving and just enough time to pull his trousers over his pyjamas.

Czech police and soldiers saw to it that no man remained hidden in a house in Saaz. All the men, including the infirm, the disabled, the sick were beaten up for the slightest irregularity. If someone was not standing in line or had turned up in national costume (as they were used to under Hitler) or for no reason at all, the maltreatment that they received was so severe that three Germans who witnessed this from their flats or houses, before joining, committed suicide. There must have been between 4-5000 men and boys being led away like sheep to the slaughter.

....

There were many towns and places all over the country, whose names echo with horror down the corridors of history, where men, women and children had to undergo unspeakable suffering for the next few months before the blood had cooled a little and voices and muscles were exhausted from screaming, kicking and beating the helpless. This was particularly bad in Prague, where the radio station had been taken over a few days before the end of the war by Czech partisans, inciting the population to violence with the words:

"*Smrt nemcum!*" (Death to the Germans)
"*Smrt vsem nemcum!* "(Death to all Germans)

The situation was similar in other towns and even small places. The worst core of Czechs who beat and murdered Germans at random might have been partisans who had suffered under the Gestapo or SS in the war for working against the regime in the underground movement. It seems likely that they used the same methods, adding a few to the ones used on them, because all over the country, wherever there were Germans - be they soldiers, men, women or children - the treatment they received was more or less the same. A kind of revolution took place, with the new black-uniformed police, called SNB, doing their 'duty' with regard to the Germans. Many young Czechs dressed up in whatever uniform they could find; old SA and German officers uniforms were popular. To exercise their returned power in these outfits seemed ironical and very disturbing.

No exception was made, even if people had been Socialists, German anti-fascists or German Communists[1], nor shown any signs of sympathy towards the regime. Even people from the Reich, or Austria, or any other foreigners, including Germans who could identify themselves as Americans, were not exempt. PoWs who had just been released were in danger of being treated like SS men on account of their uniform. Czech Communists took over everywhere. Dispossessed non-Czechs, including Jews, whose surviving members of their family tried to regain their possessions and businesses were lucky to get away with their lives.

The 'treatment' consisted of beatings, followed by more beatings. Many who escaped death were permanently disabled, i.e. deafened in one ear, or blinded in one eye. They were beaten on the head, punched in the mouth, causing them to lose teeth; kicked, (especially whilst prostrate), beaten with rubber truncheons a metre long, or any other weapon available. A common punishment was hammering of the toes and hands, beating the bare soles or forcing people to walk on broken glass. Thousands of people were clubbed to death or near death and then left to die or were shot to put them out of their misery.

Any Czech citizen was free to unleash any sadistic feelings on any German. Looters even began to pull the victims fingers off with the rings they stole.

In some towns, as in Prague and Aussig, children and babies in prams were pushed into rivers with their mothers; a common torture was also to kick people down a flight of stairs to the amusement of comrades without even looking at the injuries caused. Many people were hanged in public or in houses, including the lawyer Dr R. Schicketanz, who was accused of high treason for working out the legal expert opinion of the Sudeten German Party for the British Lord Runciman in 1938. Certain Czechs were also accused of high treason and hanged or punished for collaboration with the Germans.

The *Brünner Todesmarsch* (Brno death march) on 31st May 1945 was particularly gruesome. Some 25,000 inhabitants of Brünn with no luggage, mainly women and children, were force-marched to Austria. 1,500 of them died on the way as no provisions were provided or plans of any kind made.

This continued for about a year, gradually becoming less frequent, with radio appeals now discouraging this uncontrolled rage and atrocity, dampened by the allies, who had met in Potsdam from 16th July to 2nd

---

[1] They had to show that they could be just as cruel to their compatriots (as a man called Stroebel in Saaz)

August 1945 at Cecilienhof, formerly the home of Crown Prince Wilhelm Hohenzollern. Here, the USA, Britain and the Soviet Union agreed to the expulsion of the Sudeten Germans to, what was now, West Germany and East Germany.

· ·

All these men from Saaz were marched off to Postelberg, every time the town square filled up with them. Postelberg was a small place near Saaz, about 15 km (about 9 miles) away. It prided itself on barracks that were, at that time, a hundred years old and had served the cavalry. It comprised numerous stables, a riding school, the barracks, a Czech school, and some dried out ditches that were to serve as mass graves and latrines.

The prisoners from Saaz prison, who were still able to walk, had been ordered by police constable Captain Marek to march to the Ringplatz, where the beating was resumed until the group had reached the periphery of the town. At midnight, these men also reached Postelberg. Together with the other thousands of men, who had arrived there earlier, they lay in the yard all night until a certain command was given. Those who knew Czech obeyed, the others were shot. Some of those were dead, others only wounded. Some prisoners had to carry both dead and wounded to a ditch - a few shots with a machine gun, and all was silent. The ditch also served as a latrine for thousands.

New commandments were given. All money and jewellery was to be handed over; again as everywhere else, the penalty for not obeying orders was death. Important documents were thrown away. Everyone was thoroughly examined, (even shoes removed), but nothing more was found, although the beating and shouting continued.

The same evening, doctors, chemists, priests, in short, people with important professions, also half-Jews, husbands of Jewish and half-Jewish women and people who had been in concentration camps in the war were marched to the SS camp in Saaz. A monk, Max Hilbert, was shot dead as he could not walk fast enough.

The ones left behind were herded into stables, no food or drink had been given and the closeness of bodies was oppressive. There was no question of sleep. Shots were heard outside throughout the night

The next morning, 5th June 1945, the stable doors were opened, and shouts of "*Rychle! Rychl!*" (Quickly, quickly) were heard as shots were fired. Whoever ran too slowly was a death candidate. The injured bled to death during the day, then they were thrown into the latrine with the dead. A few more shots; 'mercy shots' as Captain Marek called them. Then the serious business of selection began. The captain wants the SS, SA, NSKK, Army, political leaders, members of the party and former members of the SDP in separate groups. Within minutes, chaos reigned supreme. Nobody knows what is going on. In one place workers were selected, in another someone was beaten up, dragged away and shot. Some were put behind barbed wire, others in stables - the entire yard echoed with screams, gunshots and beatings.

As the sun set, the prisoners who had had nothing to eat or drink for the last three days, settled their lives in the stables and in the yard, and faced death. Shots continued throughout the night. The prisoners outside envied the others in the stables, but the following night, they change their minds.

On 6th June, further endless organizing of work forces. About 120 boys from 13-18 years of age sit around by the gate. Hunger is written all over their faces. Five of them try to get out by mingling with a departing work troop. They get no farther than Postelberg itself (which had been evacuated). They are brought back and the men in the yard are warned: "Any critical remark, and there will be gunfire." Everyone is prepared, but not for this. First they are led to the riding school; their trousers are removed, then the Czech crowd queue to administer the beatings. The sticks and whips raining down cause the blood to run down their legs and their voices give out heart-rending whimpers. The soldiers disperse. The boys remain facing the wall with a guard next to them. The excitement and agitation subside as the prisoners believe that the boys have been punished enough. After half an hour, someone shouts: "Anyone who tries to escape will be shot like these boys." Disbelief can be physically felt. The boys turn round anxiously.

Herbert and his friend Walter Bauernfeind[1], who have been trying to hide as best they could, are drawn to the scene. They recognize three of the boys. They see the soldiers turn the boys to the wall again, but one boy keeps turning round to face the soldiers. Two of the soldiers aim from only a short distance away and shoot the first boy. His blood reddens the wall behind him. The other boys shout "Herr Kapitän, we won't do it again." The second boy runs towards his executioners in an attempt to push the rifles up and away from himself, but it is too late. They have already been loaded again. The odious sound cuts the air and the boy falls lifeless to the ground. Plaster sprays up as fine dust and the wall there is splashed red once more. The other boys now submit to their fate; one calls his mother before he falls. The fourth remains upright after being shot. Silently he looks into the raised barrels, which fire another

---

[1] Walter Bauernfeind had deserted just before the end of the war and was hiding in our cemetery. Herbert found him and brought him some civilian clothes, so that he could come across to his house. He was not found by the German authorities, but by the Czechs, the same as Herbert. They stayed close together at Postelberg until they were separated in the chaos and never saw each other again.

volley at him, making him collapse in a   heap. The fifth goes down
silently whilst everyone looks on. Resistance would be futile. Machine
guns are placed all along the gate, and rifles, clubs, whips, truncheons,
sticks, belts are facing them from all sides. The boys are about fifteen
years old, yet not one spectator makes a gesture to help, or raise their
voice in protest. The prisoners are prepared to die, but fear the methods of
destruction. In the stables at the back of the yard, those destined to be
killed, await their murderers. Punctually on the hour, a contingent of
Czechs set out to do their 'duty.' Equipped with sticks and whips, they do
their level best; then for ten minutes or so, the groaning, beating and
whimpering can be heard. This continues until nightfall.

And now a new spectacle begins. About twenty men with spades are
led through the back gate. They are followed by police and soldiers armed
with pistols. Evidently, more executions. But an hour later, all twenty
men return. They must have been forced to bury bodies.

On that fourth day at midday, one loaf of bread between ten
prisoners is distributed for the first time since their arrival. Again, the
afternoon is a mixture of beatings, (some on exposed bottoms), kicks,
shootings, wild swearing, ordering a dog to attack the prisoners. In
addition, prisoners are ordered to beat each other with sticks, while
guards supervise the merciless severity of it. Now and again, some Czech
women amble across the yard, enjoying the spectacle.

That same evening, relief for hundreds of men comes in the shape of
buses to transport the men away to the hydraulic works at Brüx, where
labour is needed. All over the country, slave labour to the point of
exhaustion and death begins for German women and men.

More torture is in store for the rest of the men and boys at
Postelberg. At dusk, they are squeezed into a stable so low that the
ceiling can almost be touched, and whose only window above the door is
shut tight. The 275 people can hardly stand up, let alone lie down. Lack
of oxygen produces streams of perspiration; in weak-hearted people,
unconsciousness. Screaming, roaring and raving begins that makes the
guard outside threaten to stop with a hand grenade. Some, who have
managed to keep their heads, calm the rest down and try to talk to the
guard. Their request to open the door is turned down. After repeated
begging, the guard goes to get permission to open the door, but returns
with the report that this is not possible. Renewed frenzy seizes the men,
and some show signs of insanity. The heat is unbearable, making normal
thinking increasingly impossible. One man imagines being at home and
invites the others to come in. Another one speaks with Americans on the
phone and quietly tells his fellow-sufferers that American tanks and

rescue are quite near. Dr. Wurdinger loses his mind there. My uncle Karl nearly loses his reason in that hell-hole.

At midnight, the door is opened and the fresh night air brings instantaneous relief. Soon the door is shut again and the agony continues until seven o'clock the next morning, when the door is opened.

People with wild, distorted faces and bulging eyeballs stagger out and throw themselves to the ground. Some utter a string of insults and invectives, others want to speak, but their mouths just open and shut without a sound. The first to emerge throws himself towards the guard and tries to wrench the machine gun from his hands. He is shot immediately. Another man dances out of the building on his toes like a prima ballerina, hands on waist and stark naked. How did he manage to undress himself in the squeeze during this most abominable of nights?

A German officer approaches Captain Marek and asks to be killed.

"You want a mercy-shot, do you?" The captain leads him to a ditch, makes him kneel down and aims at the back of the neck. A shot is heard. The officer turns round. "Can you not shoot better than this?" A second shot hurls him to the ground. It takes a third shot to kill him.

After five days, the man-hunting game must have lost its novelty. Many men were sent to help out on farms or in factories, and some were sent back to Saaz, including Herbert and Tante Marie's husband Karl. Herbert had been outside in the yard, hiding behind the wall to avoid flying bullets from outside the compound. He counted himself lucky to be 15 and not 14 years old. At 15, you were useful for work.

What happened to the rest is unknown. Some people claim that about eight hundred men and boys were killed at Postelberg - a name that sends shivers down the spine, like Prag, Landskron, Brünn-Pohrlitz, Brüx, Komotau, Aussig and Theresienstadt to the people who escaped from those living nightmares, in the same way that Auschwitz, Flossenbürg, Belsen, Dachau, Sachsenhausen, Theresienstadt, Warschau and Ravensbruck make us all shudder. Everywhere were casualties and tortures, but the afore-mentioned places witnessed the foulest crimes against people whose worst indictment was that their mother tongue was German. It was genocide, if not on the same scale as the German Reich's odious slaying of millions or Stalin's irrational eliminations of his own people.

How true were now the words of the British Prime Minister Lloyd George after the First World War that the terms and reparations demanded of Germany were so harsh that "we shall have to fight another war all over again in 25 years at three times the cost".

A notice reached us that everyone must return immediately to their own home. My mother left all valuables, ie. bank and savings books, jewellery, and cash at her sister's, and returned home with us. We had hardly arrived, when a Czech opened our door and informed us that we had to be out of the house within ten minutes.. The only luggage would be hand luggage. In our case, it meant that my mother could take what she could carry; the bare essentials and nothing very heavy - a set of spare clothes for each of us, a thin blanket, some food, a few photos... It was 13th June 1945.

We were told to walk to the Kaserne, the military barracks that had housed the SS. Others were transported to different towns; there were simply not enough facilities in Saaz, although later schools and the swimming pool building were used.

At the Kaserne, we met Tante Marie and many other people we knew. Years later, I saw a printed poster in a book in Czech and German, which my mother had not seen at the time; otherwise she would have been better prepared (maybe by a couple of hours) for our evacuation. The notice said:-

'Herewith the order is given for all females of Czech and German nationality and regardless of their age, also children, to report immediately after publication of this notice to the former SS Kaserne in Trnovanerstrasse in Saaz.
Germans must bring the following:
1) The minimum and the most essential travelling kit, including blankets and food. Maximum weight =25kg per person.
2) Enough food for three days.
3) All identification papers.
4) All keys on a keyring, labelled with the house number and flat.
5) All valuables, money, savings, bonds, securities, investments, precious jewellery, with an exact inventory of these objects.
These measures are taken to establish the exact identification of persons with German nationality, and their distribution to labour employment.
The concealment of any of the aforementioned valuables, or the non-observance of this order will be punished by death.
'NARODNI VYBOR'

We had heard this important sounding name of 'narodni vybor' a few times after the Czechs took over from the Russians. But now it meant life or death, torture or reprieve; in fact, it was the new power which held our lives in the palm of its hand. Czech females had also been asked to turn up, but in a different capacity.

Tante Anni had been allowed to stay at home with the baby. She came to see us, but was not allowed into the camp. Someone told us that she wanted to give us some cocoa over the fence. She told us that she had avoided walking through the town, but made her way through the fields in a semi-circle up a steep hill to our camp for the following reason. Firstly, because it was too dangerous and secondly, because a few days before, when she had to go into town with the baby, a Czech suddenly approached her and told her to take Reinhard out of the pram. She never saw the pram again. Yet she was lucky. In other places, small babies lived in camps for months under the most hair-raising conditions without milk, and many of them died there or, even worse, they were killed as in Prague and Aussig.

Frau Rauscher had to go to work like all able Germans with no small children. Herbert and all the survivors of Postelberg, including my uncle Karl, were used as slave labourers all over the country. Herbert, because of his age, was sent back to Saaz to the SS camp, where the infamous Marek had taken over the regime, but later, after being exhibited on the 'slave market' at the Ringplatz, finished up with a bachelor, called Laschtovska, who was looking for a young willing helper to do various menial jobs in his firm. This man eventually managed to get the Narodni Vybor to agree that Herbert could live in, instead of in the camp. He was very fortunate in this, as the wife of his boss's business partner, called Fischer, was German. She used to press him to her ample bosom and stroke his hair till he thought he was in heaven. Herbert was able to sneak out one day and look, unsuccessfully, for his mother, but found out that Herr Seifert was in charge of the keys to the sealed flats. Herbert pleaded with him to give him the key, but in vain. Finally he forced open the door to their flat. He searched for food and clothes, and went down to the cellar, where he found the coal one sticky mess. The Russians had emptied some jars of loganberry juice over the coal during their search for alcohol.

Everyone seemed to be searching for something or somebody. For the Czechs it was their lost republic, gained at an opportune moment after the First World War in 1919. They now wanted to start again from scratch (minus any 'undesirables' - had we not heard this somewhere before?) They needed money for this, and a workforce. Both of these they had now. For the rest of the Germans, they had different plans. These were looking for the necessities of life, which they had lost overnight, for relatives, and for a way out of this predicament that could only end in catastrophe, the way things were going.

The Communists amongst the Czechs were seeking and finding a way of taking over the country with the help of Stalin, who had supported the Czech Exile Government during the war to draw up plans, which dealt with the future of the Germans in Czechoslovakia. Benes would have to show his gratitude to Stalin, who was now in the strongest position amongst the Allies, and without whose help he could not now take these measures. Also, aligned with such a strong ally, who would dare to oppose Czechoslovakia?

The Russians themselves were a minority in the USSR, like the Czechs in their Republic.[1] There were more than one hundred ethnic groups, which Joseph Vissarionovitsch Dschugaschvili Stalin brought under one hat, teaching them the doctrines of the 19th Century German Jew Karl Marx and the Russian revolutionary V.I.U. Lenin in the Russian language, which was not Stalin's mother tongue. He was born in Gori, Georgia.

The communist doctrine of 'People Power' sounded much better than Hitler's, which had been purely nationalistic. Hitler had opposed it, but now it was back and stronger than before. After the turmoil of the terrible war, it sounded even better than after the First World War. Fraternity, liberty, and equality in all communist countries sounded even better than in the French Revolution. Surely, there was nothing better in the world than aiming for these three ideals. The difference between the two doctrines was that one was concerned with one leader of one Ayrian race conquering and controlling as many parts of the world as possible, whilst the other **promised** a proletarian leadership, embracing the world. Stalin was well on the way to it, capitalizing on the enormous effort and sacrifice of the Soviet Regime, to conquer Germany from the broad Eastern front, and for his doctrines to infiltrate the world. In the end, the two doctrines had the same goal – world domination.

****

As we walked up the stairs of the barracks, an uncomfortable feeling came over me. When we entered the sleeping quarters, I looked straight at the small, rectangular windows with the brown knobbly wire mesh across them. I remembered that I had refrained from looking through these windows when Onkel Eugen had shown me his living quarters, but now I went over and looked down into the camp. Thousands of bewildered women and children were searching for a spot where they could rest at night. The old people's home and patients from the hospital had been evacuated into our camp as well. They stayed outside or on the floor of unfinished barracks. There was not enough room for everyone to sleep in

---

[1] If the Czechs were not exactly a minority, the other ethnic groups in Czechoslovakia were there in equal numbers.

a bed. I watched a woman wearing white knee socks, her teenage daughter and her grandmother climb into an old, broken-down bus, placing their few belongings on some seats and trying to find a private corner somewhere inside, so that, in their agony, they did not have to share their life with anyone else. I watched this family over successive days, climbing in and out of the bus, either for collecting their bread and soup, fighting with thousands of others for access to the latrine or for water to wash themselves or to drink. But I never saw them talk to anybody. After a few days, only the middle-aged woman and her daughter left the bus, and each time, they looked very concerned. Within minutes, they would be back again.

One day, I noticed that they had been crying and from then on, these two figures looked utterly dejected and hopeless. The woman's white socks looked grotesque on her, but she had nothing else, just as we had only the bare minimum. If anyone went near the bus, these two would become alarmed and anxious. It was quite clear that the old woman had died in the bus and they did not want to tell the commander, in case he threw her into a mass grave. I did not tell anyone about my observation, but I have never forgotten any detail of the whole sorry incident.

A boy we knew, called Heinz Kuppert, picked up some explosives that were still lying around from the SS men. There was an explosion which rocked the building we were in. His mother had to take him to hospital in a makeshift pram, but he died soon after.

Onkel Karl came from Postelberg one day with some other men. They had to clean out the latrine and build a bigger one, as far as I remember. This latrine, used by old and young, sick and well, side by side, was one sea of worms. Karl's expression was half mad, with big, bulging eyes, and the whole man was hardly recognizable as Karl. He only gave us the briefest of accounts of what had happened in Postelberg. I knew nothing about it until much later, but wondered what could have happened to him. These men did not sleep at our camp, they were stationed in town.

After a fortnight in the camp in an impossible situation, people were asked, if any wanted to leave for an unknown destination. My mother volunteered. She said that if we stayed here much longer, we would become skeletons and have lice. She would rather go anywhere than stay here. Tante Marie was allowed to go with us. Most people did not respond to leave under escort for fear of being killed. After we left, 76 children died there in five days. Lists made of victims from Saaz, Postelberg and surrounding villages showed that 1,585 men, women and children were murdered just after World War II. Herr Steigenhöfer from our house, a socialist, had been clubbed to death in Postelberg.

On 28th June, the "first transport", as it was called, left the camp. We walked past our house, through the avenue with the 'tree roofs'[1], past the cinema and the Lauben (arcades) of the market square for the last time. Now we would have to keep these familiar and reassuring pictures of our town, only in our minds. Situations change, but our childhood memories stay the same for ever. Now, everything seemed menacing.

Herr Schmidt had come from Postelberg to the camp and was allowed to join the first transport like us (who could blame him for wanting nothing more than to get away from what he had just gone through), but his wife had to remain there, because she was a valuable worker. Frau Rauscher was sent to vegetable fields to work, like my godmother and her daughter Gerti. We spent a night in what was called the 'Glaspalast', then the first transport was led to the station and squeezed into a goods train, which had recently carried coal. The train already contained invalids from the First and Second World Wars. The residents of the old people's home were also with us. In the station was a train which had wounded German soldiers on board. It had been standing there for two days without attention. The carriages of our train had no roofs, so that the sparks of the funnel, (which looked like glow worms in the night), burnt holes in us and our precious clothes; my mother sat on her rucksack and we sat between her legs covered with the one blanket we had brought.

Before the train left Saaz, a Czech tore a cross off a woman, who had been decorated with this award by Hitler for producing so many children. What was she going to do with them now, not knowing where her husband was, whether he was dead or alive, and being left in the dark about where she was going and what was to happen to her? Where was the wall that we had built around ourselves like an impregnable fortress, with Hitler and his men as guards and protectors? Can any of us ever be sure of security of any kind, however much we work towards it, and in whatever way we think we might gain it? In the dimness of the light, after having been held up behind Komotau for a long while, and with the monotonous rhythm of the train bumping over the tracks, our minds perceived a glimmer of truth, maybe not bigger than a grain of sand. There was bitterness, hatred and confusion, but there was also a spark of an awakening reality stirring us to the core, although there were many unpalatable facts about our Reich to be revealed.

The next day, the train stopped at Obergeorgenthal, where everyone had to alight. From there began the long steep climb across the Erzgebirge mountain range (Ore mountains) that separates Czechoslovakia from Germany (Saxony).

---

[1] The arch made from joining tree branches.

Everyone started to walk, carrying their few belongings as well as they could. The scenery was breathtaking, and had it not been for the heartbreak of seeing so many people unable to cope with their situation, I would have enjoyed myself on that first day. I saw much more impressive 'big green roofs' here than in Saaz. There was a road cutting through a mixed forest, which could pride itself with the lightest green tree tops that met above our heads.

There we saw a professor's wife who cried and broke down. But no one had time to console her, because if you did not hurry, there would be no room to sleep at the next place. It was quite clear by now what the punishment for us was: Expulsion! We could not all be thrown out at once, anyway. That would have been impracticable for the Czech authorities. Also it had not been made legal yet.

We were the lucky ones, indeed, but we did not know it as our compatriots 'at home' were facing more torture.

A little wicker pram stood sadly by the roadside. Tante Marie went up to it.

"Look at this pram, Peppi, there doesn't seem anything wrong with it. Why don't we put our stuff in it?"

No sooner had we done this, did we realize the unreliability of its wheels. Every five metres or so, they would come off unless Liesl and I, on either side of the pram, banged them back into place with a big stone.

We stopped at a place called Gebirgsneudorf, and were led into a big hall, which was not big enough to contain all, who had managed to arrive there, comfortably. We slept like sardines on the floor. There was a frightening moment before we fell asleep. All the doors and windows were locked, but no one dared mention their anxiety in case panic broke out for no reason at all. Everyone looked scared and only the strenuous march, lack of food and the burden of pushing the pram load, made sleep possible in the end.

CHAPTER 37
For whom the bell tolls

The next morning, the partisans boiled some maize in an old German army pot, and my father and comrades were given their first food. It was very hot now, and the dust rose high as they were given the order to march from the Austrian-Jugoslav border through the whole of Jugoslavia to Belgrade, eventually joined by many others. On the way, they were given nothing to eat and had no opportunity for washing and seldom for drinking. On Easter Sunday, the bells rang wherever they passed, mostly small villages. People stood, expecting them. Some jumped forward and pulled shoes and uniforms off soldiers and abused them, others stood behind a fence with drinking water and meant well. But as soon as a soldier ran over to accept the water, he was shot in the back of the neck. First the guards were on foot. As the march dragged on, they were mounted on horses. Someone demanded my father's old army boots, so that he had to walk barefoot. Many German soldiers collapsed from the heat, exhaustion, thirst and hunger. They were all shot immediately.

Where they walked, the population was very poor. It was only in Slovenia, where some Germans (from Swabia) had settled under Prinz Eugen, that the land had been made to produce enough for a decent living.

The exhausted prisoners of war arrived at Semlin, a former prison of the SS for partisans. There, within a short time, 30-50 ex-soldiers died of dysentery. In the beginning, they were only given water, which was the worst possible thing after a long march without any food and so little to drink. Opposite the prison, two big mass graves had to be dug for the numerous dead to be buried.

The camp beds in the wooden barracks could not be sat on before 10 o'clock at night. This was the rule. 'Every German is a bad German and must be destroyed' did not have to be said aloud. Every morning at 4 o'clock, the commandant in person stood the prisoners in front of the barracks, which were situated on a plateau, on one side of which was a sheer drop. Fortunately, the weather was good, but if anyone collapsed near a big, Russian-style latrine with a few holes in cement, he was pushed down the sheer drop and red earth, (which was prevalent there) was thrown on top of him. This happened before the mass graves were dug.

It must have been a sort of rollcall that went on for hours, as concentration camp victims had had to experience. My father was horrified. The red earth appeared in his dreams and he was determined not to collapse. He noticed that the ones who drank the most, died. Dysentery produces an unquenchable thirst, so it was easy to give in to the compulsion to drink water. When the first morning's bread rations were handed out, my father would chew a crust for as long as he could, thus producing saliva, which eased the thirst. Had he not done this, he would have accompanied those who died like flies there.

He was there for a very long four weeks. One day, he was put in a convoy to Mitrowitza, a notorious prison that had held many partisans behind a high barbed wire fence. The sleeping quarters consisted of round tents with a pointed top in the middle. The soldiers lay inside on the floor in the shape of a star.

Again, dysentery resolved the space problem in a very short time. There was a German soldier amongst them who was a grave digger. He dug a grave for each body, and a doctor made a list of the dead. The partisans wanted to shoot him, but the guards, who were Mongolians, would not allow it. There were also Serbs as guards at times. Some guards fled to the mountains one day.

Rumour had it that an old German farmer from Yugoslavia had been nailed to his own barn door when he refused to be interned. These indigenous Germans (incl. woman and children) had to pull buildings down and erect them again, so it was said. These rumours reached them via prisoners who had to help with the harvest. Only a few could go due to most soldiers' unfitness; my father helped with the potato crop. The fields were covered with weeds. He put some potatoes in his pocket like everybody else. One soldier was caught in the act and was going to be shot. After a while, the overseer reconsidered his decision, probably because he realized he would have to shoot everyone who came from Mitrowitza, and he needed the workers.

Needless to say that the dead were buried naked, as there were no clothes available when one outfit fell to pieces. On May 8th, they were told the war had ended, although it had been fairly obvious, anyway. What my father did not know was the fate in store for us and himself.

From Mitrowitza, a whole company (comprised of many different ones) were transported to a small, deserted German village, where they stayed for the winter outside the village in an open barn. It had a roof, but was open all round. They had to sleep on the ground, with a fire in the middle to keep them from freezing to death at night. There were no blankets or shoes. My father made himself some wooden soles, which he tried, somehow, to attach to his feet. When he had found some bits of old leather for straps, he could not fix them on the soles for lack of nails. Eventually he found some short ones, but they kept coming out. He then found some old rags, which he tied round the wooden soles and his feet. The whole undertaking was rather unsatisfactory, but he had something on his feet at last. No one had socks by this time.

One of them cooked a thin maize soup without salt every morning at 3.30. Some maize bread was also handed out, which would turn mouldy if kept overnight. The rations only just prevented their sudden death. Instead, the decline in health was gradual, but unavoidable. Those who had survived the first weeks had already been seriously weakened and suffered from dysentery. Now, they were forced to fell enormous trees in the forests with no mechanical aids such as an electric saw. Everything had to be done manually. Being a lumberjack requires great strength and skill, which they lacked totally in their present emaciated state. But somehow they battled on like mountaineers who cannot afford to renounce their efforts halfway up the cliff face, although they knew that a gust of wind or icy crevice, rockfall, etc., could blow them out of existence. The wood they made available was essential, especially in Germany, and exporting it there brought badly needed foreign currency. The march to the forests took three-quarters of an hour. For as long as the weather permitted, my father went barefoot. Their underclothes had been thrown away a long time ago; their uniform was full of lice and becoming threadbare. They were walking scarecrows by now.

One day, the order came for the ones who had survived the winter, to go to a particular farmhouse and lie down on the floor while a woman doctor, who handed out some medication, examined them. They were allowed to stay there for a few days. The idea must have been to enable the release of some PoWs from Yugoslavia before they all died. They had been prisoners for one year now, and out of four companies, only one remained.

Their own group had dwindled down to a handful of people. Those few were now placed on a goods train transporting coal. Lying on the coal in March 1946, they reached Jesenice on the Austrian border once again. From there, they were squeezed into an American Red Cross train with two people to one bed.

My father was placed in a bed with his friend, the Austrian cook who had prepared their miserable maize soup for so long, when he did not even have salt to make it even slightly tasty - a terrible humiliation for a cook, but greater for this one, because he knew that people were dying from malnutrition and exposure. As the train moved very slowly into Austria, this native man in his thirties died quietly next to my father in the secure knowledge that he was back in his homeland.

CHAPTER 38
Young Karl's confrontation with stark realities

They were led to Bresnice prison, thirty to a cell, with no thought of sleep for three days and nights, after which they were told of a transfer to Prague, from where they were promised they would be released. No one believed this. Karl and another man from Saaz wanted to escape, come what may.

In front of the Hybernce station waiting room in Prague, they were sorted into three groups. Six of them had belonged to the SS; (Karl had advised one of them to remove the threads which had fastened the SS eagle on his sleeve, but the man did not care, and went on picking lice) they were led away by Czech and Russian soldiers.

The middle group was classified as Army, and interned. The last group consisted of Austrians and civilians. Karl was lucky to be placed in this last group, thanks to his clothes.

While the army group was put on lorries, the six SS men, including a 17 year-old, who had joined four weeks before the end of the war, were beaten by civilians and guards alike (with guns) until the blood began to flow.

The civilians, who had been herded on a lorry by now, saw a drunk Russian soldier order the SS men to quickly get washed. As the lorry started moving, Karl observed the six candidates walk towards a park. The Russian told them to put their arms up and run. Suddenly he told them to stop ("Stoy!") and at the same time let his machine gun loose on them, so that they were all killed in an instant. Karl thought to himself that, in Prague, torture and certain subsequent death would have awaited them.

In a former riding school in Prague, Karl spent the first night with women, children, old people and soldiers, trying to find a dry spot (it had begun to rain) under a roof which resembled a sieve. Up to that point, Karl had been the proud owner of a change of underclothes and a blanket, but in the morning, all this had disappeared.

Every night after dark, both Czech and Russian guards strolled through the big hall, taking a pair of boots off an old man, a watch off a protesting old woman, dragging screaming girls away from their mothers and out of the hall. No woman was safe, but young girls were preferable. The food for the day consisted of twice 50g bread, a cup of malt coffee in the morning and an onion soup at midday.

This went on for three weeks, until one day, they were ordered to stand in rows. A doctor inspected their arms for SS tattoo marks, and also checked to see whether they were fit enough to be used as a workforce. Karl qualified for the latter. On a lorry, they were taken back to the station again. This time, they were merely spat at and verbally abused. A train took them to an exclusively rural area. At the little station where Karl had to get off, ten to fifteen people were put on waiting tractors or wagons pulled by oxen. They all went off in different directions, bigger loads to bigger villages.

Karl immediately became more optimistic; a bit of freedom of movement, fresh air, the prospect of plenty of fresh food and healthy exercise. Darkness fell, but the journey on the rubber-wheeled trailer continued till after eleven o'clock at night, when they arrived in the village square of Melnicky Vtelno.

Although Karl was greatly relieved to be out in the country, in familiar surroundings once more, what he had witnessed and experienced had made him fear the future, and mistrust new surroundings and people.

Now, they were made to stand under lights, so that the farmers could take their pick. Karl, who was now nearly twenty-eight, and a forty year old man from Hamburg were selected by a thirtyfive year old farmer who asked them if they knew anything about farming. Karl answered in Czech that he had grown up in the country, but was not a farmer. They were given milk and bread and shown their straw beds with no bedlinen. The lack of bedclothes did not bother them, of course, after what they had been through, but exhausted as they were, they could not manage to go to sleep.

Early in the morning, an old man hobbled in and told them in broken German that if they worked well and fast, they would be well treated. They had breakfast standing in the hall, but Karl was contented. He knew what to expect, and what was expected of him. His fears vanished. He wanted to do his best, as did Richard, his comrade. They worked out in the fields with a retarded farm hand, and the farmer's mother-in-law, who used to run a shop. When she heard of Karl having managed a fairly big shop with assistants, she became quite friendly towards him.

The soil there was rich, and yielded beautiful wheat and enormous sugar beets at harvest time. Now the fields had to be nurtured, sowed, weeded, aerated, and everywhere Karl looked, it was mostly German labour providing the necessary work free of charge, but not free of will.

Ironically, they had been given the former ration cards for Jews, but when nobody looked, the farmer's wife would give them extra titbits to eat. The German labour force was not allowed to work without a Czech 'watch dog', someone who saw to it that the work was properly done, and that nobody escaped.

Karl found himself evermore involved in interpreting between Czechs and Germans, listening to both sides of the story. He was inclined to think: "Never mind the Nationals, the red partisans who want all Germans behind bars, or at least to have them under their thumb for the moment. There's a row of cherry trees on either side of the road, the grass is fresh and fragrant, the air is clean, and I'm neither hungry nor afraid."

He got used to farming quickly, enjoyed it and was grateful.

It must be said that Karl had always been a natural-born optimist, which can spur people on under the most extreme conditions. Indeed, half the battle is won, if one is so blessed. But Karl went further, to the point of denial. He did not want to believe in the fundamental lowness of man, if given a chance. If he had seen the set-up of a concentration camp under the SS, he would have erased it from his memory and believed it had been a nightmare. He looked the other way, believing that people would behave differently under different circumstances. For the moment, he was grateful, and had goodwill.

The catholic festival of Fronleichman came. It had always been a great day in Gerten, and something to look forward to now. Here was something they had in common; also, after the chaos and misery of the war and its aftermath of shock and anxiety, which brought home to him the apparent fruitlessness and evil dominance in life, Karl longed for permanence and eternal values, for strength that did not exist for its own sake.

They were not allowed to join in the devotion or festivities, but helped to make the village festive and prepare it for the big day. Karl cut more grass for a green, natural carpet in front of the farmer's altar. This carpet extended to the next farmer's altar, and so on through the whole of the village.

Suddenly a partisan came to take Karl and Richard through the village to a villa, and locked them in a cellar there. A guard with a red armband outside the building frowned at them as they were pushed in, as though it was their fault that he was missing the celebrations. As they felt their way down the cellar steps in the dark, they heard crying and sobbing. In the cellar on some damp straw sat some elderly women and men, and two young girls. The men clenched fists and ground their teeth. An old man with a leg prosthesis complained through the girls'wailing that, after the chicanery in Prague, they were trying to do the same here.

"Can't they leave us alone at last?" he said. "Look through this window." He pointed towards a little window at the top of the room, covered with spider webs. The procession was seen moving down the road accompanied by music and hymns. "I bet most of those people don't know we're here, and even if they did, they couldn't do anything about it, and the ones who do know, don't care. And yet we say we believe in the same God. They're lucky to be allowed to worship in this way," and after a pregnant pause: "Maybe one day, they'll be glad to have the Germans back as equals."

For weeks, they were taken only to the farm to work there. Every night, their cellar prison awaited them. On 8th August 1945, the deportation of Germans from eastern European countries (which had accepted help from Russia in liberating them from the Fascist regime and oppression) was made legal at Potsdam; a poster by the First National Council of Czechoslovakia (Erster Volksrat) appeared:

'To all Germans: Everyone must be in his quarters by 8 pm. Patrols (Razias) will be held. No more than three Germans are allowed to gather. No beer or other drinks are allowed to be sold to Germans. Extra food rations must not be given. Wages will not be paid to Germans, but 200 Kronen must be paid monthly to the National Council (Nationalrat) for male Germans, and 300 Kronen for female Germans.'

By now, Karl was very frustrated. He felt that the cows were far better treated than any German. He missed his own profession and social life. Sometimes, he would get up at the customary time of 4.30am, and scream and kick at the docile cows lying mournfully on the urine-drenched straw.

Richard got ill. His face and legs were so swollen that anyone would have to come to the conclusion that he suffered from heart trouble. His illness was initially ignored. Germans did not usually have the privilege of treatment when ill, but now more Czech doctors started to help them, following their Hippocratic oath and conscience. "If we are going to help the sick, it must be all the sick, regardless of creed, colour or nationality.' This notion grew stronger after they had witnessed the brutality and violence inflicted on the Germans nationwide. By 'nationwide', I do not mean that every Czech took part in this sudden and long, drawn-out slaughter, but that it took place almost everywhere in the German borderlands of Czechoslovakia.

Eventually, ministers from other countries started to investigate for themselves, and the Red Cross tried to alleviate the suffering with essential medicines, dried milk powders etc, so that at least the small children had a chance of survival.

The British MP, R.R. Stokes wrote a letter to the *Manchester Guardian* in October 1945, relating some impressions gathered on his visit to Czechoslovakia in September 1945. He actually refers to the German work force, from the 51 camps of the kind he visited, as 'slaves,' who, at the slightest sign of dissatisfaction at selection time each morning, were beaten up mercilessly. He mentions that all of them, who found it at all possible, wanted to work for the prospect of more, and better food. Their normal food ration, which he does not deem sufficient to keep body and soul together, was around 750 calories, which he says was lower than at Belsen. He concludes:

"The civil servants (officials) who gave me the information regarding the quantities did so without shame and I would be interested to know if Dr Benes is aware of it that these terrible things are happening. As he was absent from Prague, I could unfortunately not see him, but I have left reports with the Foreign and Home Office."

Earlier in this account, he mentions that when he told the Home Office about this matter, an investigation was promised.

This letter shows quite obviously how little anyone knew, and still do not know what 'game' was being played. It is clear now that Dr Benes knew; indeed he was the originator of this well-prepared plan, which he had presented to the Western powers at Potsdam. The only stipulation made from their quarters was that the evacuation should be done 'under humane conditions,' but this was never monitored for the simple reason that nobody could have prevented or stopped the violation of this 'clause.'

In fact, as early as 5th May 1942, a letter was written by Jan Masaryk to Max Weinreich in New York City, who was research director of the Yiddish Scientific Institute there, assuring him that only Germans would be "got rid off" in Czechoslovakia, not any Jews.[1] He writes in glowing terms about his boss Benes, which indicates Benes initiated this plan.

Stalin stood in the background, smiling his inscrutable smile, which facilitated the transfer of many German prisoners from Russia to Czech camps with even less food.

R.R. Stokes mentions some of these victims in his letter to the *Guardian*. They were Sudeten German Social Democrats, and an old Russian professor of dramatic art who was nearly blind. He had left Russia in 1911 and settled in Yugoslavia; when, on visiting an eye specialist in Vienna, he was put in prison, and now, he and his wife were detained by Czech officials, probably for their White Russian nationality.

Karl did the heavy work for Richard, until the latter's feet were so swollen that they would no longer fit into his clogs. Eventually, he was sent to a hospital in Melnik, where there were a few beds for Germans in the corridor. After a fortnight, Richard came back, apparently healthy, but was told to rest.

By now, the harvest was in full swing and the Germans were allowed to stay at the farms, even at night. For the whole day and half the night, all people, tractors, horses and oxen worked overtime. Richard felt he could not comply with the doctor's orders to rest, so he worked like everybody else. After a short time, he was hardly recognizable. He looked bloated and grotesque. The farmer took him back to the hospital, and in four days he was dead.

Karl wrote a letter to Richard's sister in Hamburg, making sure that she wouldn't live in the hope of him ever returning, like so many thousands who would always hope for their missing relatives to come back.

After the harvest, when work resumed its normal pace, the young Germans were determined to have some kind of social life. They started meeting secretly at weekends and on special occasions like birthdays, and on Sunday afternoons. Old and young met together at an old, isolated house that now housed a German family from Deutsch-Gabel. Twelve other families had been brought from there to Melnicky Vtelno to be unpaid servants for the farmers. Karl's farmer Cervinka had twelve such people working for him now.

---

[1] But I have heard of Jews who lost everything, the same as the Sudeten Germans with no compensation.

Karl acted as interpreter. The best off were the German children. They did not have to work, and as there was no schooling for them, they did not have to learn anything either.

One of these families were the Simmlers. He was sixty-five, badly asthmatic and a perfectionist. If the barn floor had been swept, and he spotted one remaining piece of straw, he would stoop down elegantly and pick it up with great élan, asthma or no asthma. He had been a tax inspector. His wife, who had snow-white hair, thick glasses and a goitre, could not get used to farm work. Her, her daughter's and youngest son's fierce tongues were feared, as they could give hell to anyone they cared to focus on. The couple had three grandchildren. One boy, Heinz, had learned commerce for two years, but was now an apprentice to a Czech plumber who treated him well.

Autumn set in, wet and cold. The women (mostly German) took the leaves off the sugar beet. After these enormous roots were dug up, they were carried by oxen to the 5km distant factory. Karl talked to the factory director one day, who was proud of being a partisan. "I killed sixteen homeward-bound German soldiers just after the war to free my country." The gory details were too gruesome to mention.

Winter had always been an easy time in Gerten, as far as work was concerned, and Karl anticipated it with longing. Cervinka did not have to pay the government during winter, but, as he saw it, had to feed his workers for nothing. So he provided work. Trees had to be felled, which the women had to chop up at home, providing enough wood for three winters.

Karl made use of his hobby, ie. repairing faulty wires, irons, hotpoints, thus putting himself in the farmer's wife's good books.

One Saturday evening, when the youngsters met up as usual to sing and dance together in secret, a patrol from the Naradny-Vybor turned up at the Cervinka house to check if the Germans were all present. They found Karl missing. After two hours, they called again and found Karl fast asleep. He always sneaked home clandestinely in the dark. They asked him where he had been. He mumbled something about a place with a carved heart in the yard, but they were suspicious.

It was now early March 1946. Still, the evacuation of thousands of Germans continued. People from the camps had no clothes by now. The ones they had worn for nearly a year were in shreds. Parcels from abroad with used clothes were distributed, one set of clothes for each person, if they were lucky. Wild rumours spread. One was that they would be allowed home soon, another popular one was that on 15th, there would be a transfer to Germany.

Finally, Karl got a letter from his parents in North Bavaria. They had had to leave Gerten with 50kg of hand luggage each, their feather beds and all essential crockery by means of a train journey directly to their destination in Bavaria. Everything had been much easier for them, although for a year they had lived in fear of what was in store for them. They had to leave Gerten on 26th February 1946 with Anna, their son Emil's wife. She helped her mother-in-law with the luggage, because my grandfather, now 78, had gone straight into hospital at Forchheim in West Germany. Her husband Emil was lucky to be a prisoner of war in Italy. He had never asked for much, and later looked back nostalgically to his time in Italy. He had even been up Mount Vesuvius, escaping the turmoil and hell of post-war Czechoslovakia, of which he knew nothing.

Tante Antsch and her five children, (the youngest being only a year old, whom his father, now a PoW in Russia, had never seen) were somewhere near Nuremberg, called Grossengsee[1]. Traudl, the youngest daughter of my grandparents, finished up in a little village, called Unter-Ehring, in the richest agricultural part of Lower Bavaria (die Kornkammer Bayern's). This village consisted of six farms. Traudl, her husband Otto and the boys[2] lived in two small rooms in a tiny house which had been built for the retirement of the farmer (the bigger farms could afford to do this).

Where the others were, no one knew.

Now, something happened to Karl that is one of the mysteries in life. A Czech man who knew Karl as a boy, when he had worked at Pladen, and was now a policeman in Melnicky Vtelno, told him that all former prisoners of war were going to be sent, as slave labour, to work in the coal mines; in Karl's case, it would probably be Brüx.

"You know what to do, don't you?" He winked at Karl out of the corner of his eye. Karl knew all right.

Why had the policeman given him this hint? Why did some Czech people choose to be unpopular amongst their own kind for helping Germans? Why had thousands of people risked their lives in the war, hiding hunted people or helping them escape? (I refer to individuals rather than whole organisations). One could give different reasons for this, but these would, no doubt, vary from case to case. The great force behind it all must be the individual's realisation that we are all in the same boat, as far as life as a whole is concerned. The real issue must not be avoided and we should not deceive ourselves or waste time, building an artificial security barrier around ourselves. We all know this subconsciously, but only when we are face to face with it, do we make a

---

[1] She never saw her husband again; my mother saw him last as a Russian prisoner of war in Saaz.

[2] one of them had been born just before the end of the war. There was no fresh milk during the transport to Bavaria and he nearly died from the strong tinned milk that she had acquired on the "black market".

decision. Most of the time, we are too afraid to make the right one, and this makes us feel guilty and unhappy, which may spill over to others. The avoidance of responsibility, (which may be cumbersome and even harmful to our lives) can be seen in marriages, in the task of bringing up children, in one's work, and in some people, who have to make big decisions for the common good. Personal pride and brinkmanship take principal roles in life. These are felt to be attacked from all sides at all times. Partial, twisted truth to oneself and others is therefore seen as a necessary defence mechanism. The consequences are dire. But it does not have to be like this.

Karl now decided to act upon his "enemy-friend's" warning.

CHAPTER 39
Franz adapts himself

Franz made his way (on his newly-acquired bike) from the Danube up to the north of Bavaria to Bayreuth, and on to Birkenhammer, where he encountered Russians for the first time.

On entering Czechoslovakia, he expected to see a more encouraging picture in Bohemia than the ruins he had encountered in Germany. The truth is always hard to face.

When he arrived at his uncle's surgery (Dr Beer), it was full of women who wanted to know if they were pregnant, and, if so, what could be done about it. They had been raped by Russian soldiers, and found their ordeal difficult enough to come to terms with, but the prospect of having an unwanted baby in these harrowing times filled them with despair. Dr Beer was powerless to help them.

When Franz arrived at Lauterbach (my grandmother's birthplace), he discovered that it was occupied by the American army.[1] A piano stood in the street, black and mournful; but not for long. Franz had never been able to see a piano without playing it. Soon everyone gathered round him to listen to his singing and playing. He stayed there a few days and saw how some women made close relationships with Americans for the prospect of better food in greater quantities. One of his relatives had followed suit.

---

[1] only for a short time until they had to make way for the Russian army, who, in turn, left it to the Czechs.

2 Whoever was captured by the Russians, was transported to Russia as workforce, mostly never to be seen again. Very few survived there. One of them was Herbert's uncle Hans. Hitler had also given the order to kill Russian officers instead of imprisoning them.

Between Eger and Falkenau he encountered about 200,000 German soldiers including BdM people, who had been American prisoners of War during the fortnight the Americans had stayed in Bohemia. They had left these PoWs to the incoming Russians with the result that their fate was then sealed.[2] Between Pestiek and Trnovan (near Saaz - two German villages in spite of their Czech sounding names), Franz witnessed a German boy being shot by a Czech. Franz knew the boy's mother. He pedalled on, full of foreboding.

In Saaz, at home with his family at last[1], it was the same picture as anywhere else at the time. Confusion and tragedy reigned supreme. Some Germans who were married to Czechs, also became Czech. One such person was elevated to become the Mayor of Saaz. For the moment, the Russians dominated the scene. A tall, handsome Russian major, who spoke good German, was Commandant. Franz went to the town hall and asked if any musicians were needed for entertaining the officers. He was accepted as a pianist and played at the 'Altes Rathaus' (the Old Townhall-Café) for the Russians.

On 3rd June 1945, when all men were herded together from all corners of Saaz, and mounted police paced up and down the Ringplatz, a woman came running to warn Franz of the imminent danger. This was only possible, because his father-in-law's house stood isolated outside the town walls. When they came to take him, he had already gone into hiding. Once again, Don Juan had escaped the worst, thanks to his lady friends.

But when the time for registration at the SS-Kaserne came (13th June 1945), his luck had run out. He and his family had to go, but his Communist mother in-law was allowed to stay at home while his father in-law was once again in a camp as he had been under the Hitler Regime. If they had been Socialists[2], it would not have helped them now, but they were known as anti-Fascists, which sometimes helped.

At the camp, the worst thing that could have happened to Franz (at least, as far as he was concerned) occurred. He was made to remove a dead cow, which had been lying in a room of the SS camp for days or even weeks, with the help of two other men. Long before they even reached this room, the pestilential stench took their breath away, but when faced with the cadaverous remains, including the foul, ripped-out intestines, he felt that Nemesis had finally caught up with him. Even with a handkerchief over his mouth and nose, Franz found the task in hand

---

[1] comprising his young wife Trudl, his 2-year old son Peter, his 2-months old son Franz and his mother in-law Frau Kühnl.

[2] The socialist, Herr Steigenhöfer from our house, was clubbed to death at Postelberg for professing his political stance.

quite impossible. They had to dig a hole, and drag the slimy body out to bury it. Franz had always been adept at avoiding unpleasant work, but this time there was no way out of the situation. He told a friend who had to do jobs in town, to go to the town hall and report that the pianist they had engaged was imprisoned in the Kaserne.

He did not really hold out much hope of a miraculous rescue, or sudden demand for his release. But again, luck was on his side. He and his family had been in the camp for two or three days, when a Russian official arrived on a motorbike and collected Franz to come and play music at the cafe 'Zum Löwen' in town. His family was also released and allowed home. Although the marauding Russian soldiers had disappeared from the streets since the Czechs had begun their 'revolution,' Russian officers were still celebrating the end of the war and the fact that they were far away from 'little Father Stalin', as they called him, who had their every step monitored when they were in Russia.

While Franz and family had been at the camp, his wife wondered how her mother was getting on at home on her own. She wore a red armband, so as to be recognised as a Communist, but for some time now she had been behaving strangely. The Russians coming and going, people committing suicide, the present terrible, the future unthinkable; all this had been too much for her. People said that for weeks, she had been shaking all over. She would stare into space, and no longer seemed to be in touch with reality. She could not face what she was experiencing and put an end to it all. When Franz and his family returned home, they could not find her anywhere in the house. They searched in the big vegetable garden, where they found her dead in the well; she had drowned herself. Her daughters, Trudl and sister were heartbroken.

Franz continued to play the piano and accordion for the Russians, so that Trudl was alone at home with her thoughts and fears, caring for her two little boys.

The Russian soldiers who guarded the Kettenbrücke (suspension bridge) across the Eger, which Franz had to cross after work, were bored to tears by now. They were missing their families and homeland. There was no entertainment of any kind, and heavy drinking was no fun anymore. So, one day, they invented a new game, in which Franz figured quite heavily, although he did not know it yet.

With his slight limp, he crossed the bridge one early morning, tired from playing through the long night. He passed the guards and found nothing unusual. Suddenly, in the stillness of daybreak, shots rang out. The bullets whizzed past him, missing him by inches. He began to run, feeling his heart in his mouth. He noticed that no bullet went higher than his knees.

"So, they're just having a bit of fun with me," he thought. Finally, he had to hop and jump to avoid the dangerous mini rockets that were coming his way relentlessly, and at terrifying speed. He heard the laughter of the guards as he left the bridge and ran toward the fields and gardens. All was quiet again there.

For days, they played this game with him. He would pass them, and all was well until seconds later when the salvo of bullets whooshed past him again as anticipated. The trouble was that there was no other way home than over this bridge. He could not swim, but even if he had been able to cross the Eger somehow, it would have been foolish to do so. Anyone doing something as suspicious as that could have been shot without warning.

Eventually he played for the Czechs, with Czech civilians at the Cafe Altes Rathaus, where he had played when he was younger. He earned 2,000 Kronen a month.

On 26th February 1946, he and his family were deported as part of the process of the German expulsion that was still going on. By that time, they were allowed to take more of their possessions with them, ie. feather beds, not as in 1945, when we were only allowed hand luggage. Also, they were transported by train as far as Furth in Bavaria, from where they made their way to a refugee camp in Günzburg - the town he had passed through as a hitchhiker in the Spring of 1945. They arrived there on his 36th birthday, the leap year day of 29th February 1946

By now, these refugee camps were all over Germany, East and West. They were hastily set up in converted schools, inns, community halls; in short, any relatively large and available building, mostly unsuitable for the purpose. Germany, through the heavy bombing raids by the British and Americans - intensified in the last year of the war, had 8 million homeless and 2 million maimed.

The strange thing was that these camps called themselves 'Flüchtlingslager' (refugee camps) and those inside them were, and are to this day, called 'refugees,' people who flee from danger. The Germans who had come from East Prussia, the Memel(land), and part of Silesia, from Lithuania, Estonia, etc., were refugees. They fled, because they had been made 'stateless', whereas the Sudeten Germans from Czechoslovakia and Silesia were deportees. They had had no choice. They had been deported, exiled, expelled, etc. to where they did not want to go and with no basic provision for their survival. Who wants to be expelled into utter chaos with nothing? Germany was a wasteland with people living under the heaps of rubble everywhere and hanging onto any means of transport as there were too many people inside. Nobody knew where to go. They all thought that it might be better somewhere else within Germany, until many gave the search up and decided to apply for a transit to Canada, Australia, America etc. Canada was the favourite.

For Franz, and 15 million refugees and deportees who had arrived in devastated Germany in 1945, a new phase in life had begun. Franz for one was not going to look back, but would look for the many opportunities, life has to offer.

CHAPTER 40
The new life

On the way from Gebirgsneudorf to Deutschneudorf, my mother and her sister Marie worried increasingly about my sister. They even put her in the little pram we had found for a while, but my sister refused to stay in it, not just because the sight of a thirteen year-old beanpole in a wicker pram was ludicrous, but also because the wheels continued to come off every few minutes.

Some amputees suffered from soreness caused by their protheses; in severe cases the blood trickled down into their artificial legs. Eventually, a lorry arrived with some old people on top. It picked up one or two of the worst hit. My mother tried to get Liesl onto one, but it seemed impossible. There was simply no room.

We stopped by a brook to refresh ourselves. My mother produced a glass jar of our preserved pet rabbit from a bag, and this time I was not the least bit squeamish about eating it. The trouble was that there was not enough to go round between the four of us. We had some water to drink from the sparkling murmuring brook and felt grateful for our food and drink. Somewhere along this journey, my mother told us to stay put in a meadow while she rushed to the next place to secure a nightshelter for us. She feared that by the time all of us arrived, there would be no more room. I cannot remember this, but I am told that both Liesl and myself began to cry after my mother failed to return within a reasonable time. Tante Marie tried to calm us down, but we were not happy until we saw my mother's face again, worried as it was. In Deutschneudorf, a miserable, filthy hut, which had housed some French Resistance fighters, greeted us. We had to sleep on the floor. The beds had probably been removed due to vermin. The women cleaned the floor with fir branches. There was little thought of sleep.

The next day my sister's feet hardly fitted into her shoes. They bulged menacingly over the edges, which upset my mother and aunt even more. I thought they looked unusual, but failed to see what all the fuss was about. Liesl told them not to worry, and so we walked all day again to another place, used for our accommodation, called Nenningmühle.

This was a disused mill, and looked promising. It was reasonably clean and had beds. All of us had a bed to ourselves. In the middle of the night I woke up scratching myself here, there and everywhere. I called my mother who pulled the bedclothes off me. There, in the light that had not been switched off, black bugs were crawling on my bed and all over my body. My mother screamed and began hitting them. I knocked the 'beasts' off myself onto the bed and helped to wipe them out of existence. Meanwhile, everyone else examined their bed, but nobody was quite as 'riddled' as I was.

The next morning, everyone set off as usual. By now, the walking routine had been established and everyone pushed on as a matter of course. Sore or swollen feet, sickness, disability, raw flesh, crippled toes, aching corns and bunions had to be endured. Liesl's breathing was getting more and more laboured and the way seemed endless. What mattered now was to get out of this hell. We were still in Czechoslovakia, where orders still had to be obeyed. After trotting on for half an hour or longer, I watched an old couple ahead come to a sudden standstill. Concerned, the woman looked over at her husband. "What's wrong, love? Why did you stop?" The old man mumbled: "I left my pipe in that mill." Without another word, they turned round to go all the way back to Nenningmühle to find the precious pipe!

Now, there was hardly any incline. From Nenningmühle on, we were made to go backwards and forwards several times, probably just for the fun of it. As we reached the border, all the exhausted travellers threw their white armbands, marking them as Germans in Czechoslovakia, away; glad to be out of that hell that had been our homeland. We were handed over to the Saxons as ' people who had refused to work'.

Eventually we reached Flöha in Saxony. I recollect, Liesl being transported on a lorry for part of the way.

After we had reached the other side of the mountains, my mother found a truck driver who gave us a lift to a town in Saxony, called Freiberg. She had to pay him 20 Reichsmarks for it. We had not been allowed to take any money, jewellery, or valuables of any kind. Some bank books and certificates, my mother had left in Tante Marie's house before the end of the war, some things she had tried to smuggle out unsuccessfully, but no one had checked her suspender belt, inside which she had put some cash. She had withdrawn the last remaining money from the bank as late as 22nd May, 1945 (Reichsbahn Spar-und Darlehenskasse Dresden 69258, starting with RM 261.95, on 2nd November 1942). It was only RM 40,-; all the money that was left in the account, except for 64 Reichsfennig. It was little enough, but now it was a godsend. She now had RM 20,- left.

Freiberg was and is to this day a German treasure; an old, interesting town with many sights worth visiting. It had been a silver mining town and could be proud of its imposing ancient buildings and churches. The cathedral's portal, die Goldene Pforte (the golden, arched gate), and the beautiful pulpit in the shape of a tulip were famous all around. Some houses had been bombed, but on the whole, the town made a favourable impression on anyone who had the money and means to explore and enjoy it. We were not in that category. We were seen as 'the last straw' in East Germany's present situation. After the last disastrous war, the indigenous population of Saxony were now communists overnight under the Russian Regime, (the grimmest of the Allied Zones), whether they liked it or not, which meant that they had been under a dictatorship since 1933. And how long was this going to go on? Nobody knew. The indoctrination to communism was already under way.

It was now the beginning of July 1945, and nobody showed any interest in what was left of the architecture and beauty of the few towns left intact in Germany. We had finally arrived in Germany. The slogan that had caught on under Henlein rung in our ears: *'Wir wollen heim ins Reich!'* (we want to go home to the Reich). Our wish had been granted. We, the Germans that had left Germany at the request of powers who thought that we could be useful workers in Bohemia hundreds of years ago and help make it great, were now back in our original homeland. The Czechs said: "You wanted to be 'home'; we have made your wish come true." But where to go now? As before, several schools, pubs with big dance halls or any public building that the Russians had not occupied were used to provisionally accommodate us, the German-speaking 'foreigners'. And what a funny German it was. Not like theirs.

A camp called Himmelfahrtslager ('ascension camp', and how appropriate was this?) apparently had plenty of room. It was pouring with rain and we were desperate for shelter and rest after the harassment, shock and exertion of the past month. As we arrived at the door, a one-armed man appeared and told us that we could not possibly stay there. My mother and aunt tried to change his mind, pointing out that there was indeed enough room for us, but all in vain. Someone told us about a school, which had been turned into a camp for evacuees. We dragged ourselves to the Theodor Körnerschule, as it was called, and fell into a corner of one of the corridors there. The rooms could not accommodate any more people; they were full to the brim. Everyone's feet were swollen, but my sister's health had taken a serious turn for the worse. Not only were her feet and legs in bad condition, her breathing was also giving cause for concern.

We spent the first night on the floor on our one thin blanket (from our sofa at home), grateful that it was now summer. We awoke the next morning cold and ill, only to discover that the loaf of bread my mother had bought from someone with her last money for an exorbitant price had been stolen from under our noses during the night.

The following day, a few "Bürger" of Freiberg came to give us a few presents in our hour of dire need. I received a hat made from a furry, grey material with two brightly coloured rosettes on either side, so that I envisaged myself in winter looking like a mouse with lurid orange ears. I hated the thing. My mother said something about 'being thankful for small mercies' and put the monster away for when it would be needed. She also said that she could not stay in a place where your food was stolen from under your pillow and immediately corrected herself, muttering that the food had actually been the pillow itself. My aunt added that if we slept another night on the floor with no cover, we would all catch pneumonia. So off we went in search of yet another shelter. This time, we found a gymnasium, again, full of homeless evacuees. We were given a bed each with no mattress. Most of the windows were broken or missing altogether, so that in a very short time my sister contracted rheumatic fever in her joints. She had had it before, which probably accounted for her heart problems. This second occurrence, subsequently, made her heart even worse. She had to be rushed into hospital on 8th July 1945, a place of relative safety, warmth and care, if overcrowded. My mother and aunt gave a sigh of relief. My mother visited Liesl there as often as she could, which was sometimes every day. It turned out that the doctor in charge of this hospital in Freiberg was a member of Hitler's National Socialist Party[1], and all such people in public employment had to be replaced, including Nazis who had worked for the government, even railway workers and post office employees. This doctor was replaced by none other than Dr. Schally from Bad Teplitz (Spa), who had been seeing Liesl once a month for RM50 over the last few years. She was to remain in hospital for the next six months. This could not be achieved without a continuous fight on my mother's part, every time Liesl was to be released due to the shortage of hospital beds, after her acute illness had subsided.

From the Turnhalle (gym) we were moved on to a former public house with a beer garden, ironically named the Bayerischer Garten (Bavarian Garden) throughout the length of our stay there. The image evoked was one of Bavarian merriment, swinging frothy beer jugs, while singing earthy tunes in harmony. The reality was something completely different.

There was one enormous dance hall and another smaller one, both of which were full of bunk beds with straw mattresses. There was no room for anything else whatsoever. Our few belongings had to stay on the bed,

---

[1] As most Germans were, not wanting to be suspect.

and by now it was patently clear that it was every man was for himself. Nothing could be left anywhere for fear of being stolen. It was a painful adjustment that my mother had to make at the time, ie. "you can't trust anybody any more." Feeble attempts were made to hide possessions under mattresses. The alternative was to carry, whatever you held dear, with you at all times. In front of the building stood some chestnut trees in the beer garden, which must have been a nice, restful place during peace time. Now it was a yard which separated the main building from the little brick-built kitchen next to the gate. Goodness knows what it had been before it became a makeshift kitchen. The left entrance to the building led to a corridor, to the left of which were a few wholly inadequate toilets, to the right, an office, and straight on, the hall. Apart from all the bunk beds on the left, there was a row of single beds by the right wall for sick and old people, which you had to pass to get out by the back door. Where this led to, I cannot recall, except for a little room where people used to comb the lice out of their hair and generally use as a kind of private closet. It could not be locked, but at least you were not exposed to hundreds of people for a few moments. I liked being in this part of the premises, whereas I could not bear to go near the toilets, which were in a permanent unspeakable mess until my mother was 'privileged' to get the job of cleaning them regularly. As far as I can remember, there were only three toilets to so many people. The big hall must have had some more, but not ten horses could get me near that big hall. Ours was frightening enough with all those beds and occupying people, but the big hall seemed like a bees' nest to me.

It soon became clear that the single beds accommodated the dying. I remember their feverish, bewildered eyes staring around them as if to say: "What's happening to me, where am I?" Soon, the will to carry on faded, and at that stage, the mostly old and worn bodies began to disintegrate.

There was one old gentleman, who was far away from that phase. Herr Walther had white hair, a friendly face and a zither that he had carried all the way from some remote village in Czechoslovakia instead of a blanket or some underwear. And now he sat on his bed and played the most wonderful tunes. The grim hall transformed itself instantly; bent backs straightened, sunken, sallow cheeks reddened as the brilliantly clear sounds filled the hall. He also sang some simple, yet expressive songs to his accompaniments; lyrics that expressed grief, joy, exaltation over our homeland and vivid descriptions of it. One songwriter, who was particularly talented in this kind of tune was a man, colloquially known as 'Der Günther Tonl.' His name must have been Anton Günther. His songs now became increasingly popular. They had already been well known, but now his name was a legend. His most famous song was: 'S'is Feierab'nd, s'is Feierab'nd, dös Togwerk is vollbracht...' (It's the end of the day, the day's work has been done). Whenever this was sung now, all faces became devout, almost as if a hymn was being sung, and many people broke down and wept. For this reason, it could not be sung too often.

Now that we had a roof over our head, the main problem was food. It was obvious that we could not survive on the camp diet, which consisted of soup, and more soup. I had always liked soup, but this one was nothing more than water with some enormous sugar beet leaves, and the odd globule of fat floating on the surface. Lina, the camp cook, who had seen better days on the streets of Freiberg, could not even be bothered to cut the leaves up. One day we had a kind of Camembert for supper. Few had ever seen this strange cheese before. Some people threw it away, saying: "How dare they give us mouldy cheese. On top of everything else they want us to get food-poisoning." Others, like my mother cut the 'mould' away, so that there was only a morsel of cheese left. Lina and co. were probably not familiar with this cheese either, otherwise we would never have seen it; like so many other goodies that must have come occasionally from other countries via aid agencies, and which never saw the light of o u r day.

"I want to see the commandant," my mother said feebly to the one-legged man who belligerently guarded the office door by hobbling in front of it with the aid of a crutch. He had a crew cut hairstyle, and looked menacingly at the queue of people who wanted to see 'the boss', to air their feelings and ask for favours. My mother had reached the Holy Grail and was in danger of being stamped on the toes by the ever-shifting crutch. "Retour! Retour!" he screamed all day, every day. The door opened and a woman appeared with red eyes; another request had been denied. After being pushed through the door, my mother disappeared to ask the invisible power to request the favour of cleaning our halls' toilets for a few pennies; this was most graciously granted.

In order to earn some money, my mother tried to get as many jobs as possible. She cleaned and washed for people and was a general dogsbody. Money opened the door to many otherwise inaccessible doors, just as it had always done, with one difference. The likes of us, with no connections, could not get food, even with our few coins. "We shall never go begging," she would say. "I'd rather see us starve to death."

Some people sent their children out to beg. They would return with the odd potato or apple. Three bricks and a few twigs was all that was needed to bake these potatoes out in the yard. More and more of these makeshift barbecues sprang up and the smell of burnt potatoes evoked nostalgic memories later on in my life. Personally, I could see nothing wrong with begging. All you had to do was hold out your hand and look appealingly into someone's eyes. Incredibly, there were still some people with something to spare. It must be said, however, that even though some did not have enough for themselves, they could not bear the misery all around them, and it was for this reason that they shared the little they had. It was here that man rose above himself.

Once my mother had some money, the three of us ventured out one day, by train, into the nearest villages around Freiberg to buy some food. Unfortunately, everyone else had had the same idea; most of them did not have any money, but wanted to 'acquire' something edible nevertheless. So farmers did not even want to talk to us, let alone sell us something. They had lost hundreds of kilos of potatoes, cabbages etc, in fact, anything that had not been permanently fixed and could be eaten or turned into money.

The only benefit from our trip was half a cabbage. It had not really been worth the shoe soles we had wasted in the process. From a culinary point of view, it made a change from the leaf soup, although we had no means of cooking it.

"I bet you wished you could have all the food you rejected at home now," my mother said meaningfully with a sideways glance at me. I did not wet the bed anymore, which would have been a disaster under the circumstances; instead, I had acquired a nervous tic. My facial muscles would suddenly be pulled in one direction, which made me look absurd beyond belief. Tante Marie was quick to try and put a stop to this. Each time my face twitched, she slapped me across the face, so that as a consequence, the tic occurred more frequently when she was near. By now, I was the benefactor to a whole commune of lice which had taken over my hair.

One evening, as I got undressed on my top bunk bed, my mother discovered a louse on my vest near the armpit.

"Body lice now, is it?" she murmured, and her face grew dangerously red. "It'll have to go on the fire, I'm afraid; this really is the limit." She pulled the vest over my head, and I never saw it again. Of course, not long afterwards, she regretted having thrown away one of my two vests. Now I had lice in my only vest, which, with winter approaching, could not be discarded. However clean and careful you were in your personal hygiene, (despite the scarcity of water taps), the bugs were always present.

My favourite spot, apart from the closet at the camp, was a big glass lamp across the road. It belonged to a petrol station, and was one of two lamps on either side of the entrance to it. The other one was broken, but mine offered a warm shelter and a feeling of security. When I pulled my legs up, it was just big enough to house me. Most impressive was the little glass door that opened this 'sesame' and allowed the occupation of the lamp. Inside it, I was an observer, never tiring of watching life go by, close enough to be part of it, and yet separated from it. My only fear was that I might be thrown out of my newly found oasis; I would glance anxiously at the garage employee from time to time, but he pretended I did not exist, which suited me fine.

When my mother washed our few clothes, I had to guard them from being stolen. There was a big meadow nearby, on which people dried their laundry. I remember one afternoon in August or September 1945. The sun was out, and the breeze blew the clothes which hung from strings (others were just spread out on the grass); yet it took hours for these garments to dry. I had been told to keep my eyes on our few slowly drying garments. Taking my responsibility seriously, the hours dragged on, as my favourite occupation of observing life was not possible. All I was able to 'observe' were a few miserable looking clothes which showed signs of gross depreciation. I thought of school and how nice it would be to go there now. Because of my 'lousy' state, I was not allowed to attend. I would not need the toilet key now. In Saaz I did not have to ask for permission to go to the lavatory; I was allowed to just take the key from the hook and go. The functioning of my bladder had improved a lot; in spite of having had to lie on so many cold floors.

As soon as I even thought about my waterworks, I felt the urge to relieve myself. But how could I? My post could not be left, otherwise the hours I had spent 'doing my duty' would count for nothing, if anything went missing during my brief absence. I waited a little. "It's no good," I thought, "something, 'in particular', will have to be done." I spotted an old enamelled cannister, the size of a shopping bag, lying around. Oval, grey outside, speckled inside and open at the top, it seemed the ideal container for my purposes. People minded their own business, which was only natural these days, so without losing sight of the washing, I did mine.

On the whole, I was as happy as ever, or perhaps just content. Somehow I felt that the inner structure of my life had not been shaken. The outer struts and supports had suffered and some had been broken, but it was only superficial damage that had been done. My mother was always present; anything else was not so important. I also still hoped and knew somehow that my father would be found. My sister's hospitalization had once more removed the otherwise perpetual jealousy that pervaded my thinking. I did not even feel guilty about Liesl being in hospital, for the simple reason that I heard every day that it was the best thing that could have happened to her. I agreed; it was. I followed her progress with interest, and listened spellbound when my mother told us about this girl in Liesl's ward who had to have a bone behind her ear chiselled open to release the pus which had accumulated there. I was taken to see Liesl a few times after persistent demands to be able to do so. Each time I was only allowed a few minutes there, and only on condition that I wear the dreaded hat to cover my cranial residents. I would stand outside in the flower garden and marvel at the big, clean glass windows, the flowers, the general spotlessness of the hospital, and the ailments and cures of the patients.

When Liesl was due to be discharged, and the camp commandant warned my mother of our imminent transferral to another town (I think ours had only been a transit camp, but for various reasons some people could not move on. The rest did. We had been 'allowed' to stay because of Liesl's hospitalization), my mother marched to the hospital and told them that she would kill herself and us, if Liesl could not remain where she was at the moment. I know she was desperate, but, I am sure, she only said this to give Liesl the best possible chance of survival. Endowed with an exuberant nature, goodwill and an eagerness to help others, she now began to show more initiative and patience. Our lives were in her hands and she knew it. She had to think quickly and correctly and apply her newly found life- skills as the next situation required it. As they say, life is the greatest teacher. What she still lacked was humility, which removes and replaces pride. Her pride was not the kind that produces arrogance, but the pride that does not want to ask for help. She thought it was obvious what our need was. In this respect, it was early days yet, if only we'd known it.

Men were emerging from Czechoslovakia with reports of the greatest humiliation and tortures inflicted on them as prisoners in Czech camps. They were glad to be deportees now. They had been forced to lick up spittle, blood and even excrement. They were destitute, and tried to earn money through selling self-made household articles such as graters or ladles. The graters were made from a piece of old metal, into which a nail had been hammered numerous times, and the ladles were carved from a piece of old wood. The most ingenious ideas sprang to life, epitomizing the saying 'necessity is the mother of invention.'

One of these 'craftsmen' was from Saaz; his name was Fritz Wawra. Forty years old and a car mechanic, he could not rest in Freiberg, and insisted on returning to Saaz. Tante Marie called him a fool and told him that other people were glad to have escaped with their lives, and did he know what would happen to him if he were ever caught?

"I don't care. I have to go back home." He said simply. "Who wants to stay here?"

One day, Elli and her five children turned up at the 'Bayerischer Garten'. She had not been allowed to enter Holland with this Dutchman who was her baby's father. They had stayed in Wesel on the Rhine for a while, where there was at least as much fruit as they could eat. Most of the children's clothes had fruit stains on them. My mother gave Elli an old pram that Frau Patrovsky, a music teacher's wife from Saaz had given us. It had been broken, but my mother had it repaired so that Renate (now eighteen months old) could have it. The new baby was expected in February 1946.

Elli managed to get a room in an old people's home in Pirna. (Pirna, near Dresden, was the hometown of her father's cousin). She and her mother, Tante Marie, and all the children moved in there. The older children went to the kindergarten during the day whilst Tante Marie looked after the little ones, and Elli went dressmaking and mending clothes in people's houses. Once a day, they managed to get some food from a place that helped the very poorest.

When Fritz Wawra decided to make his way to Saaz for the umpteenth time, my mother gave him a letter addressed to Onkel Franz[1], her brother, to inform him that Onkel Karl, Tante Marie's husband, was being held as a farmhand in a village called Lenneschütz, so we had just heard. Subsequently, Onkel Franz visited Lenneschütz and brought his brother-in-law some clothes. We did not know this until much later.

Another place I used to visit while 'residing' in the 'Bayerischer Garten' was a posh villa at the bottom of our road across a junction. The imposing corner- bay window was part of a big room occupied by the aristocrats Herr and Frau Weinertsgrün (real title Major Meier von Weinertsgrün), their granddaughter Trude, and her governess Fräulein Else. At home in Saaz they had had servants for everything and were not used to any practical work whatsoever; now they were fortunate enough to be able to afford this comfortable room, and buy a little food on the black market. They probably had some money invested in the Reich and good connections before the end of the war, which came in handy now.

I can see Frau Weinertsgrün now, leaning against a big tiled stove and talking in a fast, sophisticated way, a woman in her sixties with courage and a past, mixed with wealth and grief. They had owned nine houses in Saaz alone, a big estate and other assets. Now, they lived in one room and a little kitchen down a long corridor in this villa, full of tenants. Trude, Liesl's friend, was about thirteen like my sister; a blond, shy girl who lacked companionship with children her own age. She was surrounded by adults, who guarded her path twenty four hours a day, so that she dreaded every step alone for a very long time, even in later life.

Herr Weinertsgrün, her grandfather, resembled Lenin with his white pointed beard and sharp face. He had little to say for himself, now that his houses and shares and all other assets had disappeared overnight. He and his wife depended entirely on Else, the practical one, who knew what to do on a day to day basis. He was not, however, a broken man. Else soon

---

[1] He and his family had not yet been transported to Germany.

realized her newly acquired power and exercised it with firmness and tact. She was a clever woman from a good background, well educated, and now in full charge of the family.

At home in Saaz, she only had to look after Trude, but now everyone depended on her, and what counted was basic living, and where the next meal and rent were coming from. Good common sense and practical ability were now more precious than fine clothes, the right accent and choosing of your words. Unfortunately, Else had never cleaned a fire place out or cooked a meal either. So, although she had a good head on her shoulders, the terrifying responsibility for her noble employers, thrust onto her over night, proved too much for her. At first, she had been dependent on them in exchange for her loyalty and pedagogic qualities. Now her superiors were entirely in her hands. It must be said that she did manage to keep the wheel turning; she was at the helm because she was the one who made everyday decisions, which counted for a lot. She did not make big decisions, admittedly, but her voice was very clearly heard.

The outcome of this shifting of positions was the total disappearance of Else as we used to know her. Her well groomed appearance made way to a disintegration reminiscent of a vagrant. Within weeks, she took to wearing a grey woollen coat, regardless of the atmosphere and temperature, which she was to wear for the next two years. Her legs began to swell and infections set in, so that she kept them permanently bandaged. Her hair grew thin, her teeth began to fall out and her eyes looked vacant in sockets now far too big for them. As far as she was concerned, she mattered little in this new 'set-up', but she now felt personally responsible for her employers. Their wellfare was paramount to her, and the task seemed to overwhelm her.

All this was not just gross neglect of her personal appearance. She also preferred to give every spare morsel of food to Trude and her grand-parents, rather than have it herself every now and then. She was middle-aged, but now looked like an old, haggard woman. Whether she had to share the kitchen with some other tenant, I would not know, but I remember her trudging along the long corridor with her big old boots, on her feet all day long with little effect. Soon, there was just a narrow path through the room, leading from the door to the table and beds, and from there to the stove. You could not walk from the door to the stove, which heated the room, or from the table to one of the windows, unless you scrambled over pots and pans, bottles and piles of paper, shoes and all kinds of paraphernalia.

I used to sit on a dusty chair, staring at this chaos and longing to run to the window to widen my view. Naturally, the occupants of this domicile became increasingly dissatisfied with life. I am sure that, if they had been able to keep the place clean and tidy, they could have added a little here and there in time, which in turn would have made for a brighter outlook and hope for the future. But in this place of total disorganisation, there could be no thought of anything ever improving. Although they were not snobs, they had been used to a certain way of life. They missed their servants, their high-class social gatherings, their visits to cultural events etc. They were utterly lost.

I went there for a number of reasons; firstly, I knew the Weinertsgrüns, albeit not too well as yet, unlike my sister. Secondly, Trude was always glad to listen to me, while no one else had the time or inclination to do so. Thirdly, it was a 'home' of some kind. They occupied it alone, and did not have to share it with hundreds of others. They could not have endured that.

One day, as Else trundled to and fro, and everyone else sat in their own corner, depressed and forlorn, I felt the urge to cheer them all up. Humming first, I began to sing some of my mother's songs that she had learned from her own mother. They were cheeky little tunes from the Egerland, where my maternal grandmother had come from. I had never sung them in a strong dialect before, but now they escaped my vocal chords as if I were well-practised in singing that way. The pronunciation of those difficult words also came easily off my lips. When I was half way through the first one, I noticed a strange transformation in the room; everything looked so jolly, not just the people, who appeared surprised and alive once more, but also the disorder in the room, which was now a cheerful chaos. Everyone clapped when I had finished, and I was requested to sing as many as I knew. I pulled a few surprises out of the bag, like some of my mother's solos that she had sung on stage in peace time; show pieces such as 'Schurl von Herr Nols'[1] in the middle of which one had to give a piercing whistle. Unfortunately, I could not oblige in this, because I had had trouble enough learning the ordinary whistling technique from my ever-patient sister Liesl. I had been more than fascinated by how such a marvellous sound could be produced by a mere mortal, whereas my mother repeated her mother's comment on this subject: "*Mädchen die pfeifen, und Hühner, die kräh'n, soll man beizeiten die Hälse umdreh'n*", (meaning, "Girls who whistle and hens that crow, should have their necks twisted in the nick of time.") Still, I knew that my mother enjoyed whistling herself. When I had finished the last tune and nothing else came to mind, everyone looked disappointed and yet pleased that a bit of music combined with words, which only they could understand (I was too small and inexperienced!) had been able to change their lives in an instant, (if only temporarily) reassuring them that the sun

---

[1] About a Viennese rascal, showing off with his charm and wit.

was still there above the clouds. Frau Weinertsgrün mumbled something about 'precociousness', but smiled happily and magnanimously, while I felt as light as a feather, taking two steps at a time and whistling contentedly as I made my way 'home.'

CHAPTER 41
Karl escapes the shadows

One night around midnight, Karl, my father's youngest brother, left the farm on tiptoe with his shoes in his hands and a rucksack on his back, heading for the garden in the shadow of the stables. There he put his shoes on and jumped over the wall into a potato field. The night was clear with summer in the air. His plan was to follow the Pole Star, sleeping in cornfields during the day and forging ahead under cover of night. After three nights, he found he had run out of water. Thirst began to plague him and he could stand it no longer. Up to now he had avoided all human habitation, but towards the morning his craving for water was so unbearable that he threw all caution aside and approached a nearby station in the knowledge that they all had a fountain or water tap. Greedily he gulped two bottles of water down, after which he cautiously looked for the name of the place. To his horror, he realized that he had only covered 13km so far and had practically marched round in a circle.

Clearly, it was useless trying to follow a star. He would have to walk during the day, heading for a mountain between Melnicky and the German-Czech border. When the weather was clear, he could make out this mountain quite well. Picking up his rucksack, he made his way towards his objective, finally reaching it under cover of darkness. A light drizzle set in, so he wrapped his blanket around himself and settled down to sleep in some undergrowth. Before sleep enveloped him, he thought that it must be Sunday, as he not encountered anyone.

Very early the next morning, the coldness, which seemed to have penetrated every bone in his body, forced him to get up, stamp his feet and fling his arms about to get warm as he waited for daylight. After what seemed hours, he was able to make out the contours of his surroundings. Regardless of the rain which fell heavier now, he pressed on, longing to leave his homeland that had become such a nightmare to his family and his countrymen.

It was now raining torrentially, so that he was forced to shelter under some big trees, but he was soon soaked to the skin. Sitting under an enormous fir tree, a sorry sight with the rain dripping down his nose and hair, he watched the path of the wood and two buildings which nestled, as if in a picture, in a meadow surrounded by forest. Suddenly, a bearded middle-aged man, barefoot, with a big cape around him, emerged from the lower house with his dog. He sharpened his scythe and began to cut the few blades of grass, which had managed to grow on the slope on one side of the meadow. The dog watched his master with obvious interest. Both seemed oblivious to the obnoxious weather conditions. Karl looked out for the white armband on the left upper arm, which every German was forced to wear (former antifascists had to wear red armbands). Thinking that he could detect something white under the cloak, he approached the man timidly and cautiously, greeting him in Czech.

"*Pomahay Pan Buh*," (May God help you), to which the the reply came:

"*Tay to Pan Buh*," (May God grant this). The man looked up and waited for Karl's request.

"How do I get to the next village?"

"You're German and you want to get across the border, don't you?" the man asked kindly. "I'm Czech, although my name is Sperlich (a German name), but you don't have to be afraid, I'm really a cosmopolitan. Come indoors and I'll tell you all about it when I've finished here. My wife will see to you in the meantime."

Karl fetched his rucksack and hesitantly opened the door to the rambling house. Could he trust anybody after what he had experienced in the past few months? Putting down his bundle, he knocked on one of the doors. A young, well-groomed woman came out, not in the least surprised to see him, and asked him in German to take his wet shoes and socks off after leading him into the room. "Put a pair of my husband's trousers and slippers on, while I dry yours. Here's some lunch, left over from ours; be my guest."

Karl did not know what to say for a moment. He could not believe his luck, and suspected that there must be a catch somewhere. He stammered something about following the sun for days etc, until her husband came in and started a conversation with Karl.

"I'm sorry that my compatriots are hunting you down like this. I'm an artist and lived a long time in Reichenberg till we came here to this lonely place to get away from it all. These are terrible times. We're happy here, and have made some friends already." He pointed to the window, where two dwarf hens were sitting on the sill, waiting to be let in. The view from the open window, through which the hens had now come into the kitchen, made it easy to believe that the couple had found what they had been looking for: peace and contentment. Idyllically, a pony and donkey grazed together on one side of the meadow, while a flock of sheep - just waiting to be painted - minded their own business on the other side near the woods. Time and again, Karl recognized the beautiful scenery in the artist's pictures shown to him. The lady told him that they were Christians, not belonging to any particular denomination, but that they were finding fulfilment in Christ's teaching, and longed to tell others about it. She gave Karl a booklet called: 'The path to Christ' just before he left, with her husband walking a good bit of the way with him. He explained the map, handed Karl a compass, and shook hands with him heartily.

Karl had had a good sleep while his clothes were drying. He had shared an evening meal with his newfound friends, who had left him feeling refreshed in mind and body. What an oasis to reflect on in the wilderness of past and future times.

As he walked steadily on, a feeling of impatience surged up in him at this twisting, long-winded path. So he left it, and made his way through meadows, brooks and fields once more. He stumbled along all night through forests, avoiding a lake, and finally, wet through again, fell into a thicket with his blanket wrapped around him.

As soon as the morning dew and mist lifted, he was off again, wandering in the shelter of the trees through the day and night till he reached Deutsch-Gabel near the border. He straightened his clothes a little and decided to take a huge gamble. Boldly, he stepped out into the road, hoping to meet some Germans, identified by their white armbands, who could point him in the right direction.

Some of his workmates had been transported from Deutsch-Gabel to Melnicky. One of them, Adam, had described the area to him. He recognized some of the landmarks he had been told about. He worked out where the border must be, passing several Czech farmers, who were now most likely the proud owners of German farms. They glanced at him suspiciously. The path, he had been following, led back into the forest, where he met a group of German woodcutters who were horrified to see him there. They warned him about coming into contact with Czechs. They had the right to arrest and even shoot him if he tried to escape. The border turned out to be farther away than he had thought. The task ahead of him was to trek around a mountain, then climb another, and find a brook already in Germany whilst avoiding arrest in his own fatherland.

He ventured on, hurrying from tree to tree, but by now his nerves were beginning to play tricks on him. Hidden figures lurked in the shadows, noises and voices could be heard, sharply and clearly. Suddenly, a border guard confronted him, motionlessly pointing a gun at him at a distance of only about fifteen metres. Karl began to shake and strange sounds escaped his parched mouth. Would he pull the trigger now, right now? He felt his heart stop, his facial muscles contract and his knees give way. Yet, somewhere in his mind, there was the knowledge that if this were reality, the man would have shouted at him. He sat down and tried to calm himself. Was he having hallucinations from lack of sleep, food and drink? Was he ill from being soaked through day and night? Or was the ordeal he had gone through for several years taking its toll, now that he was on the point of leaving it all behind? Could it be all these factors combined? He would have to be strong now.

As he sat there, he was forced to look at his life as he had never done before. Karl Boremäus Schroll, registered at Jechnitz am See at the Dekanat, eight years at school in Gerten under head teacher Kabat, high school (Bürgerschule) in Jechnitz, apprentice at Ernst Papsch grocer's at Kriegern (a small town in the heart of the Saaz hopland). His brother Franz had been an apprentice there, but was now in the famous hop town of Saaz. He and Franz were lucky. Being the youngest boys of the family, their father had saved enough money, (most of the others had gone out into the world with nothing, to fend for themselves) to send them to a higher school and better apprenticeship in order to become merchants. They wouldn't have to dirty their hands like their older brothers. They had to work hard, of course; the bachelor boss used Karl for doing the shopping, dusting, cleaning, dishwashing, packing, weighing and selling goods etc, for which the reward would be a profession of knowledge combined with honesty, pleasure and profit, or so he was told. His boss married and the house was filled with precious carpets and expensive furniture; there was a hustle and bustle right up to the moment the bride whispered "I do"- but two days later the young wife left, and the house was emptied by heaving, swearing removal men. What an anticlimax! Karl and Boss had to manage by themselves again. The place seemed like a ghost house now. It had a chip on its shoulder; an indelible stain, and Karl was afraid of it. He never shut his bedroom door and worked tirelessly all day. By night time, (the boss was out most evenings) he would be falling asleep whilst having his tea. On waking, he would run up to his attic room, look under his bed, fall into it and into a dreamless, coma-like sleep until the unrelenting alarm clock rattled a new day into being.

One evening, while making his way up to his room past his master's bedroom, he heard the fierce crackling of flames from inside. On entering, he found the bed on fire, flames shooting up to the ceiling. He took the mattress and flung it through the wide window onto the cobblestone courtyard. He saw the cause – a red-hot electric iron dangling from the window sill, where the flex had been caught. "So this time the good man has paid with his bed, nearly with his entire home, for his carelessness," Karl muttered, proud of his heroic act.

He asked his brother Franz, if he knew of a job for him, now that his apprenticeship was nearing its completion. Through a salesman, Franz had heard of a vacancy in the Egerland, in a place called Luditz. Karl asked to be considered and was accepted to his great joy.

On his last day in Kriegern, he put his best suit on and went to the station, only this time, without the customary cart for collecting the goods. It was a damp, cold day and his friend, Herr Banch, enquired about the whereabouts of the cart.

"No more carting for me," Karl answered emphatically. "I'm just off to Podersam to collect my apprenticeship certificate," he added proudly. On it were the wise words: 'Save, learn, work, then you can do something and be someone,' which became his motto for life. But there is another saying, which is equally true: 'The road to hell is paved with good intentions.'

He went home by train, watching the Petersburg parks, where he had spent many a happy hour with his friends. Then came Alberitz, and the small railway junction, Pladen. From there, he could see the church and a few houses of his slightly higher positioned village of Gerten. His heart jumped and he felt hot all over. He grabbed his suitcase and ran down into the still dewy meadows of Pladen in the direction of Gerten. He could have waited for the train from Karlsbad, but did not want to waste any time, having been away from Gerten and his parents for half a year. It was Sunday. The countryside lay still, beautiful and fragrant, free for anyone to enjoy its splendour and peace. He walked a few feet alongside the little brook into the sandy courtyard of his parents' house.

Father was at church; Mother was, as always on a Sunday, preparing the juicy roast joint with the popular potato dumplings. She embraced him. Through tears of joy, repeating over and over, how happy she was that he had come back. Soon, some malt coffee with goat's milk and a piece of cake was placed in front of him.

Father came home. His head was a little balder, but he still looked noble. His slim figure was greatly enhanced by the black Gehrock that he only wore for church. They shook hands warmly.

"Well, my boy, you've finished your apprenticeship now. Let's hope you get a job soon. You can stay a few more months in Kriegern, but getting another job will be hard with so many men unemployed."

Karl was not yet certain that he would be accepted at Luditz, but with his usual optimism, told his father not to worry.

On 15th May 1935, he was supposed to start at Herrn Fischer's impressive looking store. His mother had made the sign of the cross on his forehead and chest, and his father had taken him to the station, helping him with his feather bed and suitcase, and telling him to be good and honest.

"You're still far too excitable at times. You're also very gullible. So don't mix with bad, irresponsible characters - and write as soon as you get there."

These words had such an effect on Karl that he began to have mixed feelings. He did not really want to leave, but at the same time, he was looking forward to the new, exciting life.

The Schnella valley was beautiful, and led to Luditz, a town nestling peacefully on a mountain slope. As soon as he saw Frau Fischer - a calm, clear-headed woman - he liked her. The boss, grey-haired, but still quite youthful-looking, arrived in a blue Skoda, which Karl had the misfortune to have to clean every Sunday morning. The two apprentices lived away. The unmarried employees lived in the house and ate with the family. Ria, a relative of the Fischer's, played the bagpipes, and was a very interesting young lady.

Karl loved working there. He had to learn the new prices, about the customers, and how this particular business was run. The manager Edi, was tall, good-looking and older than Karl. He was more experienced with women, and Karl envied him. In fact, he developed quite an inferiority complex, but soon found that not everything that glitters is gold.

Business began to go downhill, and Edi was sacked for being untrustworthy. Some young friends of Edi had started to hang around the shop and mock customers. So, after half a year there, Karl took over from Edi as branch manager. He was eighteen and enormously proud of his position. The store was immaculate, and sold chocolates, delicatessen, wine and fruit among other goods. Soon the sales figures rose and he felt justified in buying himself a new bike and some tailor-made suits. He got on well with everyone, including the long haired dog, Scholli.

Karl now saw himself on top of the Schlossberg, looking from a clearing onto the town with its narrow corner streets. His memory weakened. There were only flashes through his mind now. There he was with Annemarie, a brown-eyed young girl from Slovakia (could those eyes be faithful, he wondered?) who stayed with a relative, a doctor, to look after his children. When her mother fell ill, she returned home, and their love died.

There were flashes of Toni, a barber, working for the biggest men's salon, whom he had met while at the gymnasium twice a week; Christmas at home with Willi, Josef, Franz, Traudl, Mina and Gustl: father serving in church; afternoon walks through the snow-laden woods nearby, which the sun transformed into millions of diamonds decorating each tree.

Back in the Egerland, which has almost the same coarse, but lovable dialect as across the border in North Bavaria, he learned how to ice-skate and dance.

The people there were very friendly. The younger ones were addressed with 'Du' and the older ones with 'Ihr.' Ria was pursuing him, and he knew he was falling in love with her. She had asked him to help her run a hot dog stall at a traditional folk festival that was taking place on 12th July 1938, to which the whole population of the Egerland was invited. Already on 11th July at night, a torch procession with two bands playing, opened the festivities, and there were celebrations at 'Hotel Post' (almost every house accommodated visitors). The next morning everyone was awakened at 6am by drums and fanfares made by the gymnasts; at 7am there was a concert on the festooned square, and long before 9 o'clock there was no more room in or outside the church, in which a wedding was to take place. The procession hardly had room to make its way through the thronging crowd, which was immediately calmed as the priest's address 'in dialect' boomed through the loudspeakers. Everything 'völkisch' (traditional) was appreciated, so that after the wedding, two farmers' bands accompanied the married couple to the Markt and Festplatz, where everything was happening.

Karl now saw himself working hand in hand with Ria, selling sausages and rolls. He could actually smell the mixture of all the different food stalls and the perspiration from human bodies; he could hear the joyful sounds of the jostling masses and the bands. He longed to be there again, to be part of humanity with all its weaknesses, aspirations and potentials, its cruelty, perversity and cowardliness, as well as its inspired charity. He hated to be apart from this seething activity.

Ria and he worked non-stop at the stall. It was too hot to wear his costume top. He took it off, but his knee breeches and white woollen socks still bothered him. Ria wore a tight-fitting coloured top, a navy blue pleated skirt, and a hat with long silk ribbons.

In the afternoon, someone took over the stall, because Ria and Karl were engaged in demonstrating the traditional folk dancing on a raised platform. He could still hear the shouting and yodelling, and after the dancing, people singing folksongs. Everyone enjoyed themselves that day.

They left the merry crowd and escaped into the sweetly fragrant meadows nearby. They walked closely together holding hands. Never again would he be so happy, so fulfilled, so satisfied. He was going to marry Ria in two years time and buy a business.

But everything had turned out differently in the end. Maybe it was for the best, who knows? He knew that he was gullible, yet, he could not believe that he would have to join the Czech Army by 1st December... and had Ria really been unfaithful while he had been away?

"No!" he screamed, "no, no, it's not true! These things never happened. The war never happened! The atrocities on both sides never happened. I'm not alone here! Ria!"

He fell to the ground, crying and sobbing until he felt better. When he looked up, the crouching figures had disappeared and became tree branches once more. He now felt exhausted. With tremendous effort, he crawled up a steep slope covered with what looked like lava. At the top, in the twilight, stood a hut, just perfect for sleeping in. There would be nothing nicer than to drag himself inside and sleep as long as his mind and body demanded. But then he remembered how close his was to his goal. There was not a minute to waste. He might still be caught. His agonies had to compensated by the reward of precious freedom. He stumbled and fell down the other side of the mountain. Seeing the described brook in the dim light, he began to run toward it, not looking for the best place to cross it. Wading through it, he fell to the ground on the other side, thankful for 'having made it' into Germany.

After a while, he scrambled to his feet and steered himself towards the next small village. To his horror, his ears registered Czech sounds again. Surely, it could not be. He was desperate. Walking on, he did not care what was going to happen to him now, until reason prevailed once more. The best thing to do, he decided, would be to hide in the woods until some Germans passed by who could tell him the way. There would be little chance of this happening now, however, because of the curfew for all Germans.

It wasn't long before two women talking in German walked past his hide-out. Karl, half mad at this stage, his clothes torn, dirty and steaming – as was his body - jumped out into the road to ask them the way. But the poor women, startled and perplexed by the sight of this apparent lunatic, screamed and began to run away as fast as their legs could carry them. Karl pleaded with them until they halted their sprint away from him. Their fear gave way to charity, especially when they heard that he was a German. They informed him that the border was six kilometres away, and that there would be no guards.

He thanked them and went off into a wood so dense, that to his mind, a jungle could not be worse. At times, the only way to get through was to crawl on all fours, scraping along the hard, knobbly tree roots. The branches tore the clothes from his body, and his trousers were mere shreds by now. All during this tortuous journey, he had never once considered throwing his rucksack, with clothes, blanket and bread away. He dragged it behind as if his life depended on it.

The first firing line became visible. The border must be near now. He listened for a long time for any sounds of guards. It was pitch dark, the silence so penetrating that he felt a chill reaching the very marrow of his bones.

Suddenly darkness clouded his mind, and he knew that the time had come to fight his worst enemy – himself. He had fought the elements, people, hunger, thirst, sleep, but now he would have to fight his mind, the toughest of all battles.

"You must jump across; the end of this agony is in sight." He jumped, and new strength returned to him. "I'm going to make it," he thought triumphantly, as he crept on his raw, swollen knees through the thicket to the second shooting line. "This must be the border at last." With the last effort he jumped again and disappeared into the never ending forest.

In the distance, he heard Russian songs being sung by dark, sleepy voices, contrasting with the shrill laughter of women. This must be East Germany. Upright, he walked through a moonlit forest of oak trees. How splendidly they stood their ground, solid and majestic. He was free now, and no one could touch him. No more crawling, no more fear. What was 'home' now?

Hearing a dog bark, he went towards the sound. The moon bathed some clean, mansion-like houses in a diffused light, which gave them a fairy tale appearance. Some had lights in the windows. Karl knocked on a door. Someone looked down from one of the windows and asked testily what he wanted. After Karl's request to stay the night, the voice replied that Russian orders would not allow this. "But try a hotel or pub." The window shut with a bang, just as someone came along the road. Karl enquired after the name of the place. It was a small spa town, called Johnsdorf. His knock on the door of the public house met with no success. With his last reserves of energy, he dragged his body to the hotel, where a window was opened on the second floor, and a woman looked him up and down with open suspicion. This was hardly surprising, for the man she saw down there looked was an awful, pathetic sight. His speech was slurred, not only because his brain had almost ceased to function, but also because his tongue and lips were swollen due to dehydration. Only after assuring her of his willingness to pay, did she agree to give him a room.

It was 10th July 1946. Karl drank as much water as he could possibly accommodate and fell into bed like someone jumping into a river on a hot day. When he woke up the next day around noon, he wanted to get up, but found that it was simply not possible. All his muscles seemed to be on strike and protested violently each time he moved. Finally, after a struggle, he sat up in bed and reached for his rucksack, out of which he pulled a piece of bread. After munching it contentedly, he fell once more into a profound and long sleep.

CHAPTER 42
The open gate

Continuing his train journey in a dazed state, my father learned that Germany was now divided into four sectors; the American zone in the South, the French in the West, the British in the North-West, and the Russian in the North-East, all occupied and controlled by the former enemy. A look through the window sufficed to convince him that there was nothing much to occupy, but rather to control - bundles of rags that walked around aimlessly, hollow-eyed and starving.

The released PoWs were taken into an American military hospital in Göppingen (Swabia), converted from a Flakkaserne (Flakbarracks); where they were fed with luxuries like powdered eggs and milk, which were to become much sought after on the black market. But before they did anything, they were stripped of their lice-riddled rags hanging from their bones, and showered (my father had not had a shower or bath for a whole year), disinfected, and put into black American tunics and trousers, his best and only suit.

Everywhere in Germany and by now in Czechoslovakia also, Red Cross and 'Care' parcels, containing mainly clothes, were handed out, (if they had not disappeared into the black market), and the staff of the camps had to issue departing 'inmates' with one outfit each, because their old ones could no longer be described as 'decent.' One man in Czechoslovakia, a German on his way to exile, was handed an evening suit in immaculate condition. It is easy to visualize the tragi-comic figure he cut, being sent from one camp to another in Germany, gradually collecting more and more body and head lice as constant companions, before getting ration cards, work and a roof over his head, competing with millions of other 'foreigners' in a Germany that was totally ruined and mutilated, with many of the indigenous population killed, and utter confusion and desperation whereever one looked.

On Easter Sunday 1946, my father stood outside the gate of the Military Hospital, which had given him food, rest and shelter for the last fortnight, wondering where to go from there. All he had was a train ticket valid for one month, enabling him to find his relations, work and accommodation. Of course, he had no clue whatsoever of his loved ones' whereabouts; neither did he know, where his next meal or bed could be found.

In a way he felt exhilarated and grateful. He had escaped death by a hair's breadth. Life did not seem quite real. For years, he had been doing what he was told every minute of the day and night - and now he was free. But this newfound freedom, of which he had dreamed for so long, now frightened and confused him. The gate before him was the gateway to the world, as far as he was concerned. But what world, what prospects? Also, he was responsible for his own life now, he and he alone. He was not used to this and it scared him. "Where do I go from here?" he thought, and automatically turned toward the station. It was the usual picture. Hundreds of people were milling about looking for something, and yet, their expressions were devoid of purpose.

As he approached the timetable to orient himself as to where to go, some men, sensing his intention, approached and advised him not to waste his time travelling this way on these overcrowded trains (people clung to the steps and buffers), looking for relations. They, themselves, had tried in vain. Everything was ruined, and finding work was out of the question.

He remembered that everything would be shut until Tuesday because of Easter. "I haven't any ration cards," he thought in terror. Without them, he could get no food. He noticed a group of men standing round a noticeboard. While reading it, a glimmer of hope swept through him. A Protestant home offered newly released prisoners of war short term accommodation and food. The men around him, obviously, had the same idea. Panic had been averted at the last moment. He began to talk to an ex-army officer from Eger, Czechoslovakia who was in the same predicament, and the two of them accepted the home's hospitality of a camp bed (pure luxury), and a couple of potatoes, and bits of vegetables until Tuesday morning.

My father's release papers, issued to him by the Americans on 16th April 1946 stated the following, amongst the essentials: 'Disabilities: dysentery and rheumatism of joints. Able to do light work.' Signed: Donald Sterner, Captain, M.C.

With this piece of paper, he and his new-found companion went to the *Lebensmittelamt* (the food distribution centre), the most important authority at that time, where they were issued with ration cards for three days, after having their papers stamped. The only thing they could do with the coupons was to go to a public house or cafe, and get yet another watery soup there. My father's health was still in a very precarious state, and he could not really afford to upset it again with a diet of this kind. But there was no choice. All that Tuesday, 16th April 1946, they looked for work in Göppingen; my father sought a job as a mechanic, and his friend looked for work in a garden nursery in the vague hope of a vegetable crop there. No one wanted them.

As the day faded, they walked to the next village, and after yet another unsuccessful attempt at finding work there, they went onto the adjacent village of Heiningen, (a walk of about forty minutes) - this time, directly to the mayor. Luckily, the mayor knew of a farm where they needed a hired hand, as the only man of the house was still a French prisoner-of-war. There was no other work. Labouring was out of the question for the Army Officer; he was over sixty. He knew that his wife lived in the English zone, but he said that he was not allowed to go there, as yet. He said goodbye to my father and walked back into the unknown.

When my father arrived at the Fries farm, where he had been sent, the two unmarried middle-aged sisters in charge looked him up and down, and asked many questions. Their only brother had still not come back from the war and they could not do the hard, physical work on their own. They still had hope that their brother might be returned to them safe and sound. Meanwhile, they had employed a young German from Yugoslavia who was sacked for knowing nothing about farming. After long ruminations about his farming capabilities, and on hearing that he was a blacksmith, they accepted him.

He had not been there long, when they asked him if he could do something about Muli's feet. Muli was a big, young horse, which could not be used for work due to his flat feet, which felt every stone through his hooves.[1] The two sisters, Christine and Bärbel (short for Barbara; she was slightly hunchbacked) had some help at night from their brother-in-law, who had tried getting Muli to pull loads by hitting him, but he would never budge. My father, thus, found himself in a challenging situation, in which he was supposed to prove himself and justify their feeding him. He could not have looked very impressive in his one outfit of clothes, thin and sickly-looking, his face drained of all positive emotion; but here was his chance.

There was one more horse on the farm, a small grey, which had to do all the work alone, while Muli got stronger every day and played up at every opportunity; he had even ruined the brother-in-law's cutting machine.

My father spoke to the neighbour, a young blacksmith, whose father had just died. Together, they decided that Muli's old shoes would have to be removed. They spread cow manure onto a sack and wrapped it round Muli's feet. This was renewed every day for weeks to make his feet soft, and ease the pain. Then my father fixed some special shoes, which consisted of a wider iron and a piece of tin which covered the whole hoof.

The Fries' had a beet-pit outside the village for the cows. After Muli had been fixed up, he was put next to the little grey under strong protests from Christine and Bärbel, who repeatedly said: "Anspannen, das dulden wir nicht!" (We won't tolerate him being hitched up to and pulling the cart). Unconcerned, he made the horses trot off, with Christine running after him, telling him not to fill the wagon full. "Half full will do!" she

---

[1] There are about 24 different foot-abnormalities in horses.

screamed. She was the one who slept in the stables, so that no harm could come to the animals.

Out in the field, my father heaved fork after fork of beets onto the wagon until it was full. But Christine would not have it. Grumbling and scolding, she began to remove half the load, but my father simply put the beets back on again and gave the command for the horses to pull away. The grey obeyed, but Muli moved backwards instead of forwards. This went on for several minutes.

My father now found himself in an uncomfortable position. This obstinate horse was jeopardising his efforts to gain the respect and confidence of the village people. He had never used a whip, but now he broke off a small branch from a bush, and proceeded to hit Muli with it. Each time, Muli shot forward and then back again, until he felt a longer branch between his ears. Then he pulled away, angrily and wildly. Christine calmed down, and the first battle was won.

The second job for Muli was to bring clover home from the fields after my father had cut it with a scythe. Then the serious business of ploughing and preparing the fields in autumn began. The village folk were surprised indeed and impressed that the Fries farm could actually use its horses now.

My father enjoyed the farming. He never knew how he had managed in the beginning, being so undernourished and ill. In one way, it was a good thing that he was not given a lot of rich food; his system would have broken down. In summer, he saved his black tunic and only wore his trousers. When he felt a little stronger from the sunshine and fresh air, and after making cider (Most) from the many apple- and fruit trees they had in their meadows, the heavy winter work started and he complained about the food. The main diet consisted of soup and Spätzle (a kind of homemade pasta, very popular in Swabia). The first time he tasted a glass of cider, he felt decidedly tipsy. He obviously needed more nutritious food now, and in greater quantities, but the sisters responded with: "Our late father was always satisfied with a piece of bread and cheese."

In October 1946, the village vicar came to the stable to see my father one evening. My father had taken to going to church on Sunday mornings. He washed his clothes on Saturday night, so that they would be clean for Sunday service. Once, his clothes were not ready to wear, Christine said: "You can borrow one of my brother's suits for church, as long as you give it back after the service. I don't suppose Hans-Jörg would mind." From then on, he could wear this suit each Sunday morning until they even said, he could wear it all day every Sunday. But my father declined the generous offer.

The vicar handed my father a letter with a broad smile. "Herr Schroll, I have good news for you. The Protestant Search Service

(Evangelischer Suchdienst und Hilfswerk) has found your family." There was no reply. The vicar looked into a white face, and within half a minute he witnessed a man shake from head to foot as a result of these few simple words. He went over and spoke quietly and reassuringly to the startled figure.

My father had spent the best years of his life serving the wrong cause. Now he was trying to cope with the present - no easy task, because he could not shake off the past, however hard he tried. When Muli played him up a bit, as he still did now and again, when he fed the animals, when he walked next to the plough, absorbed in admiring the clean, fertile furrow, he was able to forgot the bad memories for a while. At those times, he felt grateful to be alive, although he could not even begin to think about us. Sometimes, the thought crossed his mind that something awful might have happened to us, especially when he thought of Liesl. No, he had to banish all such thoughts from his mind, and concentrate on what he was doing.

He had, of course, written to the Protestant Search Service like everyone else who had lost contact with their family. A few millions wrote to the Catholic Service, called 'Caritas' and many others to the Red Cross. It was probably the biggest and most extensive search operation in human history, and much was achieved in the first two years. After that, during the next eight or ten years, things moved very slowly, but, nevertheless, effectively.

My father had almost forgotten about his efforts to find us. There was not much that could be done. My mother must have written to this service too. We had suddenly entered the picture in his viewfinder, but he was not ready yet; he was in limbo, desperately trying to hold onto reality. It was hard. How could he be responsible for three more people, even though they were his next of kin?

The fear in him was evident as he spoke faintly to the vicar. "Where are they", he asked weakly.

CHAPTER 43
New Beginnings

It was now Autumn 1945. The transit-camp 'Bayerischer Garten' in Freiberg, Saxony was about to be dissolved. My mother spent many hours looking for a room. The hospital had also warned her that they could no longer keep my sister. Her heart condition could never be improved, and they needed every existing bed urgently.

At this time, we had news from Tanta Anni, my mother's youngest sister, who was somewhere else in Saxony. My mother decided to visit her, while I was being looked after by friends. The description of her experience was quite impressive. After the usual battle to find a space on the train, she reached her destination and eventually found the camp, in which her sister and her son Reinhard had found refuge. Hundreds of people were milling about the place, inside and out, some begging, others baking potatoes between bricks (there were plenty of them lying about), or anything else they had managed to get hold of. From this, my mother concluded that things must be more or less the same all over East Germany. She knew by now that conditions were considerably better in West Germany under the Americans.

As she entered the big hall of the camp, a sight engraved itself on her memory. There - amidst all the squalor and misery – lay baby Reinhard on a heap of straw, evoking a two thousand year-old image. His mother sat beside him on the floor, attending to his needs as best she could. There was no milk and no clothes. Sometimes milk powder would be distributed; but for a substitute of clothes, any old rags had to do. In the course of the two women's conversation, my mother learned that Eugen (Reinhard's father) was lucky to be alive (having been an SS man), and that he was married with four children in Mannheim, where he now lived. My mother was shocked to the core. Eventually, my aunt moved to Mannheim, where his family had lived for many years. Eugen's first wife and the by now older children were very pleasant to my aunt. Eugen, being an eccentric, was not an easy person to live with, and they must have been glad to keep in contact with him, but from a safe distance. Eugen soon got a divorce, married my aunt and 'adopted' his son.[1]

My aunt's immediate future seemed little more than hopeless when my mother saw her.[2] They might starve, or freeze to death soon. Winter was fast approaching and only rapid changes in their circumstances could save them from disaster.

My mother was immensely worried about their prospects.

"I can try and get some work and fend for myself, but Anni's hands are tied with having to look after the baby. God knows what will happen to her and her baby son, if Eugen has deserted her now in her hour of need."

My mother set about finding a room, and was finally successful in her venture. The camp-commandant's wife also agreed to employ her once a week for general alterations, mending clothes and, if I remember correctly, for doing the washing. Most of her income was to be derived from being a 'washer-woman' for quite a number of families who could

---

[1] Who later became an electro-engineer and later still, a doctor of medicine.

[2] Eight million of the indigenous 60 million Germans were homeless and two million had been disabled.

afford her services. Doing the washing was one of the hardest manual jobs at the time for a woman.

There was Frau Seifert, for instance, whose husband either owned a factory, or was its director, now that everything was state-owned as in Russia. She was very kind to us, but I do not think that she had an inkling as to the way we existed. Communists in leading positions were also relatively well off. A young woman from the house where we now lived wore black, soft, long boots - luxuries we stared at in wonder, when all the refugees and deportees wore shoes from 'home' (referring to their homeland), which were fast wearing out.

The house we had moved into was situated in the Bergstiftsgasse 31. It was occupied by several tenants on several floors, with the landlord downstairs. 'Landlord' might not be the right word, as the house belonged to two unmarried sisters called Martha and Gertrud, who worked in offices all day every day (except Sunday), and who were rather 'wise old owls' in their early forties.

I liked the house, which was now our new home for more than one reason. Firstly, we had our own room again, and were 'private' once more; secondly, our road was lined with trees which reminded me of Saaz. Only one thing, (apart from the toilet, which was a latrine in a little room inside the house on the ground floor) struck a discordant note in my newfound happiness. The house next to ours had been bombed out during the war. The rubble had been cleared, so that the row of houses resembled a set of teeth with a gap in the middle. Some parts of the side of our house had been blackened by smoke, but something else was even more disconcerting. Across the road stood a tall tree, which had caught a piece of net-curtain from the destroyed house in one of its branches, as the blast had ripped through it. Every time I left our house, I saw this curtain flutter in the wind and imagined what must have happened to the tenants of that house at the time. Also, how hard people must have worked to stop the roaring fire from spreading to the adjoining properties. Freiberg had accumulated a number of damaged buildings, but the harm done was never on such a scale that the debris could not be removed soon, or that whole areas of the town had disappeared overnight.

As you entered the front door, there was the same vestibule as in our house in Saaz, with only one difference. The passage next to the stairs led not to the basement, but to the minute lavatory that did not even have a light of any kind. Opposite Martha and Gertrud Schäffner's flat, just before you reached the stairway, was our door. It was the flimsiest door I had ever seen. The material used for it could hardly be called wood. Two or perhaps three pieces of plywood might be a good description of it. At the top corner it looked as if someone at some time had tried to prise the fragile thing open, at which point it had made up its mind never to return to its original position, but remain in its present state of gaping.

Our room consisted of two beds, a small stove, painted with silver-paint, and a table with one chair and a little bench. Later on, some kind soul gave us a trunk with a divergent top. My sister was collected from hospital just before Christmas on a sledge pulled by my mother. Liesl and I slept in a fairly comfortable bed with a feather duvet (what luxury!) near the only existing window, facing North into a little yard and wild garden. My mother's bed, minus a mattress, with only a latticed wooden surface with menacing springs visible underneath, was less inviting. At the end of every day, we saw her dragging her tired limbs into this weird contraption. The only cover she had, with winter fast approaching, was her coat and a thin sofa-cover from "at home".

I remembered how strenuous a washday had been in Saaz[1] with all the soaking over night, wringing, boiling, stirring, scrubbing by hand and on a washboard, then re-rinsing and re-wringing. There was an awful lot of washing each time, as it was collected over a period of time. Not many people owned their own house in those days, so people took it in turns with the other tenants. In each block of flats the washroom with the necessary equipment was provided. In Saaz, a rich town, many people who owned houses owned several ones, which they rented out. It was hard enough work for my mother's washing in Saaz, but now, she earned her living with it and had to do this procedure every few days for different people. From then on, my mother's hands looked permanently red and chafed.

Her first priority was food, the second, fuel to keep us warm. For the latter purpose, she had to buy a fairly big hand-cart – a necessity at that time - which she and I loaded with wood from the nearest forest (a considerable journey). Most of this fuel consisted of fir-twigs, which crackled with an alarming intensity in our little aluminium-painted stove, but as soon as the fire had devoured the fragrant branches (and it was very soon), the collapse of this previously bulky structure meant imminent extinction of our precious heat. New fuel had to be found quickly. Eventually there was no more wood of any kind to be found in the forests. On entering, it appeared as though the ground had been swept with a very effective broom, and all the tree branches had been cut off within reaching level. Within days, some clever inventor began to use a saw tied to a long pole. Thus equipped, it was now possible for a whole army of copy-cats to reach the next level of branches and saw them off. And so it was that everyone became very inventive (as well as less law-abiding) through sheer necessity.

---

[1] It lasted all day, with the soaking done the night before.

On many occasions, we had no choice but to huddle together in our coats or go to bed, due to lack of fuel. Although we possessed ration-cards like everyone else, we had no 'connections' of any kind, unlike the indigenous population of Freiberg. Liesl still had lunch with Dr. Schalli and his wife once a week, which was very much appreciated, but her health deteriorated once again, and she had to go back into hospital, where she remained on and off for the next eighteen months.

From our ration-cards we could buy greyish-brown bread, which tasted no better than saw-dust. It had just one endearing quality - it filled you up, if you ate a few slices of it as a meal. The only trouble was that we could not afford to do this. Liesl had invented a brilliant system of good 'bread-keeping' right from day one. Each of us marked every slice on our individual loaves with the blade of a knife, so that we would not run out until the next ration was due. This way, we all knew exactly how many slices we could eat per day. Liesl always adhered to her self-imposed restriction; I did not. On the mournful discovery that I had come to the end of my ration, I would beg for some of her bread. It was infuriatingly humiliating. Occasionally she would oblige, but more often than not she would articulate:

"Does that seem fair to you that you have so little self-control and can't stick to your ration, and then ask for mine?" I had to agree that it definitely was not fair, but argued that what was 'fair' at a time like this? "Well, if everyone thought like you, Erika, where would we be? I'm sure we'd be even worse off, with anarchy taking over sooner or later."

I was not impressed unless I had more than one slice of bread at a time, even if I had known what 'anarchy' meant. I think it worked out at three slices a day, and with little else to supplement them, they were no more than tastebud-teasers.

Occasionally, my mother brought home 'Grütze', a brownish mixture of what looked like minced meat in a sauce. There was more sauce than meat, and to this day, I don't know what we were actually eating. For everything, one had to queue for hours, and it was not uncommon that, having stood for so long in the freezing cold, the supply of a particular item had run out.

The longest queue was always for meat. If there was no more available, you had to accept a little cottage cheese instead. Meat-rations were almost nonexistent in any case. Most of the time, the aforementioned 'Grütze', probably made from cereal and made to look like minced meat, substituted for meat. Potatoes were also a rare commodity. Occasionally, carrots had arrived by train from somewhere. After having queued for hours in the bitter cold, a little shovel full of frozen carrots with the odd dead mouse in it was thrown in your bag.

One day, a letter arrived to inform us that someone had sent us a parcel, and we were to collect it as soon as possible from the Post Office. I had begun to attend school once more after being deloused. In Germany, school usually begins at 8am and finishes at midday. As soon as I came out of school, I ran to the station where all the parcels were distributed. I poked a hole in the thin cardboard in order to get 'to the bottom' of this big secret. Tante Anni had sent us two or three pounds of potatoes! How wonderful and miraculous! This became a regular occurrence whenever she could afford it. Needless to say, we had a feast that evening. How warm-hearted Tante Anni was to think of us in this way, when she herself was in such a predicament.

Frau Krieglstein also used to give us some potatoes now and again. My mother had made several friends by now, and she was one of them. She was an old lady of great humility and strength, whose face showed many wrinkles and creases, but also much determination and kindness. Her eyes were small and her nose too big, but her heart was in the right place. (Her son Rainer was to make a name for himself as a Sudetengerman poet a few years later). She was a Catholic and came from a small village in the Sudetenland. Whenever she and my mother met, there was an abundant exchange of war experiences and reflections about our lost homeland, which lifted them out of their present circumstances and helped them to digest the past.

With other friends, like the Aulitzkys or the Bergers, the discussions used to get very heated. The theme was usually the brutality and injustice they had all suffered, in minute detail and described in vivid colours, so that it became once more 'alive'. With Frau Krieglstein the conversation was gentle, the description of their respective birthplace and its people inspiring them with feelings of pleasure and happiness that no one could take away from them. Sometimes they would even laugh as they recalled funny incidents, and they always parted strengthened and cheered. I used to love being a silent observer and listener to all these different conversations, specially as they always took place in the rooms of these friends, never in our one room. Their rooms were better furnished, bigger and warmer. They could not offer us food, but there was always a hot drink and sustenance for the heart and brain.

It was now the spring of 1946. If we had known that my father was just about to be released as a PoW from Yugoslavia, we naturally would have rejoiced. By now we felt that, if he did not turn up soon, any hope of seeing him again, would fast ebb away. My mother was nearly 45, my sister 13 and a half and I had just reached the grand age of 9 and a bit.

When my sister was out of hospital the first time, she was allowed to go to school too. There she learned English and Russian, amongst other subjects. Russian was compulsory for all children in East Germany. To my surprise, I got on very well with it, and at the end of the school year, managed to come top of the class in it. The fact that these Russians had to have a different alphabet to our own, did not bother me. What did slightly annoy me were the dull textbooks.

"What is this?" "This is Anton. This is a tomato",etc. (The word 'tomato' seems to be the same in many languages, but where we came from, it was, translated from the French, called 'apple of paradise' and a potato was an 'earth-apple'[1]). To my mind, languages were interesting, and this incentive spurred me on to master them. My sister loved English. She tried to convey this to me, and urged me to put my faith in her teaching ability. I refused point-blank. Yes, admittedly, I got on much better with her now, but I still resented her, as I saw it, condescending manner toward me, and the way in which my mother gave her preferential treatment.

"Look," Liesl would say to me, "it's easy, almost like German." She pointed to a sentence, which she had written out for my benefit. 'We have a house and a garden.' I looked at it for a while, then translated it into German. Liesl was triumphant. "You see, I told you it was easy. Come on, let's do some more." I agreed reluctantly, when the similarity of the two languages could not be ignored, even by me, but eventually the teaching sessions, which had begun so ardently, died a quiet death, due to Liesl's departure to hospital once more.

I attended a girls' school, which buzzed with a thick Saxon dialect. My classmates were nice enough, but I felt miles apart from them in many ways. Their meaningless chatter often revolted me, so that I became isolated and frustrated. Our teacher, Fräulein Lehman noticed this and tried to help me as well as she could without making it too obvious. I sensed her sympathy and loved her for it, but my mind wandered so much that I had trouble following the lessons. Once, for instance, she explained a grammatical point in a German lesson and subsequently gave us an exercise on it. My work showed the exact opposite of what she had so patiently explained beforehand. Yet, she understood. One day, she asked if she could see where I lived. My heart gave a little jump at the prospect. Before she arrived I was as nervous as when I had eaten some jam that my mother had been given by the camp-commandant's wife from the plentiful stock that she had 'hamstered' away from the camp into her own cupboard over many months. My mother had hidden this treasure behind the curtain in our room; I had inadvertently found it on one of those afternoons after school when no other thought could be accommodated in my brain but 'F O O D.' This was a different kind of nervousness, of

[1] Again, this came from the Napoleonic occupation of Austria to which we belonged until 1919.

course. The one I experienced now was apprehension and embarrassment. Why would she want to visit me of all pupils, and what would she think of our abode? The other one had been naked fear of what my mother would say when she found out that I had eaten the jam.

Fräulein Lehmann was, as always, kind and considerate, although I noticed a certain pallor and rigidity about her; which seemed to indicate shock. She did not stay long, so that I had plenty of time to work out why she had been so near-paralytic, until I could tell my mother when she came home from work. But no answer came to me, no reason could be found, and my mother would not help me in finding one either. Fräulein Lehmann soon got married, (she was quite young) and we never saw her again. Everybody missed her dreadfully when she left - even the navy-blue suit that she wore every day, and her blond hair that she brushed back so vigorously and twisted round and round at the back of her head, so that it hurt to even look at it. Her blue eyes would no longer look at us in that familiar, penetrating, yet caring way, to which we responded as requested every time.

During this period of time, I made a few friends in my class; we had found common ground at last. Naturally enough, the topic of conversation was now the arrival of the new teacher. What would she look like, how would she treat us, and many other questions hung in the air. Even our most interesting occupation of exchanging objects of varying desirability (eg. Cards, pictures) subsided at this time, which was too bad as far as I was concerned; for my seemingly inborn tendency for collecting natural objects of beauty had surpassed unforeseen heights.

"You remember the black stains on my teeth, when I first got them?" a plump, thick-haired brunette shouted out from her seat at the back of the class for all to hear. "I was told to eat plenty of apples, which I did. And now look.." She bared her white, spotless teeth to us, and I was in the process of wondering where she had obtained all these apples from, (although I would never have asked her) when the door opened and our new teacher entered.

She was an impressive sight, and the opposite of her predecessor. Whereas the latter had been simplicity itself, the emphasis here was on elaboration, superfluity, ornateness. There were bangles and beads jangling at every flick of her wrist, artistic hair-styles, which accentuated her long, pitch-black hair; beautifully flowing dresses made from the finest materials (obviously from pre-war times; she was in her thirties). For once, there was complete silence in the classroom.

She said a few introductory words, perched casually on one of the front desks (which was empty) with her feet on the chair, apparently 'at home.' We were spellbound, and the fascination we felt continued and flourished as time went on. Not that we thought one was better than the other, rather, that our apprehension about our new teacher, comparing unfavourably with the old one, was instantly swept under the table. That said, Fräulein Lehmann would always have a special place in our hearts; her sincerity and warmth could never be forgotten.

My mother had always tried to speak *Hochdeutsch* (High German) with us, so that we spoke 'quite nicely' and not with that horrid Saaz dialect, which I grew to love in later years. Slowly but surely, I now began to learn the native Saxon dialect, not with intent, but almost subconsciously. With this increased confidence, I felt less like an outcast. No child wants to be different from its peers.

Coming out of school one afternoon, I ran directly to a little funfair. It seemed a long time since my last enjoyment of such an occasion. Everything was there on a smaller scale. Some small children sat merrily riding these haughty, nostril-blowing carousel horses, others were not so sure of what to make of this new situation. Should they laugh or cry? Anxiously, they looked around for their mothers, who waved and smiled reassuringly at them. The carousel spun the chained seats around like a top. Shrieks of pleasure, fear or both saturated the air with the little hands hanging on for dear life.

I longed to express my own frustration, fears and sorrows. I wanted to scream, howl and throw myself about just as they did, but with no money to go on one of these joy-rides, I felt unable to do so. People would have given me some strange looks, if I had simply started yelling on the spot.

Suddenly a young woman approached me, pressed six pennies into my hand and vanished into the crowd. I stared at the coins in disbelief. Then, before I might discover that it was not true, I jumped hurriedly onto the carousel, which was just about to set off. But as we went faster and faster, I found that I could not utter one sound, let alone emit a loud scream. Yet, it was wonderful to float in the air, to be lifted out of all the unhappiness, disappointments and frustrations of everyday living and transported into moments of sheer joy and abandonment. I ran home with the rest of the money, so that I could show it to my mother, when she came home from work. But when I told her about the kind lady and showed her the remaining money, she flew at me, and accused me of stealing from her purse.

"A nice little story that is," she said indignantly, "and don't think I'm going to swallow it. I haven't forgotten the last time you stole. Remember when you took that toy from that kind family?" She looked at me searchingly and I winced, thinking how utterly gratuitous it was to remind me of my misdeed. How could I ever forget it? And how many more debit-entries were going to be made in her bad books? I pleaded with her to believe me, but she would not be convinced.

The summer of 1946 brought some relief as far as food and warmth were concerned. We did not need any fuel, and much less food than in winter. Nevertheless, the latter remained a big problem. We could, of course, go to any restaurant or café and order something, provided we handed in the required ration coupons. For a special treat, my mother used to take us there sometimes. Especially in winter, it felt like pure luxury to sit in a warm, comfortable room on soft chairs, and just ask the waiter to bring something to eat, instead of racking your brain to work out where the next meal would be coming from. This could not be afforded very often, as our rations would have disappeared very quickly. When we did go, it was always felt to be a special celebration, maybe just of being alive against all odds.

Our ordered 'meal' invariably consisted of bread with a thin layer of anchovy paste spread onto it. The taste was delicious. Even to this day, anchovies mean something out of the ordinary to me. I don't know if this delicacy was the only menu available to the likes of us, or whether my mother requested it for economy's sake.

Across the courtyard, at the back of our house and as an extension to the courtyard was a small garden. How I longed to wander around in it, examining every plant and flower to discover their well-hidden secrets and enjoy their beauty and fragrance. Somehow, I could not muster sufficient courage to ask Martha and Gertrud for permission to enter this little haven. From our window, mint-plants with mauve flower-heads were visible. The rest of the garden remained a mystery. Occasionally, I would go out and play with the children from the house and next door. Upstairs lived a girl of my age, Irene Hofmann, and her brothers Werner and Manfred, aged about sixteen and seven, respectively. They had an old, blind grandfather, who was always very cheerful and sometimes sat in the courtyard next to some small sheds, which provided shelter from the wind. Now and again, he would sing a song or two from his younger days. The other children showed little interest; they must have known these tunes by heart by now. I found them so fascinating that I still remember the lyrics and melody of one of them. In his cheerful voice he would sing: *'Kartoffel in der Schal', ja, ja, dazu ein Pfündchen Butter, ja, ja Ihr Leut', Ihr wisst es ja, ist ein ausgezeichnet's Futter. Drari, drara, Kartoffel in der Schal', ja, ja; drari, drara, Kartoffel in der Schal.'* Small wonder that this impressed me so much; did it not echo my own sentiments on the subject 100%? 'Potatoes in their skins, o yes, with a little pound of butter, o yes you people, as you know, is simply excellent fodder.' If I had been less inhibited, I would have joined in wholeheartedly.

One Sunday afternoon, (my mother's only free day) we went down to the river Mulde, which was extremely shallow and narrow, so that we were able to walk across and back again as many times as we pleased. It was a wonderful day; the water was crystal-clear, and our spirits high. I skipped across the stream from one boulder to the next, anticipating disaster sooner or later, my heart beating fast from all the excitement. My mother sat on the riverbank talking to my sister, and as I approached, I heard her say:

"You know Frau Angermann, for whom I work, don't you? Well, she's got a very sharp tongue." This sounded interesting. I wondered what a person with a sharp tongue looked like. I could not remember ever seeing someone with a tongue that could cut like a knife. I shook my thin, white legs one after the other and sat down next to them.

"She calls me 'Schroll' all the time instead of Frau Schroll as any decent person addresses a woman. The other day, she called me an idiot, because she sent me to collect a parcel from the Post-Office and they wouldn't give it to me. I was furious, I can tell you. But what could I do? Just clench my fists and teeth and get on with some more work. The humiliation is just too much sometimes."

I was speechless. My mother, who was quasi-omnipotent as far as I was concerned, had been reprimanded and insulted like a silly child! I knew Frau Angermann only too well. Quite a few times, I had gone to my mother's workplaces while she was at work there, with the result of being scolded for it on each occasion, but at least I knew now the kind of people my mother worked for. My feelings with regard to Frau Angermann were unequivocal. Everything about her was objectionable. Her hot temper, her impatience and constant anger and often rudeness to anybody near her, her cynicism and her insistence on being treated with respect and tolerance, did not endear her to me. I had many grudges against my mother, yet I did not think she deserved this kind of treatment. My sister spoke quietly:

"Mama, don't grieve about her. You can see how unhappy she is, behaving in this way. It's like a vicious circle. The worse she feels, the more she antagonizes the people around her. You wouldn't want to be like that, would you?" she glanced at my mother sideways.

"I can't afford to lose my job with her, that's all I know," my mother sighed as she got up, helping Liesl up at the same time.

My mother heard by chance that her cousin Franz Langer, who had been a professor of music in Prague and a piano-virtuoso of some renown, was due to give his second Meisterkonzert in Freiberg. Coming from the same musical family, she did not want to miss this opportunity of listening to some good music again. She dressed us as best she could, and led us to the huge, impressive Konzerthalle. I enjoyed the warmth and general atmosphere (by now it was autumn again), but the music went mostly over my head, although I got a tremendous thrill from just watching the orchestra. The banging of the drums and cymbals, the tumultuous crescendo which ebbed away into the small, plaintive voice of one violin; the ear-piercing sounds of the woodwind-section; all this was implanted for ever in my memory. What I found quite unbelievable was that this conductor, controlling all this power at the flick of this little baton, was my mother's cousin! We queued up to see him at the end of the performance after tumultuous applause, at which Franz, bowing repeatedly to his audience, creased his beautiful black suit. When every 'important' person had finished talking to him, it was our turn. He was so close now that I could have touched him, if I had had the courage. Was he really made flesh and blood? I looked hard at him, but could detect no difference between him and anybody else, except a certain aloofness, which was instantly perceptible. In fact, he gave one look at us, which said it all. "How dare you miserable creatures turn up at my concert. Have you had a look in the mirror lately? To attend my performance in this apparel is an insult to me, especially when I'm pretending to be affluent." He dismissed us quickly, excusing himself before disappearing into the crowd.

"Why didn't he invite us to his house, Mama?" I asked, disappointed.

"He's trying to build up his career over here. He had to leave his home like us and has to start all over again, but I'm sure he'll make it with his talent and ability."

I could not see what this had to do with his coolness, and even embarrassment at the sight of us. I had envisaged us amidst posh furniture and people, with mountains of sumptuous food before us. This was a bitter disappointment indeed and I made up my mind that this Franz Langer was not a very nice person to know, whatever his celebrity status.

I looked down to inspect my clothes. Yes, I had to admit, none of us came up to scratch; on the contrary, we looked a sorry sight, probably more like scarecrows, but these were the only clothes we possessed. I didn't know what my face looked like, as we had no mirror, but I knew that, at least, it was clean. My mother was very particular about cleanliness. How nice it used to be to sit at her dressing-table and look in the big mirror in Saaz, brushing my lips and cheeks hard with a little eyebrow-brush, so that they became a fierce crimson colour, mimicking the effects of make-up.

We had started to go to church services in the big Gothic cathedral. Protestants were predominant in Saxony, and after the war the churches were well-attended. Herr Mitscherling, the minister, was a friendly man, whose son I liked very much. There were special classes (Sunday School) for children in a building adjoining the church and I had plenty of time to observe him there. What we were actually taught was of little interest to me. Infinitely more absorbing was this vicar's son, who could look like a tramp one day, only to appear neat and spotless the next. He did not care what people thought of him, he dressed as he liked, when he liked.

The congregation was friendly, but not caring enough in my opinion. As far as I remember, no one ever enquired as to how we as deportees managed to live, unless they were too embarrassed to do so. One person gave us a thick, old Bible and a prayer-book containing a gospel text and prayer for each day of the week. My mother began to read from these two books every day in bed before she got up. At first, she would meditate on them silently until one day, she read the following text from the prayer-book aloud:

"Therefore,' he said to his disciples, 'I bid you put away anxious thoughts about food to keep you alive, and clothes to cover your body. Life is more than food, the body more than clothes. Think of the ravens: they neither sow nor reap; they have no storehouse or barn; yet God feeds them. You are worth far more than the birds! Is there a man amongst you who by anxious thoughts can add a foot to his height? If, then, you cannot do even a very small thing, why are you so anxious about the rest?

'Think of the lilies: they neither spin nor weave; yet I tell you, even Solomon in all his splendour was not attired like one of these. But if that is how God clothes the grass, which grows in the field today, and tomorrow is thrown on the fire, how much more will he clothe you! How little faith you have! And so you are not to set your mind on food and drink; you are not to worry. For all these are things for the heathen to run after; but you have a Father who knows that you need them. No, set your mind upon his Kingdom, and all the rest will come to you as well. Have no fear, little flock; for your Father has chosen to give you the Kingdom. Sell your possessions, and give to charity. Provide for yourselves purses that do not wear out, and never-failing treasure in heaven, where no thief can get near it, no moth destroy it. For where your treasure is, there will your heart be also."

Far from finding this text from Luke Chapter 12 ironical, we experienced a deep conviction of the truth of this teaching. If we had not been at rock-bottom, this text would have been hard to believe. After all, is not our whole energy and mind geared towards providing more than the essentials of life, to create a warm nest, acquiring ever more objects to make it even more comfortable? If this does not quite fulfil us, there are our ideologies into which we fit the arts and science. In the end, it is all about security. We want to make sure we are secure in every way. But having gone through the collapse and chaos of all this, what is left? Some people in this situation either give up or throw themselves afresh into the river of materialism with a slightly different ideology. You have to believe in something after all! Or why not just believe in yourself, to the exclusion and usually detriment of everyone else. We had already seen this ideology fail on a huge scale; a fine mess they had got us into. Or why not believe in humanism, full stop. The posters in the streets were full of wonderful slogans and soundbytes: 'Communism = equality + solidarity, power for everybody with less responsibility.' We felt as if the posters and top-elite had just made room for different ones - fascism, Communism, let's wait for the next doctrine.

At school, we were bombarded with a different propaganda, with different slogans, but had we not seen and heard them all before? Pressure was applied to listen to this talk, or see that film. I began to dislike these propaganda films intensely. They made no sense to me at all, and lacked variety. They were mere horror-stories of the worst kind; three or more heads sprouting from a headless body, macabre happenings accompanied by loud, gruesome music, which overwhelmed the mind and senses.

Even at my age, I began to understand that man was his own worst enemy. I started to read the old Bible, which grew to be the most treasured of our few possessions. I learned that the whole trouble had started with the distortion of Truth. The serpent asks the woman, "Is it true that God has forbidden you to eat from any tree in the garden?" knowing full well that only the tree of life and the tree giving knowledge of good and evil was forbidden and would bring death. When the serpent is corrected, he says, "Of course you will not die. God knows that as soon as you eat from it, your eyes will be opened, and you will be like gods, knowing both good and evil."

Through believing a lie, it is much easier to disobey one's conscience. An infinite number of excuses have been made throughout history in order to twist the truth and adapt it to the desired action taken. All through the Old Testament, this theme unwinds itself; also that there is a purpose in everything, although it might take a long time to be revealed. God has patience with us, he is Love itself after all, but he is also just. After we had paid for our disobedience, he prepared to send us a part of Himself - the Truth personified in Jesus, for no man can approach God without the Truth - so that we could receive Life everlasting. We tried to kill and bury the Truth, but it cannot be buried for long; triumphantly, visibly, it rose again. And all who believe this and let the Truth penetrate, will be led towards Love and Righteousness. This releases a tremendous power, which renders the impossible possible. Many have experienced and died for it, and their lives testify to it. God cannot be present where there is no truth.

Every day we felt happier in the knowledge that we had found the right path at last. We were, of course, just starting out on our journey. It was not going to be easy, but we had found the Truth. This was our lifeline, whether we lived or died. Life would be a living death without it, a groping in the dark, a drifting along, following anyone with the biggest mouth and the most powerful fists, or the ability to fulfill our worldly desires.

We had nothing to lose anymore. We had nothing to secure and protect anymore and it was precisely this which had led us to the new and only life. We now saw everything we had previosuly valued in a different light. It all seemed so clear at last. Mountaineers must feel like this. First, they must trust the mountain. They must be convinced that to conquer it must be worth risking their life. They must feel the excitement of the undertaking, which will carry them at least half way up before they start to feel the strain. From then on, they will feel the anticipation of the summit, from where everything can be seen in its true perspective.We had the best guide, who could be trusted at all times. This was life, and there was nothing in the way anymore, that hindered us from living it in full spiritual freedom, which brings peace.

To an outsider, nothing about us had changed. We were still in a miserable state of poverty to the point of starvation, and there seemed to be no end in sight. This was the way we saw it too, but with a different attitude that permeated all our thinking. We were happy - life was a state of mind. We felt unimaginably free.

CHAPTER 44
Karl's Journey

It was night time again. Karl collected himself, shaved and washed, pulled a dark-brown suit and clean shirt out of his bundle, put them on (creased as they were), and went to see the hotel-owner. His request for something warm, after having eaten only bread and water for seven days, was promptly granted with a bread-soup, which required no ration-coupon in return. He had imagined that food would be scarce in East-Germany, and this assumption turned out to be true. He reasoned that the best thing would be to go to his parents in the American Sector. This should not be too difficult after what he had gone through, getting here. He knew that he would have to go to Oelsnitz/Vogtland, a kind of checkpoint between East and West Germany.

A horse and cart took him six kilometres to the nearest station of Zittau, from where he caught the Dresden-Chemnitz train. In Plauen, he changed for Oelsnitz, where people scurried about like ants. Some were pulling little hand-carts with luggage up the hill to a transit-camp in a castle. Karl asked the castle guard what was required to get into a so-called convoy of people travelling to the American Zone. The answer was short and final:- 'No hope.' Karl had no permit allowing him to leave the

Russian Zone or enter the American one. Sending a telegram to his parents, in which he asked for a permit from the Americans, he settled down to wait for it. Soon he got acquainted with Heinz and his wife, a couple originating from the Böhmerwald (Bohemian Woods), who were in the same predicament as himself. They discussed their problem, and came to the conclusion that the only way to get across was to stow away inside a train-convoy. They had no rationcards. Their only option was to barter for food in the villages. Most people possessed some money, but as there was very little available to purchase, one had to offer something 'special', like cigarettes, spirits, jewellery etc. Karl eventually bartered his pullover for a five-pound loaf, which turned out to be bitter, crumbly bread of sawdust consistency, the only type available in East-Germany. Still, it was something to eat.

They spent the next day in Oelsnitz. At night, after having seen all there was to see in town - utility-hardware and posters galore - they tried to settle down on the floor of the station waiting-room, ready to board the train, bound for West-Germany the next morning. As everywhere else, the place was full of people, and they were lucky to find room to rest. At about 10pm, Heinz decided to look for a hotel-room in town. He had not gone long, when he returned upset and dishevelled without his jacket. Apparently, a Russian soldier had come up from behind in a dark alley and demanded his money. There was a struggle during which the Russian ripped the jacket off Heinz and disappeared with the money into the darkness. On hearing this, Heinz's wife burst into tears; this was clearly the last straw. They had had to leave their newly-established home, she was pregnant and wanted to go to her parents, which now presented seemingly insurmountable difficulties, and now this. She sobbed inconsolably. The 10 Reichsmarks in her handbag was all the money they had. Karl and Heinz had to leave her in this state as they made their way to the railway-police, who promised to enquire at the Russian commandant's the following day. On their return, they had to step over bundles of human misery, some asleep, some worrying or crying.

At dawn, two policemen cleared the waiting room for cleaning, just as the three had managed to fall into an uneasy sleep. It was raining and everything was draped in grey. The money had not been found, which was a foregone conclusion. The train taking the privileged to the promised land began to fill quickly. The three decided to try their luck and climb inconspicuously into an attached freight-carriage. They waited an hour behind some boxes, growing stiffer and hotter every minute, until they heard the guards approach, responsible for checking every cavity and crevice of the train. Sure enough - after standing on top of the boxes and looking behind them, they discovered the stowaways, dragged them out and reprimanded them. "Don't try it again", they warned.

They immediately tried their luck in another waggon, but exactly the same fate befell them. After that, Karl gave up; he would sit it out and wait for the proper papers to arrive. According to a letter which Heinz later sent to Karl, he and his wife had succeeded at the third attempt. They were both very happy now; their persistence had paid off at last.

Karl had reached the end of his inner resources. Officially he was a 'nobody' with no papers, no roof over his head, no work and no food. He decided to rectify the two last handicaps, if possible, and found a job as a farmhand in Eichicht, Vogtland. Frau Zöpfel, the farmer's wife, shook his hand perfunctorily and showed him to his bed in the attic, which looked more like a mould than a bed. The straw inside it had not been renewed for years. Everything looked and smelled fishy and neglected. He had never seen anything like this as a soldier throughout all the war years. The hopelessness of his situation overpowered him at this point, and he sat down on the only rickety chair and cried.

By now it was harvest-time, and every hand was needed. It was strange to think that despite all the dilemmas and chaos everywhere, with so many people's worlds having collapsed, the seasons never ceased to come and go, whatever happened. It was a comforting thought. A voice came up from downstairs, reminding him to feed the animals. He took all the bedclothes and flung them on the floor in disgust, giving vent to his frustration and bitterness. Then he changed and went down to help, and became his old self again. At night, after a long day's work, they tucked into a hearty meal, and since the whole family, two boys and two girls, had a good appetite, Karl's ravenous intake of large quantities food was not particularly noticed.

The next day, the corn was cut. Karl behaved as if he had done this kind of work all his life. He thought that it would be quite safe to mention his real profession. But strangely enough, the farmer watched him closely after that. His distrust only subsided after Karl managed to produce a wagonload of wheat as symmetrical as a matchbox. On Sunday he had the privilege of playing cards at the pub with the locals.

He had given his address to his parents straightaway, and in due course a letter from his mother arrived, informing him that it was not possible for them to obtain a permit for him. Everybody wanted to be in West Germany, occupied by the Americans, or emigrate far away from this nightmare. Resignation began to get the upper hand once more. It crept up on him like the autumn cold under his blankets, which half - paralysed him during the brief hours of sleep at night.

Then, one day, a telegram arrived from his sister-in-law Hilde. Franz, Karl's brother, and Hilde had traced Karl through the Catholic organisation 'Caritas.' The telegram was succinct:- "Come to us immediately. Hilde." These few words had an unbelievable effect on

Karl. Someone cared enough to put themselves out for him. They were thinking about him right now. He would have to collect some food before leaving.

It was obvious from the hoards of townspeople roaming the countryside that the urban food situation was catastrophic. The farmers tried to protect themselves by setting up a patrol rota to guard the fields.

Karl knew that he would have to brace himself, but the anticipation of seeing some of his family again, overrode his apprehension.

On 3rd September 1946 he arrived in Neumarkt, a small textile town in Saxony. His spirits were high as he stepped off the steam-train on this sunny, glorious morning. He found his way to Gartenstrasse 18, a proud-looking villa surrounded by a well-cultivated garden boasting tobacco-plants, which were much sought after. Karl wondered how they hoped to reap the fruit of their labour without a patrol pacing up and down the garden path day and night.

Just after he had rung the bell, his sister-in-law Hilde, a kind and attractive woman, arrived with a shopping-basket in her hand. She was 8 years older than her husband Franz, Karl's intelligent and dextrous older brother. When the war ended, Franz had had the rank of railway-inspector, but on account of his having been a party-member, the German railway would not employ him now. No former party member could be employed with a job in an official capacity, even if he had occupied this post throughout the entire war.[1] He now worked as a weaver in a large factory, doing shiftwork. Hilde had been ordered by the Russians to work a 36 hour a week dayshift, followed by an eight hour nightshift each week at the same factory where her husband worked.

While Hilde and Karl were talking, Evi, their little brown-eyed girl of seven with her mother's black curls, joined them. She could not remember her Uncle Karl, but immediately implored him to stay with her. She was left alone a lot and was naturally unhappy with the situation, but it was obvious that Karl would not be able to look after her. He would have to go out to work too. Already the next day, he started at the same factory, where Franz patiently taught him how to weave. Karl began to have doubts as to whether he would ever be able to master the skill of weaving, or for that matter, tolerate the din of 300 machines in one room for longer than a few days. In spite of everything, he managed to receive a certificate as a qualified weaver after the trial period was over and began to earn enough to make ends meet with the help of Hilde, who let him stay cheaply with them and even got some clothes for him.

---

[1] It was not until the fifties that the authorities had determined who the real war-criminals were. Hitherto no former party member could be employed without documentary evidence of all their wartime movements.

Everything continued peaceably, until an unforeseen event happened that changed their lives overnight.

Karl had noticed that Hild appeared to be very nervous and unsettled. On the surface it looked as if the outer circumstances of her life were getting her down - the sudden, brutal deportation from her homeland to another country, the loss of all they had worked so hard for over many years, the daily worry of where the next meal would come from, the enforced neglect of her child Eva (she had been married before, and had a grown-up daughter, Edith, from her first marriage), the endless toil day and night to obtain essentials which left them short of money each time, the onset of the menopause and the incessant smoking to try and ease her stress - was it really surprising that she sometimes appeared to be at her wit's end? Yet, Karl detected deeper reasons than the obvious ones. He could not help noticing that Franz neglected Hilde more and more. It had always been clear that Hilda attracted men, but nobody actually knew if she ever made use of her power over them. No one had ever seen her do anything 'immoral'; on the contrary, she was kind and helpful to anyone in general. She was a very emotional person, and was deeply grieved by her husband's infidelity, which could no longer be ignored. The age difference between them must have also played a role. If Hilde was admired by men, Franz was adored by young women, who constantly offered themselves to him. The rift in their marriage widened, so that the chance of reconciliation was no more than a hope expressed, solely by Hilde. Franz eventually fell ill and saw a doctor, who wanted to see Hilde for a check-up. She told Karl that she had been given a clean bill of health by the doctor, but her crying and fainting fits continued. One night, she ran out of the factory to Karl's horror, whose first instinct was to follow her.

"Take no notice," Franz said stoically, "this has been going on a long time. She's been talking about suicide for years." Franz was not a bad father or provider. He was a charming, calm man, who was pursued by admiring women.

Karl hurried out of the factory gates in pursuit of Hilde. He could not understand his brother's callous attitude. He was familiar with never-ending arguments between marriage partners, even jealousy and bitterness, but never such indifference. What else was he going to learn about marriage? There were so many variations of unhappiness and disappointment that it hardly seemed worth contemplating as a future aim or ambition. It was an awesome responsibility when all was said and done. But for children, he thought, a proper family was very important. How nice it must be to come home to your wife and children and belong; to help in the creation of this precious unity with all your energy and zest, to share good and bad times together, to discuss and debate issues in love and with respect for each other.

Karl caught up with Hilde who had been wandering aimlessly through the dark streets and alleys of the town and asked exactly what was wrong. She would not tell him. By this time, they had reached the outskirts of Neumarkt, and Hilde suddenly fell unconscious into the road. Karl was overcome by a sense of panic and helplessness. What was he to do?

He pulled her over into the grass and put her on her side. After a short while she came to, and looked around curiously, as though she had no idea as to where she was or how she had arrived there. She was quieter now, and Karl was able to lead her home without any protest from her. He laid her on the sofa in the kitchen and talked quietly to her. Soon, Franz returned from work, shrugging his shoulders. "You shouldn't worry about her," he told Karl, "its pure hysteria, that's all!"

The 20th October 1946 was a dripping wet and cold Sunday. In the morning, they had decided to go to the cinema later on, just for a change. Hilde went to the bedroom in the attic to have a rest, and Franz followed. Karl ventured out into the rain to get some tickets for the film. Edith, who had come to visit and little Evi were busy in the kitchen when Karl returned, soaked through. Franz told him that Hilde had asked for him. He went up and knocked on the door. There was no reply. He ended up banging the door and shouting until he was red in the face from agitation and strain, but only a menacing silence answered.

Frantic and distraught, he raced downstairs and the landlady was informed. They tried every key they could lay their hands on, but all to no avail. The landlady begged the two men not to break the door down. The only available handyman prepared to come on a Sunday (under a shower of protest about his peace being disturbed by such a triviality) was a plumber. Karl, fearing the worst, stayed downstairs. Franz came down shortly after, pale and shocked. Hilde had hanged herself and he had had to cut her down.

She had put an end to it all without a word of explanation. There was no note or letter that could have given a reason for this irreversible deed. Everyone was stunned, and followed their own trail of thought. Franz obviously realized how insensitive he had been. But it was all too late now. Soon, the police arrived and made their inquiry. On the third day she was cremated. There were few mourners. As the coffin disappeared slowly behind a curtain, the minister ended his consoling words with: "From dust you came, to dust you return."

Little Eva had no idea of what had happened. She sang her short, carefree songs as before, and was reprimanded for it. Edith and her two-year-old daughter moved in with them and looked after the household. The two men went back to work, never to be the same again.

Karl decided that he would have to try once more to reach his parents, now that he presented an extra burden to the changed family circumstances. In any case, he could not bear to be in that house any longer. Everything reminded him of what had happened, especially Evi. He had to get away, and soon.

CHAPTER 45
Visitors

We had at last had news from my father. In one way, we were disappointed that he was 'in another country' ie. in West-Germany, which meant that he would not be able to come and see us easily. On the other hand, there might be a slim chance that we would be allowed to follow him - a prospect which excited us. As we could not visit him, he would have to try and visit us first.

I had started to suffer from ill health once again, but this time it was nothing psychosomatic. Shortage of food and its consequences had caught up with me. I suffered from colitis, an intestinal inflammation which flared up from time to time, accompanied by a piercing, cramp-like pain. Whenever the pain occurred, part of the lining of the colon was shed. My jaw glands began to swell, so that my skin-and-bone appearance changed to a slighty more pleasant one. I felt my face getting rounder, which made me look as if I had mumps. (I had already suffered that disease in the transit-camp). I could not go to school and, with Liesl back in hospital and my mother at work, I found myself alone in our room. Someone had given me a few magazines from bygone days, when girls and boys were content to read about explorers, how people in other countries live, and similar literature. I think it was a monthly loose-leafed magazine with the extra bonus of a continuous book publication in serial form, so that no one would ever dream of discontinuing the subscription payment unless they were in serious financial trouble. In any case, I was glad that there were so many of them (about ten) and not less. When I had finished reading them, I would go back to reading the Bible, of which I never tired, although I did not understand a lot of it. Yet, a string had been plucked and the resonance echoed on. The urge to hear more, grew. I wanted to learn more about the visible and unseen elements of life. People had always fascinated me. The word 'boredom' was nonexistent in my vocabulary.

As I was burying myself in the incredible violence and immorality of some of the Old Testament characters one day, there was a faint knock on the door. Three long hooks pulled the gaping door towards some fixtures on the doorframe. (In this way, the draught was only minimal.) I had to stand on the bottom hook in order to reach the top one. After I had unhooked all three, I cautiously opened the door, and my heart stood still. It was my father. He had changed so much that he looked more like an apparition than my beloved father. He was thin and lifeless, with a questioning look on his haggard face. He was a broken man. I did not understand why he had changed so much, nor why he stared at me in such a distraught fashion. We faced each other, motionless, then we clung to each other as strangled sounds escaped from our parched lips. He said very little, but stared into space, as if the answers to his unspoken questions were hanging around somewhere in the atmosphere. I was disturbed by this, but at the same time happy that he was back, physically unharmed. He could only stay a few days.

My sister was coming out of hospital for the length of his stay, so when my mother wanted to be alone with him for a few hours, she sent us to some friends on an errand. They all seemed better off than us. The Bergers, a middle-aged couple, occupied a flat with lovely furniture, whose former owner had left in a hurry. His young wife had died in childbirth, and her husband could not bear to be in the flat any longer. The Aulitzkys, an elderly couple with a son in West Germany, had been squeezed into a   tiny room, which prided itself on a sofa and kitchen-cabinet, amongst other 'essentials.' All this luxury may have been the reason for its minute appearance. We used to sit there often with the adults discussing the past, present and future. Their door had a big gap at the bottom, so that, in spite of sitting on that wonderful sofa of theirs, one's feet felt as if submerged in a bowl of icy water.

Later on in life, I learned that my parents had been unable to communicate with each other on that occasion, their first meeting for a long time, and for the unspeakable experiences for both of them during their enforced separation. My father was not even capable of speaking more than a few words. After he had left, he sent us little parcels, containing oats directly from the mill. The husks had been retained, but we thought that these 'presents' tasted better than any delicacy. He also wrote lovely letters. What he had not been able to say in words to us, he now expressed wonderfully on paper. He later expressed his shock at seeing us in such an emaciated state. He knew then that we would not last much longer if left. To rescue us was uppermost on his mind from then on and a plan slowly materialized. The problem was that the authorities insisted that the breadwinner had to join the family, which meant that my father would have to leave West Germany and share our starvation in East Germany.

One day, my mother was queueing for food for Frau Angermann, when her midriff began to itch. This proved to be the onset of shingles halfway around her waist, a very painful and lingering disease of the nerves, but she had to go to work every day, nevertheless.

The winter of 1946/7 lives on in many people's memories as exceptionally severe. Continuous snow and frost crippled the normal flow of the local population's lives, but for people like us, this weather condition was a killer. Now, many people were dying of starvation and cold, and if it had not been for friends and relations, we also would most likely have fallen victims to it.

Herr Berger had been employed by the railways. For this reason, he could claim old sleepers for firewood from them. These wooden sleepers had been replaced by new ones. The Berger's asked us if we could help with transporting them from the station to their house on our little handcart. My mother could not take the day off work, so she sent me. The guilt she felt about this remained with her for the rest of her life. In my condition,[1] I was hardly able to support my own feeble frame, not to mention some heavy wooden beams. I cannot remember much about it, only that we benefited through receiving some of that wood after it had been cut up.

Through our rations, we were able to buy my mother a pair of clogs, and for Liesl and myself a pair of horrible-looking leather ankle-boots. The three of us considered ourselves the luckiest people alive. The only trouble with my mother's clogs were that, after a few steps of walking in the snow with them, the wooden soles of these clogs accumulated a little mountain of compressed snow and ice, making it impossible to walk at all. If she hobbled on in spite of this, the whole 'snow-ball' would suddenly detach itself and she would reel about as if drunk. She had a good laugh about this, and so did we. Life was really very exciting, all in all. That she could have broken her bones and the state we were in, was not worth considering. We had nothing to lose, literally, having reached rock bottom in every way. Every day was a bonus.

The second visitor we had that winter was my Uncle Karl, Tante Marie's husband. He appeared one day, out of the blue, a shadow of his former self. His confident manner, which had bordered on arrogance at times, had completely disappeared. He had lived the life of a lord when young, borrowing money and asking some of his relatives to be guarantors, which brought them untold grief. Now, he looked like a skeleton with some old, frozen skin wrapped around it. He had no overcoat, and his feet, already frostbitten from the First World War, were

---

[1] I had started having very painful, light-sensitive eyes

blue and swollen. His now protruding big, blue eyes looked haunted from the experience in Postelberg, and for a few days we believed he had lost his mind. Apart from that, he suffered from exhaustion, starvation and severe frostbite, as the lady-doctor who came to   attend to him, confirmed. We did not know how he had found us. My mother was able to obtain rationcards for him, and tell him where he could find his wife and daughter. No one knew for a long time where his son Erich was.[1] He could not absorb anything that was said to him at first. My mother gave him her bed, while she slept on the little bench with her feet on the only chair in the room, her head sharing my pillow. He did nothing but sleep and groan for a few days. His clothes resembled those of a tramp, which was hardly surprising when you consider that he had walked every inch of the way from Leneschütz (a small village in Czechoslovakia) to Freiberg/Saxony in sub-zero temperatures, in constant fear of being detected. Obviously, he had had to sleep rough for weeks on end in these unusual arctic conditions.

Eventually, he was able to eat the food we had fetched from his rations. We gained the impression he had regressed right back to childhood; he was totally bewildered and terrified, but the doctor assured us that he would be all right, given time. He would begin a sentence and suddenly stop. The tears running down his sunken cheeks would prevent him from continuing.

On the fourth day, he wanted to get up, wash and shave. To give him some privacy, we went upstairs to stay with the Hofmanns. He seemed much better. My mother had obtained a brush, razor and some clothes for him. Most materials were now made from a kind of fibreglass, which itched considerably when close to the skin. He was happy to be alive, to have food and clothes, and to know where he was going. He could not wait to be reunited with his family. He also did not want to be a burden to us any longer. Before he left, he told us some of his story.

"You know how we were treated at Postelberg," he began on the sixth day, his voice shaky and his glance unsteady, "how they squeezed us in low, arched stables overnight, where it got unbearably hot, so that men lost their minds and began to attack others. I can't tell you about all the cruelties and murders the militia inflicted on us". His voice trailed off into a groan.

"Don't say any more about it", my mother said, soothingly. She had heard from other men in the camp who had managed to escape and come out alive or at least half-alive. They could not talk about it without breaking down halfway through, either. "Just tell us how you escaped, if

---

[1] His ship had been captured in the North-Ostsee Canal. Later he married a girl from East Prussia and settled in Schleswig Holstein

you can." She put her hand on his shoulder and, taking a deep breath, he continued, hesitatingly.

"Well, I was only wearing trousers over my pyjamas when they found me that Sunday morning, on 3rd June 1945. When some of us were sent back to Saaz to clean out the latrines in the camps and do other jobs that no one wanted to do, I went to fetch some tobacco from my house. I was going to go back to the job, because the chances of escape were too slim, and the risk of going to prison or being shot were very high. Opposite our house were the headquarters of the Czech commandant. They must have seen me entering the house, because straightaway a guard came with a whip and threw me out. He said I was lucky, as his father had nearly been beaten to death in the war by the Nazis, and he should do the same to me. Later we were transported to the countryside, where we were allotted to farms as slave labourers." He began to tire quickly now and had to take a rest. After a while, his voice now very quiet, he resumed his story.

"Every day we had potato soup, and very little else. Our job was to feed loads of pigs. The only way we could survive was to go through the pigswill and pick the best bits out. Last winter we nearly froze to death. If it hadn't been for your brother Franz, who came and brought me some clothes, I wouldn't have made it. He might be a rascal in other ways, but I shall never forget how he risked his own skin for me like that. Anyway, who am I to talk? I haven't exactly been angelic myself. But we never want to admit that we have been wrong. It will be very difficult for us as a nation. We have been lead astray through propaganda, once conditions improved after the last war. This comes through always looking for a strong leader. We certainly got it" His voice had become louder and more determined, although pearls of perspiration from exhaustion began to appear on his temples. My mother stopped him abruptly.

"But Karl, it can't be that we've spent the best years of our lives following a wild beast and his gang on the wrong course and making so many sacrifices for it. Nand is totally devastated now. How can we pick up the pieces and try and put them together again?"

"That's it," he moaned, "we can't sort ourselves out, so we throw ourselves into something else and hope that the original problem will go away. Sometimes it even looks as if we've achieved our aim until the truth catches up with us and we have two massive problems on our hands instead of one. And then .... the excuses. Of course, we didn't know the ins and outs of high politics and what goes on behind the scenes. But knowing eventually what these people - and every nation has them - were like, we could have had a good guess, hm?" He raised his hands and stuck his neck out towards her. "Do you think it was right to throw the Jews into work-camps and deprive them of everything they had? We know

now what that is like, don't we? That was just one outrageous act that screamed to high heaven as an injustice, the same as what happened in Russia!"[4]

My mother shrunk back in horror and covered her eyes. He knew he had said too much for the time being. It would take years to face up to what had happened in the last few years, and it was a very painful process. Many people could not do it at all. My uncle was a broken man physically, but he was 'intact' otherwise. He left us on the seventh day to join his wife and daughter in Pirna, where his grandson Werner had been born the previous year. Toni, his son-in-law eventually turned up, and they all finished up in the Western Zone somehow.

Trixi stayed in contact with the family until she committed suicide in the fifties. She had been unhappily married and could see no other escape from it. We have never forgotten her.

Before Uncle Karl left, my mother reminded him that he still had not told us the story of his escape. "There you have it", he said unhappily, and his wrinkled face became more furrowed. "There's my Truth I can't face at the moment. This other German and myself fled from the farm into the forests, where we hid in the fir-trees. The only thing we had to eat and drink was snow. When we reached the frontier, we heard shots being fired. I just hurried on as best I could, but I never saw him again."

CHAPTER 46
Feelings

It was now Spring 1947 and I was 10 years old.

In the summer of the previous year, I had made friends with the children of the neighbourhood, but my best friends were Irene and Werner Hofmann from upstairs. During a ball game, I had accidently knocked my knee against the boy's from next door. I felt as if an electric current had shot through me, and he seemed to have felt the same, judging by the look on his face. But we remained just playmates, not special friends. Irene became a confidante and close friend, and her brother Werner suddenly filled a large gap in my life without being aware of it. By the spring of 1947 I felt both guilty, and 'in love' on separate levels. Guilty, because a feeling of remorse about being so jealous of Liesl in the past had set in; and in love, because Werner was so kind and understanding, and showed such goodwill to everyone.

---

[4] The full horror of the Jewish tragedy was not known yet to most Germans. - Many Russian villages were destroyed in the war, burned and people killed, although the Russian Army itself was ordered to take revenge on the "White Russians", who often sided with the Germans. There is much we do not know yet.

Although he was only a teenager, he was similar to my sister in his 'all-knowing' wisdom. At least, that was how I saw it. His modesty and pleasant manner made him stand out immediately from the rest of the youngsters. He compared favourably with Herbert, except for one thing. Herbert could never be beaten in his forthrightness, vigour and courage, and most of all, in his strong expression of feelings he might have at any time. But love for Werner grew like the spring-flowers, which peeped through snow and ice and could not be held back by them, so strong was their beauty and purity.

I was now a pitiful sight without being aware of it. My body was just skin and bones, my swollen face permanently framed with a tied-up scarf (to keep the inflammation under control, as we incorrectly assumed), my painful eyes protected from sunlight by a pair of dark goggles. It was relatively dark in our room, but my eyes still hurt without these 'glasses', which an eye-specialist had prescribed for me. There was no question of attending school anymore. So, apart from reading the bible with my bad eyes, I used to visit the Hofmann children upstairs whenever I could. Irene had thick, auburn plaits, a transparent, longish face and braces over her teeth. She was softly spoken, and very shy. Werner had an oval face with a mop of blond hair, and blue eyes into the bargain. Since being aware of my new feelings for Werner, I tried to impress him, whenever I saw him.

Someone had given me a frilly little apron, which I tried repeatedly to press with an ancient iron – without success. This iron had a metal block inside which had to be removed and heated up somehow. Our little stove hardly had enough warmth to heat itself, let alone a room or an iron. No wonder the apron remained creased, no matter how many times I tried to flatten it with the iron.

I removed my goggles and put my apron on to make myself look respectable for the occasion of visiting Werner and his family. I now felt nervous and apprehensive each time I prepared to see him, but it was an exhilarating feeling. The last few days of my school attendance had seen great excitement. Our teacher had told us either to ask our parents about matters of sex and love, or to attend the classes offered by the school for this vital part of our education. I was too embarrassed to stay at school. My plan was to ask my mother to hold the candle in the lavatory one evening, and in this 'exclusive' spot with no one else to overhear us, I would pose the relevant questions. No sooner had I done this, all hell broke loose.

"What do you think I am?! Some kind of idiot you can trap in a corner and bombard with things like that?! No, my lady, and don't you do anything like that again, you hear?" With this parting shot, she and the candle disappeared from view. I sat there in the dark, feeling awfully ashamed of myself. How could I have dared, what audacity to ask my mother about such a subject, my mother of all people! I did not go back into our room until I was stone-cold and shivering all over. My mother would not let the subject rest; she brought it up over and over again until I bitterly regretted my strategic plan.

On rare occasions, I went over to the Schäffner's, our landladies. I would have liked to see them more often, as they had a lovely, old-fashioned home; very comfortable, with an assortment of goods from their father's shop. Their parents had died during the war, but the two daughters still stored lots of bedlinen, tea-towels and handtowels, some of which they gave to us. I still have some in my possession now, many years later. They used to look dark brown, because the linen was unbleached. With use and many washes, the colour changed to white.

The infrequency of my visits was due to the spinsters' full work-schedule, which necessitated being out all day.

"Be considerate, don't pester them when they come home from the office at night," my mother would advise urgently, "they have other things to do than talk to you."

Almost every time I went there, they were preparing ragout, a mixture of different vegetables, nicely diced and simmering gently on the gleaming kitchen range – what a peaceful existence, capturing the 'good old days' at home. A little vinegar and sugar had been added to this treat that they could afford so often; just the taste I loved the best. Anything sweet and sour was my favourite food... and yet so unreachable for me in our present position. Once, I managed to be there at the right moment. The Ragout had just been cooked and they had to give me a little taste of it while they were eating theirs.

In a bucket, something indescribably revolting was soaking in water. I dared not ask for a definition of these blood-stained articles, remembering how my mother had told me something about a monthly occurrence in a woman's life, after she had placed a heavy shopping-bag with a strange article in it on the table in our home, arousing my curiosity at once.[1]

The only time I left the house now was to regularly attend an eye-specialist and clinic, where I had to lie under an ultra-violet lamp on one day, and an infra-red one the next. Plenty of drops and ointments were put into my eyes, but the opthalmist always stressed that, all that was needed, was food. My ailments were all caused by a lack food, certain vitamins, minerals, warmth and attention in general. I was growing fast, but my intake of food was now less than before. My body was being

---

[1] Every woman had a "soaking bucket" like this, but usually in a much more private place.

exposed to every possible assault and it began to protest violently. Yet, we never asked ourselves the question: "How much longer can we last?" Not that my mother avoided her responsibilities; she did everything she could to keep us alive.

My father, in the American Zone, was repeatedly told that the breadwinner, who in those days meant the man, must join his family, wherever they might be found, which would have meant starvation for him too. We had to somehow join my father, and other relations in West-Germany, even if it meant going illegally. The longer we waited, the slimmer our chances of survival and a successful crossing of the border became. Would my sister be able to walk such a long way under difficult conditions, her heart already overstimulated at the prospect of the whole venture? Death became an integral part of our lives; another truth and reality to face. We were not afraid of it, neither did we ask for it. Now that we had nothing to lose, now that we were free from fear and anxiety, now that we were free to enjoy what was left of our lives from day to day, we wanted to hang on to that happiness of living, a little longer.

At that stage, I had reached the New Testament in my Bible reading. What language, what stories, what Truth! The whole thing vibrated with Life and Spirit. The word Truth was mentioned innumerable times. Jesus seemed to be Truth itself. "I am the way, the truth and the life ...Verily, verily (in truth) I tell you... there is no truth in you... He who sent me speaks the truth... If you dwell within the revelation I have brought, you are indeed my disciples; you shall know the truth, and the truth will set you free... The words which I have spoken to you are both spirit and life. And yet there are some of you who have no faith... Let the dead (in spirit) bury the dead... You must be born again...You must work, not for this perishable food, but for the food that lasts, the food of eternal life ....my task is to bear witness to the truth. For this I was born; for this I came into the world, and all who are not deaf to truth listen to my voice... Where there are two or three gathered together in my name, there I shall be amongst them..." Pilate stared the Truth personified in the face and asked: "What is truth?" He was no better or worse than anybody else, in fact; he had tried to find out the truth about this particular case; but his position was threatened by it, so he pretended not to see what was right. Could we ever close our eyes again and be blind to realities that represent spiritual life or death? Would we be like Peter, who said, "Lord, to whom shall we go? Your words are words of eternal life. We have faith, and we know that you are the holy One of God," but soon afterwards turned round, finding himself in a tight corner, and denied his Lord and Master, which was not held against him, yet made him realize how limited man was, despite his enormous intelligence and ingenuity.

On the first Sunday of May 1947, Mother's Day in Germany, I remembered what a big day it had been in previous years. It had meant weeks of planning ahead as far as Liesl and myself were concerned. We had our own individual plans for this special day, and neither of us knew what the other was doing, which added considerably to the excitement. One year, I had saved up enough money to buy a beautiful pot-planted hydrangea, eagerly anticipating my mother's delight, only to be bitterly disappointed by the fact that Liesl had bought an identical one. Before that, Liesl's flowers had 'outshone' my own tenfold. So, this year, we would be equal at last; neither of us had anything to give, but it seemed a shame not to have a present as a token of our appreciation. In the end, Liesl bought a few cut flowers for both of us to give to my mother from the few pennies she had saved. My mother was touched:

"You shouldn't have done that. Times are too hard to think of things like that. I wasn't able to give you anything for Christmas; how do you think I felt? It was bad enough having to give you cut-out dolls in the last year of the war."

I remembered my big paper doll with some nostalgia. I had had to cut her out of a little booklet, each page of which contained a different set of clothes for her. It had been fun making a whole 'wardrobe' from underclothes to fur-collars and boots for my very own doll. Little did my mother realize that the paper doll had pleased me far more than 'Rosalind,' the big, expensive real doll she had bought for me, or the cushion, she had made for me, in the shape of a cat.

My father kept us regularly informed about his welfare. He knew he had to rescue us as soon as was possible, but he could see no way open to him, to actually do it. We could all have been shot while crossing, or my sister could have died having to walk for miles without stopping. Time was passing and he could not come up with any solution to the problem. While reading one of his letters one day, my mother's colour changed. She put the letter on her lap and stared into space.

"Papa has lost his right index finger," she said in a voice devoid of all emotion. "It happened on the fourth of January this year, while he was putting some food for the animals through a machine. His gloved fingers were stiff and numb with the cold, so that he didn't even realize at first that his finger was only hanging on by a thread. It had happened early in the afternoon, and the doctor didn't arrive until 8 o'clock at night. The two sisters had not taken much notice of the accident, seeing my father as a 'foreigner', although he spoke the same language, albeit with a different accent. They had just informed the Protestant district nurse (Diakonisse), who came late in the afternoon, and told him off for leaving the hand in water all afternoon. Apparently it was the worst thing he could have done. She bandaged it up and waited with him for the doctor to arrive. Bärbel and her sister must have wondered what was going to happen as far as the threshing and woodcutting were concerned, but looking after the animals would not be too difficult; they could do that themselves.

My father had deliberately kept quiet about all this until he had felt able to cope with and write about it without upsetting himself or us too much. What had upset him the most was the sisters' callousness. By the time the doctor came in the evening, (the snow had made the road impassable for a time) my father had lost a considerable amount of blood. The doctor's car was unheated, and the temperature outside was sub-zero. When the doctor asked for a blanket, his request was met with stubborn resistance until he warned them that they would be made responsible if anything 'serious' happened to my father. Due to the heavy blood loss, the doctor was afraid that if they were 'snowed in' on a steep, wind-exposed slope, my father might freeze and bleed to death. The hospital in Göppingen was expecting them, and no time was wasted in amputating the finger. They put sandbags on him to keep him still while under anaesthesia. He spent a terrible night throwing the sandbags off time and again, but worse was to come. For the next 3 days, he experienced unimaginable agony without any painkillers. It could well be that they were not available at the time. The food was miserable, which was also not surprising. He spent about a fortnight there; time enough to ponder about the Frieses, and to make up his mind that wild horses would not drag him back there. He had applied to the railway for a job in Göppingen, but they correctly assumed that he must have been a former Nazi-party member. They deduced this from the short period of training he had received in Saaz, when he first joined the railway. It took years to sort out who did what during the war years and be 'denazified'.

He started work in a garden nursery, residing in some former barracks. His luck was short-lived. One day, he was caught hiding some potatoes in his pockets, and sacked on the spot.

Frau Edle Maier von Weinertsgrün had told Tante Schroll (who had owned the smithy in Saaz) of our whereabouts. Tante Schroll was in contact with her nephew Karl, my father's brother, who gave us his parents' address. In this way, we were able to tell my father that his parents now lived in a small village in Bavaria, 20 km away from Regensburg. I remembered that Herbert had been picked up in Regensburg after he had run away from home. Regensburg would also have to be our destination, because the only southbound train from East-Germany went through Hof (near the border) down to Regensburg with all the legally permitted travellers into West-Germany. My father discovered that there was a transit-camp in Regensburg. The slowly emerging plan was for my father to come and visit us again, taking us and our few belongings back with him on the train as far as the border, which we would cross on foot, illegally, and then meet up with him at the first station in West Germany.

Before this plan became a possibility, my father ran from village to village around Ehring, where his parents lived, to look for a job on a farm in exchange for a flat or room for his family. Labour was urgently needed on many farms, as many farmers' sons were either dead or missing. The problem was that nobody wanted to know about having one of 'those foreigners' living under the same roof with them, even if they put them up in an out-house. In the towns, one could understand the reluctance of the authorities to welcome more people. Most towns were badly bombed and could not support their own people. Berlin, for instance, had been bombed 90 times in the last 60 days of the war. One wonders, what there was left to bomb. The Allies, not even the Russians when they entered Berlin, realized that Hitler and his advisers had constructed a vast network of underground tunnels, with several super-strong flak towers emerging out of them. These tunnels stored tonnes of munitions and thousands of Berliners, who lived in small compartments, specially designed for this purpose. The flak towers were able to shoot at the Russians non-stop and could not be destroyed, so strong was their structure. The tunnels even contained a hospital and many other essential features for survival.

Eventually, my father came to a village, called Taimering on the Regensburg-Straubing Line, about 4 km away from Ehring, where he heard the same old story. He finally accepted a job offer from a farmer, called Beck, who was well-known for his fairness and Christian way of life. He had been Mayor during the war. Once, he had sent a farmer his conscription papers from the Ministry of War; the man took a shotgun and wounded him, fortunately not severely. It spoke in Herrn Beck's favour that he would not reveal the culprit's name. The Mayor of the adjoining village had been stabbed to death on his way to church for the same reason.

Farmer Beck could not accommodate us, if we managed to come across the border from East Germany, but he was hopeful that eventually someone in the village would. First of all, we would have to go to a camp in Regensburg in order to get our ration-cards. We might then have to squeeze into my grandparents' two-roomed flat in Ehring until a room was available for us. The good thing was that we would not need a permit to stay as we were the family of my father, who already had a permit. The East German rule that the breadwinner had to join the family did not apply in West Germany. We were allowed to join our breadwinner in the American Zone, if we could only get across there.

This plan seemed the only way out of our dilemma, and now that the warmer weather had set in, it looked quite acceptable. Risks have to be taken in life; both physically and emotionally. Constant security is in itself a threat to 'good living.' The risk did not affect anyone else, and in our position, we had no other choice.

CHAPTER 47
Karl's Perseverence and Reward

K arl, my father's brother, had found his brother Oskar not far from Neumarkt. The two of them decided to try their luck and cross from East to West Germany across the border together. It was December and winter had caught up with them, although there was no sign of snow as yet. One dismal evening, they found themselves walking along the asphalt road leading straight to the border, just two kilometres away.

A figure approached them in the dark, and Oskar, who had ten years more life experience than his brother, suggested they avoid the road and walk through the muddy fields. Karl had other ideas; this man would only be someone with the same intention as themselves. As they approached him, the middle-aged man told them that he had just come 'from there,' and that there was absolutely no danger, as there were no guards to be seen anywhere. Oskar still wanted to go via the fields, but Karl could not face this, and begged his brother to stay on the road. Cautiously they moved forward, not believing their luck that they had actually reached the border (in the shape of a barricade across the road) without being stopped.

They were just about to climb over it, when a mighty voice boomed through the darkness: "*Stoy!*" (stop), and the loading of a machine-gun could be heard. Karl's heart sank. Nothing was ever straightforward in life, Karl thought and sighed. Suddenly, there were several Russian soldiers surrounding them and no chance of escape. They were marched into the little wooden hut where they had to raise their arms as they were searched for weapons. Karl tried to explain that they were brothers, whose aim was to see their old parents in Bavaria, but could not obtain the papers to cross legally. One Russian asked: "Why you want go to German America where is no food?" Karl did not answer, but was glad that they could not read his thoughts, otherwise he might have been in even greater trouble. Everyone knew that conditions were better in West Germany, rather than East Germany.

Throughout the night, men, women and children were caught, fourteen people in total. It was a busy night; no doubt, business as usual. Karl thought of the endless streams of Germans from the East, (mainly from Poland and Czechoslovakia) still flooding across, a year and a half after the end of the war. Where could they go? The Russians knew that if they let them across, everyone (even the indigenous population) would leave the Russian Sector. There would be nobody left to do the work. On the other hand, the shortage of food and everything else for the German people, did not worry them too much. The elite had enough. They had to be rewarded for their loyalty. The rest would work harder just to stay alive, and those who did not, were too weak and useless anyway. The Russians had their own problems after that war, which had brought them to their knees.[1]

All the prisoners stood for hours outside the guard house with their luggage, waiting to be transported somewhere and trying to keep warm by stamping their feet. At 10am the next morning, the new guards arrived. The old ones took the prisoners by car to the next village for RM 5.- per person. From there, they had to walk 15 km to the next Russian commandant. Some had to throw their precious bundles away. The weight was just too heavy for them. One woman could hardly walk, because, as she admitted later to Karl, she had hidden some of her jewellery in her shoes.

The guarded, and by now thoroughly miserable prisoners finally arrived at a lonely farm. The farm house itself was occupied by Russian soldiers and their superiors. There were also some out-houses, stables, and some servants' quarters a short distance away from the main building. In the foyer there, the prisoners waited an eternity to be interrogated one at a time.

In the evening, they were escorted to a former wine-cellar. Some rotting straw and an army of rats 'welcomed' the weary captives. They had hoped for at least a bowl of soup, but nothing was given to them.

The next day, the Russians looked for volunteers to help in the kitchen. Karl was one of the first to offer his help. He was sure that something edible would come his way during the course of the day. The deliciously greasy pancakes, succulent roast pork on giant dishes and shiny big pans full of bubbling, aromatic soups were almost too much for his senses, especially since not so much as a breadcrumb fell under the table to be eaten. Towards the evening, after having cut some wood for the fire, fetched some water and cleaned the kitchen, he felt faint from pangs of hunger. One of the prisoners confessed to having a loaf of bread in his rucksack, which he took out and shared with everyone to the delight of his fellow-sufferers.

---

[1] Manpower was needed. Russia appropriated goods, manufactured in East Germany until Communism fell in 1989. The population in East Germany was shrinking drastically through people fleeing until the border was secured properly with mines and guards all along , and the Berlin Wall was erected in 1961.

When day broke, another interrogation took place. The commandant wanted to know the exact reason for this weird notion of wanting to escape from the 'liberated Russian part of Germany.'

"It's much worse over there," he told them, "you'll all starve to death in the end."

Another 12 km long walk stretched in front of them to the next commandant, housed in a big villa with an even bigger basement. No one actually knew how they had managed to arrive there, with their last reserves of energy slowly draining away. When was the last time they had had a proper meal? Could anyone remember? By now, they were 30 people. They were told to leave their luggage upstairs and settle down in this former coal cellar, divided by wooden boards. There was no thought of sleep. Everyone was exhausted, starving and frozen to the core.

The next morning, they were split up into work parties. Karl and Oskar had been chosen to make a new fence around the villa; in the afternoon, they reported for stable duty in the faintest hope of getting something to eat in return, but their hopes were dashed once more. At 5pm, they gathered again in the cellar, but this time they were allowed to have a chat together before entering their cells. There was a young woman there who was suspected of being a spy, because of her knowledge of the Russian language. She had been there for 6 weeks and had received some food. She was molested and raped by the guards almost every day. Others were kept for 3 or 4 weeks, then set free without being interrogated.

As the church-clock struck six, a guard appeared and called Karl upstairs. He had just enough time to tell his brother that if he was released, he would be waiting for Oskar at the station. Sure enough, after having been given a serious warning and being handed his luggage, he was allowed to go.

Knocking on the door of a nearby house, he was lucky to get something to eat without exchanging any of his ration-vouchers, and was able to wash and shave himself. He watched the street outside through the window the whole time, in case Oskar came along. Finally, he thanked the charitable lady and went to the heated waiting-room of the station, where Oskar appeared within half an hour. They did not waste one minute, but immediately bought tickets for another agreed crossing-point. It was understood that they would have to be more circumspect this time. It spoke for Oskar's patience and long-suffering that he did not utter one word of reproach to his brother Karl, who was responsible for the last few days' hardship and had by now been fed and groomed, whereas Oskar himself had had no opportunity to do so.

At 8.45pm they had reached their destination, which consisted of a few houses built on the side of a hill like swallows nests under the eaves of a house. Lower down in the valley, four lit-up farms could be seen, with a brook threading its way through their gardens. Karl plucked up courage and went into one of the farms to ask for a glass of milk and a slice of bread in exchange for money. When the farmer's stout wife agreed, he called in his brother. Both of them devoured all that was put in front of them as the woman chatted to them. For Oskar it was the first food for four days. She informed them of all the necessary details of the crossing in that region. Just then, a patrol passed by outside.

"You see, here he comes from his tour of the area. Up there-" (she pointed to some felled trees in the distance) "is the Czech border. This area stretches for one kilometre, after which you'll be in the American Zone." They thanked her, and rushed on in anticipation of the 'promised land,' with the end of their ordeal now in sight. The woman had seemed so honest and reliable; she had described each landmark and tree so accurately. They just had to trust her; there was no other way now. They trudged in silence through all the places that would mark the difference between happiness and misery for their future. The burning question was: would they be caught again after all this effort (as in the past) or would they finally get the break they needed to reach their goal. What was in store for them if the Czech officials caught them now? This prospect made them shudder. Their fast pace slowed down considerably, and after reaching the next village without a hitch, their anxiety had reached such a pitch that they hardly dared to look at the signpost with the aid of a torch. Yes, it was the right village, they were indeed in paradise instead of hell. The two brothers were close to tears; their happiness knew no bounds.

As soon as dawn broke, they hurried to the next station to catch a train to Bavaria. There, they were reunited with their parents the same evening after so many years of separation. How grateful they all were, remembering that countless families had not been so lucky. Many of them had died, and those left had committed suicide. To the parents, it had been a euphoric surprise to see their long-lost sons again, and to be able to celebrate Christmas with them.

In the New Year, they had to think of how to obtain a permit to stay in the American Zone. If you had a job, a permit may be granted, along with ration cards. But everybody wanted to be in this limited space of the American Zone, bursting at the seams. Everything was in chaos. People lived under the rubble of their houses in the cellars until the debris was cleared and the Wiederaufbau, with the vital help from the Germans from Eastern Europe, could begin in early 1950, when the Marshall plan came into being. It was only then that the Allies realized that Germany represented an important strategic point in the "cold war" that was emerging between Russia and the Western Powers. Until then, not much had been done, except by charities and private individuals abroad, to alleviate the suffering of the people in an almost "moonscape" Germany.

Meanwhile, people had to find ways to survive. Big families squeezed together in one room, highly trained specialists and academics worked as farm-hands or on building-sites, the black market was booming, but everyone was optimistic and anticipating a bright future. All the refugees and deportees were evenly distributed right down to the smallest village, so that there would be no ghettoes or problem areas. In retrospect, this turned out to be one of the best ideas in post-war Germany. The indigenous population did not see it that way at the time, because they had to deal with the problems as they arose. Each village and town had their fair share of them. Of course, there was a lot of initial resentment. These 'foreigners' had brought their own culture and way of life with them. The many different German dialects presented a communication barrier for a long while. In time, integration took place through the commencement of the re-building of Germany ('*Wiederaufbau*'). It became clear that without these 'intruders', the economic miracle of West-Germany (*Wirtschaftswunder*) would not have become a reality. The only way Karl and Oskar could get a permit was to join, or at least be active in this rebuilding program. Their brother Emil had settled in Munich, having been released from Italy after a long period as a PoW. He advised them to take their chances in Munich, where many hands were needed for the reconstruction of the city.

They got a job in a building firm there, and lived in a wooden hut. They wore clogs, the weather and work conditions were bad, but they were free, and would be allowed to stay in the American Zone. Their mother had brought their reports and references from home, so now there was hope.

One day, as Karl fought his way through the sludge in his clogs, a bucket of cement on his shoulders, the future owner of the house stopped him.

"You haven't exactly grown up on a building site, have you?"

"No, certainly not," Karl answered, smiling.

That was how he began work as a sales representative for the well-known German import/export firm of 'Dallmayr', whose owner, Herr Randlkofer, had literally picked him out of the mud on 7th July 1947.

CHAPTER 48
Our Escape

On the way to the eye clinic one day, I had to do a favour for one of our friends and pass on a message to someone. It was dark and unfamiliar in the passage of their house. There were many name signs, but none of them the right one. Some of the rooms had been sub-let, due to the shortage of accommodation, and there was no indication of who the sub-tenant was. Suddenly I stopped. A subdued bass-voice interchanging with high peals of laughter reached my ear through one of the doors. Since there seemed no one else about, I knocked on the door and waited timidly.

When nobody answered, I knocked again, but only the puzzling sounds from behind the door penetrated the silence. I took courage and gingerly opened the division between myself and 'them.' One glance told me who they were; some startled movement in a bed alongside the wall made it clear that these were 'lovers.' I felt the blood rush to my cheeks, and without a word of apology, I was out of the room, before I could take a second glance at them. Who knows, they might be naked, I thought in panic. I rushed out of the house, not having delivered the message and not caring what my mother would say to me at night.

The Weinertsgrüns had left Freiberg some time ago now. They had been the only friends who had children (although Trude was about 4 years older than myself). I was not really strong enough to go 'visiting.' If I had been, I would have gone to the Bergers or to Frau Krieglstein, but not to Aulitzkys by choice. Frau Aulitzky was suffering with arthritis. She could hardly walk and her hands looked more like awkward tools, or pincers. This never bothered me, on the contrary, I sympathized with her and wished her an instantaneous recovery. What did slightly irritate me, was the fact that she was always complaining about her bad fortune. Her face had a singularly young appearance, like that of a young girl, smooth-skinned with long, black hair framing it. Her husband was a thick-set, balding man with little to say for himself.

One Sunday morning, while my mother was at church with Liesl, I was preparing the feast of that week, namely some potatoes, which I had been told to peel and boil. As I dug out the 'eyes' (impurities), I recall wishing that mine could be erased, or disposed of in the same way. I cut them away mercilessly to the detriment of the precious potatoes, but for my satisfaction, the more the better. When my mother and Liesl arrived, I felt much better. The two of them immediately began to tell me that they had 'dropped in' at the Aulitzkys, where they had been told of Herrn Aulitzky's plan.

"What plan is that?" I asked, with some trepidation. I could not imagine that Herr Aulitzky had ever had a plan in his life. It just showed how wrong you could be about people. Nevertheless, 'his plan' disturbed me before I even knew what it was about. All I knew by now was that it had something to do with us, and that was bad enough.

"Well, it might not be such a bad idea," my mother said confidently. "He wants to try and cross the border with us, so that he can visit his son in the American Zone. He wouldn't be allowed to see him legally - they'll just assume that he won't want to come back once he's over there. We'll make our arrangements and he'll just have to fit in with them. As far as I can see, we have nothing to lose."

"I wouldn't be too sure," I mumbled, looking into the new cast iron pan, we had been able to buy in a shop, to check if the potatoes were done.[1]

In July 1947, my father arrived as planned. We were all glad to see him, especially since he looked so much better. We had already packed our few belongings, and said 'farewell' to all our friends and acquaintances, so that there was nothing else to hold us back a moment longer. I looked around the room. When Liesl was at home and not in hospital, we used to play 'Stadt, Land', an exciting quiz game, in which a letter from the alphabet was chosen. The contestants then had to fill the columns on their paper, headed with: town, country, flower, occupation, vegetable, bird, river, etc. beginning with that letter. Who finished that round first, stopped that round. Then the points were counted. Whenever we played that game, we forgot everything around us and I never tired of it. I remembered my sister asking me: Erika, what is heavier? A pound of feathers or a pound of lead? Of course, I did not think about it for one moment and answered 'lead', only to feel extremely silly, when she pointed out the obvious.

Just before we set off, I rushed upstairs to see Werner one last time. I was more than surprised to find him there with a young girl, whom he introduced as his fiancée. I left feeling quite flabbergasted, but also happy in a way, because he had looked so content and had wanted to share his joy with me. I felt bewildered for some time afterwards. Not that I felt 'replaced' in any way, I just could not understand that he could be engaged at his age. He was only a teenager. I had been more than satisfied to just look at and talk to him, and wondered why he wasn't. Why did he have to get engaged exactly at the time of my departure?

All of us, including H. Aulitzky, boarded a train to Gutenfürst near the border, where we parted from my father. Before that, we had arranged

---

[1] Who would have guessed at the time that this saucepan would be useful for decades to come.

to meet up again on the other side of the border at a station behind the town of Hof in West Germany. I can't remember if my father got off the train too in order to let us go across first. He must have wanted to safeguard a successful crossing, otherwise we would still have been in East-Germany, while he was in West-Germany with no hope of seeing us in the near future. Herr Aulitzky did not say much as usual, but seemed nearly as tense as my father.

We lost no time at all and proceeded straight towards the border. We met a man who told us that we should go back immediately, as he and three others had been caught and held prisoner for four days.

"It's no good," he said, shaking his head sadly, "you won't make it. You might as well save yourselves the trouble and disappointment, not to mention four days in prison." My mother looked at him, speechless for a minute, while Herr Aulitzky appeared to disintegrate before our very eyes.

"I'm not going to be put off by anything. I'm sorry you were so unfortunate, and thank you for the information, but we can't turn back now. My husband is waiting for us on the other side." With this she walked doggedly onwards, neither looking to the right, nor to the left. We trailed behind her like sheep following their shepherd. After a while, my sister, who did not like the idea of doing anything 'illegally,' said demurely: "But, Mama, if the gentleman says it's no good, why are we still walking?"

"My child," my mother half turned her head towards us without faltering in her step, "how can we turn back now? He who hesitates is lost."

It was a miserable morning. Slowly, it began to drizzle, and a greyness like dirty cotton-wool enveloped us within an hour. Mentally, we fluctuated between total despair and a glimmer of hope that all was going to be well. We reached a wood and passed a barricade across the path, at which point my mother murmured, "I wonder if this is it?" Leaving the forest, we saw a long stretch of unattended grassland stretching out before us, with woods on either side. Keeping close to the wood on the right, we walked as fast as my sister's condition would allow. My mother kept glancing anxiously at her and took note of her lips and fingernails, which had turned from blue to almost purple. At any other time, she could not have ignored these warning signs, but now, as everything was at stake, she had no option. Even long before we had set out on this dangerous journey, I could see that my mother was getting more and more worried, not so much about the outcome of this risky undertaking, but about how my sister was going to survive such a long, continuous march.

The rain came down heavily now, and just as Herr Aulitzky pulled his collar up, shots rang out nearby. Our hitherto valiant protector disappeared without trace into the woods in a flash. My mother found no time to even look in the direction he had run. Indeed, she marched on with renewed determination and energy. She must have thought that the German Policeguards could not live with themselves if they had to shoot a woman with two children in cold blood, even when their orders were otherwise. Anyway, what hope of survival did we have in East Germany? My mother, after two years of hard labour with hardly any food, and having to cope with one of the severest winters on record without proper protection against the cold, neither by day or night, by now looked like a scarecrow. Her skin stretched over tight sinews, specially visible on her long scraggy neck, her arms and legs just bones determined to manoeuvre her stick-like body in the right direction.

"This has to be no-mans-land," she whispered to us. "Not long now, and they won't be able to touch us." Herr Aulitzky made a rapid reappearance. Seeing that no more shots were aimed in our direction, he must have experienced tremendous mental turmoil and being forced to make a snap decision for once, which could mean life or death for him. What had he let himself in for? This woman was crazy and he had thought he knew her. All odds were against this venture right from the start, but especially after they had been warned by someone who should know. He was only going to visit his son, after all. He should have turned back in Gutenfürst. Yes, why hadn't he done that? He was a man, he should have known better. Trust an illogical woman to get him into such a mess. The trouble was that he had to go with her now. If he tried to go back alone, he might be shot or caught anyway. He had a better chance risking it with a woman and two children.

In the distance, a lonely farm could be discerned through the misty air. Soon, we entered the friendly farm-kitchen, where we begged the farmer's wife for something to drink, since my mother dared not pose the vital question outright. The woman seemed to read her mind.

"It's all right. You're in the West now." She put her hand on my mother's shoulder, then rushed off to bring us some fresh milk, which we had not tasted for years. We embraced each other, and even Herr Aulitzky grinned all over his face. These were hectic times, where one emotion followed another in quick succession. It was often hard to keep up with them.

As soon as my sister had recovered a little, we left for Hof, the Inter-Zone Train's first stop on West-German soil. Why we did not meet my father there, I do not know. He probably knew that many people were picked up there without legitimate papers and sent back where they had come from. I suppose my parents thought that it would be safer to reunite at a small station beyond Hof.

Hof appeared to be a happy place. Everybody in the street smiled, and looked content with their lot. Some women wore lipstick, a spectacle I had not seen for a long time. What a contrast between Gutenfürst and Hof! And yet, they were only a few miles apart. They could have been on different continents, for all I could tell. A young man bit heartily into a white roll. I could not remember ever having seen one before. It looked delicious. My mother assured us that we would soon be able to tuck into one, as well as many other undreamt-of delicacies.

We still could not believe that our troubles were over. Of course, many difficulties awaited us, but we were confident that now we had tasted the milk, the honey would surely follow. We would be united, happy and alive. We felt gratitude for Saxony, where we had learnt how to be truly alive, when we had found ourselves at the bottom strata of human society, having lost everything and being in danger of losing our very lives. We would never, ever forget this; but now we knew we wanted to have a second chance. You can only go up, after you have been right down, if you have not perished, or learnt from your experiences. This was life at its best, when your outlook on it had made a 360 degree turn.

We walked through the pouring rain to a place called Moschendorf. This was where we had arranged to meet my father. To our horror, we saw a big barbed-wire fenced camp there, with people swarming around like ants in and outside its gates. There was nothing for it but to walk on to the next village or town. Herr Aulitzky had already left us and was on his way to his son.

We were soaked through, exhausted and hungry, yet nothing would have stopped us from reaching our goal. As we made our way along the railway-line, the rain stopped. The name of the next station was Oberkotzau. My mother asked the station-master to ring through to Moschendorf to enquire whether her husband, who was wearing a reddish-brown jacket and dark knee breeches could be detected in the waiting-room. When the answer came back in the negative, my mother conferred with Liesl, and back we marched again to Moschendorf. Just after we arrived at the station, the train arrived[1], but it was obvious that it was not going to stop there.

Suddenly, I spotted my father on one of the little platforms, typical of the trains at that time. I waved my arms frantically and shouted:- "Papa!!" with all my might. My mother then saw him too, and shouted "Next station!" so that the next step for us was to trot back the same way

---

[1] still steam trains at that time. They moved much slower, specially past stations.

we had gone twice before, a third time. Still, the overwhelming joy of meeting each other in the West made up for everything. My father gave us some real bread; no more sawdust to eat from now on. There was a lot to talk about. We had plenty of time on our hands, as the next train was not due until 5am the next morning. My parents sat at a table, and Liesl and I lay on a bench all night in the waiting-room. We were soaked right through, but happy. Liesl put on a brave face, but we all saw in what bad physical condition she really was. She had to fight for every breath, and my parents, in spite of the joy they experienced, kept on looking at her, with "worry" written all over their faces.

CHAPTER 49
Conclusion

The next morning, without any breakfast, we clambered stiffly into the train, which made its way down to Regensburg, an old Celtic settlement, which had been a chosen Roman site, with many Roman walls, bastions, medieval towers, arches and a 2,000 year old bridge still standing to this day.

When we arrived there, we naturally had no eye for such ancient beauty. It was surprising that not many more houses lay in ruins there as the plane-producing Messerschmitt-works on the outskirts of the town had been bombed, and also that life seemed so different there compared to Freiberg. Trams, for instance, represented a thrilling novelty that we made use of in order to reach the camp. I gazed in wonder at the awe-inspiring cathedral with two beautifully high spires, and a wide river called the Danube, which took my breath away.

An old, familiar scene was the campsite. My father deposited us at the Commandant's office, where, at the point of departure, he asked casually: "When will my family be getting their ration-cards?" (after all, that was the reason we were there), also "When can I come and visit them? I can only come at the weekend. Will next Sunday be all right?"

The commandant, sitting behind his desk, looked grimly over his glasses and said sternly "You will not be seeing your family here next Sunday. They are going back to the Russian Zone as part of the next convoy which will leave tomorrow. We are full to the brim in this camp, as in most camps in Germany. You must understand that we cannot cope with an indiscriminate number of people, especially when they have no proper papers."

There was absolute silence in the room. My father looked as if all the blood had drained from his balding head in an instant. My mother jumped up, pulled a small bottle out of her bag and went over to my father. She had not quite reached him before the commandant jumped over his desk and snatched the bottle away from her before anyone could say a word.

"We are not going to poison ourselves, Herr Commandant," she said in a loud, deliberate voice, "Not after what we have been through. I was only going to give my husband some drops (Hoffmannstropfen) to calm himself down."

The commandant mumbled something about "....wouldn't be the first time here ...." and my mother answering that he would not have any trouble with *us in this way*. With this, my father beckoned us to follow him as my mother picked up her bag, and out we went from the stuffy office into the fresh air outside, free, but once again, not knowing where the next meal would be coming from. We heard some apologies mumbled about everybody wanting to be treated as an exception, then the door shut.

We travelled by train to Taimering, from where a little country road with the odd crucifix here and there stretched ahead of us, taking us first to Ober-Ehring and then to a minute village, which was now my grandparents new domicile, Unter-Ehring. The five or six farms there showed considerable prosperity, which was by no means reflected in their owners' appearances. These people were clean, industrious and forthright Bavarians, who said little, but lived and let live. Of course, by that time, each village had been allocated a number of *Flüchtlinge* (refugees), or deportees like us[1], according to its size, and I suspect the Mayor was responsible for a fair distribution of these occupants in their houses. It was natural that virtually no one initially welcomed the idea; indeed, some refused to cooperate under any circumstances.

In this part of the world, any farmer who could afford it, had a small house built near his farm with the prospect of moving into it at the time of his retirement (*Austragshaus*). At first, the refugees were crammed into these houses, since they were mainly unoccupied. Once the 'intruders' were housed, they had to find work. The farms needed helpers; many farmers had died along with their sons in the war. Necessity commanded therefore that intellectuals and manual workers alike laboured alongside each other for a while. It was clearly not an ideal situation. A countryman's heart bleeds when he sees someone holding a pitchfork the wrong way round. Equally, an accountant or professor is not exactly enthralled at the prospect of loading a highly pungent-smelling heap of manure onto a cart. It took nearly two generations for the integration process of these different peoples to be completed, when they realized

---

[1] 15 Million of us had first to be accommodated in the totally destroyed Germany before other countries were willing to accept some of these people.

how much they had learnt from each other, and how beneficial it had been.

My grandparents were very surprised, but also happy to see us. They stared at our emaciated faces and bodies as if we had just risen from the dead. They thought that my sister's survival after such a horrendous, dangerous trek in her condition was a miracle. My grandmother immediately smuggled one of those desirable bread-rolls into our hands before her husband could see it. They themselves were literally 'on the bread line', but life out in the country had many obvious advantages, and many a good thing came their way unexpectedly from their landlord's house next door. They too lived in their landlord's "Austragshaus".

With them in the same house lived my Aunt Traudl with her husband Otto and their two little boys Dieter and Otti. They occupied two rooms next to my grandparents downstairs; upstairs lived a Bavarian family with three children, one girl was my age. I was to become quite friendly with all of them.

The distribution of these incoming 15 million people was very arbitrary. Sometimes, after the train deposited the people on its route, people soon left that place and went near other relations. In my grandparents's case, there were no relations in that area, except their daughter, who must have come with them on the train from Bohemia, from where they were evacuated.

Although my grandparents had not expected us, they made room for us as far as was possible in these crowded conditions. In the 'living-room,' my grandmother slept on one side of the room with uncle Willi's picture hanging over her bed, on the other side my grandfather occupied a bed next to an old cooker, for which he had to gather wood and saw it up. A straw-mattress on the floor provided a resting place for my mother. During the day, this mattress was kept in a little shed outside. Liesl and I slept in one bed again in a tiny room, in which my grandfather kept his shoemaking equipment. There was just enough room to turn round, when he was not repairing or making shoes as a favour for someone. When Karl and Oskar came from Munich to visit their parents, I had to share the bed with my grandmother, and Liesl the straw-mattress with my mother. All the beds were very primitive with straw-mattresses.

As expected, my sister developed an inflammation of the heart once again, but there was no question of going into hospital this time. It would have been impossible to visit her regularly from where we were now; also the fare would have swallowed up all our financial resources. My mother now devoted herself almost entirely to nursing my sister back to whatever health she still had in her, with some degree of success, which surprised us all. Although my sister had not been as undernourished as my mother and myself, she had had to go through an ordeal, namely our journey here. The undertaking had been a big risk and we were grateful that she had survived it.

With no ration-cards in our possession, our diet consisted mainly of potatoes and malt-coffee, which, to us, meant nothing less than luxury. We could eat to our heart's delight, and we would never be hungry again. What a prospect! Our zest for life continued undiminished. Even my grandparents, who were still quarrelling as before, became infected by it. My grandfather used to tell us jokes from his youth with such relish that the tears ran down his cheeks. This was probably also a sign of the release of tension and extreme anger that life had dealt us such a blow. But, at least, we were safe now and he could relax a little. Meanwhile, Grandmother (we called them by their oldfashioned title of 'Grossmutter and Grossvater', but my small cousins called them by the modern names of 'Oma and Opa') looked on in amazement. Many a happy hour was spent with her teaching us how to play card-games that we had never even heard of. But she could still not lose with dignity, and I learnt a great deal from this. Now, I certainly did not want to be seen as in Saaz a few years ago - leaving the room abruptly and sulking until I won a game.

My father used to visit at the weekend and stay with us a few hours. He still worked for the Becks, ploughing the fields with a couple of fine horses in front of him, enormously long stretches of land demanding preparation for a rich harvest, taking the elements in full measure, whilst concentrating solely on the task in hand. It also gave him time to 'digest' the past little by little with the help of the healing power of mother Nature.

Herr Beck apparently collected 'treasures,' antique finds in the soil, some of them for the museum in Regensburg. He had drifted into this hobby without really knowing how. I suppose, during his long life, he had come across more and more interesting artefacts in the furrows of his long fields. In his china-cabinet behind glass-doors were some ancient small skulls, tools and vessels. He never overstated it, but was always pleased, when someone showed an interest in them. When I first saw these exhibits, I was excited and bursting to shoot a barrage of questions at him as to the exact details of where and when his findings had taken place. But knowing that he was a man of few words, I had to restrain myself and only ask a few. To my surprise, he answered them all with pleasure and a smile on his face.

I started having the most repulsive sores all over my face. Purulent and crusted up, they hurt each time a muscle twitched or my lips moved. A sudden increase in nourishment must have thrown my system out of its declining rut with upsetting consequences. My condition would have been worse, had we had a richer diet. It was months before they slowly healed up, leaving behind big, red blotches, which took a long time to recede.

It was now the summer holidays. My mother would have to look for a school for me. The nearest was in Riekofen, another larger village about two or three km away. Watching the cows graze peacefully in the still, endless meadows just outside our village, listening to the cheerful chatter of the well-fed birds and generally soaking up the atmosphere, my days were spent in blissful happiness. With Ady, short for Adolf (nobody wanted to be called that name now), a young relation of our landlord Herr Stierstorfer, and Elfriede, the girl from upstairs, I 'investigated' every corner of the farm and its surroundings. Our favourite meeting place was an old green-house in the landlord's garden. We were in nobody's way there, and equally, no one disturbed us in this hide-out, filled with cracked flower pots, broken tables and rusty garden tools. Earnest disussions and an endless exchange of past experiences took place in there.

Each time I thought of Ady's departure (he was only there on holiday), a pang of fear and sadness shot through me, only mitigated by the thought of Elfriede, who would still be with me. She assured me that she was going to take me to school soon.

When the big day came, my only dress had been washed and pressed, my ankleboots repaired by my grandfather with patches sewn on here and there, and my wavy hair parted and tied up with two elastics. The walk with the few other village children and Elfriede was pleasant, and led through meadows, paths and over a brook, which became flooded in Autumn and Spring.

Just after entering the village of Riekofen, a solid, well-maintained building came into view. It was the school, whose headmaster was Oberlehrer Mooshandl, well aware of his position, but also of his responsibilities. (If I was to return there now, the crucifix which he presented to us with an inscription on the back on the day before his retirement would probably still be hanging there between the two windows). The same old problem I had faced in Freiberg reared its ugly head yet again.

Apart from my outlandish and threadbare clothes, I could not speak the same dialect; indeed, mine was now as authentic as any child's in Saxony, and a greater divergence between that and the one here, one could not imagine. What trouble I had taken to learn it, albeit subconsciously! In Saxony, I had listened so carefully to every nuance, every intonation. Now I had to erase it all from my memory and learn something completely different. Even Elfriede made fun of me at times. She had to slightly modify her broad Bavarian dialect when she spoke to me. Fortunately for me, Herr Mooshandl did not tolerate broad Bavarian, but he himself could do little about his own intonation, just like most Bavarians who try to speak 'Hochdeutsch.' All four classes were taught by him in one room. While he taught one class a certain subject, the other classes worked 'quietly' away on some other subjects. In another big room of the building were 'the little ones' being taught in another four classes by a pleasant young woman in the same way.

If our other classes worked less than quietly, 'public' caning was a constant reminder that the required silence had not been achieved. I do not think that Herr Mooshandl was in any way a sadist. This measure of punishment was the accepted one at the time, and the children themselves would have been very surprised, had it stopped overnight.

He told us one day that a bishop in Regensburg had been hanged in public just before the American troops took the town in 1945. He had been against the town council's decision to blow up the Steinerne Brücke, the oldest stone bridge in Germany, in order to prevent the Americans from entering the town. He had wanted a peaceful capitulation to save lives. They labelled him a traitor and managed to destroy him and part of the ancient bridge.

The highlight of the day came just before we went home; we would walk across the road to a big farmyard, where we were given soup and grapefruit juice. None of us had ever tasted this bitter-sharp flavour before. We were told that it had come all the way from America, like the gift-parcels from the American Charity "Care" that some people had heard of. So, after an initial reluctance, we got used to it and later even enjoyed it. The soup was always very good and immensely satisfying to all, even the dinner-ladies. The whole enterprise was called 'Schulspeisung', which roughly translates as 'schooldinners.'

My sister's future occupation posed a real problem to my mother. Liesl had lost out on so much schooling, and yet, she was so thirsty for knowledge and generally interested in everything. She was now fifteen, and at that age, elementary education had come to an end. The only option open to her would have been to attend the Berufschule (career training school) once a week, which was aimed at teaching every day life and work experience. But my sister had her mind set on becoming a needlework teacher.

My parents' dilemma came to an end when my sister became so ill that there was no choice but to take her to a hospital in a converted school (Augustenschule) in Regensburg. An ambulance came and took her away. A small crowd of villagers and relations stared at this frail, gasping teenager, whose every intake of breath could well have been the last. Onkel Emil and his wife Anna (who had come to Ehring to be near my grandparents and who lived and worked next door) stood watching, moved to tears. My father came with his horses and a heavy cart in order not to miss her departure. The three of us had seen her many times 'on death's door' which did not mean that we took it less seriously; rather, the shock of seeing her like this did not have such an impact on us now. My mother reproached herself for not having been vigilant enough. She had gone to Sünching, (another village nearby) and on her return was horrified and angry to find Liesl sawing wood with my grandfather. She was panting heavily by the time my mother reached her, but looked happy in the knowledge that she had been able to be of some use for once.

One day, on my regular visit to my uncle Emil and aunt Anna in their one-room flat at Stierstorfer's, they surprised me with the news that they were going back to Munich, where Tante Antsch with her five children, and Onkel Karl and Oskar lived. I was very disappointed to hear this. They had no children, and had given Liesl and myself books, jigsaw-puzzles and small games, which we would never have had otherwise. We always greatly appreciated their gifts as well as their love and affection. We could not blame them for wanting to leave Ehring. The community was too small to be able to offer anything but hard work. My aunt and uncle, (both born and bred in Gerten, having been in charge of the post-office there) had begun to be interested in the arts, and were generally aiming towards improving themselves culturally. The younger people in the village felt a need for some kind of culture, or just recreational facilities, which were totally absent. One auburn-haired young woman, who could be seen walking barefoot over the frosty ground behind her cows each Spring and Autumn, showed great interest in Onkel Karl's visits to Ehring. No doubt, she saw a remote chance of escaping the otherwise inevitable monotony and hard labour stretching out in front of her. To become something higher than a farmer's wife was the ultimate Utopia, and was rarely achieved.

At the Stierstorfer's, our landlords, there were four bachelors and one spinster managing the farm. Their parents had died, and one brother had only just returned from being a prisoner of war in Russia. I shall never forget how he watched a sow with a litter of rosy, vulnerable and squealing piglets, suckling her off-spring, while she grunted contentedly and reassuringly. There were tears in his eyes as he stared spellbound into the pen. He was probably thinking: "Where have I been so long? How could I have forgotten something so simple and moving?" He did not know that he would be married within the year. Yet in the adjacent stable, his sister was busy killing a number of pigeons, ducks and hens. The pigeons had their necks wrung, the ducks' necks were pierced for the blood to drain away (they twitched and shook all over for a long time), while the hens had their heads cut off with an axe. Invariably, they did not find out about this until later, and ran off headless.

One evening, Elfriede and I were gleaning a field. I felt terribly guilty about it, because there was a lot of wheat - as far as I was concerned- to be picked up. It felt like stealing from the farmer who owned the field. Elfiede chattered on, unaware of my feelings.

"Do you know, my sister's getting married to a sailor soon, but they can't have any children, ever." I looked at her in surprise, and visualized her sister, who was an attractive young girl with brown eyes and wavy, long hair of the same colour.

"Why not?" I asked indignantly. She straightened up from her stoop, came over and whispered to me: "He can't, because..." and then she raised her eyes meaningfully to heaven. We both resumed our gleaning as before, but I thought to myself that no man deserved that kind of a sacrifice. Children, to me, were an essential part of a marriage. I had seen Tante Mina and Onkel Gustl and Tanta Anna and Onkel Emil fret over not having had children. Their lives seemed somehow incomplete without them, and I myself could think of nothing better than a whole bunch of children sitting around the dinner-table, enjoying a meal together with their parents, as I had seen at Elli's. There was no jealousy amongst them., because what little they had, was shared equally between them, and there was no time to give one child preferential treatment. What is perfect in this world? I thought to myself. It's probably different things to different people, and they might all be wrong in the end, who knows? Personally, I liked pushing my two little cousins, Tante Traudl's children, around in a small wicker pram through the countryside. We would stop at a maize-field, and I would break off a young cob and admire with them the soft-flowing, light-green hair, that hung down from it.

We all felt very homesick at times, but the older people in particular increasingly looked back, rather than forward. What had happened to Herbert and his parents and all my friends and my parents' friends and acquaintances from Saaz, I wondered. We were lucky and thankful that most of our wider family had survived the ordeal.

I watched my grandfather make himself a beautiful pair of ankle boots from scratch. With the help of his last and tools, some sheets of leather, wooden and metal nails, and some glue, the boots materialized bit by bit, until they stood in the corner awaiting the big event for which they had been created. My grandfather was going to walk 'home' to Bohemia in his new boots.

Every nail hammered into the inner and outer sole told of its purpose, and my grandfather's determination to walk all the way from Bavaria to Bohemia, from Ehring to Gerten across fields and meadows, over hills and mountains, brooks, rivers and boundaries, even through endless thick and impenetrable forests and frontiers. He was only just able to patch up my old shoes in between working away on his masterpiece, the culmination of a lifetime's experience, meticulously perfecting his already near-flawless craft for the 'sole' purpose of producing a pair of boots that would take him 'home'. Here, he was an old man with nothing to call his own, living at the mercy of a few people; there in Gerten, he was (or at least had been) a respected figure, doing important jobs and living in his own house, having brought up nine children independently. His boots in the corner represented the means to fulfil his dream of regaining what he had lost. He could not tolerate the present situation. The pain was too great.

One day, he actually set off on his mission, without telling anyone of his intentions. When he returned two hours later, he cried and took to his bed, where he remained for days on end. He had walked as far as Sünching, when the sense of futility of his venture overwhelmed him. He was never going to make it; he knew that now. My grandfather was one of those thousands who had lost everything, including people who had lost whole estates and fortunes, and could not come to terms with the loss of a lifetimes work and achievement. They soon died of a broken heart.[1]

The winter, as seen from our little room, was wonderful. My grandmother was in the habit of putting crumbs on the window-sill. Soon, there was a rapid response to this invitation. All different kinds of tits, finches and robins frequented this little feeding-table, never taking any notice of me on the other side of the window. The garden beyond looked more like a park with a small pond, on which colourful ducks and and other waterbirds enjoyed themselves all year round. Sometimes in winter, the water froze over so thickly that we children could slide on it. Someone even brought a pair of skates on one occasion, and everyone who wanted to, was allowed to have a go on them. I held on to the trees surrounding the pond, then pushed myself away from them into the centre of the pond. Everything looked as though dusted over with icing-sugar, and there was I, gliding on ice. I went indoors as darkness descended and wrote a poem, which my mother kept and showed to relations and friends. Life was so wonderful and precious.

Meanwhile, my sister was due to come out of hospital. My mother insisted that a flat of our own had first to be found. During December of 1948, she slept in some barracks next to the station in Regensburg, run by the Lutheran Home Mission, so that she could be with Liesl over Christmas. In America, the very first heart-valve replacements were being performed, but this had not yet reached Europe, and we did not hear of it until much later, when it was too late.

---

[1] A few years later, I came across a number of people who found it impossible to make a new start, even with the German Government's Lastenausgleich and Wiedergutmachung (a relative small compensation).

My sister died of her condition on 1st April 1950, a young girl of seventeen. As she had always seen death as a reality of life, she was able to look far beyond our human mortality, and made it possible for us to have a glimpse of it also.

BIBLIOGRAPHY

Dokumente zur Austreibung der Sudetendeutschen,
Herausgegeben von der Arbeitsgemeinschaft zur
Wahrung Sudetendeutscher Interessen

The Third Reich by D. G. Williamson,
Published by Longman Group UK Ltd.in 1982

A Pictorial History of Nazi Germany by Erwin Leiser,
Translation fist published in Pelican Books in 1962

**1945 – 1995, 50 Jahre Flucht, Deportation, Vertreibung;
Unrecht bleibt Unrecht**
Published by Bund der Vertriebenen – Kreisverband Regensburg

Tschechen und Deutsche in Böhmen und Mähren 1920 – 1946
By Ingrid Kaiser-Kaplaner, published by Hermagoras in 2002

The Fire, The Bombing of Germany 1940 – 1945,
By Jörg Friedrich, translation copyright in 2006
By Columbia University Press

Lightning Source UK Ltd.
Milton Keynes UK

174679UK00001B/17/P